Variation in South Asian Languages

Pritha Chandra

Editor

Variation in South Asian Languages

From Macro to Micro-Differences

 Springer

Editor
Pritha Chandra
Department of Humanities and Social
Sciences
Indian Institute of Technology Delhi
New Delhi, India

ISBN 978-981-99-1148-6   ISBN 978-981-99-1149-3   (eBook)
https://doi.org/10.1007/978-981-99-1149-3

This Springer imprint is published by the registered company Springer Nature Singapore Pte Ltd.
The registered company address is: 152 Beach Road, #21-01/04 Gateway East, Singapore 189721,
Singapore

Preface

Preparing a collection of essays on language variation in South Asia seems an obvious task to undertake. The South Asian linguistic belt, with a considerable portion lying within the Indian borders, is home to multiple language families, each with multiple languages and their varieties. Archiving and analysing this immense variety, to whatever extent possible, is a challenge, but it is an important engagement for researchers who are interested in not just knowing how varied the South Asian linguistic landscape is, but also in understanding the reasons behind this variation. The current volume is a small step in the direction of recording the huge variety that currently defines the South Asian linguistic belt. It also captures the rich array of theories and methodologies adopted by researchers to examine linguistic variation and thereby provides readers with a glimpse of the reasons and processes underlying variation.

Most of the contributions in this volume came out of talks delivered at the 'Workshop on Approaches to Language Variation' that was held at the Indian Institute of Technology Delhi in 2019. I am immensely grateful to the Indian Council of Social Science Research Delhi for sponsoring the two-day event, and to the engaging audience which included both young, upcoming researchers and more established scholars in the field. We were so enthused by the response we received at the workshop that we decided to publish a collection of articles that truly showcases South Asian linguistic variation and would serve as an essential reading for students and researchers in the future. I have several people to thank for helping me complete this task.

This volume would not have seen the light of the day, had it not been for the support we got from the editorial team of Springer Nature. Right from a rigorous review process to all logistics related to publication and printing, the Springer Nature team made sure that all due processes were followed to create a strong and meaningful academic product. The comments from four anonymous reviewers also helped the contributors to sharpen their arguments with more empirical data and better conceptual clarity. We are grateful that the reviewers went through the entire manuscript and provided very insightful comments on individual chapters that guided us in the preparation of the final copy.

As the editor of the volume, I must also thank those, without whose research and writing, this volume would not even exist. The contributors have been a patient lot, writing, rewriting and resubmitting, whenever they have been asked to, and most of all, meeting strict deadlines while managing their hectic work schedules. Those who were graduate students at the time when the idea for the volume was conceived have successfully defended their theses and taken up teaching jobs. These scholars should be separately acknowledged for multi-tasking and concurrently working on their dissertations and articles during the very challenging COVID times.

A special word of thanks for Preeti Kumari, Chandni Dutta and Sayantani Banerjee for not just helping me organize the 2019 workshop but for also keeping me engaged with this topic with their own research on language variation. Their enthusiasm for languages of South Asia gives me an unending hope that there will be more books in the future on linguistic variation in the region.

I close this note remembering Prof. Rahul Balusu, one of our contributors whose sudden death left a void in South Asian linguistics that is hard to fill. Rahul was not just a brilliant linguist; he was a wonderful person, very modest and ready to help whenever he could. While we slowly come to terms with the painful truth, I get closure from the fact that the last long conversation I had with him was on the topic of language variation. I dedicate this book to the memory of this wonderful linguist and to his undying love for languages.

New Delhi, India   Pritha Chandra
December 2022

Contents

Editor and Contributors

About the Editor

Pritha Chandra is Professor of Linguistics in the Department of Humanities and Social Sciences at the Indian Institute of Technology Delhi. She has a Ph.D. from the University of Maryland, USA. Her research is mainly centered around the theoretical constructs of case, agreement and formal features in South Asian languages; her more recent publications are on feature variation and language change in Indo-Aryan languages.

Contributors

Apurva is Assistant Professor in the Indian Institute of Management at Jammu. His research interest is sentence processing, where he primarily focuses on the interaction of working memory and expectations in Hindi sentence processing. His research methodology involves the use of sentence completion, self-paced reading (SPR) and eye-tracking experiments.

Rahul Balusu was Assistant Professor in the English and Foreign Language University at Hyderabad, India. He held a Ph.D. degree in Linguistics from New York University. He was a very eminent semanticist working primarily on South Asian languages. Both during his graduate days and during his term as a professor, his work received global recognition.

Sansuma Brahma is Assistant Professor in the Institute of Chartered Financial Analysts of India University, Tripura. He is interested in the syntax of Tibeto-Burman languages, especially the negation and negative polarity items found in them. He has presented his research at several conferences in India.

Kamal K. Choudhary is Associate Professor at the Department of Humanities and Social Sciences, Indian Institute of Technology Ropar. Kamal completed his Ph.D. from Max Planck Institute of Human Cognitive and Brain Sciences Leipzig, Germany/University of Leipzig, Germany. Before joining IIT Ropar, he worked as a visiting faculty at the Centre of Behavioural and Cognitive Sciences, University of Allahabad, India. He works primarily in the area of the neurophysiology of language comprehension. His broad areas of interest include psycho/neurolinguistics, language and cognition, neurocognition/neuroscience of language comprehension. Currently, his research focuses on ergative languages.

Mayuri Dilip is Assistant Professor of linguistics at Central University of Rajasthan. She received her doctoral degree from IIT Madras in Chennai. She works on syntactic typology of Austo-Asiatic languages. She has presented her work at various professional meetings in India and abroad.

Ambalika Guha is Assistant Professor in the Department of English at Adamas University (Kolkata). Her research interests are in generative syntax and semantics. Particularly, she investigates the uniformity between nominal and clausal left periphery. Recently, she has also been intrigued by the semantics of questions, showing how a language speaker uses a question particle as a disjunction marker.

Mahima Gulati is currently Assistant Professor at the New Delhi Institute of Management, New Delhi. She has completed her doctoral degree from the Department of Humanities and Social Sciences, Indian Institute of Technology Ropar. Her dissertation titled 'The Role of Case in Incremental Argument Interpretation: Evidence from Punjabi' is an ERP study exploring the treatment of nominative and ergative case in Punjabi. She has formerly completed her Masters in Philosophy with a dissertation titled 'Sluicing in Hindi: A Psycholinguistic Study' from the Centre for Advanced Studies in Linguistics (CASL), University of Delhi in 2014. She did her Masters in Linguistics from the English and Foreign Languages University, Hyderabad, in 2012, and her Bachelors in Literature from University of Delhi in 2009. Her areas of interest include exploring case and agreement from linguistic, neurolinguistic/psycholinguistic and cognitive science perspective.

Samar Husain is Associate Professor in the Department of Humanities and Social Sciences at IIT Delhi since 2014. He teaches courses to undergraduates and postgraduates in the areas of linguistics, cognitive science, statistics, and psycholinguistics. He completed his Ph.D. in 2011 from IIIT-Hyderabad, India. Subsequently, from 2011 to 2014, he was a post-doctoral researcher at the Vasishth lab, University of Potsdam, Germany. His broad areas of research are human sentence processing, natural language modelling, natural language parsing and dependency grammars. These topics lie at the intersection of psychology, computational linguistics and theoretical linguistics. His current research investigates the sources of sentence complexity (such as working memory, orthography, grammatical representation and parsing strategy) during real-time language comprehension and production using behavioural, corpus-based as well as computational methods.

Thapasya Jayaraj is currently Assistant Professor in the Indian Institute of Technology Indore. She completed her doctoral degree from the Department of Humanities and Social Sciences, Indian Institute of Technology Madras in 2020. Her dissertation was on 'Dynamics of Malabar Mappila Malayalam and Projecting Identity: A Sociolinguistic Analysis.' She did her Masters in Applied Linguistics from the Centre for Applied Linguistics and Translation Studies, University of Hyderabad in 2015. She has formerly completed her Bachelors in Functional English from University of Calicut in 2013 with first position in the university. Her areas of research interest inclined towards sociolinguistic perspectives of language variation and identity.

Sonal Kulkarni-Joshi is Sociolinguist and Professor in the Linguistics department at the Deccan College, Pune (India). She holds a Ph.D. from the University of Reading (UK). Her research interests include language variation and change, migration and language, language contact, dialectology and dialect mapping. Sonal is currently heading a government-funded project for creating a digital database of regional and social dialects of Marathi. The bilingual project website (under construction) can be accessed at www.sdml.ac.in. She has served as Treasurer of the Linguistic Society of India (2005–2014). email: sonal.kulkarni@dcpune.ac.in, Address: Dept. of Linguistics, Deccan College (Deemed University), Yerawada, Pune [India] 411006.

Rajesh Kumar is Professor of linguistics in the Department of Humanities and Social Sciences at the Indian Institute of Technology Madras, Chennai. He serves as the associate editor of the journal Language and Language Teaching. The broad goal of his research is uncovering regularities underlying both the structural form (what language is) and sociolinguistic functions (what language does) of natural language. He works on the structure of South Asian Languages. He is also interested in issues related to language (multi-lingualism) in education; politics; human cognition; and landscape.

Preeti Kumari is Assistant Professor at the Institute of Technical Education and Research, Siksha O Anusandhan University in Bhubaneswar. Her Ph.D. thesis from the Indian Institute of Technology Delhi investigates the syntax of honorificity in the Eastern Indo-Aryan languages such as Maithili, Magahi and Bangla. Specifically, she looks at the phenomenon of referent honorifics and its interaction with allocutive honorifics in these languages.

Sh. Francis Monsang is Assistant Professor at the English and Foreign Language University, Shillong. He is interested in the syntax of Tibeto-Burman languages in general and the structure of Monsang in particular. He has presented his research at several conferences in India. He has published his work in several journals of repute.

Karumuri V. Subbarao is formerly Professor of Linguistics at Delhi University, and former Radhakrishnan Chair Professor in Humanities at the University of Hyderabad. His research work is focused on the syntactic typology of South Asian languages in general and Tibeto-Burman and Austro-Asiatic languages in particular.

One of his recent books *South Asian languages: A Syntactic Typology* (2012) is published by Cambridge University Press, Cambridge. He has been an **elected member** of the Linguistic Society of America since 2003, and the Linguistic Society of Nepal since 2005. He has taught at several universities in India and abroad. He was Visiting Professor at the University of Hamburg, Hamburg, Germany, and Tokyo University of Foreign Studies, Tokyo, Japan. Currently, he is working on the grammars of three Tibeto-Burman languages, namely Mizo, Rabha and Saihriem. He has published in international and national journals. Some of his publications are available at: www.academia.edu & www.Researchgate.edu

Usha Udaar is Assistant Professor of Linguistics in the Dept. of Humanities and Social Sciences, Indian Institute of Technology Kanpur. She works on underexplored Western Indo-Aryan languages such as Haryanavi, Mewati, Marwari and Mewari. Her work, which tries to explain the mechanisms of micro- and meso-level variation, has been presented and published in multiple fora.

Chapter 1
Introducing Language Variation

Pritha Chandra

Objectives

The current volume brings together various aspects of language variation in South Asia, viewed from different theoretical lenses, especially the generative or mentalist account and a collection of non-mentalist approaches including sociolinguistics and experimental linguistics. To the reader, this may initially appear as an eclectic collection. However, the selection of the approaches and the chapters was done for two primary reasons. The first motivation behind proposing a work with multiple theories is to introduce to the readers the richness of methodologies currently in practise in the South Asian space. I believe that though the perspectives are most often diametrically opposite to each other, scholars, specifically students and young researchers should appreciate how variation can be studied from multiple perspectives. Language is a complex construct, and to understand it in its entirety, all its aspects (whether mental or social/pragmatic usage) must be studied carefully. The second is more of a hope that in the future, a more fruitful dialogue can be initiated between divergent theories, and an attempt can be made to close the gap between the abstract and mental approaches to languages, and those directly dealing with its empirical and social aspects.

With these two aims in mind, this volume has contributions from linguists working in different subfields—sociolinguistics, typology, semantics, experimental linguistics (psycholinguists, neurolinguists) and theoretical/generative syntax. Without giving any one approach prominence over the other, this volume seeks out the opinions of these researchers on the scope and the limits of their methodologies in explaining language variation.

There are two primary contributions of the current volume. The first contribution is that this is the first collection of essays from the Indian subcontinent

P. Chandra (✉)
Indian Institute of Technology Delhi, New Delhi, India
e-mail: pritha@iitd.ac.in

© The Author(s), under exclusive license to Springer Nature Singapore Pte Ltd. 2023
P. Chandra (ed.), *Variation in South Asian Languages*,
https://doi.org/10.1007/978-981-99-1149-3_1

which directly touches on the topic of linguistic variation. While linguists work-ing with South Asian languages have always highlighted the impressive number of language varieties found in the area (cf. Abbi et al., 2001; Dayal & Mahajan, 2007; Subbarao, 2012, among others), there is currently no existing work that directly addresses the topic of linguistic variation. Here, we have chapters that introduce variation at multiple levels—macro/typological level where languages belonging to different language families in the South Asian landscape are com-pared, meso-level variation where typologically related languages and their variations are discussed, as well as micro- or dialect-level variation within a sin-gle language. The second contribution is that it is one of the first works from the Indian subcontinent to bring together different perspectives and methods employed to understand language variation. The present volume fills up an exist-ing lacuna in the literature, by bringing in mentalist and non-mentalist accounts on the same page, and therefore providing a bird's eye view to the reader about the multi-faceted nature of linguistic variation.

Language Variation—What Is It?

One question to break ground with is, what is language variation? The literature registers various levels of linguistic variation—at the level of the individual, the community, the region and the nation. Previously, we have seen very productive studies on language types created through comparisons of structures between mutually unintelligible and genealogically unrelated languages such as English, Japanese, French and Swahili among others. Based on these structural differences, linguists have broadly classified languages into types, some examples of which are head-final languages versus head-initial languages, classifier languages versus non-classifier languages and configurational versus non-configurational languages. Differences also abound within typologically related languages. Within what are known as the Germanic languages, English, German and Dutch exhibit ample variation in sound, structure and meaning, while also sharing many common fea-tures inherited from a shared lineage. Furthermore, even within a single language, there are differences based on the area where a particular variety ('dialect') is spo-ken, who speaks it, and in which (formal/informal) contexts in which it is used. Language variation is therefore not a homogeneous term with a single meaning. This explains why there is such a wealth of studies related to language variation, and variation research continues to grow at an exponential rate, while adopting dif-ferent methodologies and approaches. Oftentimes, theoretical silos created around language variation studies restrict the inquiry to either the mental or the social. Such studies are not without merits since rigorous investigations sometimes require sidestepping for the moment, some variables that are not of immediate impor-tance. When looking at individual variation, one may look at variation as either grammar-internal or as arising from the social variables dictating the individual's behaviour. At the community level, the factors considered would naturally change, since the domain itself would be governed by community-level variables, and the same holds for regional variants. While such partitioning is natural, it is, however, important to be cognizant that neither the object of language nor the phenomenon of language variation can be delimited to a single domain—the mental versus the social. With its roots deep in mental operations and brain and neural connections, language is also constantly shaped by its performance among individuals working in social and cultural contexts. In the discipline however, we find very little effort made in the direction of formulating a holistic approach while working with different viewpoints on language variation. This calls for a thoughtful intervention that can curb these one-sided answers to the phenomenon of variation.

Views on Language Variation

The Generative View

In order to formulate a holistic understanding of language variation using lessons from multiple approaches, it is important to understand the different theoretical assumptions for the phenomenon. The big, traditional divide in linguistics is between the formal, generative approach developed in Chomsky (1957, 1965 among others) that is centred around universality rather than variability on one hand, and on the other, empirical, data-driven approaches covered by diverse subfields such as non-generative typology (cf. Comrie, 1989), experimental psycholinguistics, neurolinguistics (Stemmer & Whitaker, 1998) and sociolinguistics and variationist linguistics (Hymes, 1962, 1964; Labov, 1966). Generative linguists dissect languages, reducing them to their bare essentials that constitute a special cognitive device (Faculty of Language/FL) entrenched deep into the crevices of the brain/mind. For a generativist, language is a cognitive ability, and understanding it requires us to probe the phenomenon in its mental abode, away from its actual use in a social context. The focus is on an individual's knowledge or competence (or *I-language*)—the generative capacity of the universal language organ placed in the speaker's mind—rather than her actual performance or expression (or *E(xternal)-language*). Linguistic variation is understood to result from the limited hypothesis space available within the generative machine and partly from externalization (morphological) pressures and constraints. With the formulation of the principles and parameters architecture of grammar (cf. Chomsky, 1981), the language organ is conceptualized with invariant and innate principles and open parameters with binary values, only one of which is chosen by the language-learning kid based on her linguistic experience. Grammar or more precisely, linguistic knowledge is a machine with mutually exclusive options, and the problem of linguistic variation is tackled in terms of parametric choices. This approach to linguistic variation resembles binary-valued switches that have only a single, obligatory value at any given point of time (best exemplified by James Higginbotham's famous switch-board metaphor; see Rizzi, 2014: 17).

The Sociolinguistic View

On the other side of the spectrum, there are scholars who view language as a phe-nomenon in continuous flux. The dynamics of a language correlate primarily to its performance in real, socio-cultural contexts. Language, with its primary role of communication, organizes itself according to the appropriateness of its forms and expressions in different cultural milieus. Diversity is therefore a defining charac-ter of language, and its examination is grounded in the diversity of human users, the real-world situation in which they live and grow and the different social and cultural variables at play. Sociolinguists therefore strongly object to the idea of restricting language studies to the epistemology of language, or to simply lan-guage sciences or linguistics. Instead, language is taken as part of ethnographic studies (cf. Gumperz & Hymes, 1964). This school of thought which understands language as more than epistemology also includes Labov (1966, 1972); also see Weinreich et al., (1968) among others. Termed as 'variationist (quantitative) soci-olinguistics,' Labov's approach to linguistic variation addresses systematic and inherent variation in language—both diachronically and synchronically—and explains it through an examination of external phenomena like societal and cul-tural heterogeneity. The heterogeneity of language, as per Labov, constitutes the core of language studies. Labov also embraces the practice of enhanced statistical processes and quantitative modelling of large swathes of linguistic data collected directly from real-world contexts. Ever since his seminal work on New York class-based dialectal variations, he has continuously asked for an increasing sophistica-tion of statistical procedures to decode the patterns present in big linguistic data sets. Corpuses are as central to understanding patterns of language change for vari-ationist sociolinguists, as are the statistical tools to decode them.

The Experimental Approach

Variationist sociolinguistics has its roots deep in experiments in the actual society among the speakers themselves. Labov's original work was a pioneering exper-iment done on salespeople in New York's departmental stores—which constitute the prototype settings for naturalistic and varied speech. But variation studies are not always conducted in real/external contexts. Variation experiments conducted in well-controlled lab settings are also becoming common, where informants or par-ticipants are prompted to respond to accurately designed and targeted questions. Experimental methods naturally vary from psycholinguistics to neurolinguistics to language acquisition studies, with researchers modifying them or accommodating new ones to fit in new paradigms and factors related to the age, and identities of the informants (adults/children) as well as to the specific domain of investigation (cognition/brain). Experimentalists judge the abilities of young and adult speak-ers in comprehending sentences in real time, and their handling of ambiguous and indeterminate inputs. They also attempt at unravelling mechanisms underlying language production when speakers express their communicative intentions via a series of articulatory (verbal) gestures. One defining feature of experimental linguistics is that language is studied in its engagement with other cognitive systems. To illustrate, experimental work may research on how language processing utilizes short and long-term memory; or the role of attention in making lexical and sentence parsing a highly automatic and routine process (see Ferreira, 2003).

Over the last few decades, there have been efforts to build associations between experimental and theoretical linguistics, most notably with generative syntax. However, the journey has not been without hiccups. One of the biggest challenges for this dialogue has been posed by the question of whether language is a special cognitive device with its own computations and functions or it is merely a part of our general cognitive mechanism. Are the language-specific cognitive systems/ models proposed by generativists too abstract and difficult to reconcile with experimental tests and results?

These questions have been variously framed and answered in the past years in notable works presenting models that capture linguistic performance algorithmically. Following the generative trend of understanding human language competence as a transformational system, psycholinguists initially displayed immense enthusiasm in understanding language performance as a type of information processing. To illustrate, the language processing models of Kimbal (1973) and Fodor et al. (1974) work with phrases and constituents of the type that are presented by theoretical linguists. Sidestepping their differences for the moment, it is noteworthy that both Kimbal and Fodor et al. separately proposed models with two-stage parsers, where the first-stage parser connects each lexical item that it encounters into a phrase marker on the right, while the second parser associates transformationally moved constituents with their deep structure positions in the phrase markers. This close association however took a beating in the 1970s, primarily with the emergence of the Derivational Theory of Complexity (henceforth, DTC; Foss & Hakes, 1978), which correlates sentence processing directly to the number of transformations involved in yielding surface strings. One reason for this split often cited by experimentalists is that the analyses of generative syntacticians could not meet tough experimental scrutiny. Structures and structure-dependent rules postulated by them found no experimental correlates. Thereon, the general consensus in the field was that generative linguists dealt more with abstract structures, while the psycholinguists attempted at unravelling the 'psychological reality' of language constructs and behaviour (Halle et al., 1978). Their goals were different—one dealt with unverifiable, untestable theoretical constructs, and the other dealt with empirically/lab-tested observations. Then came the 'psycholinguistic renaissance' (Clifton, 1981), when multiple influences from different fields of cognitive science came together to reignite the association. Chomsky's (1981) Government and Binding (GB) Theory promised a descriptively and explanatorily adequate model of linguistic competence, and psycholinguists were quick to realize that GB's features have the potential to capture language processing abilities as well. One telling instance is the shift in the theoretician's understanding of passive structures that were now considered outputs of a movement operation (Move-a), rather than a set of derivational rules. For experimentalists, this suggested that the complexity of certain structures including passives could now be decoded as the relation between the moved/surface phrases and, their traces/logical positions, rather than by traversing back to the original kernel sentences and the number of transformations that lead to the present forms (Frazier et al., 1983). This understanding synced perfectly to the left to right comprehension of sentences, where the perceiver first identifies the filler, holds it in working memory and then relates it to the gap once it is identified. However, this tie-up between the two fields was not to last too long. Doubts again emerged on the cognitive feasibility of theoretical tools, augmented further by the growing popularity of connectionist models or 'Parallel Distributed Processing' (PDP) explanations of cognition (Rumelhart et al., 1986). The connectionist models rejected ruled-based explanations of language, replacing them with processes involving activation over a set of simple units, stimulated by the frequency rates of linguistic inputs. These deep philosophical differences widened the gap between the two camps, with the theoreticians assuming language as a specialized, innate, mental capacity or knowledge and, the psycholinguists working more on language as tools to understand the general cognitive architecture and learning mechanisms. In short, the relationship between theoretical and experimental work has been, to say the least, a roller coaster ride over the years.

The Semantics Question

Another domain which has been a bone of contention between the two camps relates to semantics. In Aspects (Chomsky, 1965), the generative system for the first time incorporated a semantic component, alongside the syntactic and phonological components, with the tacit understanding that sentence meanings obligatorily draw upon their syntactic forms. The semantic component is a crucial interface between the language machine and the thought module. This syntactico-centric approach to semantics was for the first time, stated clearly in Katz and Fodor's (1998) seminal work, which lays down the aim of a semantic theory as the determination of 'what a fluent speaker knows about the structure of his language that enables him to use and understand its sentences (pp: 171).' The seventies brought in new tools and an interesting new dimension to our understanding of natural language. Without relinquishing the idea that semantics piggybacks on syntax, generative linguists now turned to a Montague-inspired project of devising natural language semantics with the same tools used by logicians for artificial languages of formal systems of logic. The leitmotif was Montague's own belief that there are no fundamental theoretical differences between natural languages and the artificial languages of logicians. With its use of model theoretic semantics and a string adherence to the principle of compositionality, Montague-style semantics increasingly became an extremely popular enterprise in generative linguistics and continues to dominate most discussions on generative semantics (see Heim & Kratzer, 1998 for a detailed exposition).

The generative approach to semantics, and the tools used for interpretation thereon, have been challenged by many linguists, including those who work within sociolinguistic frameworks. For the latter, information or interpretation of sentences correlates to the multi-faceted identity of the speaker and her social and cultural milieus (see Eckert, 2000, 2012; Labov, 1966, 2001). Linguistic meaning is equally varied and emanates from the actual linguistic performance in the real world. Eckert (2012) mentions three specific types of variables that underlie social meanings. The first variable is implicitness which is rarely overtly constructed. It is present in those subtle signals of speakers that do not find expression in words. Implicitness varies from one speaker to the other, allowing ample variation in what they want to imply about themselves and their contexts. The second variable is underspecification, which enables speakers to communicate multiple kinds of information via a small number of forms. The meaning potential of each form is therefore completely contingent on the social contexts—no form has just one inherent meaning attached to it. The third variable is combinativeness, which allows the semantically underspecified forms to take on meaning as stylistic components. They relate to the outside contexts through enactments and re-enactments of different personae. Since the personae change with changes in the social contexts, meaning also becomes fluid and ever dynamic. These three properties make meaning variable and challenge the static nature of meaning assumed by generative linguists through their logical analysis of sentences.

How do these three differences reflect on language variation studies? Prima facie, generative linguists seem to undermine language variation—whether in structure or in semantics completely by their insistence on the a priori existence of a language-specific organ. Their models appear abstract and dissociated from real-world usage, where the variation is usually assumed to lie. Sociolinguists and experimental linguists, on the other hand, who are invested in language either as a social phenomenon or as part of the overall cognitive ability of humans, emphasize on the immense variation found in language production and comprehension. These are the received views in the linguistic literature and seem to indicate the total absence of a point of convergence between these approaches, especially in the inquiry of language variation.

There is one ground where the received view can be contested immediately—and that is the domain of data collection. While non-generative typologists have traditionally been very active in creating large databases, generative grammarians have, in more recent years, contributed equally to data-archiving. Some notable examples are the Syntactic Atlas of Dutch Dialects (SAND), *Atlante Sintattico dell'Italia Settentrionale* 'Syntactic Atlas of Northern Italy' (ASIS), etc. The allegation about missing performance data from generative studies no longer holds, at least for those theoreticians who are actively seeking out and analysing copious amounts and kinds of data. Additionally, there are several ongoing efforts to bridge some of the questions that have divided the linguistic community over the last many decades. I elaborate on some of these attempts at integration below.

Possible Integration Among Methodologies?

Perhaps in a volume such as this, a natural expectation is an integration of approaches. It is indeed true that integration is a very desirable goal in the sciences, and linguists have also variously argued that it is possible and of utmost importance in their discipline as well. Integration is however not an easy task since the gaps between approaches are sometimes too deep and irremediable. The difficulties associated with integration have been taken up by various scholars in both generative and non-generative camps (cf. Christiansen & Chater, 2017; D'Allesandro & Oostendorp, 2017). The biggest challenge is finding the correct correspondences between abstract/mental constructs and their physical, performance-based forms. Similar obstacles arise while integrating the mental constructs with neural correlates, as has been ardently presented in Poeppel and Embick (2005). The first problem they note is 'granularity mismatch.' Theoretical constructs (distinctive features, syllables, morphemes etc.) are more nuanced and fine-grained and their computations (concatenation, linearization) more explicit. Neuroscience on the other hand operates with broader conceptual constructs (dendrites, spines, neurons, long-term potentiation, receptive fields, etc.). This brings in the problem of ontological incommensurability, with theoretical constructs and operations on one hand, and neuroscience constructs and operations on the other hand, and there being no common language to translate one from the other.

Ontological incommensurability is definitely one of the hardest challenges to all attempts at integration. Different linguists work with languages at different levels of abstraction, and none of its various facets can be avoided. We cannot sidestep linguistic competence since it defines a speaker's knowledge of her language—her capacity to produce and comprehend novel sentences despite having never encountered them in the real environment. We also cannot undermine the fact that language is shaped equally by usage and environment. If communication is an obligatory end-result of the language organ, the external factors influencing performance must be considered carefully too. However, is integration ever possible between the mental and the physical, and even more so, is it desirable at this stage of development of the discipline?

Rather than an integration, a modest and doable goal would be to learn from each other—if linguistic variation happens in an urban setting more than in a rural setting, what does it tell us about the structures and grammar of the language(s) under change? If individual grammars show a certain pattern of change, do we expect a collective to also follow the same trajectory? Learning from the other approaches is therefore extremely important to keep refining one's own research questions, albeit without changing some theoretical commitments.

What is therefore very important to ask is—where does the explanatory power of one theory end, and that of the other begins. This seamless approach potentially allows us to isolate and appreciate the benefits and the limits of each approach, and also enables us to pose challenging questions so that the research within each approach is also carried forward.

This multi-pronged approach has similarities with Newmeyer's (2005) distinction of possible and probable languages. This dual differentiation, according to Newmeyer, is crucial because it shows us the constraints that the abstract, theoretical constructs and the processing mechanisms separately impose on language. Possible languages constitute the set of languages permitted by universal, innate constraints and probable languages constitute the set that is allowed by function and usage. This possible-probable language distinction, triggered by two different kinds of constraints (mental versus usage), allows us to study language, and language variation, in particular at two different levels, without diluting the rigour of a given method, and without side-lining the results of any approach. To illustrate, the two most prominent word orders in world languages—SVO and SOV, as per Newmeyer, are outcomes of Universal Grammar, whereas the other less attested word orders are fallouts of other processing and performance-based constraints. Under this approach, linguistic characteristics arise from both language-specific and general constraints, thereby confirming the validity of multiple and sometimes diametrically opposite theories and methodologies.

Fortunately for us, despite the contentious issue regarding the ontological status of language, there have been multiple joint efforts made in recent years by generative theoreticians, sociolinguists and experimentalists to better understand language. One very relevant collaboration in this regard is between David Adger, a theoretical syntactician and Jennifer Smith, a sociolinguist, who try to explain variable data with the theoretical apparatus at hand as laid out in Adger (2003) (see Adger & Smith, 2005). They argue that sociolinguistic variable data, such as the alternation between 'was' and 'were' in English and Scottish dialects (in their case, Buckie), which are generally thought of only in terms of social constructs, arises from the mechanisms of feature manipulation within the narrow syntactic computational workspace. Adger and Smith question if a pure social-cultural perspective is necessary in these cases or if such variation can also be accounted for in theory-internal terms. There has also been a substantial increase in the number and types of experiments conducted by generative grammarians. Psycholinguistic research from a generative perspective has been happening for some time (see Lewis & Phillips, 2015; Phillips, 2003, among others). There is another relatively new subfield that has emerged in recent years—which true to its spirit is called Experimental Syntax, its primary objective being to test out whether the acceptability judgements of speakers collected through conventional methods replicate in experimental set-ups as well. With a view to this objective, experimental syntacticians (Schutze, 2016; Sprouse, 2015) have devised a set of formal methods for collecting data, complementing the traditional, informal judgement collection methods generally deployed by theoretical syntacticians. A larger pool of participants are now tested in tightly controlled experimental settings, thereby engendering a larger corpus of data reflecting more nuanced acceptability judgements of speakers. Other than evaluating the correctness and accuracy of the data collected through conventional methods, experimental syntacticians emphasize on the nature of the mental space in which language is located. One of their primary concerns is, therefore, about the adequacy via comparison of two opposing theories of language/mind—the binary-categorical theories (Chomsky's binary-valued param-eters) and the weighted-constraint theories (cf. Keller's, 2005 Linear Optimality Theory and Boersma's 2004 Stochastic Optimality Theory, among others). Which of these language/mental modules account for gradient values and language var-iation in the most optimal way? If variation is not captured in these models, are differential acceptability judgements the result of other cognitive modules, most specifically those that deal with processing/parsing, pragmatics, etc.?

These attempts ameliorate many of the concerns that non-generativists have expressed regarding the significance given to data or acceptability judgements in generative linguistics. Large swathes of data collected from multiple speakers and their relative acceptability rates are analysed as closely as in any other approach. Structural and semantic differences are not side-lined in these analyses. Similarly, the engagement of language with other cognitive systems is not undermined, since the purpose is to capture various facets of the data set collected through experiments.

In the end, we recognize that despite differences, there is a burgeoning need in the field for interfaces and interactions. However, we also acknowledge that in order for us to have meaningful exchanges, it is important that we ask the right questions for integration, and not succumb to spurious alliances. One way forward that we present here is to seek the limits of our own theory or framework and take the unexplainable to the next level or domain.

The contributions in this volume therefore consciously avoid making any hasty conclusions about integrative language sciences. Rather, the task for every contrib-utor is to try to explain (to the extent possible) variation observed for any linguis-tic phenomenon within the confines of one's own theory and with conventional theoretical tools. The efficiency and limitations of each approach get highlighted in the process of data explanation. It is here, at the limits of an approach or theory, that we feel that the maximum possibility of integration lies.

The Selected South Asian Landscape

In this volume, we take up a selected portion of the South Asian linguistic land-scape to answer some of the questions raised above. Some specific questions asked by the contributors are as follows. Which kinds of variation do we observe among languages belonging to different major language families of the area, namely Austro-Asiatic, Dravidian, Indo-Aryan and Tibeto-Burman? Are there differences between languages belonging to the same language families? In other words, what kind of differences does one observe between Dravidian languages such as Kannada and Telugu, or between Bangla and Assamese of the Eastern Indo-Aryan family? Last but not the least, we also take up the very challenging issue of intra-language or dialectal variation, such as the differences one may observe between so called dialects of Hindi (Awadhi and Bhojpuri), or of Rajasthani (Marwari, Mewari) or of Malayalam (e.g. the Mappila variety).

Along with extensive data surveys and expositions, all contributors detail out the methodologies they adopt and the theoretical implications of their studies. There are some papers that are sociolinguistic in nature, some that report results of laboratory experiments, some that are more descriptive in nature and yet others whose analyses are couched in generative terms. The range of approaches found in this volume is therefore quite wide, as is the range of South Asian languages covered in the chapters.

The selected South Asian languages are mainly spoken in India, though these languages can also be found in other parts of the world, in varied degrees, due to wide-scale migration of communities to foreign lands. While the Indian states which provide the main source of data for these chapters are mostly tied to linguistic identities, it is also well-accepted that that are no pure linguistic areas. People and communities move between these states and have done so for many centuries, which has resulted in the formation of a fluid linguistic state, showcasing considerable amount of bi/multi-lingualism, linguistic admixtures, and common lexical, morphological and syntactic properties (cf. Subbarao, 2012 for a very recent work detailing out many such interesting aspects of South Asian languages).

Contributions

The volume is organized in the following way. We begin with chapters that give an overview of structural phenomena in multiple languages of South Asia, covering different language families. The first cohort of chapters helps in familiarizing the readers with typological or macro-level differences found in South Asian languages belonging to different language families (Indo-Aryan, Dravidian, Tibeto-Burman, Austro-Asiatic), whether that be in the domains of relative clauses, negation, word order, etc. The next set of chapters look at meso-level variation between languages of the same family. The empirical phenomena covered range from correlatives, polar questions to honorification patterns. The last set of chapters deal with intra-language variation. The chapters on ergativity and agreement variation are arranged together to enable the reader to get an understanding of different approaches adopted to understand small-changes changes in languages.

The first chapter is by Prof. Karumuri V. Subbarao's titled 'A Panorama of South Asian Relatives: A Case of Structural Convergence, Divergence, Innovation and Syntactic Change.' The chapter examines variation, structural commonalities and innovations made in the formation of full-fledged and participial relative clauses in Tibeto-Burman languages, Dakkhini Hindi-Urdu (Indo-Aryan), Bhālāvali Bhasha, Karnataka Saraswat Konkani (Mangalore Konkani; Indo-Aryan) and Saurashtra (an Indo-Aryan language spoken in Tamil Nadu). Subbarao's main thesis is that in contact situations, specific functional categories are reanalysed to accommodate newly acquired syntactic phenomena.

Rajesh Kumar, Sansuma Bramha, Sh. Francis Monsang and Mayuri Dilip in their paper 'Negation in Select South Asian Languages' give a typological analysis of negation and negative polarity items (NPIs) in Hindi, Oriya, Assamese, Santali, Khasi, Monsang, Bodo, Tamil and Telugu. They closely examine the morphological structure of Negation in the clause structure as well as the licensing conditions of negative polarity items (NPIs). They also study the occurrence of NPIs in constructions with long-distance licensing. The root of the NPI can be a wh-element, a quantifier or an idiomatic expression. Keeping in view the structural restrictions on NPI licensing, they analyse NPIs adopting Kumar's (2006) c-commanding strategy, feature checking and alternative-based approach to NPIs (Chierchia, 2013), where the NPIs inherently possess a quantificational scale.

Apurva and Samar Husain, in their paper 'Effect of Non-canonical Word Order and Argument Proximity on Processing of SOV Languages,' consider the role of prediction during sentence comprehension in SOV languages. Robust clause final verbal prediction and its maintenance has been argued as a processing variation in SOV languages vis-à-vis SVO languages. They examine verbal predictions in Hindi (an SOV language) to investigate its robustness and fallibility using a series of completion studies. They provide new data to show that increased working memory load (operationalized as increased preverbal complexity) adversely affects prediction in an SOV language such as Hindi. Using a series of sentence completion studies, they show that clause final verb prediction suffers with increased embeddings as well as with addition of preverbal adjuncts. Together, the results show that while preverbal cues are effectively employed by the parser to make clause final structural predictions, the parsing system breaks down when the number of predicted verbs/relations exceeds beyond a certain threshold. The results suggest that processing in SOV languages is susceptible to centre-embeddings similar to that in SVO languages. This highlights the overarching influence of working memory constraints during sentence comprehension and thereby on the parser to posit less complex structures in both SOV as well as in SVO languages.

Rahul Balusu in his paper 'A Correlative Typology Mixing Syntactic and Semantic Parameters' looks closely at Dravidian correlatives that are formed with a wh-item containing sentence with -oo at the clause edge. The disjunction marker -oo in Dravidian languages participates in coordinating elements, forming indefinites and questions. In the literature, the typology of correlatives has been proposed to have two syntactic parameters—one, the kind of relative clause it originates from—EHRC, IHRC, FR; and two, the kind of left dislocation involved—HTLD, CLD, CLLD. Balusu proposes to add to this typology a third and semantic parameter, its denotation—property or propositional. He contends that the Dravidian correlative is built out of the semantic choice of a proposition-based denotation. This semantic parameter itself is located in the denotation of the wh-items of the language, its lexical semantic entry—as sets of alternatives or as property free variables. This paper has substantial overlaps with Balusu's (2021) paper.

Ambalika Guha in her paper 'A Comparative Study of the Lexicalization of the Bangla Polar Question Particle ki and the Assamese Polar Question Particle ne' investigates the relation between polar question particle and disjunction in three Indo-Aryan languages Hindi, Bangla, and Assamese. The polar questions in these three languages indicate disjunction in the answer space. This further leads to the proposal that there exists a disjunction operator in the polar questions of these languages. Under the principle and parameter approach of generative grammar, this paper studies the property of identity relation between interrogative disjunction operator and polar question particle and shows how it varies across three languages which originated from the same language family. In the paper, it is proposed that the [+Q] disjunction operator is lexically realized as a question particle in Bangla and Assamese. But in Hindi, the [+Q] disjunction operator remains null.

Preeti Kumari's paper is on 'Comparing Honorificity Agreement in Maithili and Bangla.' The system of honorifics in languages has been understood in the form of honorification agreement (Harada, 1976; Toribio, 1990; Boeckx & Niinuma, 2004). This work contends this idea and claims that honorificity, despite being a feature in the DP, needs valuation from a functional head in the discourse domain, owing to its context-sensitive and relational nature. Kumari adopts Portner et al. (2019) in assuming that the 'context' head licenses the honorificity feature in the DP. In the light of this account, Kumari's paper looks at the honorification system of Maithili and compares it to that of Bangla (Eastern Indo-Aryan language). For this comparison, this paper takes up Maithili honorification cases of subject agreement, addressee agreement and multiple argument agreement, i.e. with both subject and object. This comparison shows that honorificity differences can be understood as a parametric difference.

Thapasya Jayaraj and Rajesh Kumar's paper 'Towards an Understanding of Micro-variations: Decoding the Hierarchical Module of Variation and the Correlates of Mappila Malayalam' demonstrates the effects that linguistic and extralinguistic factors have on the structures of languages. They illustrate the notion of a hierarchy of variation with instances of language change from Mappila Malayalam, one of the dominant sociolects of Malayalam. This language has two dominant phases of variation, one denoted as 'first wave variation' and the other denoted as 'second wave variation.' The paper identifies three significant domains influencing the hierarchy of language variation in its contexts and describes the interweaved system of layered hierarchy influenced by the level of linguistic expression, visibility of the variant and the progressive transition of variants.

Sonal Kulkarni-Joshi's paper is titled 'Dialect Variation and Dialect Change: A Social-dialectological Approach.' Working with case marking and agreement in the transitive-perfective clause in regional varieties of Marathi, including Konkani and Ahirani, Kulkarni-Joshi demonstrates how language variation is treated using the methodological tool of socio-historical linguistics and modern dialectology. She also studies the implication of these variations for language change.

Usha Udaar's paper 'Parametrizing Ergativity: Insights from Western Indo-Aryan Languages' aims to find out the underlying parameters that bring about differential ergative patterns in languages. Ergativity is a salient, well-attested phenomenon in many Western Indo-Aryan languages, which is manifested as an overt case marking on the subject and object verb agreement. However, a closer observation of the ergative patterns across some languages such as Haryanavi, Mewati, Marwari and Mewari reveals that there is no one feature that solely defines ergativity, except as an opposition to the default nominative-accusative alignment. This paper argues that the ergativity differences emerge from differential values of the v-heads, and the resultant DP-movements.

The paper by Mahima Gulati and Kamal K. Choudhary is 'Cross-linguistic Variations in the Processing of Ergative Case: Evidences from Punjabi.' This study explores case-based violations, tested previously in Hindi, in order to ascertain if typologically similar languages are neurocognitively equivalent. In contrast to the previously reported N400-P600 pattern observed in Hindi (Choudhary et al., 2009), as well as in Basque (Zawiszewski et al., 2011), the authors observe only a positivity for both nominative as well as ergative case violations in Punjabi. They argue that this difference in the ERP components might have arisen from the idiosyncratic properties of the language, namely the restricted use of the ergative case in Punjabi.

Pritha Chandra's paper 'On Gender Micro-variation' looks at variation in Hindi 'dialects' Awadhi and Bhojpuri. Her main claim is that dialects with nominalizers enable gender morphology; those which lack a nominalizer fail to display gender agreement. The gender-nominalizer association is taken to indicate that there are underlying structural signatures for gender morphology. Language-learning children must use these structural cues to grasp structural schemas that are conducive to its expression. The paper then goes on to discuss how languages shift between nouns and adjectives during the course of their development.

References

Abbi, A., Gupta, R. S, Kidwai, A. (2001). *Language structure and language dynamics in South Asia* (p. 432).

Adger, D. (2003). *Core syntax: A minimalist approach.* Oxford University Press.

Adger, D., & Smith, J. (2005). Variation and the minimalist program. In L. Cornips & K. Corrigan (Eds.), *Syntax and variation: Reconciling the biological and the social* (pp. 149–178). John Benjamins.

Balusu, R. (2021). The Dravidian Correlative and the Disjunctive Marker. In D. Alok & S. Raghotham (Eds.), *Proceedings of Formal Approaches to South Asian Languages (FASAL) 9.*

Boeckx, C., & Fumikazu, N. (2004). Conditions on Agreement in Japanese. *Natural Language and Linguistic Theory, 22*: 453–480.

Boersma, P. (2004). A stochastic OT account of paralinguistic tasks such as grammaticality and prototypicality judgments. Rutgers Optimality Archive.

Chomsky, N. (1957). *Syntactic structures.* Mouton & Co.

Chomsky, N. (1965). *Aspects of the theory of syntax.* MIT Press.

Chomsky, N. (1981). *Lectures on government and binding.* Walter de Gruyter.

Choudhary, K. K., Schlesewsky, M., Roehm, D., & Bornkessel-Schlesewsky, I. (2009). The N400 as a Correlate of Interpretively Relevant Linguistic Rules: Evidence from Hindi. *Neuropsychologia, 47*(13), 3012–3022.

Chierchia, G. (2013). *Logic in grammar: Polarity, free choice, and intervention.* Oxford: University Press Oxford.

Christiansen, M. H., & Charter, N. (2017). Towards an integrated science of language. *Koine Greek.*

Clifton, C. J. (1981). Psycholinguistic renaissance? *Contemporary Psychology, 26*, 919–921.

Comrie, B. (1989). *Language universals and linguistic typology: Syntax and morphology.* University of Chicago Press.

D'Allesandro, R., & van Oostendorp, M. (2017). On the diversity of linguistic data and the integration of the language sciences, *Frontiers in Psychology, 27.*

Dayal, V., & Mahajan, A. (2007). *Clause structure in South Asian languages.* Kluwer.

Eckert, P. (2000). *Linguistic variation as social practice.* Blackwell.

Eckert, P. (2012). Three waves of variation study: The emergence of meaning in the study of sociolinguistic variation. *Annual Review of Anthropology, 2012*(41), 87–100.

Ferreira, F. (2003). The misinterpretation of noncanonical sentences. *Cognitive Psychology, 47,* 164–203.

Fodor, J. A., Bever, T. G., & Garrett, M. (1974). The specificity of language skills. In *The psychology of language.* Mcgraw-Hill.

Foss, D. J., & Hakes, D. T. (1978). *Psycholinguistics: An introduction to the psychology of language.* Prentice-Hall.

Frazier, L., Clifton, C., Randall, J. (1983). Filling gaps: Decision principles and structure in sentence comprehension. *Cognition, 13*(2), 187–222.

Gumperz, J. J., & Hymes, D. (Eds.). (1964). The ethnography of communication. *American Anthropologist, 66*(6), part 2, 186.

Halle, M., Bresnan, J., & Miller, G. A. (Eds.). (1978). Preface and knowledge unlearned and untaught. In *Linguistic theory and psychological reality* (pp. xi–xv and 294–303, revised version of No. 86–87). MIT Press.

Harada, S. I. (1976). Honorifics. In M. Shibatani (Ed.), *Syntax and Semantics 5*, 499–561. Academic Press: New York.

Heim, I., & Kratzer, A. (1998). *Semantics in generative grammar.* Wiley Blackwell.

Hymes, D. (1962). The ethnography of speaking. In Gladwin, T. & Sturtevant, W. C. (Eds.), *Anthropology and human behavior* (pp. 13–53).

Hymes, D. (1964). Introduction: Toward ethnographies of communication. In Gumperz, J. J. & Hymes, D. (Eds.), *The ethnography of communication. Am. Anthropol.* (Vol. 66(6), Part 2, p. 186)

Katz, J. J., & Fodor, J. A. (1998). *The structure of a semantic theory.* Massachusetts Institute of Technology.

Keller, F. (2005). Linear optimality theory as a model of gradience in grammar. In Fanselow, G., Féry, C., Vogel, R., & Schlesewsky, M. (Eds.), *Gradience in grammar: Generative perspectives.* Oxford University Press.

Kimball, J. (1973). Seven principles of surface structure parsing in natural language. *Cognition, 2*(1), 15–47.

Kumar, R. (2006). *Negation and Licensing of Negative Polarity Items in Hindi Syntax.* Routledge: New York & London.

Labov, W. (2001). *Principles of linguistic change* (Vol. II: Social Factors). Blackwell.

Labov, W. (1966). *The social stratification of English in New York City.* Centre for Applied Linguistics.

Labov, W. (1972). *Language in the Inner City* (p. 412). Univ. Pennsylvania Press.

Lewis, S., & Phillips, C. (2015). Aligning grammatical theories and language processing models. *Journal of Psycholinguistic Research, 44*(1), 27–46.

Newmeyer, F. J. (2005). *Possible and probable languages: A generative perspective on linguistic typology.* Oxford University Press.

Phillips, C. (2003). Syntax. In Nadel, L. (Ed.), *Encyclopedia of cognitive science* (No. 4, pp. 319–329). MacMillan Reference.

Poeppel, D., & Embick, D. (2005). Defining the relation between linguistics and neuroscience. In *Twenty-first century psycholinguistics: Four cornerstones.* Taylor and Francis.

Portner, P., Pak, M., & Zanuttini, R. (2019). The speaker-addressee relation at the syntax-semantics interface. *Language, 95*(1), 1–36.

Rizzi, L. (2014). On the study of language as a cognitive capacity: Results and perspectives. In Cardinaletti, A., Cinque, G. & Endo, Y. (Eds), *On peripheries* (pp. 61–99). Hituzi Syobo.

Rumelhart, D. E, Hinton, G. E., & McClelland, J. L. (1986). A general framework for parallel distribution processing. In *Parallel distributed processing: Explorations in microstructure of cognition* (Vol. 1, pp. 45–76). MIT Press.

Schütze, C. T. (2016). *The empirical base of linguistics: Grammaticality judgments and linguistic methodology* (Classics in Linguistics 2). Language Science Press.

Sprouse, J. (2015). Three open questions in experimental syntax. *Linguistics Vanguard, 1*(1), 89–100.

Stemmer, B., & Whitaker, H. A. (Eds.). (1998). *Handbook of neurolinguistics*. Academic Press.

Subbarao, K. V. (2012). *South Asian languages*. Cambridge University Press.

Toribio, A. (1990). Specifier-head Agreement in Japanese. In *Proceedings of WCCFL 9*, 535–548, CSLI: Stanford.

Weinreich, U., Labov, W., & Herzog, M. (1968). Empirical foundations for a theory of language change. In W. Lehmann & Y. Malkiel (Eds.), *Directions for historical linguistics* (pp. 97–195). University of Texas Press.

Zawiszewski, A., Gutiérrez, E., Fernández, B., & Laka, I. (2011). Language Distance and Non-Native Syntactic Processing: Evidence from Event-Related Potentials. *Bilingualism: Language and Cognition, 14*, 400–411.

Pritha Chandra is Professor of Linguistics in the Department of Humanities and Social Sciences at the Indian Institute of Technology Delhi. She works on inflectional morphology and structural phenomena from a generative linguistics perspective. Using data from a wide array of languages, her work primarily focuses on the mechanisms that underlie language variation—covering the entire gamut from micro-level to macro-level variation. Her research has been presented and published on different national and international platforms. She can be contacted at pritha@hss.iitd.ac.in.

Chapter 2
A Panorama of South Asian Relatives: A Case of Structural Convergence, Divergence, Innovation and Syntactic Change

Karumuri V. Subbarao

Abstract This paper attempts to study variation, structural commonalities and innovations made in the formation of full-fledged (the *wh*-type of English) and participial relative clauses in Tibeto-Burman languages, Dakkhini Hindi-Urdu (Indo-Aryan), Bhālāvali Bhasha, Karnataka Saraswat Konkani (Mangalore Konkani; Indo-Aryan) and Saurashtra (an Indo-Aryan language spoken in Tamil Nadu). We show that in contact situations, specific functional categories are reanalysed to accommodate newly acquired syntactic phenomena. We attempt to demonstrate that a creole may prove to be the catalyst in the innovation of a construction type that is novel to the recipient language. We provide data that show that in contact situations, a language may use the *juxtaposition* strategy as a means to express noun modification, as is the case in Nagamese, an Assamese-based creole, and the Konkani spoken by the Indian diaspora in South Africa. We demonstrate that the full-fledged relative clause found in some Naga languages is due to the influence of Nagamese, a creole that has acquired the status of a mother tongue for some Naga speakers.

Keywords Relative clauses · Generative typology · Contact situations · South Asian languages

Abbreviations

ACC	Accusative
CL	Classifier
CORR	Correlative
DAT	Dative

K.V. Subbarao (✉)
Delhi University, Delhi, India
e-mail: kvs2811@gmail.com

17

DEF	Definite
DM	Diminutive marker
DUB MKR	Dubitative marker
EHRC	Externally headed relative clause
ERG	Ergative
GEN	Genitive
IHRC	Internally headed relative clause
IMPERF	Imperfect
INSTR	Instrumental
m	Masculine
NOM	Nominative
NOZR	Nominalizer
p	Plural
PRES	Present
PERF PPL	Perfect participle
PL	Plural
PST	Past
Q	Question
REL	Relative
REL LINKER	Relative linker

Introduction

The purpose of this paper is to present a brief introduction to the nature and formation of relatives clauses in Indo-Aryan, Dravidian and Tibeto-Burman. We
argue that full-fledged relative clauses that occur in some select languages of
Nagaland, which are not indigenous to the Tibeto-Burman language family, are
a result of contact with Assamese through Nagamese, an Assamese-based creole,
used by the various different Naga language speakers as a lingua franca for communication. Based on evidence from Konkani language spoken in Southern Africa,
we hypothesize that the juxtaposition strategy plays a crucial role in borrowing
the relative clause structure. We show that as a result of such borrowing a question
word may be used as a relative pronoun and consequently, a relative linker may be
innovated as a relative complementizer. Based on such evidence, we hypothesize
that the full-fledged relative clauses that occur in Dravidian may be due to contact
with Indo-Aryan.

There are three types of *full-fledged relative clauses* in South Asian languages.
The first type is the relative-correlative clause. 'The correlative clause is associated
with a matrix clause that contains a demonstrative phrase (henceforth Dem-XP).
Correlatives can be simple correlatives (cf. 1a) or multi-head correlatives (1b).'
The embedded relative clause invariably occurs to the left of the head noun.

Hindi-Urdu (Indo-Aryan)

1 (a)   [[*jo*   *so-tā*   *hai*]   *vah*   *kho-tā*   *hai*]

        who (REL)   sleep-IMPERF   PRES   he   lose-IMPERF   PRES

        'Who(ever) sleeps, loses.'

Subbarao (1984)

1(b)   [*jis-ne*   *jo*   *kar-nā*   *cāhā*]   *us-ne*   *vo*   *kiyā*

        who-ERG (REL)   that (REL)   do-INF   wanted   he-ERG   that   did

        For x, y wanted to do x, y did that.'
        Literally: 'Who wanted to do what, he/she did that.'

Bhatt (2003: 416)

Below are given some more structures—NPs with relative clause—post-nominal relative clause (2), and those with right-adjoined relative clause (3).

Hindi-Urdu (Indo-Aryan)

2   [[*ve*   *log*]$_i$ [*jo*   *zyādā*   *cāy pī-te*   *hãĩ*]$_i$]

    which people   who a lot of   tea sleep-IMPERF PRES

    kam   *so*   *pā-te*   *hãĩ*

    less   sleep   find- IMPERF   PRES

People who drink a lot of tea sleep less

Subbarao (2012a, 2012b: 267)

3   *vo*   *kitāb*   *acchī*   *hai*   [*jo*   *sale par*   *hai*]

    that   book   good   PRES   which   sale on   PRES

    'That book is good which is on sale.'

Bhatt (2003: 488)

The second type of relative clauses in South Asian languages is labelled as the gap relative. The embedded predicate in such clauses is non-finite, and it may be in its participial form as in Indo-Aryan, Dravidian and Munda languages, or in the infinitival form as in most of the Tibeto-Burman languages (Subbarao, 2012a, 2012b). Below are given varied types of this construction.

(a) The embedded verb is in its participial form, and the head of the relative clause is outside the embedded relative clause (EHRC).

The embedded predicate *kharīde hue* 'bought (perf pple, m, p)' is in the perfect participial form.

Hindi-Urdu (Indo-Aryan)

4 [$_{S2}$*pūjā-ke*   *kal-ke*   ∅$_i$ *kharīde-hue* $_{S2}$]
   pooja-gen (m, p)   yesterday-gen   bring-PERF PPL

   kape$_i$ *bahut*   *khūbsūrat*   *the*
   clothes (m, p)   very   pretty   PST

   'The clothes that Pooja bought yesterday were very beautiful.'

In some languages, the embedded verb may also appear in its nominalized form, as in Tibeto-Burman languages. As for instance, the embedded verb *le* 'cut' is followed by the infinitival marker *-ke* in (5) in Tenyidie/Angami (Tibeto-Burman) in an internally headed relative clause (IHRC).

Tenyidie/Angami (Tibeto-Burman)

5 [*nɔ*   *kutari*$_i$*-pie*   *nhasi*   *le-ke-*] *ci-*∅$_i$ *u*   *ʒa-se*
   you   knife-INSTR   fruit   cut-NOZR-DM-ø   DEF   big-very
   'The knife with which you cut the fruit is very big.'

                                                    Subbarao and Kevichüsa (1999)

In the following section, we discuss modification strategies in Tibeto-Burman languages and see how a select set of Naga languages developed the relative-correlative clauses. Interestingly, their formation is structurally almost *identical* to the one found in all Dravidian languages.

Tibeto-Burman—Noun Modification Strategies

All South Asian languages (except the Mon-Khmer languages) are *left-branching*. Tibeto-Burman languages thus are head-final. In Tibeto-Burman languages, only the gap (participial or infinitival) strategy is the indigenous strategy. In most of the Tibeto-Burman languages, the embedded verb is [-finite], and hence, the embedded clause is in its nominalized form,[1,2] (Matisoff, 1972). The gap strategy relatives are of two types:

---

[1] That is why an internally headed relative clause (IHRC) in some Tibeto-Burman languages is ambiguous between a relative clause interpretation and a nominal clause interpretation.

[2] In Kokborok (a Tibeto-Burman language spoken in the state of Tripura), there ae participial relatives too. (cf. Gargi Roy (2021)).

Type 1: Externally Headed Relative Clause (EHRC)

In an externally headed relative clause (EHRC), the *head* is overtly present *in the matrix clause* and is coindexed with a null element in the embedded clause (8). The externally headed relative clause (EHRC) is found in all South Asian languages.

6   [- - - - - $\emptyset i$ --]   NPi

In the Tenyidie (Angami-Naga) example below, the head *khriesa* 'young man' is overtly present *in the matrix clause,* and it is coindexed with a *covert operator.*

7   [$_{S2}\emptyset_i$ *bulie*   *kemerie*   *se-ke-ba*$_{S2}$]   *khriesa*$_i$*_u-e*   *a-zemia*
              shirt   red   wear-NOZR-PROG   young   my-friend
                                                    man-DEF-NOM

'The boy who is wearing a red shirt is my friend.'

Kevichüsa and Subbarao (1998: 45, Kevichüsa 2018)

Type 2: Internally Headed Relative Clause (IHRC)

In an IHRC, the *head* is overtly present *in the embedded clause* and is coindexed with a null element in the matrix clause (8). IHRCs are not found in English, Indo-Aryan, Dravidian and Austro-Asiatic (Mon-Khmer and Munda). They are found only in Tibeto-Burman in the South Asian subcontinent.[3]

8   [- - - - NP- ---]   Null$i$

Internally Headed Relative Clauses (IHRCs) are of two types:

Type A: The Internal Head *Overtly* Case Marked
Type B: The Internal Head *Null* Case Marked

Type A: The internal head of an IHRC carries the postposition that manifests the thematic relation of the head with the embedded verb.
    The Naga languages belong to this category. In Konyak of the Naga subgroup of languages, the internal head is overtly case marked with the postposition *phasi* 'with,' the instrumental case marker.

Konyak (Naga, Tibeto-Burman)
Instrumental PP as the head of the IHRC—The postposition ***phasi*** is in bold.

---

[3] Also found in Japanese, Korean, and some American Indian languages.

9 [*naŋ-e*   *mit-phasi*   *peleak*   *watne-con-pu-*] *a*

   you-nom   knife-INSTR   fruit   cut-use-NOZR-DEF

   ø (pro)   *yəʔɔŋe*   *lonaŋ ke*

              very   sharp

   'The knife with which you cut fruit is very sharp.'

Type B: The internal head of an IHRC *does not* carry the postposition that man-ifests the thematic relation of the head with the embedded verb as is the case in the Kuki-Chin languages.
   Indirect object as the head of the IHRC.

Hmar (Tibeto-Burman)

10 [*Lali-n*   *ui-ø*   *bu*   *a-pek*]   kha]   ø(pro)

    Lala-ERG   dog (IO)-DAT   food   3SG-gave   DET

    zanikhan   *a-huŋ*

    yesterday   3SG-came

    'The dog who(m) Lali gave food to came yesterday

An example of a simple clause with the dative case marker (in italics) overtly present.

11   *Lali-n*   *ui-(kuomah)*[a] *(IO)* *bu*   *a-pek-tɔ*

     Lala-ERG   dog-DAT   food   3SG-give-PERF

     'Lali gave food to the cow.'

[a]Like in the other Kuki-Chin languages, the postposition has two forms: (i) *kuomah*—a [+finite] form that occurs in a finite clause and *kuoma*—a [-finite] form that occurs in a non-finite clause. The difference in these two forms is that in the [+finite] form the glottal stop /-h/ occurs and in the non-finite form it does not. A similar pattern is also found in verbs, adjectives, in some other postpositions and also, in adverbs. See for some discussion Subbarao (2012a, 2012b). See Subbarao & Bapui (2018)

Note that the occurrence of the dative case marker *kuomah* 'to' is optional in Hmar in a simplex clause in (11) above.
   We now discuss the nature of the full-fledged relative clauses in some Naga languages of Nagaland. Tibeto-Burman languages in general lack full-fledged rel-ative clauses indigenously. However, there is a select set of languages (Angami Sema, Khezha, Konyak, Ao Mongsen, Ao Chanki and Ao Chungli, Lotha, etc. spo-ken in Nagaland) that has full-fledged relative-correlative clauses.
   The questions that arise now are: How is it that a select set of the Naga lan-guages only has such clauses? We hypothesize that Nagamese, a modified form of

Assamese (Indo-Aryan), used as a lingua franca in Nagaland, functions as a trigger and catalyst in the formation of relative clauses in the select set of Naga languages that has the following specific features:

(i)   A question expression is used as a relative pronoun, and there are no indigenous relative pronouns as such in all the Tibeto-Burman languages.

(ii) A relative complementizer occurs to the right of the embedded clause that links the subordinate clause with the matrix clause.

(iii) The relative complementizer performs some other functions one of which is as a marker of doubt, generally, labelled as the dubitative marker in the grammars of Dravidian languages.

It is worth mentioning that the occurrence of the dubitative marker (a clitic) as the relative complementizer to the right of the embedded clause in Naga languages is similar to the occurrence of the dubitative marker and relative complementizer in Dravidian.[4] Not only does a subset of the Naga languages (spoken in Nagaland) of the Tibeto-Burman family and all Dravidian languages exhibit this pattern, but the functions that the complementizer performs are also identical.

In the grammars of Dravidian languages, this relative linker is referred to as *dubitative marker*. Note that the dubitative marker occurs when the head of the relative clause is [−definite]. In sentences (12)–(14), the head is [−definite]. The relative complementizer is *ši* in (12) in Tenyidie (Angami), *kena* in in Sümi (Sema) in (13) and *sana* in Lotha in (14).

12	*šumie*	*sɔdu*	*vɔr*	*nyi-ba*
	Rel PRON	tomorrow	come	want-PROG
	ši	*siko*	*vɔr.lierivi*	
	DUB MKR (rel linker)	CORR	come.may	

'Whoever wants to come tomorrow may come.'

Kevichüsa (2018:50)

Head [−definite]- dubitative marker overtly present

13	*khukhomɔ*	*atɨlɨ*	*ipeling*	*kena*	*prāiz*	*ithulni*
	whoever	first	comes	DUB MKR	prize	will get

'Whoever comes first will get the prize.'

(Sümi/Sema) (Naga, Tibeto-Burman)

---

[4] See Arora & Subbarao (1989) and Jayaseelan (2018) for a discussion of the relative complementizer in Dravidian.

14 *oco-na*   *zakto* *yuŋa-sana* *oci-na*   *oraŋ-ji*   *huŋ-ŋu*

    who-NOM fast   run-REL   he/she-NOM   money-DEF   get-FUT
                  LINKER

    'Whoever runs fast will get the money.'

Lotha (Tibeto-Burman)

In Sema, when the head is [+definite], the dubitative marker does not occur. The relative complementizer/linker in such cases is *akienɔ* (in bold) in (15).

15 *timi* [*khū* *axathi* *ʒie* *akienɔ*]   *itehi* *hile* *ye.li*

    man   who   fruit   sells rel linker   now   here   came

    'The man who sells fruit came just now.'

(Sümi/Sema) (Tibeto-Burman))

Unlike the English-type right-adjoined relative clauses, the embedded relative clause in a relative-correlative construction *cannot* be extraposed to the *right* of the matrix clause, as is the case in all Dravidian languages and in the Naga languages that have this construction. The non-extraposability of the embedded relative in the relative-correlative construction could possibly be a universal. Some illustrations of structures with extraposition are provided below.

Tenyidie (Angami)

Extraposition—not permitted

16 **siko*   *vər.lierivi*   *Sumie*   *sɔdu*

    CORR   come.may   REL PRON   tomorrow

    vɔr   *nyi-ba*   *Ši*

    come   want-PROG   DUB MKR

    'Whoever wants to come tomorrow may come.'

Kevichüsa (2018)

Extraposition—not permitted

17 **prāiz* *ithulni*   *khukhomɔ* *atili* *ipeling* *kena*

    prize   will get   whoever   first   comes   DUB MKR

    'Whoever comes first, will get the prize.'

Sema (Naga, Tibeto-Burman)

Another interesting commonality between the Naga languages and the Dravidian languages is that interrogative pronouns and relative pronouns are homophonous, just as in English and French. Thus, the embedded relative clause in the select Naga and Dravidian languages devoid of the relative complementizer imparts the interpretation of a simple question.

The following examples of relative clauses from Telugu and Tamil (Dravidian) demonstrate the occurrence of the dubitative marker to the right of the embedded clause. In Dravidian,[5] the dubitative marker – ō occurs to the right of the embedded clause in (18) and (19).

Telugu (Dravidian)

18 [ēdi   kāwāl(i)- ō]   adi   paṭṭu-ku-pō

   what   be-wanted-COMP   that   take-REFL-go-IMP-SG

   'Take away what you want.'

Tamil (Dravidian)

19 yār   aṅkē   mutali   vantu   cēru-v-ār-ō

   who   there   first   come.CPM   reach-FUT-3SG
                                                      HON-DUB
                                                      MKR

   avar   tikeṭṭu   vāṅkalam

   he.NOM   ticket   buy.permissive

   'Let whoever reaches there first buy the tickets.'

Steever (1987: 30)

The embedded relative in a relative-correlative clause cannot be extraposed to the right.

(Telugu (Dravidian))

20 *adi   paṭṭu-ku- pō   [ēdi   kāwāl(i)-ō]

   that   take-REFL- Go-IMP-s   what   be-wanted-COMP

   'Take away what you want.'

Tamil (Dravidian)

21 *avar   ṭikeṭṭu   vāṅkalam   yār   aṅkē   mutali

   he.NOM   ticket   buy.permissive   who   there   first

   vantu   cēru-v-ār-ō

   come.CPM   reach-fut-3 s.HON-
                DUB MKR

---

[5] The dubitative marker in Dravidian performs some other functions such as a disjunctive marker or a [−definite] marker with interrogative pronouns. (See, Subbarao 2012a, 2012b).

More on the Dubitative Marker in Dravidian and Tibeto-Burman

The dubitative marker, which is a clitic, performs the function of a marker expressing doubt in embedded questions in Tibeto-Burman and Dravidian. Sentences (22) in Tenydie (Angami) and (23) from Telugu (Dravidian) are illustrative.

Tenydie (Angami) (Naga, Tibeto-Burman)

22 *šumie   vɔr   nyɨ   ba   ši*
    who   come   want   PROG   DUB MKR
    'I wonder who wants to come.[a, b]'

[a]Mising (Tibeto-Burman) too has the dubitative marker performing similar functions. Interestingly, Mising does not have the relative-correlative clause construction.
[b]The dubitative marker functions as a disjunctive marker in Dravidian and in Mising

Telugu (Dravidian)

23 *inta.ki.i   rēpu   evaru   vastāru-ō*
    anaphoric discourse linker   tomorrow who   come.FUT-DUB MKR
    'I wonder who'd come tomorrow.'

In case the dubitative marker is not overtly present, the sentence would impart the interpretation of an interrogative clause in Tenyidie and Telugu.

22a *šumie   vɔr   nyɨ   ba*
     who   come   want   PROG
     'Who wants to come?'

Telugu (Dravidian)

23a inta ki.i   rēpu   evaru   vastāru
     anaphoric discourse   tomorrow   who   will come-
     linker

     'Who'll come tomorrow?',[a]

[a]Mising (Tibeto-Burman) too has the dubitative marker performing similar functions. See the Appendix

The dubitative marker functions as a disjunctive marker in Dravidian and Mising.

Mising (Tibeto-Burman)

24a	pədoŋə	oyə-	**soŋ**	omā-	**soŋ**	oyəji	omāji	supaŋ	lāma
	rain	will fall-	**dub mkr**	neg-	**dub mkr**	now	say	can	not
	(nominative)								

'(One) cannot say now whether (it) will rain or not.'

Taid (2010: 126)

Telugu (Dravidian) too has a parallel structure.

24b	vāna	paḍutund-	**ō**	lēd-	**ō**	ippuḍu	ceppa lēmu
	rain (nominative)	will fall-	**dub mkr**	neg-	**dub mkr**	now	cannot say

'We cannot say now whether (it) will rain or not.'

Full-Fledged Relative Clauses in Dravidian and Indo-Aryan-Contrasted

The structure of full-fledged relative clauses in Dravidian is distinct from the structure of full-fledged relative clauses in Indo-Aryan. *All Dravidian languages only have the relative-correlative construction, and so do select Tibeto-Burman languages.* Indo-Aryan languages have three types of relative clauses, namely the relative-correlative clauses, the English-type right-adjoined relative clauses and the rightward extraposed relative clauses (Bhatt, 2003). There is no linker that links the main clause and the embedded clause in any Indo-Aryan language. Relative pronouns and question expressions are distinct and are not homophonou. in Indo-Aryan. In contrast, in Dravidian and Tibeto-Burman, they are distinct.

A plausible reason for the absence of a linker in Indo-Aryan: Since question words and relative pronouns are distinct in Indo-Aryan, and the embedded relative does not impart a question interpretation, there is no need for the Indo-Aryan languages to have an overt relative complementizer like the dubitative marker in Dravidian and Tibeto-Burman. Further, Dravidian and Tibeto-Burman languages both

(i)   employ a question word as a relative pronoun,
(ii) use the complementizer or a dubitative marker as a linker to link the embedded relative clause with the matrix clause,
(iii) do only have the relative-correlative construction, and do not have the Indo-Aryan-type relative clauses, and
(iv) have clefts while no Indo-Aryan language has any cleft.

The question then is: How and why did a select set of languages spoken only in Nagaland get the relative-correlative construction? A plausible explanation is that Nagamese is an Assamese based language. According to Kevichüsa (2017),

(i)   '- - -Nagamese is the lingua franca and it is fast spreading, – -'
(ii)   ' - - -Nagamese is no longer a pidgin as most believe it to be, but it is now a creole as it has become a first language for some native Nagas [Naga language speakers speaking different Naga languages, which are mutually unintelligible to each other.KVS].'
(iii) ' - - - it[Nagamese] is a mixture of Assamese, Bengali, Hindi, and probably Nepali. It has been birthed by languages all belonging to the Indo-Aryan language family, and enriched by some words from the Native Naga languages—words like *axone* 'fermented soya bean' (origin: Sümi), and *tsamar* "person from mainland India" (origin: Ao), for example.'

Let us look at the linguistic scenario of Nagaland. Nagaland has about 30 languages and 18 tribes, and each tribe and subtribe speaks a language that is not mutually intelligible among intra- and inter-tribe. It is estimated that there are 90 languages which are undocumented, and the dialect or language status is not determined. The case of Ao Naga is an example. Ao has three 'dialects'—Mongsen, Chungli and Chanki which are not mutually intelligible. Officially and sociolinguistically, they all are labelled as 'dialects.' Wachking dialect is the standard dialect among the Konyaks. However, this dialect is mutually intelligible only to few neighbouring villages nearby and is not intelligible to villages that are a few kilometres away geographically. Such dialects include Tamkong, Wangla, etc. In such a scenario, it is Nagamese, the Assamese-based creole that functions as the lingua-franca for the entire state.[6] We hypothesize that the Indo-Aryan-type relative clause has triggered the formation of the relative-correlative construction in the Naga languages spoken in Nagaland. Nagamese uses the full-fledged relative clause and the juxtaposition of the two clauses. Nagamese, like the Naga and Dravidian languages, uses the question word as the relative pronoun. There are no exceptions to this to the best of our knowledge. The language is spoken in Nagaland and in Assam in contact situations only by the Naga speakers.

Nagamese (Indo-Aryan)

25	masi-bara	ki	kitap	boriši	i.to	kor-ti	asi
	Mhase.NOM	which (Q-word)	book	read	that.CL	home-at	is

'The book which Mhase read at home.'

---

[6]Nikay Besa, a Konyak speaker and a graduate student working on Konyak, provided this information.

The next question that requires an answer is: How is that both Dravidian and the select Naga languages have chosen a dubitative marker as a relative linker or complementizer? As discussed above, the linker preempts the interpretation of a question of the embedded clause. Further, the relative-correlative clause might have started out to modify a head that is [−definite], and in some languages, the relative clause is used to modify a head that is [+definite], as is the case in the Dravidian languages.

Most of the Tibeto-Burman languages and all Dravidian languages have the cleft construction, too. In the Dravidian languages, the verb is in a [-finite] form, and a pronominal suffix occurs to the right of the embedded cleft. In Nagamese, however, in the relative-correlative construction, the matrix and the embedded verb are [+finite].

Nagamese (Indo-Aryan) Relative Clause with the Direct Object as Head.

26 *abuno-bara*   *kitap* *i-to*   *mota-ki*   *tia-to*   *na-bai*

Abuno-NOM   book   that-CL   boy-DAT   gave-CL   not-found

'The book which Abuno gave to the boy is not found.'

(Nikay Besa, personal communication)

In (27), the matrix clause and the embedded clause are juxtaposed, and there is no relative pronoun or a cleft clitic or a linker that occurs in the embedded sentence. Note that the matrix verb and the embedded verb are both [+finite].

Juxtaposition strategy
Nagamese

27 [*yati* *mota* *ek-ta*   *ahato*] [*moi-laka* *sati*   *asi*]

here   boy   one-CL   came   I-GEN   friend PRES

'The boy who came here is my friend'

The question that arises is: why are question words used in place of relative pronouns in Nagamese and in the Naga languages? Some plausible answers are:

(i)   Economy- Q-words (*wh*-expressions) are already available and hence, they come in handy as relative pronouns.
(ii) *wh*-expressions are learnt by the Naga speakers first for negotiations in marketplaces with Assamese speakers for economic transactions.
(iii) The relative linker is needed in Naga languages. If the linker is absent, the embedded clause imparts the interpretation of a question, just as in Dravidian.
(iv) In contact situations, when a language borrows the full-fledged relative clause construction that is not indigenous to it, it employs question words as relative pronouns as it is not only economical, but it preempts the need for inventing or innovating a novel set of relative pronouns.

4. In support of the answers provided above, we attempt to provide evidence from the relative clause construction in Mangalore Konkani, Bhalavali Bhasha, Dakkhini Hindi-Urdu, Saurasthra and the Munda languages.

To substantiate our claim that the relative clause in the Naga languages is a borrowed construction due to language contact, we now discuss the occurrence and nature of relative-correlative clause construction in language contact situations.[7]

5. We provide data that show that in Mangalore Konkani, Bhālavali Bhāshā, Dakkhini and Saurashtra, the transplanted varieties of standard Konkani, Hindi-Urdu, Marathi and Gujarati spoken in Saurashtra area of Gujarat, respectively, in the Dravidian language speaking area:

   (i) a question word of Indo-Aryan is used as a relative pronoun, and
   (ii) either the Initial Complementizer (IC) *ki* 'that' of Hindi-Urdu or Konkani or Gujarati of Indo-Aryan, is reanalysed as a post-sentential linker in Dakkhini, Konkani and Gujarati or a question word is used as a linker in Bhālavali Bhāshā relative clauses and embedded questions.

Thus, when a language that lacks a specific construction-type indigenously comes in contact with another language that has the specific construction-type that is novel to it, it is likely to borrow the construction-type and then make further innovations. Such innovations may utilize some functional categories that are already available in the language, as is the case in Dakkhini, Mangalore Konkani and Saurashtra, an Indo-Aryan language spoken in Tamil Nadu.

Our data demonstrate that the principle of *optimal utilization* of functional categories plays a dominant role in structural borrowing. The case of *ki*, the Initial Complementizer in Dakkhini Hindi-Urdu (Indo-Aryan) spoken in the southern parts of India, aka, Dakkhini. as a case of Syntactic Reanalysis. See Arora and Subbarao (1989).

In Dakkhini:

(i) the question word is used as a relative pronoun, and,
(ii) the Initial Complementizer (IC) of standard Hindi-Urdu is reanalysed[8] as a post-sentential relative linker to link the subordinate clause with the main clause. That is, there is a *positional shift* and a change in the function of the Initial Complementizer (IC)

---

[7] Further, Telugu (Ramarao n.d.) and possibly, the other Dravidian languages have a second type of relative clause construction in which the matrix clause and the embedded clause are linked by the clitic -*ē*- and there is an absence of either a relative pronoun or a question word in such sentences. Such clauses are similar in structure to the juxtaposition clauses except for the fact that the verb of the embedded relative clause carries the clitic -*ē*- that also functions as an emphatic marker.

[8] The correlative pronoun of Hindi-Urdu is reanalysed as an adjectivalizer in Dakkhini, and, it performs several other functions too in Dakkhini. See Arora & Subbarao (1989).

Such change in function may be treated as an innovation.

Dakkhiṇi Hindi-Urdu (Indo-Aryan)

28 [*āp*   *kon.se*   *bacce-ku*   *dyo*   *bole*   *ki*

    you   which-DAT   boy-DAT   give.IMP   said   REL LINKER

    vo   *bacce-ku*   *detī*   *ū̃*

    that   boy-DAT   give   PRES

    'I'll give it to the boy whom you asked me to give.'

Arora and Subbarao (1989:6)

Significantly, an identical phenomenon is observed in Mangalore Konkani, Saurashtra and Bhalavali Bhasha, all of which are transplanted varieties of standard Konkani, Saurasta and Marathi, respectively.

Karnataka Saraswat Konkani (Mangalore Konkani) (Indo-Aryan)

Question word used in place of a relative pronoun with the Initial Complementizer (IC) as the linker.

29 *[khanco*   *mhāntāro*   pēpar   vaccat āssa   *kī*

    which   old man   paper   is reading   linker (COMP)
    (q-word)

    to   ḍākṭarunu   āssa

    he   Doctor   is

Literally: 'Which old man is reading a newspaper, he is a doctor'

Nadkarni (1975:674)

Mangalore Konkani (the relative-correlative clause) which is of the Kannada-type does not permit extraposition, just as all Dravidian languages do not.

30 **avanu/ ā mudukanu/to (mhāntāro)*   *doctor*   *khanco*   *mhāntāro*

    he that old man that (old man)   doctor   which   old man

    pēpar   *vaccat*   *āssa-ki*

    paper   reading   is-COMP

    'The old man who is reading a newspaper is a doctor.'

Bhalavali Bhasha

31 *kōṇi*   *āgi*   *varaḍasi*   *jāntadi-ga*   *te-ni*   *agge-ni*

    who (Q-word)   all   marriage   going-Q   they-ERF   all-ERG

    pānci   *ghəṇṭɛ-si*   *həytti*   *pāvo-[ɛvɛ*

    five   hours-to   here   reach-IMP

Those who are going to the marriage should come here at five o'clock

Varija (2018)

The use of question words in relative clauses is also observed in Goan Christian Konkani.

32 *kɔɲacɛ* *pəišɛ* *sāḍliyat* *taɳɛ* *firyad* *di-u~ci*
    whose   money   lost   he   complaint   give should'

The one who lost the money should give the complaint, Almeida (1989)

Konkani spoken by Indian speakers in South Africa uses the juxtaposition strategy, and there are no relative pronouns or question words that are used. Recall that Nagamese too uses the juxtaposition strategy.

South African Konkani

Juxtaposition—Preferred Strategy

33 [*vərsa-ni* *ti* *mulgi* *pərət* *əjli*]
    year.INS   that   girl   back   come.PST.3SF

[*ti-la* *mi* *mil-ja* *gelu*]
she-DAT   I   meet-INF   go.PST

'I went to meet the girl who returned after a year.'

Participial or Gap Strategy—Also permitted

34 [*vərsa-ni* *pərət* Ø$_i$ *əj-le-lja* *mulgi-la*$_i$ *mi*
    year-INS   back   come-PERF   girl-DAT/ACC   I
                               PPL-3SG.F

mil-ja *gelu* *hotu*
meet-INF   go.PST   be.PST.1

'I went to meet the girl who returned after a year.'

             (Ruta Paradkar & Sonal Kulkarni, (personal communication))

Since the clauses discussed are relative-correlative clauses, no rightward extraposition of the embedded clauses is permitted in Dakkhini, Mangalore Konkani and Bhālāvali Bhasha, as well. It appears that when a relative clause is borrowed by a language that does not have such construction indigenously, the juxtaposition strategy is the preferred strategy before the language fully adopts and internalizes the relative-correlative clause construction.

The next question that arises is: Why is the Initial Complementizer (IC) of Indo-Aryan used as a linker? The reason is the embedded clause with a question word in place of a relative pronoun imparts the interpretation of a question. To preempt such interpretation, a linker is needed. Such linker has two functions: (i) It preempts the question interpretation, and (ii) it functions as a relativizer to link the subordinate clause with the main clause.

In Saurashtra too, the complementizer -*gi* (< from Gujarati *ke*) is used as a relative linker.

Full-fledged sentential relative clause with -*gi* as a relativizer (RELZR).

35	*kon*	*beka*	*avāya-*	*gī*[a]	*tena*	*mora*	*singati*
	which	boy	came-	RELZR	he	my	friend

The boy who came is my friend
[a]-*gī* is also used to express indefiniteness as a [−definite] marker

(Saurashtra, Indo-Aryan) (Siva Sottalu, personal communication)

In Dravidian languages too, the dubitative marker that functions as a linker in relative-correlative clauses also functions as a Final Complementizer (FC) in embedded questions.[9] That is why the IC of Hindi-Urdu and Konkani is reanalysed as a linker in Dakkhini and Mangalore Konkani due to intense language contact. Further, functional categories in a language are very limited, and hence, the recipient language attempts to make of the existing functional categories to the maximum possible extent in a judicious fashion. Such a phenomenon may be termed as the optimal utilization of an existing functional category. To quote Subbarao (2012a, 2012b:11), '(S)yntactic convergence results in the *reanalysis of existing functional categories* to new ones, and we shall show how a contact language optimally utilizes the limited set of functional categories that it has.[10]

Telugu (Dravidian)

36	*nā-ku*	*telusu*	*mī-inti-ki*	*evaru*	*vacc- ē-ru*	*ō*
	I.obl-DAT	know	your-house-to	who	come-PST.3.PL	COMP

I know who came to your house.

Since Konkani and Dakkhini have the quotative, a grammaticalized form of the verb *say* functioning as the Finite Complementizer, the Initial Complementizer (IC) *ki* 'that' inherited from Konkani and Hindi-Urdu is in surplus. Both Dakkhini Hindi-Urdu and Konkani spoken in the southern part of India use it as a relative linker.

In the following section, we discuss how languages in contact may influence each other.

---

[9] Krishnamurti & Gwynn, Steever, Subbarao, Subhrahmanyam, Ramarao, Umamaheshwar Rao and many other scholars have discussed this phenomenon in their works.

[10] Such occurrence of the complementizer in embedded questions is also found in the other Dravidian languages too.

The Role of Contact in Participial Relatives

The dominant and preferred strategy for noun modification in all Tibeto-Burman, Dravidian and Austro-Asiatic (Munda and Mon-Khmer) languages is the gap strategy with no breaks in the Noun Phrase Accessibility Hierarchy (NPAH) proposed by Keenan and Comrie, while Indo-Aryan languages observe restrictions with regard to participial strategies with the positions that can be relativized in the NPAH.

According to the NPAH, in the formation of relative clauses:

Subject > Direct Object > Indirect Object > Oblique Object[11] > Object of the Genitive > Object of Comparison.

- stands for 'stronger than'/'more accessible than'

According to Keenan and Comrie's (1977), the three principles of the Noun Phrase Accessibility Hierarchy (NPAH) are as follows:

The NPAH constraints are:

(i)   A language must be able to relativize subjects.
(ii) The strategy of relativization must apply to a continuous segment of grammatical functions/constituents of the NPAH-scale.
(iii) Strategies that apply at one point of the NPAH-scale may in principle cease at any point on the scale.

There is a considerable variation in Indo-Aryan languages with regard to the positions that can be relativized in the gap strategy. While Hindi-Urdu, Punjabi, Kashmiri and Bangla exhibit gaps in some positions, Assamese of the East Indo-Aryan group, Konkani Marathi and Gujarati of the Western Indo-Aryan group, Oriya of the Eastern group have very few gaps in the positions that can be relativized (Subbarao, 2012a, 2012b: 272–274).

Modification of oblique objects (locative, instrumental, ablative except for the comitative) by the gap or the participial strategy in Indo-Aryan deserves mention. Oriya, Assamese, Nepali, Gujarati, Marathi and Konkani freely permit the modification of oblique objects; Hindi-Urdu, Punjabi, Kashmiri and Bangla do not permit at all. IO too does not permit modification (cf. Subbarao, 2012a, 2012b: 278–288).

The modification of the Comitative PP is not permitted in any South Asian language except in those Tibeto-Burman languages that permit Postposition Incorporation or in Mon-Khmer languages that permit a group marker and a reciprocal marker to occur with the embedded verb (Subbarao & Temsen, 2009; Subbarao, 2012a, 2012b: 299–308). Interestingly, Dakkhini, an offshoot of Indo-Aryan permits the modification of all positions except for the Comitative PP.

---

[11] The Oblique Object (OO) includes Object of Instrumental, Ablative, Locative, Comitative, Allative etc.

Our claim that the role of contact plays a dominant role gains support from the following facts:

(i) Sinhala (Gair, 1997, 2003) lost full-fledged relative clauses in toto as well as the relative-correlative clauses too that they had indigenously.

(ii) In Dakkhini, the frequency of the occurrence of sentential relatives is very low in comparison to gap or participial relatives. Dakkhini instead uses the correlative pronoun *so* 'he/she' of the source languages, namely, Hindi-Urdu and Punjabi. (Arora, 2004; Arora & Subbarao, 1989).

Dravidian languages have full-fledged relative-correlative clauses as well as the participial (gap) relatives. There are divergent views with regard to the origin and occurrence of the relative-correlative construction in Dravidian. Ramaswamy (1981) and Lakshmibai (1985) point out that relative-correlative clauses are *indigenous to Dravidian*. According to them, they are inherited and indigenous structures and are *not borrowed* from Indo-Aryan. Their contention is that the relative-correlative construction is quite widespread in Dravidian, and also, since Old Dravidian too had it, it is not borrowed, but *inherited*. In contrast, Nadkarni (1975), Krishnamurti and Gwynn (1985), Sridhar (1990: 47), Asher and Kumari (1997: 53) observe that the relative clause in Dravidian may be considered *an areal feature borrowed from Sanskrit* (Indo-Aryan). Steever (1987: 33) points out that relative clauses are found in all literary Dravidian languages from the beginning of the literature, and this phenomenon is reconstructible for Proto-Dravidian. Steever (personal communication) holds the view that the relative-correlative construction is indigenous to Dravidian and is not borrowed from Indo-Aryan. His argument is based on the fact that all Dravidian (literary and non-literary) languages have it, and, hence, it cannot be a borrowed construction,

Our view is that the relative-correlative construction is not ingenious to Dravidian and is borrowed from Indo-Aryan. Evidence for our view comes from the following facts.

(i)   Note that in the set of South Asian languages from which the relative-correlative construction is borrowed, a question word is used as a relative pronoun, and there *may* occur a complementizer/dubitative marker to the right of the embedded clause, as is the case in Dakkhini Hindi-Urdu, Mangalore Konkani, Saurastra and Naga languages such as Angami (Tenyidie), Sema. Lotha, Ao (Monsgen, Chungli, Chanki). I

(ii) Since in Dravidian too, we have a question word as a relative pronoun and the COMP $-\bar{o}$ occurs to the right of the embedded verb, it is reasonable to hypothesize that the relative-correlative construction went through similar stages in Dravidian languages too.

(iii) In Tibeto-Burman languages and Munda, the relative-correlative construction is not indigenous. The participial/nominalization (the gap strategy) is the only indigenous and the primary strategy available in Tibeto-Burman and Munda languages. In Dravidian too, the gap strategy is the primary strategy, and all the positions of the Noun Phrase Accessibility Hierarchy (NPAH) are relativizable in this strategy. (Uma Maheshwar Rao, personal communication). The argument we propose is that when a language lacks the full-fledged relative clause and since each language requires a way to modify the noun phrase that manifests each grammatical function, the one and only alternative that the language has is to have the gap strategy that permits the modification of each position on the NPAH.

(iv) Languages in contact situations prefer to use existing functional categories, and the proliferation of new categories is not preferred. Saraswat Konkani, BhalavaLi Marathi, Dakkhini Hindi-Urdu, Saurashtra, Sema and Tenyidie and some other Naga languages such as Ao (Mongsen, Chanki and Chungli), Kezha and Lotha use question words as relative pronouns and an existing marker to express doubt (labelled generally as the dubitative marker) as a relative complementizer or linker. A similar situation obtains in Dravidian too. In those languages in which q-words and relative pronouns are homophonoous, from the point of view of language aquisition, question words are acquired first and the question words acquired earlier would acquire the function as relative pronouns at a later stage in acquisition.

Based on the above discussion thus far, the stages in the acquisition of the relative-correlative construction are as follows:

Stage 1: The matrix and the embedded clauses are juxtaposed to each other.
Stage 2: A question word borrowed from the source language is used is used as a relative pronoun.
Stage 3: When a question word is used to impart the interpretation of a simple question, the language may use a complementizer or dubitative marker or some such marker as a linking strategy to link the subordinate clause to the main clause. This is to preempt the interpretation as a question.

If the stages we propose turn out be valid, one might like to use the three stages in the formation of the relative-correlative construction as a heuristic tool to see if the noun modifying construction is borrowed or indigenous.

Conclusion

In this paper, we have presented discussion on the occurrence of the various types of relative clauses in the four major language families of the South Asian subcontinent. We have shown how a creole/contact language may provide a trigger for the innovation of a novel construction that a language never possessed. We have also noticed that there are stages in the acquisition of the novel construction that include the juxtaposition of the embedded and matrix clauses in a row, the use of question words as relative pronouns and the use of a complementizer or a dubitative marker to link the subordinate clause with the main clause.

We suggested that the various stages observed may provide a heuristic clue to see if the relative-correlative construction is borrowed or indigenous. We also pointed out that a robust gap strategy in a language may hint at the possibility of the gap strategy being indigenous, and the relative-correlative clause may be a borrowed construction.

Acknowledgements I would like to thank the reviewer for her/his helpful comments, most of which have been attended to. The correspondence I have had with Uma Maheshwar Rao and Sanford Steever on the nature of Dravidian relative clauses has been very illuminating and helpful. Thanks to Pritha Chandra for organizing this conference.

I am thankful to Nikay Besa for providing data on Nagamese relative clauses, to Mimi Kevichusa for enlightening me on Nagamese, to Sonal Kulkarni for providing data on South African Konkani (collected by Ruta Paradkar), to Varija N for the data on BaLavaLi Marathi relative clauses, to Siva Sottallu for the data on Sautastra relative clauses and to Basanti Devi for her help on Assamese relative clauses. Thanks are also due to Ian Smith for his help on Saurashtra modification strategies. Thanks to Gargi Roy for her help in the final stages of the manuscript.

Appendix

In this Appendix, we provide parallel data from Lotha and Dravidian to show the similarities and differences in the functions of the dubitative marker *sana* in Lotha and *–ō* in Dravidian (Telugu, Tamil, Kannada and Malayalam).

sana 'dubitative mkr' in relative clauses with a [−definite] head

(i) As a relative linker

Lotha (Tibeto-Burman)

1	*oco-na*	*zakto*	*yuŋa-sana*	*oci-na*	*oraŋ-ji*	*huŋ-ŋu*
	who-NOM	fast	run-rel linker	he/she-NOM	money-DEF	get-will

'Whoever runs fast will get the money.'

Telugu (Dravidian)

2	*evaru*	*tvaragā*	*parigettutār(u)-ō*	*vāḍi-ki*	*bahumati*	*vastundi*
	who	fast	run-rel linker	he/she-NOM	award	get.fut

'Whoever runs fast will get the money.'

(ii) As an indefinite marker

In Tibeto-Burman languages of the Naga group and in Dravidian, an indefinite pronoun constitutes the question expression plus the dubitative marker.

Thus, in an answer to a question in (3), the dubitative marker is used as in (4) in Lotha (Tibeto-Burman) to express indefiniteness.

Lotha (Tibeto-Burman).

3 *ni-ki*   *oczo* *yĭ-co-la*
   your-house   who   come-PST-Q
   'Who came to your house?'

4 *oco-sana*   *yi-co*
   who-DEF   come-PST
   'Someone came.'

Similarly, in an answer to a question in (5), the dubitative marker is used as in (6) in Telugu and (7) in Tamil to express indefiniteness.

Telugu (Dravidian)

5 mī-   inṭi-ki   evaru   vaccēru
   your- *house-to* who   *came*
   'Who came to your house?'

6 *evar(u)-ō*   *vaccēru*
   who-DEF   came
   'Someone came.'

Tamil (Dravidian)

7 *nēṟṟu*   *yār-ō*   *uŋkaḷ-ai-k*   *kūpiṭ-t-ān*
   yesterday   who-[DEF]   you(PL)-ACC   call.PST-3SG.m
   'Someone called you yesterday.'

                                                      Lehmann (1989: 155)

8 *yār-ō*   *baruttidāre*
   who-INDEF   came
   'Someone came.'

Kannada (Dravidian)

8 *yār-ō*   *baruttidāre*
   who-INDEF   came
   'Someone came.'

                    (Sridhar 1990: 259)

Wh-expressions and the corresponding indefinite pronouns.

Lotha (Tibeto-Burman)

	Q expression	gloss	[−definite] pronoun	gloss
1	oco	'who'	oco-sanā 'who-[−def] mkr'	'some one'
2	undo/nto	'what'	nto-sanā/ unto-sanā	'some thing'
3	kothoŋ	'when'	kothoŋ-sanā 'when-[−def] mkr'	'some time ago'
4	kolo	'where'	kolo-sanā 'where-[−def] mkr'	'some where'
5	kotoli	'how'	koto.li-sanā how.way-[−def] mkr	'some how'

Telugu (Dravidian)

	Q expression	gloss	[−definite] pronoun	gloss
1	evaru	'who'	evar(u)-ō 'who-[−def] mkr'	'some one'
2	ēmiṭi	'what'	ēmiṭ(i)-ō 'what-[−def] mkr'	'some thing'
3	eppuḍu	'when'	eppuḍ(u)-ō when-[−def] mkr	'some time ago'
4	ekkaḍa	'where'	ekkaḍ(a)-ō 'where-[−def] mkr'	'some where'
5	elāga	'how'	elāg(a)-ō how-[−def] mkr	'some how'

Kannada (Dravidian)

9	namma	akka	ellig-ō	hō-giddāre
	my	elder sister	where (to?)	go-PERF.n.PST.3SG.f

'My elder sister went somewhere.'

(Sridhar 1990: 259–260)

Note that the expression *ellig-ō* 'where-[−def]' consists of the *wh*-expression *elli* 'where' and the dubitative marker *−ō* functioning as a [−def] marker.

(iii) As a complementizer (COMP) in embedded questions

Lotha (Tibeto-Burman)

10	a-na	nca	ni-ki	oco	yĭ-co	(*la)	sanā
	I-NOM	know	your-house	who	come-PST	Q	COMP

'I know who came to your house.'

Note that the question marker *–la* cannot occur which we've shown with a * in parentheses.

Telugu (Dravidian)

11 *nā-ku   telusu mī-inṭi-ki   evaru vacc-ē-rō*
    I.obl-DAT know   your-house-to who   come-PST-COMP
    'I know who came to your house.'

Lotha (Tibeto-Burman)

12 *a-na kolo   yi-co-(*la) sanā   a-na   nca*
    I-erg where go-PST-Q   COMP I-NOM know
    'I know where Mhaebmo went.'

Telugu (Dravidian)

14 *nāku   sarita ekkaḍi-ki veLL,ind(u)-ō telusu*
    I.DAT Sarita where-to went-COMP   is known
    'I know where Sarita went.'

Lotha (Tibeto-Burman)

15 *a-na   n.nci   mhabemo-na   ndoli*
    I-ERG   NEG.know Mhabemo-ERG why

    hoto   tho-co-lā   sanā
    like that say-PST-Q   COMP
    'I don't know why Mhabemo said like that?'

Telugu

16 *nāku sarita enduk(u)   and(i)   ō   teliyadu*
    I.dat Sarita why   said   comp
    'I don't know why Sarita said like that.'

Lotha (Tibeto-Burman)

17 *ete-na   n-nci   mhabemo-na   iɲi-co-sanā*
    we-NOM NEG-know Mhabemo-NOM NEG-come-PST-[−DEF]
    'We don't know why Mhabemo did not come.'

Telugu (Dravidian)

18 *inta.kii vāḍu enduku rā   lēd(u)-ō*
    well   He   why   come NEG-DEF
    'I wonder why he didn't come.'

Data similar to Telugu can be adduced from Tamil, Malayalam and Kannada too.

I have collected data similar to the Lotha (Tibeto-Burman) data from Ao (Mongsen), Ao (Chungli), Ao (Chanki), and Khezha. It is not included here due to imitations of space.

The dubitative marker -*soŋ* in Mising performs similar functions.

'Doubt or uncertainty [italics in the original] is expressed by the suffixes –*soŋ* ... -*māsoŋ* or –*ji*...-*mā ji*, each of which is a pair expressing an affirmative and a negative possibility [respectively, KVS] (*māsoŋ/māji* comprising the morphemes *maŋ* 'the negative marker' and –*soŋ* or *ji, e.g.*.' (Taid, 2010: 126).

16	*pədoŋə*	*oyə-soŋ*	*omā- soŋ*	*oye əji*	*omāji*	*supaŋ*	*lāma*
	rain.NOM	will fall-DUB MKR	will fall-DUB MKR	now	say	can	NEG

'(One) cannot say now whether (it) will rain or not.'

Taid (ibid) adds: 'Without the principal clause in the sentence the sentence with –*soŋ* would usually be interrogative in form. e.g.

19	*pədoŋə*	*oyə-soŋ*	*omā- soŋ*
	rain.NOM	will fall-DUB MKR	NEG-DUB MKR

'(Any idea) whether (it) will rain or not, etc.'

Taid (2010: 126)[12]

In Dravidian languages too, the dubitative marker –*ō* performs an identical function.

Telugu (Dravidian)

20	*vāna*	*paḍutund(i)-ō*	*lēd(u)-ō*	*ippuḍu*
	rain.NOM	will fall-DUB MKR	NEG-DUB MKR	now
	evarū	*ceppa-lē-ru*		
	anyone	say-NEG-3.PL		

Literally: 'Anyone cannot say now whether (it) will rain or not.'
Intended: 'No one can say now whether (it) will rain or not.'

---

[12] What is worth noting about Mising is the fact that in spite of having a dubitative marker that performs many functions like the dubitative marker in the Dravidian and select Tibeto-Burman languages, and in spite of having been in intense contact for centuries with Assamese that has full-fledged relative clauses, the dubitative marker did not acquire the functions of a complementizer in relativization. As a result, unlike the select Naga languages in Nagaland, Mising does *not* possess the relative-correlative construction. This fact demonstrates that though a language may possess all the morphological and syntactic ingredients in a contact situation, it is not a desideratum that the language would innovate or borrow a novel construction. This phenomenon would be of interest to linguists studying syntactic change in contact situations.

References

Almeida, M. (1989). *A Description of Konkani*. Panaji, Goa. Thomas Stephens Konkani Kendr.

Arora, H., & Subbarao, K. V. (1989). Syntactic change and convergence. The case of *so* in Dakkhini. *Studies in the Linguistic Sciences, 19*(1), p.1–18. Urbana-Champaign: University of Illinois. Also, available at: www.academia.edu.

Arora, H. (2004). *Syntactic convergence: The case of Dakkhini Hindi-Urdu* Delhi: Publication Division, Delhi University.

Bhatt, R. (2003). Locality in correlatives. *Natural Language and Linguistic Theory, 21*, 485–541.

Gair, J. W. (2003). *Sinhala*. In: G. Cardona & D. Jain (eds.), *Indo-Aryan Languages* (Routledge language family series, 2).

Gair, J., & Paolillo, J. (1997). *Sinhala* (Munchen: Lincom Europa).

Kevichüsa, M., & Subbarao, K. V. (1998). The relative clause in Tenyidie (Angami Naga). *South Asian Language Review, 8*(2), 40–64.

Kevichüsa, M. (2018). *Relative Clause Formation in Tenyidie,* Kohima: Nagaland, 14–19.

Kevichüsa, M. (2017). Status of the languages in Nagaland: An introspection. *Nagaland University Research Journal*, 10.

Krishnamurti, Bh., & Gwynn, J. P. L. (1985). *A Grammar of Modern Telugu*. New Delhi: Oxford University Press.

Matisoff, J. (1972). Lahu nominalization, relativization and Genitivization. In J. Kimbal (Ed.), *Syntax and Semantics, I* (pp. 237–257). Academic Press.

Nadkarni, M. V. (1975). Bilingualism and syntactic change. *Language, 52*(3), 672–683.

Roy, G. (2021). *Clause structures in Kokborok—A case of language contact and convergence.* Ph.D. Thesis, IIT. Madras.

Steever, S. B. (1987). Remarks on Dravidian complementation. *Studies in the Linguistic Sciences, 17*(1), 103–119.

Subbarao, K. V. (1984). *Complementation in Hindi Syntax*. Delhi: Academic Publications.

Subbarao, K. V., Dutta-Gogoi, M., & Rabha, H. U. (2023). *A Typological Grammar of the Rabha Language*.Guwahati Assam: Anundoram Borooah Institute of Language, Art & Culture.

Subbarao, K. V. (2012a). *South Asian languages: A syntactic typology.* Cambridge. New York, & Delhi: Cambridge University Press.

Subbarao, K. V. (2012b). *South Asian Languages: A syntactic typology.* Cambridge. New York, & Delhi: Cambridge University Press. www.Cambridge.org/subbarao. Also Available at https://www.academia.edu/6666513/South_Asian_Languages_A_Syntactic_Typology

Subbarao, K. V., & Kevichüsa, M. (1999). Internal relative clauses in Tenyidie (Angami): A case of hierarchical precedence vs. linear precedence. *Linguistics of the Tibeto-Burman Area, 22*(1), 149–181.

Subbarao, K. V., & Temsen, G. (2009). Comitative PP as Head in externally-headed relative clauses in Khasi. *Journal of Austro-Asiatic Languages.* Bangkok: Mahidol University.

Subbarao, K. V., & Bapui, V. T. (2018). The Syntax of Finite and Non-Finite Predicates in Mizo (Kuki-Chin). Invited talk presented at the SALA conference in the special symposium *In Memory of Alice Davison & James W. Gair* at the SALA Conference, University of Konstanz, Konstanz, Germany.

Taid, T. R. (2010). *A Dictionary of the Mising Language (Mising to Mising, Assamese, English).* Assam: Anundoram Boorah Institute of Language, Art & Culture.

Varija, N. (2005, 2018). A Typological Grammar of Bhalavali Bhasha. ms.

Karumuri V. Subbarao is formerly Professor of Linguistics at Delhi University, and former Radhakrishnan Chair Professor in Humanities at the University of Hyderabad. His research work is focused on the syntactic typology of South Asian languages in general and Tibeto-Burman and Austro-Asiatic languages in particular. One of his recent books *South Asian languages: A Syntactic Typology* (2012) is published by Cambridge University Press, Cambridge. He has been an ***elected member*** of the Linguistic Society of America since 2003, and the Linguistic Society of Nepal since 2005. He has taught at several universities in India and abroad. He was a Visiting Professor at the University of Hamburg, Hamburg, Germany, and Tokyo University of Foreign Studies, Tokyo, Japan. Currently, he is working on the grammars of three Tibeto-Burman languages, namely, Mizo, Rabha and Saihriem. He has published in international and national journals. A grammar of Rabha has recently been published in 2023. Some of his publications are available at: www.academia.edu & www.Researchgate.edu.

Chapter 3
Negation in Select South Asian Languages

Rajesh Kumar, Sansuma Brahma, Sh. Francis Monsang and Mayuri Dilip

Abstract Negation occupies a significant focus in the syntactic study of languages. The phenomena of negation in select South Asian languages reveal significant generalizations. In some languages, negation is expressed by lexical items while others are morphological. The paper primarily focuses on two aspects: first, the morphological distribution of negative markers in different clause structures including sentential and constituent negation. The morphological parsing of sentential negation shows that the negative is suffixed to the tense/verb form if the overt tense form exists. This pattern of morphological alignment, where tense occurs preceding the sentential negative is analogous to the syntactic representation, where the TP occurs above NegP within the functional domain. The sentential negation occurs below TP and above vP, whereas the constituent negation adjoins to the constituent. The second part is the distribution of negative polarity items (NPIs) in these languages and their licensing conditions. We show that there are different kinds of NPIs present in SALs such as classifier, quantifier, wh-NPIs and idiomatic-NPIs. All NPIs are marked with the emphatic particle at the word-final position having exclusiveness meaning *even* in negative and inclusiveness meaning *also* in affirmative sentences. Keeping in view, the structural restrictions of NPI, we analyse NPIs adopting (Kumar, Negation and licensing of negative polarity items in Hindi syntax, Routledge, 2006) c-commanding strategy, feature checking and alternative-based approach to NPIs (Chierchia, Logic in grammar: polarity, free choice, and intervention. OUP Oxford, 2013), where the NPIs inherently possess a quantificational scale.

R. Kumar (✉)
Indian Institute of Technology Madras, Chennai, India
e-mail: rajesh@iitm.ac.in

S. Brahma
Indian Institute of Technology Indore, Indore, India

Sh. F. Monsang
English and Foreign Language University, Shillong, India

M. Dilip
Central University of Rajasthan, Ajmer, India

Keywords Negation · Sentential · Constituent · Negative polarity items · C-commanding

Symbols and Abbreviations

1SG	1St person singular
3PLNH	3Rd person non-honorific
3SG	3Rd singular
3SGM	3Rd singular masculine
ACC	Accusative
AFF	Affirmative
ALL	Allative
AUX	Auxiliary
CLF	Classifier
COMP	ComplementizerCPM
DAT	Dative
DEM	Demonstrative
ERG	Ergative
exist	Existential
FIN	Finite
FUT	Future
HAB.MASC	Habitual. masculine
IMP	Imperative
IMPF	Imperative
Q	Quantifier
INCL	Inclusive
LOC	Location
NEG	Negation
NMLZ	Nominalizer
NOM	Nominalizer
NPI	Negative polarity itemOM
PRES	Present tense
PRF	Perfective
PROX	Proximity
pst	Past
intr	Intransitive
Q	Question marker
Q-NPI	Quantifier negative polarityUQM
WH-NPI	Wh-negative polarity item

Introduction

Negation depicts various morphosyntactic complexities as discussed in previous studies. Payne (1985), Zanuttini (2001) and Kumar (2006) demonstrate two strategies of negation; i.e. it occurs as a morpheme attached to a verb, and alternatively, it occurs as a lexical form. Chomsky (1991), building on Pollock's (1989) study, followed by Mahajan (1990) and Dwivedi (1991) note that a sentential negation occurs below TP and above AgrP within the clause structure. Nicolae (2012) and Chierchia (2013) provide a semantic approach to demonstrate negative influencing NPIs, where the negative features interact with the NPIs. In this paper, the previous studies come handy to investigate the structure of sentential negation, constituent negation, quantifier scope and the position of NegP in clause structure in select Indian languages from Indo-Aryan, Dravidian, Tibeto-Burman and Austro-Asiatic language families.

The paper primarily focuses on two aspects that are divided into two different parts. The first part of the paper shows the morphological distribution of negative markers in different clause structures including sentential and constituent negation in select South Asian Languages (henceforth SALs), whereas the second part of the paper demonstrates different kinds of NPIs and their licensing conditions. In the NPI licensing, the paper looks into the various licensing condition including local vs long-distance licensing, NPI licensing in the presence of overt vs covert negation. The root of the NPI can be a classifier, a quantifier, a question word and an idiomatic expression. Keeping in view, the structural restrictions of NPI, we analyse NPIs adopting Kumar's (2006) c-commanding strategy, feature checking and alternative-based approach to NPIs (Chierchia, 2013), where the NPIs inherently possess a quantificational scale.

The data show that in some South Asian Languages spoken in India, the negation occurs as a free or bound morpheme. The negation occurs in different positions in the sentential and constituent negation. In sentential negation, the NegP remains below TP and above vP, whereas in constituent negation, it immediately precedes or follows the constituent as an adjunct. Though the negative markers in these languages occur with certain variations, their function and projection in the syntactic tree remain similar. We have categorized four different kinds of NPIs based on the nature of the root word: classifier, quantifier, question word and idiomatic expression. These expressions allow overt licensing; however, few do not allow overt licensing (licensing in few environments other than negation). All allow local licensing and most of these languages allow long-distance licensing too (except Khasi.) Based on these distinctions, we have categorized NPIs as strong and weak.

The data for the present work comes from various sources. The Tibeto-Burman data are primarily elicited from the native speakers of Bodo (Kokrajhar, Assam) and Monsang (Monsang Panthai, Manipur) by the second author and the third author, who are native speakers of Bodo and Monsang, respectively. We have also verified these data with senior members of the respective communities. For the

Indo-Aryan, we have consulted two Assamese native speakers who are also doing Ph.D. at Gauhati University. We elicited some Bengali data from the Bengali students studying at IITM, and the Hindi data are provided by the first author who is a native speaker of Hindi. The Dravidian data comes from the fourth author's fieldwork during her stay at IITM. The Austro-Asiatic data also comes from the fourth author's fieldwork on Santhali, whereas for Khasi data, we have consulted some Khasi speakers at Shillong.

The organization of the paper is as follows: Sect. 3.2 spells out the morphological properties and occurrence of negation both in predicative (sentential negation) and adjoined (constituent negation) positions; the distribution of negation in both verbal predicates and in existential predicates; the occurrence of a negative element as a bound morpheme, following the tense marker in a verbal predicate; the distribution of negative elements in the context of light verbs and the distribution of constituent negation. Section 3.3 discusses the syntactic distribution of sentential negation and constituent negation in the clause structure; Sect. 3.4 deals with some syntactic operations of negative elements. It shows how quantifier scope and NPIs behave in the presence of negative markers. Section 3.5 provides an account of different kinds of NPIs present in South Asian Languages. It demonstrates the distribution of NPIs in different clause structures, and how certain elements such as NPIs occur only in the presence of negation; Sect. 3.6 elaborates on the licensing conditions of such NPIs; Sect. 3.7 deals with NPIs in non-negative contexts; Sect. 3.8 discusses some of the theoretical operations for NPI licensing, namely c-commanding strategy, feature checking and alternative-based approach; Sect. 3.9 is the conclusion.

Distribution of Negation

The morphosyntactic properties of negative elements as sentential negation in its occurrence in a sentence vary from language to language. In the following subsection, two forms of negatives, namely sentential and constituent negation, are discussed in terms of their morphological features, distribution and location in sentences in select South Asian Languages. As discussed by Zanuttini (1991), Progovac (1994), Hany-Babu (1996), Ouhalla (1990), Mahajan (1990), Haegeman (1995), Benmamoun (1997), Kumar (2006), sentential negation scope over the entire sentence, whereas constituent negation scopes only the constituent it negates. In other words, the negative remains around the verb in sentential negation, whereas the negative remains around the target constituent in constituent negation. Negation in South Asian languages is either free or bound morpheme in nature and can occur either in the preverbal or post-verbal positions. In some languages, it is preverbal, whereas in some it is post-verbal, and in a few cases, it is both preverbal and post-verbal. In Hindi, Santali and Khasi the negation occurs as a free morpheme in the preverbal position as in (1–3).

(1) *rājīv*   *āj*   *dillī*   *nahī̃*   *jā-egā*   [Hindi]
     Rajiv   today   Delhi   NEG   go-SUBJ.3.FUT
     'Rajiv will not go to Delhi today.' Kumar (2006)

(2) *baha*   *baŋ*   *hej-en-a-y*   [Santali]
     Baha   NEG   come-PST-INTR-FIN-3.SG
     'Baha did not come.'

(3) *u*   *John*   *ym*   *shym*   *wan*   [Khasi]
     3SGM   John   3SGM   NEG   come
     'John did not come.'

In Bodo, the negation occurs as a bound morpheme in both preverbal and post-verbal positions as in (4).

(4a) *dui-jɔ*   *da-tʰaŋ-lai*   [Bodo]
     river-LOC   NEG-go-IMP
     'Don't go to the river.'

(4b) *aŋ(-u)*   *uŋkʰam*   *za-ja*   [Bodo]
     1SG(-NOM)   rice   eat-NEG
     'I don't eat rice.'

In Monsang, Telugu and Oriya, the negation occurs in post-verbal positions as in (5), (6) and (7), respectively.

(5) *ámá*   *kítʰə̀r-té*   *sí-má:*   [Monsang]
     3SG   market-ALL   go-NEG
     'S/he didn't go to market.'

(6) *rāmu*   *rā-lē-du*   [Telugu]
     Ramu   come-PST.NEG-3SG
     'Ramu did not come.'

(7) *rāmu*   *pakkore*   *ṭikke*   *madhya*   *nai*   [Oriya]
     Ramu   with   little   also   NEG
     'Ramu does not have anything.'

Distribution of Sentential Negation

In the section, we demonstrate the distribution of negative elements as a morphological entity as sentential negation in select SALs. In all the languages mentioned
above, the sentential negation occurs either as a free or bound morpheme and
attaches adjacent to the main verb as already discussed in the previous section. In
Hindi, the free morpheme *nahĩĩ* occurs to the left of the verb *jā* 'go' as in (8a). In
Assamese, the preverbal bound morpheme occurs to the left of the main verb *kʰa*
'eat' as in (8b). In Tamil, the bound morpheme *–illai* attaches to the right of the
verb *varav* 'come' as in (8c). In Telugu, the bound morpheme *–lē* occurs to the right
of verb *rā* 'come' as in (8d). In Bodo, the post-verbal bound morpheme *–ja* occurs
to the right of the main verb *za* 'eat' as in (8e). In Monsang, the post-verbal bound
morpheme *–má:* occurs to the right of the main verb *si* 'go' as in (8f). In Santhali,
the free morpheme *baŋ* occurs to the left of the verb *hej* '*come*' as in (8 g). In Khasi,
the free morpheme *shym* occurs to the left of the verb *wan* 'come' as in (8 h).

(8a) *rājīv   āj   dillī   nahĩĩ   jā-egā*   [Hindi]

     Rajiv   today   delhi   NEG   go-SUBJ.3.FUT

     'Rajiv will not go to Delhi today.'

(8b) *moi   bʰat   na-kʰa-u*   [Assamese]

     1SG   rice   NEG-eat-1SG

     'I do not eat rice.'

(8c) *rāmu   varav-illai*   [Tamil]

     Ramu   come- PRES.NEG

     'Ramu does not come.'

(8d) *rāmu   rā-lē-du*   [Telugu]

     Ramu   come-PST.NEG-3SG

     'Ramu did not come.'

(8e) *gobla-ja   football   gele-ja*   [Bodo]

     PN-NOM   football   play-NEG

     'Gobla does not play football.'

(8f) *kə   kítʰər-tè   sí-má:-ŋ*   [Monsang]

     1SG   market-ALL   go-NEG-1SG

     'I do/did not go to market.'

(8 g) *baha*   *baŋ*   *hej-en-a-y*   [Santali]

      Baha   NEG   come-PST-INTR-FIN-3.SG

      'Baha did not come.'

(8 h) *u*   *John*   *ym*   *shym*   *wan*   [Khasi]

      3SGM   John   3SGM   not   come

      'John did not come.'

The existential verbs show different patterns of negative occurrences. The examples in (9) show the occurrence of negative with existential verbs in SALs. In Hindi, negation *nahĩĩ* occurs left to the 'be' verb *hai* adjacently as in (9a). The word *nei* in Bengali functions as a negative existential verb as in (9b). In Tamil, the word *illai* functions as a negative existential verb as in (9c). In Telugu, the negative *lē-* appears to be merging with the existential verb as shown in (9d). In Bodo, the negative marker *-ja* occurs right to the negative existential morpheme *gui-* as shown in (9e). In Monsang, the negative marker *-má:* occurs right to the existential marker m̩- as in (9f). In Khasi, the negative marker merges with the existential marker and forms don as shown in (9g).

(9a) *rām*   *ghar-pe*   *nahĩĩ* *hai*   [Hindi]

      Ram   house-LOC   NEG   EXIST.PRS

      'Ram is not at home.'

(9b) ram   bari-te   nei   [Bengali]

      Ram   house-LOC   neg.EXIST.PRS

      'Ram is not at home.'

(9c) *rāmu*   *vīṭṭ-il*   *illai*   [Tamil]

      Ramu   house-in   exist.pres.neg

      'Ramu is not at home.'

(9d) *rāmu*   *inṭ-lo*   *lē-ḍu*   [Telugu]

      Ramu   house-LOC   EXIST.PRES.NEG

      'Ramu is not at home.'

(9e) *ram-a*   *no-wao*   *gui-ja*   [Bodo]

      Ram-NOM   house-LOC   EXIST-NEG

      'Ramu is not at home.'

(9f) *ét^hwùr* *m̥-má:*   [Monsang]

   fruit   exist-NEG

   'There is no fruit.'

(9 g) *u*   *ramu*   *ym*   *don* *ha*   *ïïŋ*   [Khasi]

       3SGM   Ramu   3SGM   NEG   at   home

       'Ramu is not at home.'

The following examples in (10) show the occurrence of negative imperatives in SALs. The negative bound morpheme *na-* occurs to the left of the main verb *k^ha* 'eat' in Assamese as in (10a), the negative free morpheme *na* occurs to the right of the main verb *k^hejo* 'eat' in Bengali as in (10b), the negative bound morpheme *da-* occurs to the left of the main verb *za* 'eat' in Bodo as in (10c), the negative free morpheme *mət* occurs to the left of the main verb *k^ha* 'eat' in Hindi as in (10d), the negative free morpheme *wat* occurs to the left of the main verb *jaid* 'walk' in Khasi as in (10e), the negative bound morpheme *-nu* occurs to the right of the main verb *ca* 'eat' in Meitei as in (10f), the negative bound morpheme *-ma:* occurs to the right of the main verb *tu* 'do' in Monsang as in (10 g), the negative free morpheme *nā* occurs to the right of the main verb *k^hā* 'eat' in Oriya as in (10 h), the negative bound morpheme *alo* occurs to the left of the main verb *lei* 'tell' in Santali as in (10i), the negative bound morpheme *āt* occurs to the right of the main verb *var* 'come' in Tamil as in (10j), and the negative bound morpheme *aku* occurs to the right of the main verb *rāy* 'write' in Telugu as in (10 k) in imperative sentences.

(10a) *(tumi)* *b^ha:t*   *na-k^ha-ba*   [Assamese]

       2SG   rice   NEG-eat-IMP.INFORMAL

       'Don't eat rice.'

(10b) *k^hejo*   *na*   [Bengali]

       eat   NEG

       'Don't eat.'

(10c) *(nuɯŋ)* *uɯŋk^ham* *da-za-lai*   [Bodo]

       2SG   rice   NEG-eat-IMP

       'Don't eat rice.'

(10d) *(tum)* *bha:t*   *mət* *k^ha-o*   [Hindi]

       2SG   rice   NEG   eat-IMP.INFORMAL

       'Don't eat rice.'

(10e) *wat   jaid*   [Khasi]

    NEG   walk

    'Do not walk.'

(10f) *ca-ga-nu*   [Meitei]

    eat-IRR-NEG

    'Don't eat'

(10 g) *ámə̀   tú-má:*   [Monsang]

    this   do-NEG

    Don't do this.'

(10 h) *kʰā   nā*   [Oriya]

    eat   NEG

    'Don't eat.'

(10i) *alo=m*   *lei-a-e-a*   [Santali]

    PHB=2   tell-APPL-3-FIN

    'Don't tell him.' (Bodding, 1929: 81)

(10j) *iŋkē   var-āt-ē*   [Tamil]

    here   come-NEG-EMPH

    'Do not come here.'

(10 k) *(nuvvu)*   *rāy-aku*   [Telugu]

    you   write-NEG.IMP

    'Do not write.'

In this section, we observed the morphological distribution of sentential negation, where we find that the negative follows the tense marker. This pattern of alignment where the tense precedes the negative is analogous to the positions of TP, and NegP, where TP occurs above NegP, within the functional domain. Thus, the morphological alignment of tense and the sentential negative strengthens the fact that TP occurs above NegP syntactically. The following section discusses the occurrence of negative in the context of light verbs, where we show the implications when the negative intervenes in the root verb and the vector verb.

Sentential Negation in the Context of Light Verbs

In this section, we present a discussion on sentential negation in the context of light verbs. In all these languages, the lexical and light verbs should be adjacent in light verb formation. The infinite verb is followed by the light verbs, which are conjugated with the final verb suffixes such as tense, aspect, mood, negation and so on. In Hindi, the unmarked position of the negative marker in the context of light verbs is the preverbal position. The negative can intervene between the main verb and the light verb as in (11a-b). In Bangla, the negative marker occurs to the right of the light verb in the form of a free morpheme. In the case of displacement of the negative marker, it leads to the ungrammatical sentence as in (12a-b). However, in the two Dravidian languages, i.e. Tamil and Telugu, the negative in light verbs occur as a bound morpheme, suffixed to the main verb as in (13a) and (14a). As a result, the bound morpheme does not have the capability to move to a preverbal position, reflected through the ungrammatical sentences as in (13b) and (14b). In Bodo, the negative marker in the context of light verbs occurs as a bound morpheme, suffixed to the light verb as in (15a). This is like the Dravidian languages where the movement of the negative marker in any position other than its fixed order leads to the ungrammatical sentence as in (15b). In Khasi and Monsang, the construction with the light verb is not found in the data collected.

(11a) *raziv   ofis   saaf   nahiiN   kar-taa*   [Hindi]
       Rajiv   office   clean   NEG   do-HAB.MASC
       'Rajiv does not clean the office.'

(11b) *raziv   ofis   nahiiN   saaf   kar-taa   hai*   [Hindi]
       Rajiv   office   clean   NEG   do-HAB.MASC   be.PRS
       'Rajiv does not clean the office.'

(12a) *raziv   ofis   poriskar   kor-e   na*   [Bengali]
       Rajiv   office   clean   do-CPM   NEG
       'Rajiv does not clean office.'

(12b) **raziv   ofis   poriskar   na   kor-e*   [Bengali]
       Rajiv   office   clean   NEG   do-CPM
       'Rajiv does not clean office.'

(13a) *avan   pikpaket   adik-illa*   [Tamil]
       he   pick pocket   beat-HAB.NEG
       'He does not pick pocket.'

(13b) *avan   pikpaket   illa-adik   [Tamil]

      he   pick pocket   HAB.NEG-beat

      'He does not pick pocket.'

(14a) atanu   zebulu   kott-a-du   [Telugu]

      he   pocket   beat-HAB.NEG-3P.SG.M

      'He does not pick pocket.'

(14b) *atanu   zebulu   a-kott-du   [Telugu]

      he   pocket   HAB.NEG-beat-3P.SG.M

      'He does not pick pocket.'

(15a) sulekʰa-ja   metʰai   ruzab   laŋ-a-kʰui-mun   [Bodo]

      PN-NOM   song   sing   take away-NEG-IMPF-PST

      'Sulekha did not sing (a) song.'

(15b) *sulekʰa-ja   metʰai   ruzab   a-laŋ-kʰui-mun   [Bodo]

      PN-NOM   song   sing   NEG-take away-IMPF-PST

      'Sulekha did not sing (a) song.'

As we observe the light verbs above, the movement of the negative to the intervening position in light verbs leads to ungrammaticality in Bengali, Tamil, Telugu and Bodo but not in Hindi. Irrespective of Bangla having a sentential negative as a free morpheme, cannot move to an intervening position. From the observation mentioned above, we can claim that when the negative occurs in the post-verbal position, the displacement is not possible, whereas, in Hindi, the negative occurring in the preverbal position can intervene between the root and the vector verb.

Based on the description of facts presented above, we can make generalizations that the occurrences of sentential negation in SALs vary from language to language in terms of their position in a sentence. In Dravidian language and Tibeto-Burman languages, the sentential negatives in verbal predicates are bound morphemes, attaching to the right of the verb stem, when the tense occurs as a zero morpheme. However, the negative attaches to the right of the tense marker, when the verb has an overt tense marker. This provides us evidence, to show that tense precedes the negation, similar to the occurrence of TP, NegP and AgroP in the syntactic tree, where NegP occurs below TP, and above AgroP as discussed in Pollock (1989), Mahajan (1990), Chomsky (1991), Dwivedi (1991). In contrast to Dravidian and TB languages, Hindi and Bangla show that sentential negation occurs as a lexical element. The lexical element occurs in the preverbal position in Hindi, and in the post-verbal position in Bangla. In the case of non-verbal predicates such as the existential constructions in Dravidian languages, the negative shows three different morphological structures, where in the first case, there is a merging of verbal and negative functions; in the second case, the two functions are manifested in two different morphemes; and in the third case, the two functions are manifested in two different morphemes; however, the negative occurs in the preverbal position. In contrast to Dravidian languages, in Hindi, sentential negative occurs as a lexical element, in the preverbal position, and in Bangla, it occurs as a lexical element in the post-verbal position. As we observe, the negative markers, the strict alignment of the verbal morphemes is found only when the negative is a bound morpheme. When the sentential negation occurs in a light verb, the displacement of the negative, to a position intervening the root verb and the vector verb leads to ungrammaticality in Dravidian languages and Bangla, but not in Hindi. The canonical position of the sentential negative, being post-verbal can be a reason for the ungrammaticality in Dravidian languages and Bangla. Thus, on the basis of the data presented in the sections above, we can claim that the occurrence of a sentential negation as a free morpheme or a bound morpheme, and the position of the sentential negative in the clause structure is a parametric variation. In the following section, we discuss the morphological properties of constituent negation and its position in the clause structure.

Distribution of Constituent Negation

This section demonstrates the morphological distribution and the position of constituent negation in the above-mentioned languages. In all the languages mentioned above, the negative marker in constituent negation occurs as a free or bound morpheme and immediately follows the constituent that is being negated except Khasi. In Khasi, a head-initial language, it is obvious to expect that the negation precedes the constituent it negates.

In Hindi, the free morpheme negation *nahiiN* follows and negates only the constituent subject *main* as shown in (16a). In Assamese, the negative marker *no-* is a bound morpheme, suffixed to the be-verb *hoi*, follows and negates the constituent *doctor* as shown in (16b). In Tamil, the negative *alla/illai* follows and negates the constituent *doctor* only as shown in (16c). In Telugu, the negative marker *kādu* follows and negates the constituent *doctor* only as shown in (16d). In Bodo, the negative marker *-ja* is a bound morpheme, suffixed to the be-verb *noŋ*, follows and negates the constituent *doctor* only as shown in (16e). In Monsang too, the negative marker *má:* follows and negates the constituent *doctor* as shown in (16f). In Khasi, the negative marker *dei* precedes and negates the constituent *doctor* as shown in (16 g). In all the examples below, the negative marker has scope over the constituent that it negates.

(16a)   *main*   *nahiiN*   *skuul*   *jaa-taa*   [Hindi]
     1SG   NEG   school   go-HAB
     'I don't go to school.'

(16b)   *moi*   *doctor*   *no-hoi*   [Assamese]
     1SG   doctor   NEG-be
     'I am not (a) doctor.'

(16c)   *rāmu*   *ḍākṭar*   *alla/illai*   [Tamil]
     Ram   doctor   be.NEG.PRS
     'Ram is not (a) doctor.'

(16d)   *rāmu*   *ḍākṭar*   *kādu*   [Telugu]
     Ram   doctor   NEG
     'Ram is not (a) doctor.'

(16e)   *ram-a*   *doctor*   *noŋ-a*   [Bodo]
     PN-NOM   doctor   be-NEG
     'Ram is not (a) doctor'

(16f)   *momo*   *khà*   *dóktàr*   *má: kà*   [Monsang]
     Momo   DEF   doctor   NEG COP
     'Momo is not a doctor.'

(16 g)   *u*   *ram*   *ym*   *dei*   *u*   *doctor*   [Khasi]
     3SGM   Ram   3SGM   NEG   3SGM   doctor
     'Ram is not (a) doctor'

Based on the description of facts presented above, we can say that the occurrence of constituent negation does not vary from language to language in terms of their position and also its forms and functions except Khasi in SALs. In Indo-Aryan languages like Hindi, Assamese, in Dravidian languages like Tamil, Telugu and Tibeto-Burman languages like Bodo and Monsang, the constituent occurs as a free or bound morpheme, following the constituent that is being negated. The occurrence of the constituent negative shows a uniform distribution in these languages. However, Khasi shows a different pattern with respect to its distribution of constituent negation. The constituent negation in Khasi occurs as a free morpheme, preceding the constituent it negates.

To summarize this section, the morphological distribution of sentential negation and constituent negation is discussed. We show the alignment of sentential negative, where the negative follows the tense and precedes the agreement marker in Indo-Aryan, Dravidian, Tibeto-Burman and Austro-Asiatic languages. This morphological pattern resembles the syntactic positions of TP, NegP and AgroP in a tree structure, where NegP occurs below TP and above AgroP. This analogy in the morphological and the syntactic occurrence strengthens the phenomenon discussed by Pollock (1989) that TP dominates NegP. Sentential negation in the context of light verbs is discussed, where the displacement of the sentential negative from the canonical position to the position intervening between the root verb and the vector verb. Such displacement leads to ungrammaticality in Dravidian, Tibeto-Burman, Austro-Asiatic and Bangla due to the fact that the negative occurs in the post-verbal position, unlike Hindi. Further, the morphological properties of the constituent negation are discussed. The constituent negative occurs to the right of the constituent that is being negated in all the languages discussed above except Khasi.

Syntactic Distribution of Negation in Clause Structure

The discussion in the previous sections suggested that the distribution of the sentential negation and the constituent negation vary in their morphological properties in SALs. In this section, the syntactic configuration of the two types of negations is illustrated. Pollock (1989), Chomsky (1991), Zanuttini (1991), Mahajan (1990), Dwivedi (1991), Kumar (2006) suggest that Negative heads Negative Phrase and it occurs in the functional domain dominated by IP. According to Pollock (1989), Chomsky (1991) within the functional domain dominated by IP, the NegP occurs between TP and AgroP, based on the position of the negation in the clause structure. According to Zanuttini (1991), NegP occurs higher than TP. Mahajan (1990) shows that, in Hindi, NegP occurs below TP in Hindi. Dwivedi (1991) noted that the negation occurs as the head of NegP, located outside VP and below AspP, taking VP as its complement. However, Kumar (2006) shows that NegP occurs below TP and above AspP, ModP, whereas, in constituent negation, the negation is XP-final, attached to the constituent, through the process of adjunction to the NP that is being negated. In the light of the proposals mentioned above, the following sections exemplify the syntactic configuration of sentential negation and constituent negation in SALs.

Sentential Negation

In SALs, the negation occurs outside the VP and not inside it. Further, the negative heads its own phrase, namely NegP. The NegP occurs in the functional domain and does not occur in the lexical domain. Among the phrases in the functional domain, NegP occurs below TP and above AspP as in Fig. 3.1.

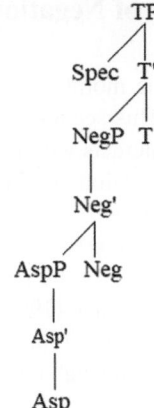

Fig. 3.1   Tree depicting the position of NegP occurring below TP and above AspP

Recall that the morphological parsing of the verb with sentential negation shows that the negative follows the tense and precedes the agreement marker. As we observe, the tree representation of the NegP, we can see that the NegP occurring below TP, resembles the morphological parsing of the verbal predicates, where the negative follows the tense. The following section deals with the syntactic representation of constituent negation in SALs.

Constituent Negation

The constituent negative is attached to the NP that is being negated, through the process of adjunction, as in Fig. 3.2.

To summarize this section, the sentential negative in SALs occurs as the head of NegP, in the functional domain, below TP and above AspP. The SALs show a morphological pattern analogous to the tree representation, wherein both the cases, TP occurs before NegP, and agreement follows NegP. Conversely, the constituent negation adjoins to the constituent that is being negated. In the following section, the quantifiers occurring in the scope of negation are elaborated.

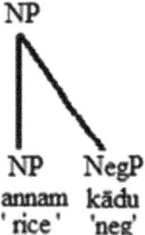

Fig. 3.2   Tree depicting constituent negation with Telugu data

Some Syntactic Operations of Negation

The previous section discusses the morphological properties and the position of negation in the clause structure. This section discusses some syntactic operations of negation, where the negative interacts with the elements in the clause structure. The two syntactic operations of negation are the quantifier scope and the negative polarity items (NPIs). In the quantifier scope, the reduction of scope, due to the presence of a negative marker is demonstrated. Further, NPIs are discussed, where they require negative licensors, either in the local domain, or long-distant as discussed in several studies such as Mahajan (1990), Progovac (1994), Lahiri (1998), Kumar (2006) and among others. In the light of the proposals mentioned above, the syntactic operations of negation are elaborated below.

Quantifier Scope

Certain quantifiers can have narrow scope when co-occurring with negation as explained in *John did not shoot many arrows.* (Progovac, 1994: 5). The quantifier *many,* which usually has a wide scope, gets influenced by the negation, and consequently, the scope is reduced to *few,* indicating narrow scope. A similar scope reduction can be found in SALs, where the wide scope of the quantifier is reduced due to a presence of a negative. The structural configuration of such quantifier scope reduction is elaborated below.

(17a)   *sab*   *hai/nahiN*   *hai*   [Hindi]
         All   be.PRS/NEG   be.PRS
         'All are there.'/ 'Nothing is there.' or 'Not all are there.'

(17b)   *xokolu*   *as-e/*   *nai*   [Assamese]
         All   EXIST-3p/   EXIST.NEG
         'All are there.'/ 'Not all are there.'

(17c)   *attanai(y)-um*   *irəkə/ illai*   [Tamil]
         all.UQM   BE.PRES/ be.PRES.NEG
         'All are there.'/ 'Nothing is there.' or 'Not all are there.'

(17d)   *anni-i*   *unn-ā-yi/ lē-vu*   [Telugu]
         all.UQM   be-PRES-3.PL.NH/ BE.PRES.NEG-3.PL.NH
         'All are there.'/ 'Nothing is there.' or 'Not all are there.'

(17e) *gasɯibɯ*   *doŋ-o-mɯn/gɯi-ja-mɯn*   [Bodo]

       All   EXIST-AFF-PST/EXIST-NEG-PST

       'All are there.'/ 'Nothing is there.' or 'Not all are there.'

(17f) *mí*   *békʰè*   *òŋ*   *nè /*   *òŋ*   *má:*   [Monsang]

       people   ALL   stay   REAL /   stay   NEG

       All are there.'/ 'Not all are there.'

(17 g) *baroh*   *ki*   *don*   *haŋtei /*   *um*   *don*   *eiei*   haŋtei   [Khasi]

        everyone   GEN   are   there /   NEG   there   nothing   there

        'All are there.' / 'Nothing is there.'

As we observe the data presented above, the quantifier that manifested universal quantification, also occurs in the presence of a sentential negation, manifesting narrow scope. It is interesting to note that the quantifiers with narrow scope, are manifesting two interpretations of narrow scopes, such as 'Nothing is there.' / 'Not all are there.' Such ambiguity of scope is not found in other types of quantifiers in SALs.

Negative Polarity Items in South Asian Languages

This section discusses different types of NPIs, namely classifier NPIs, quantifier NPIs, question word NPIs and idiomatic expression NPIs. They can occur in the subject, object and adjunct positions in the presence of overt negation in the local and non-local environments (in a few clauses). In addition, they can occur in the absence of overt negation in a few negative-like contexts such as modals, conditionals, questions, future, generic/habitual, etc. One morphological feature common among these languages is that the NPI is suffixed with an emphatic particle whose unmarked function is an inclusiveness marker *ho* in Santali, *bhī* in Hindi and *kūḍā*/vowel lengthening Telugu, *bɯ* in Bodo, *o* in Bangla, *dóŋ/-rʷú* in Monsang and so on. However, the function of these markers is 'even' in the presence of negation as mentioned in Lahiri (1998).

Classifier NPIs

The classifier NPIs are a combination of several constituents such as a classifier, numeral one, and an emphatic particle as shown in (18). The order of these constituent morphemes varies from language to language. In Bodo, the classifier NPIs are of the following order: classifier-numeral-emphatic particle, whereas it is the numeral-classifier-emphatic particle in Bangla. The classifier NPIs are similar to

English idiomatic expressions such as even a penny, even a budge, etc. In SALs, these types of NPIs may be found in classifier languages.

(18a) *sulekʰa-ja*   *duŋ-se-bu*   *metʰai*   *ruzab* *-a-kʰui-mun*   [Bodo]

PN-NOM   CLF-one-even   song   sing-NEG-IMPF-PST

'Sulekha did not sing even a song.'

(18b) *robi*   *æk-ta-o*   *boi*   *ken-e-ni*   [Bangla]

Ravi   one-CLF-even book   buy-3-NEG.PRF

'Ravi did not buy even a single food.'

Quantifier NPIs

The quantifier NPIs are a combination of a bound morpheme and an emphatic particle. These kinds of NPIs are observed in all the SALs as shown in (19).

(19a) *sulekʰa-ja*   *rao-kʰuu-bu*   *nu-wa-kʰui-mun*   [Bodo]

PN-NOM   Q-ACC-even   see-NEG-IMPF-PST

'Sulekha did not see anybody.'

(19b) *ŋkʰèʔ-zə́/-dóŋ*   *ḿ-má:*   [Monsang]

one-even   EXIST-NEG

'There is nothing.' / 'Even one is not there.'

(19c) *ēk bhī*   *nahĩĩ*   *hẽ*   [Hindi]

Q-NPI   not   be.PRES.SG

'There is nobody.'/ 'Not even one person is there.'/
'Even a single penny is not there.'

(19d) *ami*   *kichui*   *kha-i*   *ni*   [Bangla]

I   anything   eat-1P   NEG.PRF

'I have not eaten anything.'

(19e) *oruttan{-um/kūḍā}*   *illai/*iru-kkir-ān*   [Tamil]

one person-also.NPI   be.PRES.NEG/be.PRES

'Not even one person is there.'

(19f) *okkaḍu{-u/kūḍā}*   *lē-ḍu/*unn-ā-ḍu*   [Telugu]

one person also.NPI   be.PRES.NEG-3.SG.M/be.PRES-3.SG.M

'Not even one person is there.'

(19 g) *baha   miṭi hoṛ ho   baŋ   ɲel-ked-e-(y)a*   [Santali]

baha   Q-NPI   not   see-PST:A-FIN-OM-FIN

'Baha did not insult anyone.'

Wh-NPIs

The wh-NPIs in observed in all the SALs. These are of the following combination wh-word-emphatic particle. Let us consider the following example in (20).

(20a) *rāmu ne   kisī kā bhī   apmān   nahī̃   kiyā   thā*   [Hindi]

ramu ERG   WH-NPI   insult   not   do   PST.SG

'Ramu did not insult anyone.'

(20b) *yārum   ill-ai/*irəkə*   [Tamil]

nobody.NPI   be.PRES.NEG-3.PL.N/ be.PRES-3.PL.N

'Nobody is there.'

(20c) *evarū   lē-ru/*unnāru*   [Telugu]

nobody.NPI   be.PRES.NEG-3.PL.H/ be.PRES-3.PL.H

'Nobody is there.'

(20d) *sulekʰa-ja   mabla-ba-bɯ   metʰai   rɯzab-a*   [Bodo]

PN-NOM   when-PRT-even   song   sing-NEG

'Sulekha does not sing (a) song even sometimes.'

(20e) *momo*   *ák^{h}útè-dóŋ/-r^{w}ú*   *sí-má:*   [Monsang]

       momo   where-even   go-NEG

       'Momo didn't go anywhere.'

(20f) *okoy ho*   *banu-ko-a*   [Santali]

       wh-NPI   not.COP-OM-FIN

       'Not even one is there.'

Idiomatic Expression NPIs

The idiomatic expression NPIs refer to the existence of a single expression that is idiomatic in nature. These kinds of expressions are somehow similar to that of classifiers NPIs which we discussed earlier. Let us consider the following examples in (21).

(21a) *mẽ*   *tum-kō*   *ēk phūṭi*   {*nahī̃ dū-ngā*/ *dū-ngā}   [Hindi]
                    kauṛī

       I   you-DAT   i-NPI   {NEG give-FUT.1.SG.M/
                             give-FUT.1.SG.M}

       'I will not give you a red cent.'

       (Kumar, 2006: 4)

(21b) *enn-itam*   *oru*   *nayā paisa kūḍa*   *illai*/*irəkə   [Tamil]

       me-with   one   single penny also.NPI   be.PRES.NEG/*be.PRES

       'I don't have a single penny with me.'

(21c) *nā-daggara*   *cilli gavva kūḍā*   *lē-du*/*un-di   [Telugu]

       me-with   single penny incl.NPI   be.NEG.PRES-3.SG.NH/*be.PRES-3.SG.NH

       'I don't have a single penny with me.'

(21d) *iɲ*   *miṭit kaṇa tamba ho*   *baŋ*   *emam-a-ɲ*   [Santali]

       I   i-NPI   not   give.FUT-FIN-SM

       'I will not give you a red cent.'

Long-Distance Licensing of NPIs

In the previous section, we have discussed different types of NPIs in a few SALs where NPIs are licensed in the local domain. In this subsection, we focus on long-distance licensing. We will be classifying the elements into strict NPIs if they do not allow long-distance licensing, and non-strict NPIs, if they allow long-distance licensing. In such cases, the NPI occurs in the embedded clause, and the negative occurs in the matrix clause, leading to long-distance licensing of NPI. Except for Santali, long-distance licensing exists in all the SALs mentioned above as shown in (22). The sentences with long-distance licensing are provided below.

(22a) *sariitaa-ne nahiiN kah-aa ki us kamre meN koi bhii*

Sarita-ERG NEG say-PRF that that room in some even

aadmii thaa   [Hindi]

person was

'Sarita did not say that there was anybody in that room.'

(22b) *razu kotʰao za-b-e bole bol-e ni* [Bengali]

Raju anywhere go-FUT-3P that tell-PRF NEG

'Raju did not say that he would go anywhere.'

(22c) *orutan-um iruppan enru ninaikkav-illai* [Tamil]

one person-even be-PRS-3P.SG.H comp think-PST.BE.NEG

'I did not think that there is even one person.'

(22d) *okkadu-kuda un-ta-d(u) ani anuko-le-du* [Telugu]

one person-even be-PRS-3P.SG.M comp think-PST.NEG-3P.SG.F

'I did not think that there is even one person.'

(22e) *ram-a*   *raobɯ*   *pʰɯi-duŋ*   *hunna*   *san-a-kʰɯi-*
                                                   mun[Bodo]

PN-NOM   anybody   come-IMPF   COMP   think-NEG-IMPF-PST

'I didn't think that
anybody came.'

(22f) *kə-íŋ*   *john*   *tʰóʔ*   *mí*   *òŋ*   *kà*   *rʷú*   *kʰár-*   [Monsang]
                                                         mà:-ŋ

I-ERG   john   COM   person   stay   COP   not   think-
                                                   even.NPI   NEG-1SG

'I did not think that there is anyone with John.'

(22 g) **baha*   *noḍe*   *okoy-ho*   *ləi-kate*   *baŋ*   *hec-en-a-y*   [Santali]

Baha   here   wh-also.NPI   tell-CPM   NEG   think-PST-FIN-SM

'Baha did not think that there is anybody.'

(22 h) *nga-m*   *tharai*   *ba*   *don*   *mano*   *bad*   *u*   *john*   [Khasi]
                                                  mano

I-NEG   think   there   alone   who   with   3SGM   john
                                                 who.NPI

'I did not think that there is anyone/nobody with John.'

The above examples in (22) show the long-distance licensing of NPIs in SALs. The negative *nahiiN* of the matrix clause licenses the NPI *koi bhii admi* of the embedded clause in Hindi as shown in (22a). The negative *ni* of the matric clause licenses *kotʰao* of the embedded clause in Bengali as shown in (22b). The negative *-illai* of the matric clause licenses *orutan-um* of the embedded clause in Tamil as shown in (22c). The negative *–le-* of the matrix clause licenses *okkadu-kuda* of the embedded clause in Telugu as shown in (22d). The negative *-a* of the matrix clause licenses *raobɯ* of the embedded clause in Bodo as shown in (22e). The negative *–má:* of the matrix clause licenses *rʷú* of the embedded clause in Monsang as shown in (22f). The negative *–m* of the matrix clause licenses *mano mano* of the embedded clause in Khasi as shown in (22h). However, the negative *baŋ* of the matrix clause does not license *okoy-ho* of the embedded clause in Santali as shown in (22g).

NPI in Non-negative Contexts

Various non-negative contexts as discussed in Lahiri (1998), Kumar (2006) and Bhattacharyya (2012) are yes/no questions, conditionals, imperative, generic, modal of possibility and adversative predicate. We compare the NPIs in non-negative contexts in a few SALs as shown in (23–27). We notice that the occurrence of NPI in Santali resembles the structure of Telugu. In Santali and Telugu, the form of NPI in the negative context varies the form in the non-negative contexts. In contrast, the form of NPI is identical in both negative and non-negative contexts in the rest of the languages. In Telugu, the NPI in negative context occurs with vowel lengthening 'even.' In contrast, the NPI in the non-negative context is attached with *ainā* 'at least.' A variation exists in Santali too. The NPI in the negative context occurs with the particle *ho* 'even' and in non-negative contexts, no particle exists. Except for Bodo, all languages allow NPIs in a few non-negative contexts.

Modal Verbs

The data presented below in (23) illustrates NPI licensing in the context of modal verbs in a few SALs.

(23a) *tum*   *kabhii bhii*   *ghar*   *jaa*   *sakte*   *ho*   [Hindi]

     you   anytime   home   go   may   AUX

     'You may go home anytime.'

     (Lahiri, 1998: 76)

(23b) *{evvar(u) ainā/*yē pillī}*   *ī*   *tēbl*   *ni*   *etta-galugutā-ru* [Telugu]

     who at least/*wh-NPI}   this   table   ACC   lift-POSS-3.PL.H

     'Anyone can lift this table.'

(23c) *átʲʷú*   *ŋkʰèʔ-z-iŋ*   *ámɔ̀*   *é-tú*   *tʲé-vá*   *tè*   [Monsang]

     who   one-even-ERG   DEM   NMLZ-do   able-FUT   AUX

     'Anyone can do this.'

(23d) *jahay ge/*okoy ho*   *noa ṭebl*   *tul-daḍe-a-y*   [Santali]

     anybody/*wh-NPI   this table.ACC   lift-POSS-FIN-SM

     'Anyone can lift this table.'

(23e)   *raobɯ   pʰɯi-nɯ   ha-jɯ   [Bodo]

        Anybody   come-NF   can-HAB

        'Anyone can come.'

Conditionals

The data presented below in (24) illustrates NPI licensing in context of conditional sentences in few SALs.

(24a)   agar   raam   kisii-ko bhii dekhegaa   to tumheN   bataayegaa [Hindi]

        if   Ram   anyone   see-FUT   then you   tell-FUT

        'If Ram sees anyone, he will inform you.'

        (Lahiri, 1998:61)

(24b)   okavēla   ā   gadilō-ki   {evar(u)   ainā/*evarū}

        if   that   room-in   who   at
                                                                     least/*wh-NPI}

        vaste   nēnu   nī-ku   cept-ā-nu   [Telugu]

        come   I   you-to   tell-PST-3.
                                          SG

        'I will let you know, if anybody comes into the room.'

(24c)   tíʔ   kítʰər-té   sí   nə́bè   ņ̀ná   ņ́ŋnà   ŗ̐ər-váŋ   ké-tè

        sister mark-   go   if   mother   TOWARDS. say-FUT   1SG-AUX
                er-ALL   LOC

        'If sister goes to market, I will tell to mother.'   [Monsang]

(24d)   juti   rum re   {okoy   hijuk-a iɲ   am-ke
                                    ko/*okoy
                                    ho}

        if   room-LOC   who   come-FIN   I   you-to
                                   PL/*WH-NPI

        ləi am-a-y   [Santali]

        tell-PST-3.SG

        'I will let you know, if anybody comes into the room.'

(24e) *raobɯ   pʰui-bla   aŋ   nuŋ-nu   kʰuntʰa-gun   [Bodo]
      Anybody   come-COND   1SG   2SG-DAT tell-FUT
      'If anybody comes, I will tell you.'

Yes/No Questions

The data presented below in (25) illustrates NPI licensing Yes/No questions in few
SALs.

(25a) tumheN   koii bhii   kitaab   pasand aayii   kyaa?   [Hindi]
      you   any   book   like   Q
      'Did you like any book?'
      (Lahiri, 1998:98)

(25b) ā   rūm   lo   {evar(u)-   unn-ā-r(u)-ā?   [Telugu]
                              ainā/*evarū}

      that   room   in   {who-   be-PST-3.PL.H-INTR
                             even/*WH-NPI}

      'Is anybody there in that room?'

(25c) rum   re   {okoy ko/*okoy ho}   banu-ko-ge-a   [Santali]
      Room   LOC   who pl/*WH-NPI   NEG-OM-be.PRS-FIN
      'Is anybody there in that room?'

(25d) momo   ákʰútè-rʷú   é-sí   mó   [Monsang]
      Momo   where.ALL-even   NMLZ-go   Q.MKR
      'Did Momo go anywhere?'

(25e) *raobɯ   pʰui-duŋ-mun   nama   [Bodo]
      Anybody   come-IMPF-PST   Q
      'Did anyone come?'

Habitual/Generic

The data presented below in (26) illustrate NPI licensing in habitual/generic sentences in few SALs.

(26a) *koii bhii*   *aadmii   is   mez-ko   uThaa letaa   hai*   [Hindi]

      any   man   this   table   lift-PERF-take-V2 PRES

      'Any man lifts this table.'

      (Lahiri, 1998:75)

(26b) *{yē pilli ainā/*yē pillī}*   *eluka-ni   vēṭāḍu-tun-di*   [Telugu]

      which cat at least/*WH-NPI}   rat-ACC   hunt-GEN-3.SG.N

      'Any cat hunts a rat.'

(26c) *jahay /*okoy ho*   *pusi ge   guḍuj   sab-ko-a-y*   [Santali]

      any/*WH-NPI   cat   rat   hunt-OM-FIN-SM

      'Any cat hunts a rat.'

(26d) **raobɯ   gotʰo-wa   pʰoraisali-jao   pʰɯi-jɯ*   [Bodo]

      Any   child-NOM   school-LOC   come-HAB

      'Any child comes to school.'

Imperative

The data presented below in (27) illustrates NPI licensing in imperative sentences in few SALs.

(27a) *kuchh bhii   khaa   lo*   [Hindi]

      anything   eat   IMP

      'Eat anything.'

      (Lahiri, 1998: 77)

(27b) *{ēdi   ainā/*ēdī}   tinu*   [Telugu]

      anything   at least/*WH-NPI}   eat-3.SG

      'Eat anything.'

(27c) *jahna ge/*okoy ho   jom-me*   [Santali]

      anything/*WH-NPI   eat-IMP

      'Eat anything.'

(27d)   *zebu*   *za-lai*   [Bodo]

       Anything   eat-IMP

       'Eat anything.'

C-Commanding Strategy of NPIs

In this section, we examine the c-commanding strategies of NPIs mentioned in Mahajan (1990), Chomsky (1995), Kumar (2006), and finally, we adopt Kumar's (2006) analysis, since it is most suitable for analysing NPIs in SALs. We also provide evidence supporting the obligatory requirement of the c-commanding strategy.

Mahajan (1990) states that the negation moves and adjoins to the finite IP in a way that it c-commands the NPI. However, this strategy might not be suitable for NPIs in SALs as in (29) due to the following reasons.

a. There is no limit to the number of heads moving.
b. The movement of the negation is long-distance; i.e. it moves from the embedded clause to the left of the finite IP. Such movement is a violation of the head-movement constraint.
c. The negation cannot move above the adjoined NP, since the adjunction functions as a barrier for movement.
d. Before the movement, the negative only negates the embedded clause. However, after the movement of the negative, to form an adjunct of a finite IP, the negative negates the entire sentence, that is the embedded and the matrix clause. As a result, it is a violation of the structure-preserving principle, since there is a change in the scope at PF and LF.

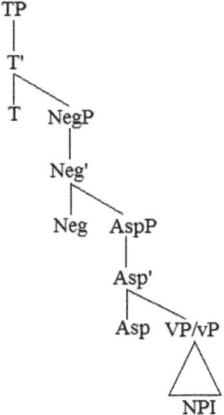

Fig. 3.3   Neg c-commanding the NPI

(28) *bang_j*   *[okoy ho]_i*   *[S_1*   *baha*   *lai-ke-a-y*   *ce*   [Santali]

       neg   anybody   Baha   tell-PST-   COMP
                  even.NPI   FIN-SM

       [S_2   *arel t_i*   *t_j*   *nyel-aka-*
                                                            t-ko-a-y]

       Arel   see-PST-TR-3.SG-FIN-SM

'Baha said that Arel did not see anyone here.'

In Chomsky's (1995) reconstruction, the NPI is reconstructed to a lower position, in a way that the negative c-commands the NPI at the level of LF as in (29a) and (29b). That is, when *[baha hataoa foto ho]_i* is reconstructed to a lower position, then the pronoun *uni* wrongly c-commands the referential expression *baha* as in (29b).

Surface Structure.

(29a) *arel*   *men-ke-a-y ce*   *[baha*   *hataoa*   *foto ho]_i*   *uni*   *bang*

        Arel   tell-PST-3.   COMP   Baha   taken   photo   her   not
                       SG.M   even

        kusi-e-d-a-y t_i   [Santali]

        tell-PST-TR-FIN-SM

'Ramu said that she does not like any photograph that Sita took.'

Logical Form

(29b) *arel*   *men-ke-a-y ce*   *e_i*   *uni*   *bang*

        Arel   tell-PST-3.   COMP   her   not
                       SG.M

        kusi-e-d-a-y *[baha*   *hataoa*   *foto ho]_i*   [Santali]

        tell-PST-TR-FIN-SM   [Baha taken Photo even]

'Ramu said that she does not like any photograph that Sita took.'

Kumar (2006) states that the NPIs in Hindi are licensed by negation prior to movement of the NPI when the NPIs occur in the VP-internal positions. This analysis is more suitable than the other analyses mentioned above since it can account for the structural distribution of NPIs as described above. One feature of SALs that cannot be analysed by other c-commanding strategies mentioned above is the occurrence of NPI in the subject position. Other analyses are not suitable because the negation licenses only those NPIs that do not move out of the c-commanding domain of the NPIs. Such analyses are suitable for English, where the NPI in the subject position is ungrammatical. We further modify Kumar's analysis into a

Minimalist-Based approach. Instead of Deep Structure, Surface Structure, Logical Form and Phonetic Form as in Government and Binding approach, we now have only Logical Form and Phonetic Form.

In the tree structure, Neg occurs within the functional domain below Tense Phrase. In the case of NPIs, the Neg c-commands the NPIs, as shown in Fig. 3.3.

Quantificational Restriction of NPIs: An Alternative-Based Structure

In this section, we discuss the feature interaction of the NPI. Adopting Chierchia (2013: 5) for NPI in negative contexts, we describe the quantificational feature of NPIs. Chierchia proposes a quantificational scale that has alternatives. The alternatives to the right entail the alternatives on the left. For example, if the scale has < *one, two, three...* > then *three* entails two; two entails one. The licensing also involves feature checking (Chierchia, 2013: 229), where the negative marker has a negative interpretable feature [iNEG] and NPIs have uninterpretable features [uNEG]. Similar to Lahiri's (1998) proposal, we state that the emphatic operator is associated with a low-point element, and this point functions as semantically the strongest alternative. By strongest alternative, we mean that the point is a threshold, where no other alternatives further entail it. For example, if there is *ēk* as an NPI as in (30), then no alternative greater than or equal to *ēk* is selected (Dilip and Kumar 2019). As a result, the number of alternatives quantified would be zero. In other words, the number of individuals coming is not one or greater than one. Further, anything lesser than or equal to the threshold is the subdomain alternatives.

(30) *ēk bhī*   *ādmī*   *nahī̃*   *āyā*   [Hindi]

      any.NPI   man   not   came

      'No man came.'

      (Chierchia, 2013: 156)

Feature interaction follows the operations such as a. origination of the NPIs in VP-internal positions; b. negation c-commanding the NPIs in the VP-internal positions. We analyse the feature interaction, keeping in view the alternative scale mentioned above.

In the feature checking, the negative functions as a goal with interpretable negative features [iNeg] and NPI functions as a probe with uninterpretable features [uNeg] as in (31). The probe receives the negative interpretable features from the goal and as a result, the element realizes into an NPI with the emphatic particle attached to it.

(31) Feature checking of negative and NPI

Before: $[_{NegP}$ NEG   [VP   NPI]]

         iNEG   uNEG

After: $[_{NegP}$ NEG   [VP   NPI]]

         iNEG   uNEG

Summing up the discussion in this section, the NPIs inherently possess an alternative scale and the alternatives get restricted based on the feature checking. For feature checking, the negative is the goal with negative interpretable features and the NPI is the probe with unvalued uninterpretable features. In the negative context, the NPI receives interpretable negative features from sentential negation. As a result, the subdomain alternatives get selected.

Conclusion

This paper presented the morphological properties and the syntactic configuration of negation in select South Asian Languages (SALs). It primarily consists of two main parts; first, it focuses on the issues relating to sentential and constituent negation. The morphological parsing of sentential negation shows that the negative is suffixed to the tense form if the overt tense form exists. This pattern of morphological alignment, where tense occurs preceding the sentential negative is analogous to the syntactic representation, where the TP occurs above NegP within the functional domain. In the case of light verbs, the movement of the sentential negative to the intervening position between the root verb and the vector verb is blocked when the canonical position of the sentential negative is post-verbal as in Dravidian languages, Tibeto-Burman, Austro-Asiatic and Bangla of Indo-Aryan language. However, the movement of the sentential negation is allowed when the canonical position of the negative is preverbal as in Hindi. In the case of constituent negation in Dravidian languages, the negative occurs to the right of the constituent being negated. We observed that the morphological properties of sentential negation varied from language to language; however, the constituent negation showed a uniform pattern among languages. The syntactic representation of sentential negation and constituent negation is illustrated. In SALs, the sentential negation occurs below TP and above vP, within the functional domain, whereas, in the constituent negation, negation adjoins to the constituent that is being negated. Negation showed an interaction with quantifiers, where the quantifier depicted narrow scope in the presence of the sentential negation. The second part of the paper shows the analysis of NPIs in select South Asian languages, keeping in view various forms of NPIs and their occurrence in long-distance licensing by sentential negation. In the distribution of NPIs, we showed that there are different kinds of NPIs present in SALs, viz. classifier, quantifier, wh-kind NPIs and idiomatic-NPIs. All NPIs are marked with the emphatic particle at the word-final position having exclusiveness meaning *even* in negative and inclusiveness meaning *also* in an affirmative sentence. Following the occurrence of NPI in the c-commanding domain, the NPI undergoes feature interaction with negative, where the NPI is the probe and the negative is the goal. Following the feature checking, the alternative scale inherent to the NPI gets restricted based on the negative interpretable features it receives.

References

Benmamoun, E. (1997). Licensing of negative polarity items in Moroccan Arabic. *Natural Language and Linguistic Theory, 15*, 263–287.

Bodding, P. O. (1929). *Materials for a Santali grammar: Mostly morphological*. Santal Mission of the Northern Churches.

Chierchia, G. (2013). *Logic in grammar: Polarity, free choice, and intervention*. OUP Oxford.

Chomsky, N. (1991). Some notes on the economy of derivation and representation. In R. Freidin (Ed.), *Principles and Parameters in Comparative Grammar* (pp. 417–454). MIT Press.

Dilip, M. J., & Kumar, R. (2019). Negative polarity items in Telugu. *Acta Linguistica Asiatica, 9*(1), 9–28.

Dwivedi, V. (1991). Negation as a functional projection in Hindi. In: K. Hunt, T. Perry, & V. Samiian (Eds.), *Proceedings of the Western Conference on Linguistics* (pp. 88–101). Fresno: California State University Press.

Hany-Babu, M. T. (1996). The structure of Malayalam sentential negation. *International Journal of Dravidian Linguistics, 25*, 1–15.

Kumar, R. (2006). *Negation and licensing of negative polarity items in Hindi syntax*. Routledge.

Lahiri, U. (1998). Focus and negative polarity in Hindi. *Natural Language Semantics, 6*(1), 57–123.

Mahajan, A. K. (1990). LF conditions on negative polarity item licensing. *Lingua, 80*, 333–348.

Haegeman, L. (1995). *The syntax of negation*. Cambridge: Cambridge University Press.

Nicolae, A. C. (2012). Negation-resistant polarity items. In C. Pin (Ed.), *Empirical issues in syntax and semantics 9* (pp. 225–242).

Ouhalla, J. (1990). Sentential negation, relativised minimality and the aspectual status of auxiliaries. *7*(2), 183–231.

Payne, J. R. (1985). Negation. In T. Shopen (Ed.), *Language typology and syntactic description. Vol. I. clause structure* (pp. 197–242). Cambridge: Cambridge University Press.

Pollock, J.-Y. (1989). Verb movement, Universal Grammar, and the structure of IP. *Linguistic Inquiry, 20*, 365–424.

Progovac, L. (1994). *Negative and positive polarity: A binding approach*. Cambridge: Cambridge University Press.

Zanuttini, R. (1991). *Syntactic properties of sentential negation: A comparative study of Romance Languages* (Doctoral dissertation). University of Pennsylvania, Philadelphia.

Zanuttini, R. (2001). Sentential negation. In M. Baltin, & C. Collins (Eds.), *The handbook of contemporary syntactic theory* (pp. 511–535). London: Blackwell.

Rajesh Kumar is Professor of linguistics in the Department of Humanities and Social Sciences at the Indian Institute of Technology Madras, Chennai. He serves as the associate editor of the journal Language and Language Teaching. The broad goal of his research is uncovering regularities underlying both the structural form (what language is) and sociolinguistic functions (what language does) of natural language. He works on the structure of South Asian Languages. He is also interested in issues related to language (multilingualism) in education; politics; human cognition; and landscape.

Sansuma Brahma is Assistant Professor in the Department of Humanities and Social Sciences at the Indian Institute of Technology Indore, Indore. He is interested in the syntax of Tibeto-Burman languages, especially the negation and negative polarity items found in them. He has presented his research at several conferences in India.

Sh. Francis Monsang is Assistant Professor at the English and Foreign Language University, Shillong. He is interested in the syntax of Tibeto-Burman languages in general and the structure of Monsang in particular. He has presented his research at several conferences in India. He has published his work in several journals of repute.

Mayuri Dilip is Assistant Professor of linguistics at Central University of Rajasthan. She received her doctoral degree from IIT Madras in Chennai. She works on syntactic typology of Austo-Asiatic languages. She has presented her work at various professional meetings in India and abroad.

Chapter 4
Investigating Limits to Processing Variability in SOV Languages

Apurva and Samar Husain

Abstract Robust clause final verbal prediction and its maintenance have been argued as a processing variation in SOV languages vis-à-vis SVO languages. Such a processing variation has been used to explain effects such as anti-locality and lack of structural forgetting in language such as German, Japanese, Dutch and Hindi. Typically, these effects are taken to show a weak influence of working memory constraints on SOV languages compared to SVO languages. In this work, we provide new data to show that increased working memory load (operationalized as increased preverbal complexity) adversely affects prediction in an SOV language such as Hindi. Using a series of sentence completion studies, we show that clause final verb prediction suffers with increased embeddings as well as with addition of preverbal adjuncts. Together, the results show that while preverbal cues are effectively employed by the parser to make clause final structural predictions, the parsing system breaks down when the number of predicted verbs/ relations exceeds beyond a certain threshold. The results suggest that processing in SOV languages is susceptible to centre-embeddings similar to that in SVO languages. This highlights the overarching influence of working memory constraints during sentence comprehension and thereby on the parser to posit less complex structures in both SOV and in SVO languages.

Keywords Parsing error in SOV languages · Prediction fallibility · Working memory limitation · Grammatical illusion · Good-enough processing

Apurva · S. Husain (✉)
Indian Institute of Technology, Delhi, India
e-mail: samar@hss.iitd.ac.in

© The Author(s), under exclusive license to Springer Nature Singapore Pte Ltd. 2023
P. Chandra (ed.), *Variation in South Asian Languages*,
https://doi.org/10.1007/978-981-99-1149-3_4

Introduction

One of the most enduring questions in modern linguistics is to understand the universal principles that underlie the variation found across human languages (e.g., Bresnan, 1982; Chomsky, 1981, 1995; Joshi, 1985; Pollard & Sag, 1994; Steedman, 2001). Psycholinguists have been trying to uncover these universal representations as well as the processes that act on these representations to arrive at a unified account of how humans acquire, comprehend and produce different languages (e.g., Bock, 1986; Fodor, 1978; Frazier & Fodor, 1978; Hawkins, 1994; Kimball, 1973; Miller & Chomsky, 1963). Cognitive resource considerations have been an important aspect of such proposals. For example, Yngve (1960) showed that right-extraposition as a syntactic phenomenon is a manifestation of conserving working memory resource. Similarly, Frazier (1985) showed that when the parser is confronted with local ambiguity it takes decision to conserve processing resources. However, language-specific properties have posed a challenge to these attempts. For example, Bach et al. (1986) showed that nested dependencies in Dutch were easier than equivalent embedded structures in German. Similarly, Carreiras and Clifton (1993) showed that relative clause attachment preferences are subject to language preferences and need not be governed by simplicity considerations alone. This line of research shows that language-specific properties plays an important role in determining processing strategies across languages (e.g., Mitchell et al., 1995). This aspect in processing has been termed 'adaptation' which in turn leads to processing variability across languages. In the context of this work, we look at variability of the processing system in SOV languages. In particular, it has been argued that, compared to SVO languages, SOV language is better adapted at predictive processing. The goal of this work is to demonstrate that certain cognitive constraints adversely affect predictive processing of SOV languages, in spite of the assumed adaptive features. In this sense, compared to other works in this volume (e.g., Gulati & Choudhary, 2023; Chandra, 2021), the current work is more about limits to variation rather than increased variation.

Processing Variation in SOV Languages

When humans process a sentence, they do not wait for it to finish in order to make sense of its meaning. Rather, they actively predict the upcoming linguistic material during the comprehension process. Experimental evidence over many decades has established this aspect of the comprehension system (e.g. MarslenWilson, 1973; Fischler & Bloom, 1979; Kutas & Hillyard, 1980, 1984; Zola, 1984; Schwanenflugel & Lacount, 1988; Schwanenflugel & Shoben, 1985; Altmann & Kamide, 1999, 2007; Kliegl et al., 2004; Ashby et al., 2005; Staub & Clifton, 2006; Rayner et al., 2011; Levy & Keller, 2013).

More recently, the role of prediction has been highlighted in the processing of SOV languages (e.g. Friederici & Frisch, 2000; Husain et al., 2014; Kamide et al., 2003; Koso et al., 2011; Levy & Keller, 2013; Yamashita, 1997, 2000). Evidence for robust verbal prediction and its maintenance in SOV languages comes from (a) antilocality effects and (b) lack of structural forgetting effects. Briefly, the anti-locality effect is characterized by a processing facilitation at the verbal head with increased linear distance between the verb and its prior dependents. The lack of structural forgetting in SOV languages, as the name suggests, is characterized by robust maintenance of clause final verb in the face of multiple embeddings.

Evidence for robust prediction in SOV languages can largely be subsumed under the *robust prediction and maintenance hypothesis (RPM)* (Hale, 2006; Levy, 2008; Vasishth et al., 2010). The RPM hypothesis states that the parser in SOV languages becomes adept at effectively utilizing the preverbal linguistic cues to make robust clause final verbal predictions. In addition, due to the high frequency of SOV word order, it also becomes very good at maintaining these predictions successfully. The RPM hypothesis, therefore, makes the following predictions with regard to sentence processing in SOV languages: (a) verbal prediction in SOV languages is quite robust, (b) additional preverbal material (arguments and adjuncts) make such predictions better and more precise, and (c) verbal predictions are efficiently maintained during the parsing process.

Role of Working Memory Constraints on Prediction

The RPM hypothesis assume a parsing process that does not lead to globally illicit parses in SOV languages due to prediction fallibility. From a typological perspective, these processing results in SOV languages can be contrasted with results from SVO languages (e.g. English) where evidence for locality (as opposed to anti-locality) and structural forgetting effect has been demonstrated (e.g., Gibson & Thomas, 1999; Grodner & Gibson, 2005). Consequently, a differential processing account based on the typological word order feature (SVO vs SOV) of a language has been posited (e.g., Vasishth et al., 2010). Crucially, this has led to the assumption that the influence of working memory constraints on SOV language is weak compared to that in SVO languages.

However, there is some evidence that predictive processing interacts with working memory constraints (e.g., Husain et al., 2014; Vasishth & Drenhaus, 2011). For example, Vasishth and Drenhaus (2011) showed that in German similarity-based interference among preverbal nominals can lead to locality effects. While these works have focused on the retrieval processes at the verb, it remains a possibility that in such configurations verbal predictions made *prior to the actual verb* suffers. In other words, increased working memory load due to structural complexity could in principle lead to prediction fallibility in SOV languages. This implies that the linguistic environment prior to the verb should be simple in order to ensure processing ease. We call this the *fallible prediction and maintenance*

(FPM) hypothesis. The FPM hypothesis predicts that while prediction in SOV languages is robust, it is also constrained by working memory pressures. In particular, it predicts that parsing errors due to incorrect verbal prediction will increase in cases such as increased structural depth. Such an account posits that both SVO and SOV languages are susceptible to working memory constraints due to increased linguistic complexity. Similar proposals have been made by Ueno and Polinsky (2009), Gibson et al. (2013), Ros et al. (2015).

Given the proposed wide-ranging role of prediction in processing of SOV languages, it is critical to evaluate the *robust prediction and maintenance (RPM) hypothesis* and the *fallible prediction and maintenance (FPM) hypothesis* rigorously. To our knowledge, such an investigation is currently lacking. In this work, we conduct a series of sentence completion studies to investigate this.

The paper is arranged as follows. In Experiment 1, we present a sentence completion study to investigate the role of preverbal complexity on verbal prediction. Following this, Experiment 2 investigates how verbal predictions are maintained when additional preverbal adjuncts are introduced. We then consolidate the findings and discuss its implications. Finally, we conclude the work.

Experiment 1

We begin our investigation into verbal prediction by investigating the role of syntactic complexity on prediction. In particular, the current experiment investigates if increase in the number of preverbal arguments and embeddings leads to increased prediction errors.

Material and Methods

Participants

Thirty-six native speakers of Hindi participated in this experiment. These subjects did not participate in any other experiment discussed in the paper. All the participants were undergraduate or graduate students from the Indian Institute of Technology, Delhi. The average age of the participants was 24.3 (SD = 3.08). Each participant was paid INR 150 for participating in the experiment.

Items

The experimental conditions are shown in sentence 1. Each condition had three proper nouns with Ergative 'ne,' Accusative 'ko' or Ablative 'se' case-marker in different order. This led to six conditions.

(1)   a   ne-ko-se

          pooja**=ne**   urmila**=ko**   suneet**=se**   **...**

          Pooja=ERG   Urmila=ACC Suneet=ABL   ...

    b   ne-se-ko

          pooja**=ne**   urmila**=se**   suneet**=ko**   **...**

          Pooja=ERG   Urmila=ABL Suneet=ACC   ...

    c   ko-ne-se

          pooja**=ko**   urmila**=ne**   suneet**=se**   **...**

          Pooja=ACC   Urmila=ERG Suneet=ABL   ...

    d   ko-se-ne

          pooja**=ko**   urmila**=se**   suneet**=ne**   **...**

          Pooja=ACC   Urmila=ABL Suneet=ERG   ...

    e   se-ko-ne

          pooja**=se**   urmila**=ko**   suneet**=ne**   **...**

          Pooja=ABL   Urmila=ACC Suneet=ERG   ...

    f   se-ne-ko

          pooja**=se**   urmila**=ne**   suneet**=ko**   **...**

          Pooja=ABL   Urmila=ERG Suneet=ACC   ...

A key motivation to select the above preverbal configuration was that it is compatible with continuations that have varying degree of complexity. Figure 4.1 shows these structures. For example, the N1ne N2ko N3se substring can be completed with a single matrix verb (Causative) which involves no embeddings. Or, it could be completed with a doubly embedded structure involving 2 nonfinite participle clauses and the finite verb.

Twelve items with the different conditions were constructed for both unique case-marker and similar case-marker experiments. In addition, 60 filler items were prepared. The filler items comprised of different construction types. These were, embedded relative clauses, correlative constructions, sentences with two proper nouns with differing case-markers, sentences with two proper nouns and an adverbial/inanimate noun with differing case-markers, sentences with two pronouns, declarative sentences with non-canonical word order, other random sentences taken from a news corpus. The items of the experiment along with the filler were presented using the Latin-squared design.

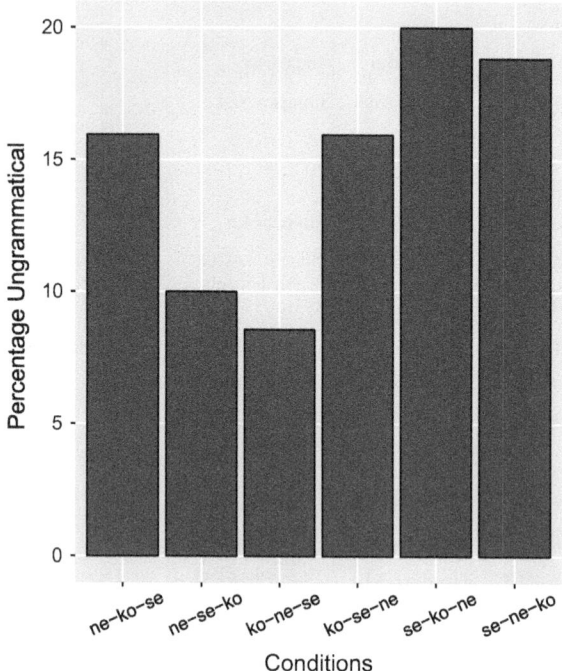

Fig. 4.1 Percentage ungrammatical completions for all the conditions in the unique case-marker experiment. Percentage values were computed by considering the number of ungrammatical completions out of all the completions in a particular condition

Procedure

The sentence completion task was employed as the experimental paradigm (Taylor, 1953). Each sentence was presented using the centred self-paced reading (SPR) paradigm. Participants were provided an incomplete sentence, and their task was to complete it such that it was meaningful. Each sentence appeared on the screen in the self-paced reading format. Initially, a '+' sign appeared on the centre of the computer screen. When the participant pressed the spacebar key, this+sign got replaced with the first word of the sentence. Successive button presses displayed the remaining words of the sentence at the centre of the screen. A ... symbol prompted the participant to complete the sentence. This was done in a text box that appeared by pressing 'spacebar' after the ... symbol. After typing in the text the participants pressed the 'enter' key to move to the next trial. The experiment was conducted using Douglas Rohde's Linger software.[1] Items were automatically randomized by Linger.

The sentence completion task is the goto paradigm to quantify predictability during comprehension. Previous studies on word predictability employing the sentence completion task have shown that completion patterns correlate strongly with

---

[1] Version 2.94.

reading time patterns found during online sentence comprehension (Husain et al., 2014; Jäger et al., 2015; Levy & Keller, 2013; Rayner et al., 2011). Indeed, it has been argued that cloze probabilities from the completion task provide the most comprehensive measure to quantify predictability (Staub, 2015).

Response Coding

Coding was done for grammaticality of the completion as well as the verb type. Grammaticality was coded as 0 if the completion was ungrammatical and 1 if it was grammatical.

Response coding was also done for verb class of the completion. Coding was done such that 3 nouns in the sentence fragments were interpreted as arguments of the verb(s) used to complete a condition. We analyse all such non-finite and matrix verbs used in the completion data. Coding was done for the following verb class: Transitive: T, Intransitive: IN, Ditransitive: DT, Experiencer: EXP, Copula: COP and Causatives: CAUS. For example, if the completion had one transitive non-finite verb and a ditransitive matrix verb, then it was coded as T+DT. Note that if the participants used additional nouns during completions, they were coded only if they formed part of the argument structure of the verbs.

Predictions

The RPM hypothesis will predict robust prediction for various conditions. As noted earlier, these case-marker combinations can lead to grammatical completions. The RPM hypothesis predicts effective usage of the nominal features to predict the required number of verbs. In particular, it does not predict use of globally illicit parses in SOV languages due to prediction fallibility. The FPM hypothesis, on the other hand, will predict high error rates in various 3NP patterns as they require positing complex structures (cf. Table 1.).

Results

The statistical analysis for grammaticality was done using the generalized linear mixed-effects model with logit link function. This has been done using the lme4 package (Bates et al., 2015) in R. Maximal models were fit when possible (Barr et al., 2013); in case of convergence failure, a less complex model was fit by successively removing the random slopes of the by-subject and by-item random effects component. We first discuss the results on grammaticality and then turn towards the verb class results.[2]

---

[2] All the data and analysis files for the experiments reported are available at https://osf.io/nj5rt/.

Table 1. Possible structures to complete N1 = ne N2 = ko N3 = se sentence fragment with various verb types

Structure	No. of verbs/clauses	No. of core relations
N1=ne N2=ko N3=se **CAUS/DT**	1	3
N1=ne N2=ko (N3=se **T.NFV**) **DT**	2	5
N1=ne N2=ko (N3=se **T.NFV**) **T**	2	5
N1=ne N2=ko (N3=se **NP DT.NFV**) **DT**	2	6
N1=ne N2=ko (N3=se (**IN.NFV**) **DT.NFV**) **DT**	3	7
N1=ne N2=ko (N3=se (**NP T.NFV**) **DT.NFV**) **DT**	3	8
N1=ne N2=ko (N3=se (**NP DT.NFV**) **DT.NFV**) **DT**	3	9

Underlined text represents possible completions. Round braces represent clausal boundaries. Green arcs represent syntactic relations between the matrix verb and its arguments. Black arcs represent syntactic relations between non-finite verb and its argument. Dotted red arcs represent implied arguments. Blue arc represents adjunct relation between the finite verb and the nonfinite verb. 'ne': Ergative case-marker, 'ko': Accusative case-marker, 'se': Ablative casemarker. CAUS: Causative matrix verb, DT: Ditransitive matrix verb, T.NFV: Transitive nonfinite verb, IN.NFV: Intransitive non-finite verb, DT.NFV: Ditransitive non-finite verb

Verb class errors were also analysed using the method discussed above. These errors were divided into the following types, (a) N1N2: when the first two nouns were used (and the third noun was not used) to predict the verbs, (b) N2N3: when the last two nouns were used (and the first noun was not used) to predict the verbs, (c) N1N3: when the first and the last nouns were used (and the second noun was not used) to predict the verbs, (d) Case-exchange: when one of the case-markers on N1, N2 or N3 was misinterpreted to predict the verbs, (e) Random: when errors could not be classified as (a)-(d).

Results

Results for the grammaticality analysis shows no difference between the canonical word order condition vs the other non-canonical conditions (see Table 2.). The average parsing error across all conditions due to incorrect predictions was around 15%. This can be seen in Fig. 4.1. Further, a comparison of these 3NP conditions with 2NP filler items[3] showed a significant difference in grammaticality ($z = 4.5$) such that the average grammaticality in the 2NP conditions was 98% compared to 85% in the experimental conditions.

Table 3. shows the different types of errors for all conditions. One prominent trend was that the N2N3 errors were much higher with N1se conditions (i.e. se-ko-ne, se-ne-ko) compared to the rest of the conditions ($z = 3.5$).

Discussion

Hindi native speakers make parsing errors due to incorrect predictions in various 3NP conditions tested. The average error for the critical items was found to be around 15%. In comparison, the average error in the 2NP filler items was just 2%.

Table 2.   glmer results for the grammaticality analysis for Experiment 2. Treatment contrast was used with ne-ko-se as the baseline

	Coefficient	SE	z-value
Intercept	1.71	0.34	4.9
ne-se-ko	0.55	0.51	1.05
ko-ne-se	0.72	0.54	1.33
ko-se-ne	0.007	0.46	0.01
se-ko-ne	0.27	0.44	0.61
se-ne-ko	0.20	0.45	0.45

Table 3.   Parsing errors classification in Experiment 1

Condition	N1N2	N2N3	N1N3	Case-exchange	Random
ne-ko-se	3	0	5	5	1
ne-se-ko	3	1	4	0	0
ko-ne-se	3	2	0	0	2
ko-se-ne	1	6	5	1	1
se-ko-ne	1	11	4	0	2
se-ne-ko	0	12	6	0	1

---

[3] There were around 7 such 2NP filler items with differing casemarkers (such as ko-se, ko-ne, ne-ko). In all, there were 245 such data points.

Table 4. Grammatical completions in Experiment 1

Completion	Count	Percentage (%)	No. of clauses	No. of core relations
CAUS	125	35.2	1	3
T+DT	115	32.3	2	5
N+DT+DT	34	9.5	2	6
T+T	14	3.9	2	5
Others	67	18.8	–	–

These results highlight a limit on predictive processing in Hindi and therefore support the FPM hypothesis. The parser is susceptible to making verb prediction errors in 3NP conditions with animate nouns. Results show that in such configurations, the parser tends to predict simple structures. Recall that the 3NP conditions can be completed using a variety of syntactic configurations with differing complexity (operationalized as multiple verbs involving around 2–3 clausal embedding and around 5–9 syntactic relations; see Table 1.). Bulk of the grammatical completions had less than or equal to 2 clausal embedding; similarly, a large amount of grammatical completions had less than or equal to 5 verbal relations (see Table 4.). Indeed, not a single instance of grammatical completion with a double embedded structure was found in the data. Such a constraint on predictive processing could be due to a need to maintain multiple heads as well as multiple syntactic dependencies in the 3NP conditions (as seen in Table 1.). It is reasonable to assume that positing such complex structure would increase the working memory load (cf. Gibson, 1998; Lewis, 1993; Yngve, 1960). On similar lines, the ungrammatical completions also had simple structures (see Table 5.).

The results found that the word order of the case-marker did not significantly affect the average number of errors in various 3NP conditions. This suggests that the parser is generally vulnerable in such cases. At the same time, certain 3NP conditions lead to specific kinds of errors, thus highlighting parsing strategy in these configurations. In particular, if the local case-marker combination is more frequent than the global case-marker combination, the local features tend to be used during the completion to form illicit parses that are globally inconsistent. A closer look at the nature of the error (see Table 3.) shows that when the *se* case-marker appears sentence initially, the number of N2N3 errors was significantly higher compared to other conditions. For example, in the *se-ne-ko* condition,

Table 5. Ungrammatical completions in Experiment1

Completion	Count	Percentage (%)	No. of clauses	No. of core relations
N+DT	15	24.1	1	3
IN+DT	10	16.1	2	4
CAUS	9	14.5	1	3
T+DT	6	9.6	2	5
N+T+DT	5	8.0	2	5
T	5	8.0	1	2
Others	50	19.3	–	–

Table 6. Experiment 1: N2+N3 errors for conditions kosene, sekone, seneko. *v1*+*v2* signifies an embedded structure with *v1* as the embedded nonfinite verb and *v2* as the matrix verb. In the case of *n*+*v1*+*v2*, *n* is part of the *v1 is* nonfinite clause, and *v2* is the matrix verb

Embeddings	Completion	Count	Example
1	N+DT	10	/N//1/-/s/e/ N1-ko N2-ne <u>kuchh kaha</u> 'something say'
	T	3	/N//1/-/s/e/ N1-ko N2-ne peeta tha 'hit PAST'
	CAUS	1	/N//1/-/k/o/ N1-se N2-ne maafi mangvaii 'apology
	DT	1	cause ask'
			/N//1/-/s/e/ N1-ne N2-ko introduce kiya 'introduce do'
2	N+T+DT	7	/N//1/-/s/e/ N1-ko N2-ne (prashna hal karne ko)
	IN+DT	6	kahaa 'question to solve ACC say'
	N+DT+DT	1	/N//1/-/s/e/ N1-ne N2-ko <u>(chup rehne ko)</u> kaha 'to
			stay quite say'
			/N//1/-/s/e/ N1-ne N2-ko (pen dene se) mana kar
			diya 'pen to give decline'

IN: Intransitive, CAUS: Causative, T: Transitive, DT: Ditransitive, N: Noun

completions that are compatible with *ne-ko* become high. This could be because *se-ne-ko* is a very rare combination while *ne-ko* is quite frequent.[4] Table 6. shows some examples of such errors. We discuss the implication of these errors on parsing strategy during comprehension in Sect. 4.4.

To summarize, the nature of grammatical and ungrammatical completions show that Hindi native speakers tend to predict simple structures with fewer embeddings and minimal number of core verbal relations. The N2N3/case-exchange errors in the experiment show a prediction strategy where the parser misinterprets rare input features (e.g., case-markers) as a frequent case-marker combination to form illicit parses at the expense of globally consistent parses. The results suggest that Hindi native speakers should find structures with more than 1 embeddings (i.e., 2 verbs) and more than 5 core verbal relations difficult to process.

The experiment discussed in this section highlighted prediction fallibility in Hindi. The nature of the parsing errors discussed above is not predicted by the RPM hypothesis. We next test another prediction of the RPM hypothesis; i.e., verbal predictions in SOV languages are robustly maintained in the face of additional preverbal elements (e.g., adjuncts).

Experiment 2

In experiment 2, we investigate the effect of preverbal adjuncts on verbal prediction and its maintenance. In particular, it tests a key claim of the RPM hypothesis that verbal predictions can be maintained robustly when additional linguistic material in the form of adjuncts is added preverbally (Levy, 2008; Vasishth & Lewis, 2006; Vasishth et al., 2010).

---

[4] In a Hindi treebank Bhatt et al. (2009), there were 0 instance of *se-ne-ko* while there were 1231 instances of *ne-ko*.

Material and Methods

Participants

Twenty-seven native speakers of Hindi participated in this experiment. These subjects did not participate in any other experiment discussed in the paper. All the participants were undergraduate or graduate students from the Indian Institute of Technology, Delhi. The average age of the participants was 21.3 (SD = 2.97). Each participant was paid INR 200 for participating in the experiment.

Items

We use the *ne-ko-se* condition from the previous experiment as the baseline condition. The other conditions added additional linguistic material of differing complexity after the 3rd noun, i.e., N3se. This was done to investigate prediction maintenance while controlling for the strength of predictability at N3. The conditions can be seen in example 2. In condition (b), two adverbials are introduced after N3. In condition (c), a non-finite clause (comprising of an intransitive verb and its Genetive marked subject) is introduced after N3. The adjuncts in conditions (b) and (c) can structurally attach only with the verbs predicted at N3. Additionally, the adjunct in condition (c) is assumed to be more complex than (b)–processing the adjunct in (c) requires creating an embedded structure while in (b) no such structure is formed. In conditions (d) and (e), a relative clause (RC) is added as an adjunct. The relative clause in these two conditions cannot structurally modify the upcoming verb and modifies N3 instead. Additionally, the RC in condition (e) is assumed to be more complex than the one in (d), as it involves a transitive event compared to the copular construction in (d). The adjuncts in conditions (b)-(e) comprise of 4–5 words.

(2) a   Baseline (ne-ko-se)

        pUjaa=ne   urmilaa=ko   sunitaa=se   ...

        Pooja=ERG   Urmila=ACC   Sunita=ABL   ...

    b   Simple Verbal modification (Adverb)

        pUjaa=ne   urmilaa=ko   sunitaa=se   kal   der shaam=me   ...

        Pooja=ERG Urmila=ACC Sunita=ABL yesterday late evening=LOC ...

    c   Complex Verbal modification (Non-finite clause)

        pUjaa=ne   urmilaa=ko   sunitaa=se   police=ke   jaane ke baad   ...

        Pooja=ERG Urmila=ACC Sunita=ABL Police=GEN go   -Part after   ...

d   Simple Noun modification (RC copula)

pUjaa=ne	urmilaa=ko	sunitaa=se	jo	dilli=me	hai	...
Pooja=ERG	Urmila=ACC	Sunita=ABL	who	Delhi=LOC	is	...

e   Complex Noun modification (RC transitive)

pUjaa=ne	urmilaa=ko	sunitaa=se	jo	hokI	khelta hai	...
Pooja=ERG	Urmila=ACC	Sunita=ABL	who	hockey	play PRES	...

Twenty-five sets of items were created with the above conditions. In addition, there were 50 filler items. A Latin-squared design was used to present the items. In all, five lists were prepared.

Procedure

Similar to Experiment 1, we follow the sentence completion paradigm in this experiment.

Response Coding

The response coding procedure was the same as in Experiment 1.

Predictions

The key assumption of the RPM hypothesis is that in SOV language predictions get better and are maintained robustly in the face of increased distance between the predicted verb and its preverbal modifiers (arguments or adjuncts). As stated earlier, this is how effects such as anti-locality and lack of structural forgetting is explained in the literature. Most experimental manipulations add such modifiers to demonstrate anti-locality in SOV languages such as German (Konieczny, 2000; Levy & Keller, 2013), Hindi (Husain et al., 2014; Vasishth & Lewis, 2006), Japanense (Nakatani & Gibson, 2010). Theories that explain lack of forgetting effect in SOV languages (Vasishth et al., 2010) predict that addition of adjuncts (e.g., an embedded clause in conditions c, d and e) will not affect the maintenance of the predicted verbs. Critically, the RPM hypothesis will not predict any degradation of verbal prediction when additional adjuncts (in the form of adverbial, participle or a relative clause) are added after a robust (and grammatical) verbal prediction has been made at *N3se*.

On the other hand, the FPM hypothesis will predict that addition of adjuncts can degrade the prediction made at N3. In particular, the degradation in robust prediction should be higher in complex adjunct conditions such as participles and relative clauses.

Results

All the statistical analyses follow the same procedure as mentioned in Experiment 1.

The average ungrammatical completions in the baseline condition were 19.7%, compared to that the average ungrammatical completions in the other conditions with adjuncts were 41.7%. Table 7. shows the breakup for each condition. The results for grammaticality of the completions (grammatical vs ungrammatical) show that compared to the baseline condition (a), the percentage of grammatical completions was significantly lower in other conditions (b)–(d) (see Table 8.).[5]

With regard to the error types, we find that bulk of the errors in the nonbaseline conditions are due to N1N2, N1N3 and N1N2/N1N3; i.e., the completion is meaningful if one considers the nominal features of the first two nouns or the first and the last nouns. Compared to the baseline condition, all the other conditions had

Table 7. Grammatical and ungrammatical completion counts in conditions a–e. Percentages shown in braces. The percentages consider the number of ungrammatical completions out of all the completions in a particular condition

Condition	Grammatical Completions	Ungrammatical Completions	Total
ne-ko-se	106 (80.3%)	26 (19.6%)	132
Adverbial	70 (55.1%)	57 (44.8%)	127
Non-finite clause	52 (41.2%)	74 (58.7%)	126
RC Copula	83 (66.9%)	41 (33.0%)	124
RC Transitive	88 (69.8%)	38 (30.1%)	126

Table 8. glmer results for the grammatical versus ungrammatical completion. The analysis uses treatment contrast, with condition a as the baseline with other coefficients signifying the difference from the baseline

	Coefficient	SE	z-value
Intercept	1.63	0.29	5.52
Adverbial	−1.36	0.30	**−4.50**
Non-finite clause	−2.04	0.31	**−6.60**
RC	−0.69	0.27	**−2.55**

---

[5] Since the percentage errors in the two RC conditions were similar, they were collapsed for the purpose of the analysis. The reported results do not change if they are analyzed separately.

Table 9. Sample verb class errors in Experiment 3. *v1* + *v2* signifies an embedded structure with *v1* as the embedded nonfinite verb and *v2* as the matrix verb. In the case of *n* + *v1* + *v2*, *n* is part of the *v1* nonfinite clause and *v2* is the matrix verb. IN: Intransitive, CAUS: Causative, T: Transitive, DT: Ditransitive, N: Noun

Completion	Example
T	N1-ne N2-ko N//3//-/s/e/ NFV chup rakha 'quiet keep'
IN+DT	N1-ne N2-ko N///3/-/s/e/ ADV baag jaane ko kaha 'to run away ask'
N+IN+DT	N1-ne N2-ko /N//3/-/s/e/ NFV ghar lautne kaa aadesh diya 'home to return ordered'
N+T+DT	N1-ne /N//2/-/k/o// N3-se RC kavita likhne ki maang ki 'poem to write request'

significantly more such errors ($z = 2.9$, $z = 4.2$, $z = 2.5$ respectively for conditions adverb, non-finite clause, RC). Table 9. shows some prominent error completions based on the type of predicted verbs found across various conditions.

Discussion

The results of the current experiment show that addition of adjuncts after the *N1-ne N2ko N3se* string increases the percentage of ungrammatical completions. This goes counter to the robust prediction maintenance assumption of the RPM hypothesis and supports the FPM hypothesis.

The average correct prediction in the baseline condition was around 80%, and the result suggests that addition of adjuncts was detrimental to the maintenance of the predicted verbs in the baseline condition. This was particularly true when the adjunct was complex, e.g., a nonfinite verb. This is not expected in an SOV language considering the proposals of linguistic adaptability that predict better maintenance of clause final verbal predictions (Levy & Keller, 2013; Vasishth et al., 2010). However, under the assumption that the parser is susceptible to errors in 3NP conditions (as noted in Experiment 1), presumably due to increased working memory load, addition of new linguistic material could lead to further increase in load and thereby lead to processing difficulty. This lends further support to the FPM hypothesis and highlights the configurations where parsing in SOV languages can suffer.

Qualitatively, the nature of predicted verb class in the grammatical and ungrammatical completions was similar to those found in Experiment 1. The dominant parsing error type observed in this experiment is also consistent with what was found in Experiment 1. In particular, when the parser is under strain due to the maintenance of various heads/relations, it can rely on more frequent nominal features that it has seen so far. For this experiment, this turns out to be N1ne N2ko or N1ne N3se both of which are much more frequent than the N1ne N2ko N3se combination.[6]

---

[6] In a Hindi treebank Bhatt et al. (2009), there were 13 instance of ne-ko-se while there were 1231 instances of ne-ko and 436 instances of nese.

General Discussion

The experiment reported in this work show that Hindi native speakers success-fully predict clause final verbs based on the number of preverbal nouns and their case-markers. At the same time, the results show verbal predictions in Hindi to be fallible. This fallibility is reflected as a significant amount of parsing errors in various experiments. In particular, the presence of three preverbal animate nouns with various case-markers lead to increased ungrammaticality. These errors further increased with the addition of preverbal adjuncts of differing complexity. Together, the experiments demonstrate a limit to robust verbal prediction and its mainte-nance. The parsing process in an SOV language like Hindi seems to suffer in the face of establishing more than five verbal dependencies and more than two verbal heads (or more than one clausal embedding). These results support the *fallible pre-diction and maintenance* (FPM) hypothesis that posits a limit to adaptabilitybased prediction in SOV languages.

Processing variability and working memory constraints

From a typological perspective, the results suggest that, similar to an SVO lan-guage like English, processing in an SOV language Hindi is adversely affected by working memory load due to syntactic configurations such as clausal embeddings.

A key contribution of this work is to also highlight the role of working memory constraint on predictive processing. For example, the conditions with three prever-bal nouns lead to more parsing errors compared to the conditions with two prever-bal nouns. One could argue that the errors in 2NP conditions are less due to their high frequency in the language compared to the 3NP conditions. However, a work-ing memory account need not be mutually exclusive to the frequency account. For example, processing difficulty during comprehension due to low frequency can be due to working memory constraints during production (e.g., Kurumada & Jaeger, 2015; MacDonald, 2013; Scontras et al., 2015). In addition, the differen-tial parsing error due to intervener complexity discussed in Experiment 2 cannot be easily explained by a purely frequency-based account. This is because all the intervener conditions in Experiment 2 are rare; however, errors are high when the intervener is more complex vs when it's simple. Indeed, the current proposal of lossy surprisal (Futrell et al., 2020) that assumes a random noise function will also be unable to correctly account for this differential prediction error. If the linguistic material of adjuncts that follow the preverbal nominals have equal length, then a random noise function will not be able to capture differential prediction patterns due to the *nature* of adjuncts. Finally, the nature of parsing error during the com-pletion task also highlights the influence of limited memory resource on pars-ing. As noted earlier, in the 3NP conditions, the parser posits structures that have fewer verbal heads and have fewer dependency relations. Tables 4., 5. show that the number of clauses in such predictions range from 1 to 2, while the number of core syntactic relations range from 3 to 6. This can be contrasted with Table 1. which shows that range of clauses and core dependency relations for grammatical completions in 3NP conditions can range from 1–3 to 3–9, respectively. A comparison of the complexity of parses in grammatical vs ungrammatical completion suggests that both the number of clauses and the number of core syntactic relations matter during the prediction process. The errors show that predicting/maintaining more than two verbs/clauses is rare. And in cases where the number of predicted verbs is similar between grammatical and ungrammatical completions, the total number of core relations in error completions is comparatively less.

Predictive processing in SOV languages has been frequently pitted against locality constraints because effects such as anti-locality and lack of forgetting go against working memory constraints during comprehension. SOV languages have been shown to have longer dependency length wrt SVO languages (Futrell et al., 2015; Yadav et al., 2020). Thus, the parser in SOV languages has been argued to be deeply influenced by certain typological properties such as the word order (Levy & Keller, 2013; Vasishth et al., 2010). While this may be true to some extent, more recent corpus studies have also highlighted constraints on this adaptability. For example, using a cross-linguistic corpus study, Yadav et al. (2020) have shown that SOV languages do not allow for more than three clausal embeddings. Relatedly, Sharma et al. (2020) show that the core verbal arguments (subject, object, indirect objects) are typically found close to the verbal head and bulk of long-distance dependencies in a language like Hindi are due verbal adjuncts. Indeed, avoidance of complex preverbal configurations due to working memory constraints has been argued to be an important feature in SOV languages (e.g., Gibson et al., 2013; Ros et al., 2015; Ueno & Polinsky, 2009). Consistent with these observations, the configurations used in the current study show that when working memory is strained, the robustness of verbal prediction decreases. The current work shows that, in an SOV language like Hindi, the adaptability of the parser to make verbal predictions and maintain them has limits. In the light of this, the processing accounts for effects such as anti-locality and no-forgetting in SOV languages need a reappraisal.

Prediction in SOV and SVO languages

While prediction is SOV language has garnered much attention, it is also known that prediction is an active feature during parsing of SVO languages. For example, we know that the properties of the verb is used to anticipate the object in a language like English (e.g., Altmann & Kamide, 1999); see Fig. 4.2. The current work suggests that predictive processing in SVO and SOV languages should be

Fig. 4.2 Prediction in SOV and SVO languages. Left panel: The properties of the preverbal arguments, e.g., subject and object determine the prediction of the clause final verb in SOV languages. Right panel: The properties of the subject and the verb determine the prediction of the postverbal object in SVO languages.

subject to similar constraints (cf. Yadav et al., 2020). While this would amount to incorrect prediction of *arguments* in SVO languages, in SOV language this would lead to incorrect prediction of *verbs*. In other words, while the *features* used for prediction in the two language varieties will differ, the influence of working memory constraints on prediction fallibility should be similar. Prediction fallibility should increase in both language varieties with increased linguistic complexity. Validation of this hypothesis will be taken up in future work.

Conclusion

Given the importance of predictive processing in SOV languages, the current study highlights a limit to prediction in an SOV language like Hindi. Using a sentence completion task, we show that Hindi native speakers make consistent parsing errors in conditions with three animate nouns with unique case-markers. Such parsing errors increase when adjuncts of differing complexity follow the three nouns. The grammatical and ungrammatical completions show that native speakers of Hindi predict simple structures with at most two embedding and five core syntactic relations, thus highlighting an upper bound to robust verbal prediction and its maintenance in such configurations. Further, the type of parsing errors suggests that the parser relies on frequent preverbal nominal features in order to make verbal predictions and form illicit parses at the expense of globally consistent parses. Together, the experiments paint a more nuanced picture of predictive processing in an SOV language like Hindi in terms of nature of verbal predictions and the possible cause of such predictions. The results highlight the need for a reappraisal of current theories that use robust prediction in SOV languages as an explanation to effects such as anti-locality and lack of forgetting. The work shows that linguistic complexity should lead to prediction fallibility in both SOV and SVO languages.

Acknowledgements This work was supported by a Department of Science and Technology—Cognitive Science Research Initiative grant (SR/CSRI/29/2015) to Samar Husain.

References

Altmann, G. T., & Kamide, Y. (1999). Incremental interpretation at verbs: Restricting the domain of subsequent reference. *Cognition, 73*, 247–256.

Altmann, G. T., & Kamide, Y. (2007). The realtime mediation of visual attention by language and world knowledge: Linking anticipatory (and other) eye movements to linguistic processing. *Journal of Memory and Language, 57*, 502–518.

Ashby, J., Rayner, K., & Charles Clifton, J. (2005). Eye movements of highly skilled and average readers: Differential effects of frequency and predictability. *The Quarterly Journal of Experimental Psychology Section A, 58*, 1065–1086.

Bach, E., Brown, C., Marslenwilson, W. (1986). Crossed and nested dependencies in german and dutch: A psy cholinguistic study. *Language and Cognitive Processes, 1*, 249–262.

Barr, D. J., Levy, R., Scheepers, C., & Tily, H. J. (2013). Random effects structure for confirmatory hypothesis testing: Keep it maximal. *Journal of Memory and Language, 68*, 255–278.

Bates, D., Machler, M., Bolker, B., & Walker, S. (2015). Fitting linear mixedeffects models using lme4. *Journal of Statistical Software, 67*, 1–48.

Bhatt, R., Narasimhan, B., Palmer, M., Rambow, O., Sharma, D. M., & Xia, F. (2009). A multirepresentational and multilayered treebank for Hindi/Urdu. In *Proceedings of the Third Linguistic Annotation Workshop* (pp. 186–189). Association for Computational Linguistics.

Bock, J. K. (1986). Syntactic persistence in language production. *Cognitive Psychology, 18*, 355–387.

Bresnan, J. (1982). *The mental representation of grammatical relations*. MIT Press.

Carreiras, M., & Clifton, C. (1993). Relative clause interpretation preferences in Spanish and English. *Language and Speech, 36*, 353.

Chandra P (2023) Problematizing linguistic variation. In: Chandra P (ed) Variation in South Asian Languages: From Macro to Microdifferences. Springer Nature

Chomsky, N. (1981). *Lectures on government and binding*. Foris.

Chomsky, N. (1995). *The minimalist program* volume 1765. Cambridge Univ Press.

Fischler, I. S., & Bloom, P. A. (1979). Automatic and attentional processes in the effects of sentence contexts on word recognition. *Journal of Verbal Learning and Verbal Behavior, 18*, 1–20.

Fodor, J. D. (1978). Parsing strategies and constraints on transformations. In *Linguistic Inquiry* (pp. 427–473)

Frazier, L. (1985). Syntactic complexity. In L. K. D. Dowty & A. Zwicky (Eds.), *Natural language parsing* (pp. 129–189). Cambridge University Press.

Frazier, L., & Fodor, J. D. (1978). The sausage machine: A new twostage parsing model. *Cognition, 6*, 291–325.

Friederici, A. D., & Frisch, S. (2000). Verb argument structure processing: The role of verb specific and argumentspecific information. *Journal of Memory and Language, 43*, 476–507.

Futrell, R., Mahowald, K., & Gibson, E. (2015). Largescale evidence of dependency length minimization in 37 languages. *Proceedings of the National Academy of Sciences, 112*, 10336–10341.

Futrell, R., Gibson, E., & Levy, R. (2020). Lossycontext surprisal: An informationtheoretic model of memory effects in sentence processing. *Cognitive Science*.

Gibson, E. (1998). Linguistic complexity: Locality of syntactic dependencies. *Cognition, 68*, 1–76.

Gibson, E., & Thomas, J. (1999). Memory limitations and structural forgetting: The perception of complex ungrammatical sentences as grammatical. *Language and Cognitive Processes, 14*(3), 225–248.

Gibson, E., Piantadosi, S. T., Brink, K., Bergen, L., Lim, E., & Saxe, R. (2013). A noisychannel account of crosslinguistic wordorder variation. *Psychological Science, 24*, 1079–1088.

Grodner, D., & Gibson, E. (2005). Consequences of the serial nature of linguistic input for sentenial complexity. *Cognitive Science, 29*, 261–290.

Gulati M, Choudhary K (2023) Cross-linguistic Variations in the Processing of Punjabi Ergative Case. In: Chandra P (ed) Variation in South Asian Languages: From Macro to Microdifferences. Springer Nature

Hale, J. T. (2006). Uncertainty about the rest of the sentence. *Cognitive Science, 30*.

Hawkins, J. A. (1994). *A performance theory of order and constituency* (Vol. 73). Cambridge University Press.

Husain, S., Vasishth, S., & Srinivasan, N. (2014). Strong expectations cancel locality effects: Evidence from Hindi. *PLoS ONE, 9*, e100986.

Jäger, L., Chen, Z., Li, Q., Lin, C.J. C., & Vasishth, S. (2015). The subjectrelative advantage in chinese: Evidence for expectationbased processing. *Journal of Memory and Language, 79*, 97–120

Joshi, A. K. (1985). Tree adjoining grammars: How much contextsensitivity is required to provide reasonable structural descriptions? In D. R. Dowty, L. Karttunen, & A. Zwicky (Eds.), *Natural language parsing* (pp. 206–250). Cambridge University Press.

Kamide, Y., Altmann, G. T., & Haywood, S. L. (2003). The timecourse of prediction in incremental sentence processing: Evidence from anticipatory eye movements. *Journal of Memory and Language, 49*, 133–156.

Kimball, J. (1973). Seven principles of surface structure parsing in natural language. *Cognition, 2*, 15–47.

Kliegl, R., Grabner, E., Rolfs, M., & Engbert, R. (2004). Length, frequency, and predictability effects of words on eye movements in reading. *European Journal of Cognitive Psychology, 16*, 262–284.

Konieczny, L. (2000). Locality and parsing complexity. *Journal of Psycholinguistic Research, 29*, 627–645.

Koso, A., Ojima, S., & Hagiwara, H. (2011). An eventrelated potential investigation of lexical pitchaccent processing in auditory japanese. *Brain Research, 1385*, 217–228.

Kurumada, C., & Jaeger, T. F. (2015). Communicative efficiency in language production: Optional casemarking in japanese. *Journal of Memory and Language, 83*, 152–178.

Kutas, M., & Hillyard, S. A. (1980). Reading senseless sentences: Brain potentials reflect semantic incongruity. *Science, 207*, 203–205.

Kutas, M., & Hillyard, S. (1984). Brain potentials during reading reflect word expectancy and semantic association. *Nature, 307*, 161–163.

Levy, R. (2008). Expectationbased syntactic comprehension. *Cognition, 106*, 1126–1177.

Levy, R., & Keller, F. (2013). Expectation and locality effects in german verbfinal structures. *Journal of memory and language, 68*, 199–222. ergative-absolutive

Lewis, R. (1993). *An architecturallybased theory of human sentence processing*. PhD Thesis, Ph.D. dissertation, Carnegie Mellon University Pittsburgh.

MacDonald, M. C. (2013). How language production shapes language form and comprehension. *Frontiers in Psychology, 4*, 226.

MarslenWilson, W. (1973). Linguistic structure and speech shadowing at very short latencies. *Nature, 244*, 522–523

Miller, G. A., & Chomsky, N. (1963). Finitary models of language users. In R. B. R.D. Luce, & E. Galanter (Eds.), *Handbook of mathematical psychology* (vol. 2, pp. 419–492). New York: Wiley.

Mitchell, D. C., Cuetos, F., Corley, M. M. B., & Brysbaert, M. (1995). Exposurebased models of human parsing: Evidence for the use of coarsegrained (nonlexical) statistical records. *Journal of Psycholinguistic Research, 24*, 469–488.

Nakatani, K., & Gibson, E. (2010). An online study of japanese nesting complexity. *Cognitive Science, 34*, 94–112.

Pollard, C., & Sag, I. A. (1994). *HeadDriven Phrase Structure Grammar*. Stanford, CA: Center for the Study of Language and Information.

Rayner, K., Slattery, T. J., Drieghe, D., & Liversedge, S. P. (2011). Eye movements and word skipping during reading. *Journal of Experimental Psychology: Human Perception and Performance, 37*, 514–528.

Ros, I., Santesteban, M., Fukumura, K., & Laka, I. (2015). Aiming at shorter dependencies: The role of agreement morphology. *Language, Cognition and Neuroscience, 30*, 1156–1174.

Schwanenflugel, P. J., & Lacount, K. L. (1988). Semantic relatedness and the scope of facilitation for upcoming words in sentences. *Journal of Experimental Psychology: Learning Memory and Cognition, 14*, 344–354.

Schwanenflugel, P. J., & Shoben, E. J. (1985). The influence of sentence constraint on the scope of facilitation for upcoming words. *Journal of Memory and Language, 24*, 232–252.

Scontras, G., Badecker, W., Shank, L., Lim, E., & Fedorenko, E. (2015). Syntactic complexity effects in sentence production. *Cognitive Science, 39*, 559–583.

Sharma, K., Futrell, R., & Husain, S. (2020). What determines the order of verbal dependents in hindi? effects of efficiency in comprehension and production. In *Proceedings of Cognitive Modeling and Computational Linguistics (CMCL)*.

Staub, A. (2015). The effect of lexical predictability on eye movements in reading: Critical review and theoretical interpretation. *Language and Linguistics Compass, 9*, 311–327.

Staub, A., Clifton, J. C. (2006). Syntactic prediction in language comprehension: Evidence from either … or. *Journal of Experimental Psychology: Learning, Memory, and Cognition, 32*, 425–436.

Steedman, M. (2001). *The syntactic process*. MIT Press.

Taylor, W. (1953). 'cloze' procedure: A new tool for measuring readability. *Journalism Quarterly, 30*, 415–433.

Ueno, M., & Polinsky, M. (2009). Does headedness affect processing? a new look at the vo–ov contrast. *Journal of Linguistics, 45*, 675–710.

Vasishth, S., Suckow, K., Lewis, R. L., & Kern, S. (2010). Shortterm forgetting in sentence comprehension: Crosslin guistic evidence from verbfinal structures. *Language and Cognitive Processes, 25*, 533–567.

Vasishth, S., & Drenhaus, H. (2011). Locality in German. *Dialogue & Discourse, 2*, 59–82.

Vasishth, S., & Lewis, R. L. (2006). Argumenthead distance and processing complexity: Explaining both locality and antilocality effects. *Language*, 767–794.

Yadav, H., Vaidya, A., Shukla, V., & Husain, S. (2020). Word order typology interacts with linguistic complexity: a crosslinguistic corpus study. *Cognitive Science, 44*.

Yamashita, H. (1997). The effects of wordorder and case marking information on the processing of japanese. *Journal of Psycholinguistic Research, 26*, 163–188.

Yamashita, H. (2000). Structural computation and the role of morphological markings in the processing of japanese. *Language and Speech, 43*, 429–455.

Yngve, V. H. (1960). A model and an hypothesis for language structure. *Proceedings of the American Philosophical Society, 104*, 444–466.

Zola, D. (1984). Redundancy and word perception during reading. *Perception & Psychophysics, 36*, 277–284.

Apurva is Assistant Professor in the Indian Institute of Management at Jammu. His research interest is sentence processing, where he primarily focuses on the interaction of working memory and expectations in Hindi sentence processing. His research methodology involves the use of sentence completion, Self-Paced Reading (SPR), and eye-tracking experiments.

Samar Husain is Associate Professor in the Department of Humanities and Social Sciences at IIT Delhi since 2014. He teaches courses to undergraduates and postgraduates in the areas of linguistics, cognitive science, statistics, and psycholinguistics. He completed his Ph.D. in 2011 from IIIT-Hyderabad, India. Subsequently, from 2011 to 2014, he was a post-doctoral researcher at the Vasishth lab, University of Potsdam, Germany. His broad areas of research are human sentence processing, natural language modeling, natural language parsing, and dependency grammars. These topics lie at the intersection of psychology, computational linguistics and theoretical linguistics. His current research investigates the sources of sentence complexity (such as working-memory, orthography, grammatical representation and parsing strategy) during real-time language comprehension and production using behavioral, corpus-based as well as computational methods.

Chapter 5
A Correlative Typology Mixing Syntactic and Semantic Parameters

Rahul Balusu

Abstract The Dravidian correlative is formed with a *wh*-item containing sentence with *-oo* at the clause edge. The disjunction marker *-oo* in Dravidian languages participates in coordinating elements, forming indefinites, and questions. Given that the canonical semantics of correlatives, (Dayal 1991, 1995) analyses them as definite descriptions, which bind the pronoun variable via predicate abstraction, the question is what *-oo* is doing here, and how does the semantic composition work. This sketch towards a compositional derivation of the Dravidian correlative based on a question denotation proves that it is not only feasible but also quite advantageous—we keep a unified semantics of *-oo*, the disjunction marker that also participates in forming indefinites, and questions, and derive a number of properties of the Dravidian correlative from the semantics of questions and answers. In the literature, the typology of correlatives has been proposed to have two syntactic parameters—one, the kind of relative clause it originates from—EHRC, IHRC, FR; and two, the kind of left dislocation involved—HTLD, CLD, CLLD. We propose to add to this typology a third and semantic parameter, its denotation—property or propositional. We show that the Dravidian correlative is built out of the semantic choice of a proposition-based denotation. We locate this semantic parameter itself in the denotation of the *wh*-items of the language, its lexical semantic entry—as sets of alternatives or as property free variables.

Keywords Correlatives · Dravidian · Disjunction · Questions · Left dislocation

R. Balusu (✉)
EFL University, Hyderabad, India

A Case for Semantic Parameters[1]

One of the primary goals of current linguistic theory is to explain and locate cross-linguistic variation in human language. What is the locus of parametric variation? There have been various proposals in the development of linguistic theory in accounting for this:

1. UG = Universal pool of features + Universal principles of derivation/interpretation. This itself has seen three stages:

    (a) Grammatical Parameters = Variation in principles + Variation in bundling of features into Lexical Items (LI)
    (b) Functional Parameters = Invariant principles + Variation in functional LI bundling (Borer, 1984)
    (c) Externalized Parameters = All parameters at PF (Chomsky, 2010, et seq.)

2. UG specified parameters versus UG underspecified parameters

    (a) UG very rich: Parameter settings and values provided by UG
    (b) Downsizing of UG: To explain sudden and recent emergence of particular properties of Human Language.

        i. Parameters not provided by UG, but 'emerge' at points where UG is underspecified.
        ii. (More) role for general cognitive processes: Third-factors (F3) of data processing, analysis and bootstrapping.

Most of these proposals have always focused on the PF or Syntactic side of things and have located variation there. In this paper, we focus on the question of whether there are semantic parameters. Semantic compositional and interpretational principles are considered invariant across languages (Higginbotham, 1986). But languages do vary in interpretation—tense/aspect, modification, comparison, complex predicates, etc. (Beck, 2018). There have been found to be remarkably few universals in semantics (Von Fintel & Matthewson, 2008). At the same time, few (if any) clear examples of parametric variation in semantics are identified. We all know of Comparative Syntax. Who has heard of Comparative Semantics? As Beck (2018, p. 3) says 'the field has not yet developed a theory of semantic variation.'

But what could semantic parameters look like? One semantic parameter that has been proposed is the Nominal Mapping Parameter (Chierchia, 1998):

1. Nouns are predicative = Romance languages
2. Nouns are argumental = Chinese

Another semantic parameter that has been proposed has to do with Polarity Items (Chierchia, 2013), (1).

---

[1] I would like to thank Pritha Chandra, the organizer of the Workshop on Approaches to Language Variation, IIT Delhi, and the audience for helpful discussion and comments.

In this paper, we explore one semantic parameter, the denotation of *wh*-items. We do this by taking the case study of the Dravidian correlative and their role of the disjunctive particle *-oo* in the correlative, while at the same time looking to unify the semantics of this disjunctive particle-*oo* across its various appearances. In unifying the semantics of the *-oo* particle in Dravidian, we end up proposing a question semantics for the Dravidian correlative. We go on to propose a typology of correlatives based on a mix of syntactic parameters—headed-ness and kind of dislocation; and a semantic parameter—denotation of *wh*-items. This paper thus becomes part of a larger approach to the issue of cross-linguistic variation: Semantic parameters.

(1)

Exhaustifying operators	Formal features	Type of alternatives	Modus operandi	Operandum	Examples of targets
$E_{\sigma A}$	$[\sigma]$	Degreealternatives, $\angle$ ordered Das	Single agree or Multiple agree	Assertive content	Give damn Koii bhii
$E_{\sigma A}^{S}$	$[\sigma]$	σAs	Single agre or Multiple agree	Assertive content + pre-suppositions	Sleep a wink
$O_{\sigma A}$	$[\sigma][n\text{-}\sigma]$	σAs	Single agree or multiple agree	Assertive content	Ever, alcun, mai
$O_{C/\sigma A}$	$[\sigma]$	C/σAs Contextually pruned σAs	Single agree or multiple agree	Assertive content	Some, and
O_{DA}	$[D][n\text{-}D]$	DAs	Multiple agree	Assertive content	Ever, alcun, mai
$O_{Exh\text{-}DA}$	$[D]$	Pre-exhaustified DAs	Multiple agree	Assertive content	Any, irgendein, some
O_{ALT}^{s}	$[[\sigma, D]]$ $[[n\text{-}\sigma, D]]$	$\sigma A \cup DA$	Multiple agree	Assertive content + pre-supposition	In weeks Strong Nwords
$O_{\sigma A/DA}^{PS}$	$[PS\text{-}\sigma, D]$	$PS\text{-}\sigma A/PS - DA$	Multiple agree or single agree	Assertive content	Qualsiasi Un N qualsiasi
$O_{\pi A}$	$[\pi]$	πAs (presuppositional alternatives)	single agree	Assertive content	Because, Know

Semantics of the Dravidian Disjunctive Particle-oo

The disjunction marker-*oo* in Dravidian languages participates in coordinating elements, forming indefinites, forming questions, and even forming correlatives. These multiple roles for this marker are by no means special to Dravidian—Sinhala Slade (2011); Japanese Kuroda (1965); among others. These have been dubbed KA particles–Mitrovic (2014), Szabolcsi (2015). A cross-linguistic pattern of KA particles is shown in (2)

(2)

Roles of -KA	TB	DR				IA			Jap	Slavic
	Mei	Tel	Kan	Tam	Mal	Hin	Ban	Sin	Jap	Hun
Disjunction	-ra -la	*-oo*	*-oo*	*-oo*	*-oo*			*-hari*	*-ka*	vagy
Polar question particle embedded								-de		
Polar question particle matrix		*-aa*	*-aa*	*-aa*				*-hari*		
Constituent question particle	*-no*	*-oo*	*-oo*	*-oo*						
Existential quantifier particle										vala
Correlative marker	*-ke*									

XP-oo

The KA particle in Dravidian *-oo* attaches at the phrasal level, as a disjunctive marker, as shown in (3).

(3) a.   *john-*(oo)   bill-*(oo)   peter-*(o o)*
         John-OO   Bill-OO   Peter-OO
         MALAYALAM/KANNADA/TELUGU/TAMIL
         'John, Bill or Peter'

    b.   *john-oo   bill-oo varum   MALAYALAM*
         John-oO Bill-OO come-will
         'John or Bill will come.'

When the disjunct is a DP with an overt case-marker, the -oo comes outside the case-marker, as shown in (4).

(4) a.   *doDDa*   *bekki-g-oo*   *chikka naayi-g-oo*

          big   Cat-DAT-oo small   dog-DAT-oo   KANNADA
                                                             (Amritavalli, 2003)

          'for/to a big cat or a small dog'

     b.   *ada-ra*   *meel-oo ida-ra*   *keLag-oo*

          that-GEN top-DISJ this-GEN under-DISJ

          'on top of that or under this'

     c.   *ada-ra*   *meel-inda-loo ida-ra keLag-inda-loo*

          that-GEN top-ABL-DISJ this-GEN under-ABL-DISJ

          'from on top of that or from under this'

The *-oo* also acts as a QUANTIFIER PARTICLE when added to *wh*-words, and forms existential quantifiers –epistemic indefinites, as shown in (5).

(5) a.   MALAYALAM (Jayaseelan, 2001)

          aar-oo   somebody
          who-OO

          ent-oo   something
          what-OO

          ewiDe-(y)oo   somewhere
          where-OO

          eppoozh-oo   sometime
          when-OO

          eNNine-(y)oo   somehow
          how-OO

     b.   *naan*   *iruTT-il*   *aar-e-(y)oo*   *toTTu*

          I   darkness-in who-ACC-OO touched

          'I touched somebody in the dark.'

As Jayaseelan (2001, p. 132) notes: 'The existential quantifiers are not polarity sensitive. They have a more restricted meaning, they can be used only when the identity of the person or thing being described is not known to the speaker.' This is shown in (6).

(6) a.   *naan*   *iruTT-il*   *aar-e-(y)oo*   *toTTu*

          I   darkness-in who-ACC-DISJ touched

          'I touched somebody in the dark.'

     b.   #   *naan innale   aar-e-(y)oo   paricayappeTTu*

          I   yesterday who-ACC-DISJ met

          'I met somebody yesterday.'

Sentence Final Particle -OO

This KA particle in Dravidian, *-oo* also occurs clause or sentence finally. When it occurs sentence finally, it forms POL/ALT questions. Malayalam Pol/Alt Qs are formed by adding *-oo* to each clause; Telugu/Tamil/Kannada embedded Pol/Alt Qs have a clause final *-oo*, as shown in (7).

(7) a.   *John wannu-(w)oo?*   MALAYALAM

        John came-OO

        'Did John come?'

    b.   *John wannu-(w)oo illa-(y)oo?*

        John came-OO   not-OO

        'Did John come or not?'

    c.   *John wacceeD-oo aDugu!*   TELUGU

        John came-OO   ask

        'Ask if John came!'

    d.   *John wacceeD-oo leed-oo aDugu!*

        John came-oo   not-oo   ask

        'Ask if John came or not!'

Unlike in Malayalam (7a), the particle *-oo* cannot be used in a matrix clause to form Pol or Alt Qs, in Telugu, Kannada and Tamil, as shown in (8) from Telugu.

(8)   **anu   uma-ki   pustakam iccind-oo?*

    Anu   Uma-DAT book   gave-OO

    'Did Anu give the book to Uma?'

In Tamil, Kannada and Telugu, a question particle, that I'll call the Polar Question Particle, **Q**, is required in Matrix Pol/Alt Qs, as shown in (9) from Telugu. There is no disjunction marker here.

(9) a. *anu uma-ki   pustakam iccind-aa?*

      Anu Uma-DAT book gave-Q_p

      'Did Anu give the book to Uma?'

   b. *anu uma-ki   pustakam iccind-aa leed-aa?*   [Polar Alt Q]

      Anu Uma-DAT book gave-Q_p not$_{+FIN}$-Q_p

      'Did Anu give the book to Uma or not?'

   c. *anu   uma-ki   pustakam iccind-aa ivva-leed-aa?*

     Anu Uma-DAT book gave-Q_p gave-not$_{+FIN}$-Q_p

     'Did Anu give the book to Uma or not give?'

   d. *anu   uma-ki   pustakam iccindaa pen iccind-aa?* [Alt Q]

     Anu Uma-DAT book gave-Q_p pen gave-Q_p

     'Did Anu give Uma the book or the pen?'

This particle *-oo* also forms *wh*-QUESTIONS in Telugu, Tamil and Kannada. Embedded *wh*-questions (and Pol/Alt Qs) are formed by adding *-oo* to the clause, as shown in (10).

10 a. *Naaku evaru wacceer-oo telusu*   TELUGU

     I-DAT   who   came-oo   know

     'I know who came.'

   b. *anu   uma-ki   pustakam iccind-oo   leed-oo   naa-ku telusu*

     Anu Uma-DAT book gave–DISJ not–DISJ I-DAT   know

     'I know if Anu gave the book to Uma'

   c. *anu   uma-ki   pustakam iccind-oo   pen iccind-oo naaku telusu?* [Alt Q]

     Anu Uma-DAT book gave-DISJ pen gave-DISJ I-DAT   know

     'I know if Anu give Uma the book or the pen.'

However, Malayalam *wh*-questions are not marked with -oo, as shown in (11).

11 a. *aar. wannu?*

     who came

     'who came?'

   b. *awan ewiDe pooyi*

     he   where went

     'Where did he go?'

   c. *[awan ewiDe pooyi enn] naan coodiccu*

     he   where went C   I   asked

     'I asked where he went.'

But contrary to this observational fact, Jayaseelan (2001) argues that *wh*-questions in Malayalam also have an underlying *-oo*.

In matrix clauses in Kannada, Tamil and Telugu, the question particle *-oo* with a *wh*-word, or in an Alt Q, gives the meaning of 'wonder,' as shown in (12).

12 a. *anu*   *uma-ki*   *eemi iccind-oo*   TELUGU

    Anu Uma-DAT what gave-OO

    'I wonder what Anu gave to Uma'

  b. *anu*   *uma-ki*   *pustakam iccind-oo leed-oo*?   *[Polar Alt Q]*

    Anu Uma-DAT book   gave-OO not$_{+FIN}$-OO

    'I wonder if Anu gave the book to Uma or not'

  c. *anu*   *uma-ki*   *pustakam iccind-oo ivva-leed-oo*?

    Anu Uma-DAT book   gave-OO gave-not$_{+FIN}$-OO

    'I wonder if Anu gave the book to Uma or not give.'

  d. *anu*   *uma-ki*   *pustakam iccind-oo pen iccind-oo*? *[Alt Q]*

    Anu Uma-DAT book gave-OO   pen gave-OO

    'I wonder if Anu gave Uma the book or the pen'

A summary of the distribution of *-oo* across the Dravidian languages in shown in (13)

13	Role of -KA	Malayalam	Telugu	Kannada	Tamil
	disjunction	-oo	-oo	-oo	-oo
	existential quantifier particle	-oo	-oo	-oo	-oo
	Pol/Atl-Q particle matrix	-oo	-aa	-aa	-aa
	Pol/Alt-Q particle embedded	-oo	-oo	-oo	-oo
	wh-Q particle matrix	–	–	–	–
	wh-Q particle embedded	–	-oo	-oo	-oo

Why Does KA Take on Multiple Roles?

On the one hand, the role of KA particles in multiple functions is taken to be homophony, and each role is treated in isolation (Cable, 2010). On the other, this is taken to signify an underlying property that justifies its many roles, and unification is attempted —Jayaseelan (2011); Szabolcsi (2015); Slade (2011), etc. The latest and perhaps most unificatory in this series is Uegaki et al. (2018).

Jayaseelan (2001, 2011, 2014) analyses coordination as being made up of the two operations: i. concatenation ii. serial substitution. The two operations are realized by two distinct functional heads in the syntax of coordination. Languages realize either one of these heads but not both. English and/or, are copies of the concatenation operator; the same appears to be true of Hindi aur/yaa. By contrast, Japanese/Malayalam coordination markers are copies of the substitution operator (choice function). Disjunction marker *-oo* which 'marks off' each disjunct is a copy of the substitution operator (choice function), and the concatenation operator has no lexical realization. A coordination operator is 'silent' (not phonologically realized) when its copies are present on the coordinands. The two parametrized structures are shown in (14).

(14)

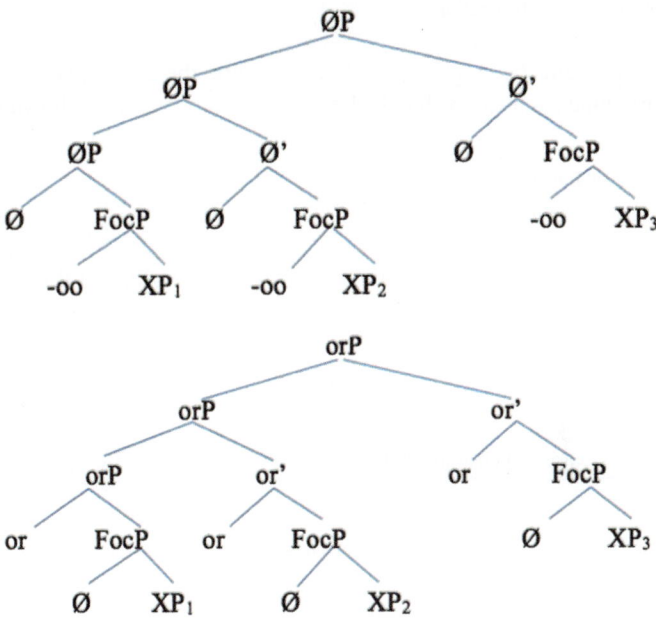

But the *-oo* that appears in existential quantifiers, correlative clauses and questions is the realization of the choice-function operator itself. For him, a *wh*-word signifies a focused variable (Nishigauchi, 1990); and a disjunction choice-function operator applied to a variable interprets it as an 'infinite disjunction' (the meaning of an existential quantifier). The operator 'applies to' the question word by 'association with focus' (Rooth, 1985). The disjunction marker doubles as the question marker because a question clause has the disjunction operator in the head position of ForceP. All Malayalam questions have a clause final *-oo*, although this is overt only in Pol/Alt Qs. The quantifier exists in two parts. Universally, says Jayaseelan, questions contain a disjunction operator generated as the head of ForceP. From this position, it applies to question words by association with focus, yielding question interpretations.

Uegaki et al. (2018) treats each appearance of *ka*, the Japanese counterpart of *-oo*, as having only one semantic role, that of copying what is in the alternative semantic dimension into the ordinary semantic dimension, in a two-tier alternative semantics *wh*-in-situ (Beck, 2006; Kotek, 2014) model, as shown in (15).

15 $[\alpha ka]^0 = [\alpha]^{alt}$ and $[\alpha ka]^{alt} \{ [\alpha]^{alt} \}$

When alternatives enter the ordinary dimension early in the sentence precipi-
tated by a low attached *ka*, they cannot be handled by the semantic composition,
and a repair strategy of folding the alternatives into a single (existential) element
kicks in, as shown in (16).

(16) a. *ka* + *wh*-item = existential indefinite

      b. *ka* + α … β = disjunction

But when *ka* attaches high, in the left periphery, the alternatives entering into
the ordinary dimension can be handled by a question operator, as shown in (17).

(17) a. clause final *ka* + *wh*-item = *wh*-Q

      b. clause final *ka* + α … β = Alt Q

This nice bifurcation in the readings, at two levels, speaks to this explanation,
as shown in (18).

(18)	*-oo* is:	subclausal	Clause final
	α … β	declarative disjunction	Alt Q
	wh-	existential quantifier	*wh*-Q

Why Is There an *-Oo* in the Dravidian Correlative?

The Dravidian KA, the *-oo*, also appears in correlatives, as a correlative marker,
as shown in (19). As Subbarao (2008, p. 64) notes 'When the head of the relative
clause is indefinite, non-specific, and hypothetical, the clause is labelled a free relative clause. In Dravidian languages and in some Tibeto-Burman languages, the
main clause and the subordinate clause in such cases are linked by a marker called
the "dubitative marker" (dub mkr) in traditional grammars.'

(19) a. *[nii eng-enge pooriy-oo] angellam* TAMIL   TAMIL
          naanum varuveen

          you where-where go-OO there-all   I-also   will-come
          I-also will-come

          'I too will come wherever you go.'

      b. *enn-e aar nuLLi-(y)oo, awan*   MALAYALAM   MALAYALAM
          duST-avan aaN

          I-ACC who pinched-OO he wick-   wicked-man is
          ed-man is

          'The person who pinched me is
          wicked.'

Interestingly, the morphosyntactic shape of the correlative is the same as the question, as shown in (20).

(20) a. *wh*-QUESTION

      eemi konnaaD-oo aDigeenu   TELUGU

      what bought-OO   asked

      '(I) asked what (he) bought.'

    b. CORRELATIVE

      eemi konnaaD-oo (adi) tinnaanu

      what bought-OO   that ate

      'What (he) bought, that (I) ate.'

The [clause final +*wh*-] cell thus gets another occupant in Dravidian, as shown in (21).

(21)	*-oo* is:	subclausal	Clause final
	$\alpha \dots \beta$	declarative disjunction	Alt Q
	wh-	existential quantifier	**wh-Q/correlative**

We can now update the cross-linguistic pattern of KA particles with the correlative role, as shown in (22), with the KA of Dravidian also playing a role in forming correlatives.

(22)	TB	DR				IA			Jap	Slavic
Roles of -**KA**	Mei	Tel	Kan	Tam	Mal	Hin	Ban	Sin	Jap	Hun
disjunction	-ra	*-oo*	*-oo*	*-oo*	*-oo*			*-hari*	*-ka*	**vagy**
polar question particle embedded	-la							**-de**		
polar question particle matrix		*-aa*	*-aa*	*-aa*						
constituent question particle	*-no*									
existential quantifier particle			*-oo*	*-oo*				*-hari*		*vala*
correlative marker	*-ke*	*-oo*								

What semantic role does *-oo* have in correlatives? Correlative semantics is standardly given a denotation of properties not propositions (which is what questions are). The canonical semantics of correlatives (Dayal 1991, 1995) analyses them as definite descriptions, which bind the pronoun variable via predicate abstraction, as shown in (23).

(23) a. *[jo laDakaa gaayaa hai]$_i$ vo$_i$ mera bhai hai*   HINDI

       REL-P boy Sang is he my brother is

       'which boy sang, he is my brother.'

   b. [[$\iota(\lambda x.x$ sang and x is a boy)] [λ_2 he$_2$ is my brother]]

The question then is what *-oo* is doing here in the correlative, and if it has the Uegaki KA denotation, then how does the semantic composition work. The correlative, with its two word order locations illustrated in (24), is thus a problem.

(24) a. LEFT-ADJOINED CORRELATIVE

       [eemi tecceen-oo] ravi adi tinnaaDu   TELUGU

       what brought-OO Ravi that ate

       'Ravi ate what (I) brought.'

   b. DEM-ADJOINED CORRELATIVE

       ravi uma-ki[[eemi tecceen-oo] adi] icceeDu

       ravi uma-DAT what brought-OO that gave

       'Ravi gave to Uma what (I) brought.'

Can we build the Dravidian correlative out of a question denotation? Our answer is: yes, as we show in the next section.

A Question Semantics for the Dravidian Correlative

Jayaseelan (2001) treats the appearance of *-oo* in questions and correlatives as the disjunction operator. This disjunction operator has the semantics of the logical boolean operator . For him, a correlative clause has the same structure as a question, but it is not interpreted as a request for information. Questions then, according to him, have an additional 'request-for-information' meaning, which could be accommodated if the head of ForceP contained, besides the disjunction operator, 'another' element. Also, the question's illocutionary force may be signalled by intonation (or other means). There is thus no 'question meaning' in the correlative. Our analysis will however take the opposite position and integrate a question denotation into the correlative, as shown below.

Demirok (2017) already proposes that the Turkish correlative is built on *wh*-question semantics and an additional conditional semantics, reflected in the morphosyntax, as shown in (25).

(25) *[John kim-i davet-et-ti-yse]₍ᵢ₎ oᵢ gel-di*   TURKISH
      John who-ACC invite-PST-**SA** DEM come-PST
      'Whoever John invited, came.'

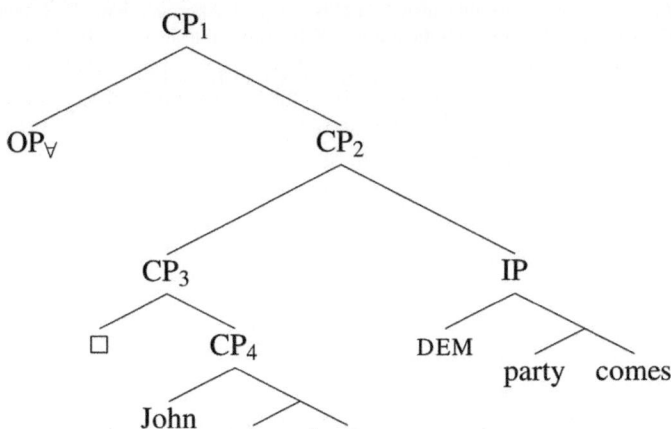

Each of the propositions in the Q-denotation pointwise restricts the modal conditional, thus delivering a free choice (FC) meaning. We get a generalized conjunction of conditional statements. The main clause DEM is given an E-type
denotation. This works for Turkish because Turkish correlatives have a FC
interpretation, but it won't work for Dravidian because they have a definite
interpretation.

Chierchia & Caponigro (2013) propose that all free relatives (FRs) are built on
top of a question denotation in two steps, as shown in (26).

(26) a. a TP ('Topical Property') operator that extracts properties from questions:
          TP(what Mary cooked?) = λx. λw Mary cooked x in w

      b. John ate[$_{DP}$ what [$_{CP}$ Mary cooked t]]

      c. = John ate D$_{rel}$ (TP(what Mary cooked t?))
          = $\exists$x [x = ιx M cooked$_w$ x] $\wedge$ J ate$_w$ x

FRs are DPs with the same denotation as short answers to Qs. The subset relation of *wh*-items in free relatives to those of questions is due to the D$_{rel}$ operator
that is a partial function from question to free relative denotations.

But in Dravidian, all the *wh*-words that occur in questions also occur in correlatives. So we don't need a partial mapping D$_{rel}$ operator and instead can build
directly on top of the answerhood operator, which occurs with all *wh*-questions.
However what we need to use is the short answer to a question (of type *e*), and
not the full answer, of type $\langle s, t \rangle$, since it has to bind the demonstrative in the main
clause.

Liu (2017) develops a structured meaning for questions in an alternative semantics framework, to explain the Mandarin *wh*-conditional construction, out of which we can easily form a short answerhood operator, as he points out, and as shown in (27).

(27) *Dayal-answer*: a possible answer of Q is a focus-background pair $\langle F, B \rangle$ belonging to Q; A Dayal-answer at w is the unique $\langle F, B \rangle$ that is the strongest true answer at w.

$$\text{Ans}(Q)(w) = \iota \langle F, B \rangle \in Q[(B)(F)(w) = 1 \wedge \forall \langle F', B' \rangle \in Q[(B')(F')(w)$$
$$= 1 \rightarrow B(F) \subseteq B'(F')]]$$

The denotation of the short answer of a question can be directly read off its Dayal-answer, which is just the F-part of the latter. We define the short answerhood operator, (28), using the Fox (2013) version of answerhood (that allows mention-some interpretations), and Liu's $\langle$Focus Background$\rangle$ structure.

(28) $\text{ANS}^s (Q)(w) =$
$$\left\{ F | F \in \langle F, B \rangle \wedge w \in \langle F, B \rangle \in Q \wedge \forall \langle F', B' \rangle [w \in \langle F', B' \rangle \in Q \rightarrow \langle F', B' \rangle \langle F, B \rangle] \right\}$$

({F| F is the focus denotation of $\langle F, B \rangle$F,B, a true proposition in Q, and $\langle F, B \rangle$ is not asymmetrically entailed by any true propositions in Q})

A Correlative Typology with a Semantic Parameter

Finally, moving to the larger picture, towards a correlative typology, we find that Cinque (2010, p. 210) posits two syntactic points of variation for correlatives: 'Correlatives (at least those that do not contain multiple wh-phrases) are embedded in a DP which is left dislocated at the beginning of the matrix clause and is resumed by a correlative pro-form (or a full DP) inside the matrix clause.' He considers Multiple correlatives as non-relative, free adjunct, CPs.

The left dislocation is of three possible types, as shown in (29).

(29) a. CLD (Contrastive Left Dislocation) = German, Bulgarian

      b. CLLD (Clitic Left Dislocation) = Italian

      c. HTLD (Hanging Topic Left Dislocation) = Hungarian

'The left dislocated DP may contain, depending on the language, either an externally headed postnominal, or an externally headed prenominal, or an internally headed, or a headless (free), relative clause.' Cinque (2010, p. 212). Thus, the kind of relative clause the correlative originates from is of the following types, as shown in (30).

(30) a.   Externally headed postnominal = Slavic, Warlpiri

b.   'Headless' /'free' relative = Bulgarian, German, Italian

c.   Externally headed prenominal = Sinhala

d.   Internally headed = Wappo, Bambara, Georgian (Bhatt & Nash 2018)

To these two parameters of variation, both syntactic, that give rise to the variety of correlatives that are found cross-linguistically, we add a third and semantic point of variation, i.e. the denotation—property-based or propositional, as shown in (31). As we saw, Demirok (2017) builds propositions out of the *wh*-phrase containing antecedents, which pointwise restrict the modal associated with the conditional operator that is suffixed clause finally to the antecedent. We maintain, based on the occurrence of *-oo* suffixed clause finally to the antecedent, that in Dravidian also, the *wh*-item containing antecedent delivers propositional meaning.

(31) a.   property-based = Georgian (Bhatt & Nash 2018), Hindi-Urdu (Dayal, 1995)

b.   propositional = Turkish (Demirok, 2017), Dravidian

We locate this semantic parameter itself in the denotation of the *wh*-items of the language, its lexical semantic entry –as sets of alternatives or as property free variables. Thus, what we are proposing is a *wh*-word semantic parameter. The semantic entry typology for interrogative pronouns that we propose is shown in (32).

32 a.   *wh*-words as property free variables (Demirok, 2017, Šimík 2018):

i. $who = \lambda x.\lambda w.x$ in human in w
Movement creates a semantic predicate:

ii. who λ_i John hit $t_i = \lambda x.\lambda w$ john hit x in w
Combining with an iota operator turns the predicate into a definite description, that forms a wh-FR or correlative, etc.:

iii. $\big[D\big[\text{who } \lambda_i \text{ John hit } t_i \big]\big] = \iota x.\lambda w.$ john hit x in w

b   wh-words as sets of alternatives:

i. $who^{\circ} = $ undefined
$who^{\,dlt} = \{x|x \text{ is } \in \text{HUMAN}\}$
Composing with a predicate:

ii. ran $^{\circ} = \lambda x, \lambda w, \text{ran}(x, w)$
ran $^{alt} == \{\lambda x, \lambda w.\text{ran}(x, w)\}$
Remember $\alpha KA^{\circ} = \alpha^{alt}$ and $\alpha KA^{alt} = \{\alpha^{alt}\}$

iii. who -oo ran$^{\circ} == \exists x.\lambda w \cdot \text{ran}(x, w)$ By [∃]$^{\circ}$ repair
whoran $- oo^{\circ} = \{\lambda x, \lambda w, \text{ran}(x, w), x \text{ is human in } w\}$

Combining with answerhood operators or pointwise restriction of conditional modals yields (definite) correlatives and Free-Choice correlatives, respectively.

Conclusions

This sketch towards a compositional derivation of the Dravidian correlative based on a question denotation leads us to conclude that it is not only feasible but also quite advantageous:

1. We keep a unified semantics of -*oo*, the Dravidian KA particle.
2. We derive a number of properties of the correlative from the semantics of questions and answers.

References

Amritavalli, R. (2003). Question and negative polarity in the disjunction phrase. *Syntax, 6*(1), 1–18.

Beck, S. (2006). Intervention effects follow from focus interpretation. *Natural Language Semantics, 14*(1), 1–56.

Beck, S. (2018). Semantic parameters and universals. In L. Matthewson, C. Meier, H. Rullmann, T.E. Zimmermann (Eds), *Semantics Companion*.

Bhatt, R., & Nash, L. *Deconstructing correlatives individuals and properties—the case of Georgian rom relatives*. Talk given at TripleA 5, University of Konstanz.

Borer, H. (1984). The projection principle and rules of morphology. In *Proceedings of NELS* (vol. 14, pp. 16–33).

Cable, S. (2010). *The grammar of Q: Q-particles, wh-movement, and pied-piping*. Oxford University Press.

Chierchia, G. (1998). Plurality of mass nouns and the notion of "semantic parameter". In *Events and grammar* (pp. 53–103). Springer.

Chierchia, G. (2013). *Logic in grammar: Polarity, free choice, and intervention*. In G. Chierchia, & I. Caponigro (Eds.), *Questions on questions and free relatives. In:Sinn und Bedeutung*, vol. 18. OUP Oxford.

Chomsky, N. (2010). *Poverty of stimulus: Unfinished business*. Transcript of a presentation given at Johannes-Gutenberg University.

Cinque, G. (2010). Five notes on correlatives. *Working Papers in Linguistics, 19*, 35–60.

Dayal, V. (1995). Quantification in correlatives. In *Quantification in natural languages* (pp. 179–205). Springer.

Dayal, V. S. (1991). *Wh dependencies in Hindi and the theory of grammar* [Ph.D. thesis, Ph. D. dissertation] Cornell University, Ithaca, NY.

Demirok, O. (2017). A compositional semantics for Turkish correlatives. In *WCCFL 34: Proceedings of the 34th West Coast Conference on Formal Linguistics* (pp. 159–166).

Fox, D. (2013). *Mention-some readings of questions, class notes*.

Higginbotham, J. (1986). Linguistic theory and Davidson's program in semantics. MIT seminars.

Jayaseelan, K. A. (2014). Coordination, relativization and finiteness in Dravidian. *Natural Language & Linguistic Theory, 32*(1), 191–211.

Jayaseelan, K. A. (2001). IP-internal topic and focus phrases. *Studia Linguistica, 55*(1), 39–75.

Jayaseelan, K. A. (2011). Comparative morphology of quantifiers. *Lingua, 121*(2), 269–286.

Kotek, H. (2014). Composing questions. Massachusetts Institute of Technology dissertation.

Kuroda, S-Y. (1965). Generative grammatical studies in the Japanese language. [Ph.D. thesis]. Massachusetts Institute of Technology.

Liu, M. (2017). Varieties of alternatives: Mandarin focus particles. *Linguistics and Philosophy, 40*(1), 61–95.

Mitrovic, M. (2014). Morphosyntactic atoms of propositional logic: a philo-logical programme. Ph. D. diss.

Nishigauchi, T. (1990). Construing wh. In *Quantification in the Theory of Grammar* (pp. 116–176). Springer.

Rooth, M. (1985). *Association with focus*. Ph.D. thesis, University of Massachusetts, Amherst.

Šimík, R. (2018). Free relatives. In D. Gutzmann, (Ed.), Semantics Companion.

Slade, B. M. (2011). Formal and philological inquiries into the nature of interrogatives, indefinites, disjunction, and focus in Sinhala and other languages. [Ph.D. thesis] University of Illinois at Urbana-Champaign.

Subbarao, K. V. (2008). Typological characteristics of South Asian languages. *Language in South Asia*, 49–78.

Szabolcsi, A. (2015). What do quantifier particles do? *Linguistics and Philosophy, 38*(2), 159–204.

Uegaki, W., et al. (2018). A unified semantics for the Japanese Q-particle" ka" in indefinites, questions and disjunctions. *Glossa: a journal of general linguistics*, **3**, 45.

Von Fintel, K., & Matthewson, L. (2008). Universals in semantics. *The linguistic review*, **25** (1–2), 139–201.

Chapter 6
A Comparative Study of the Lexicalization of the Bangla Polar Question Particle *ki* and the Assamese Polar Question Particle *ne*

Ambalika Guha

Abstract The primary discussion of the chapter is centred around the two polar question particles 'ki' and 'ne' in the Eastern Indo-Aryan languages Bangla and Assamese, respectively. Both these question particles seem to occur in polar questions and alternative questions. It is argued that the polar question particles 'ki' in Bangla and 'ne' in Assamese are interpreted as interrogative disjunction particles in alternative questions and embedded questions (I would like to thank the anonymous reviewers for their productive comments and I would also like to thank Prof. Pritha Chandra for helping in constructing the main arguments of the chapter and for highlighting that lexicalization as a constraint of language variation is the primary focus of the chapter.).

Keywords Polar questions · Alternative questions · Question operator · Disjunction operator · Lexicalization · Polar question particle · Interrogative disjunction particle · Cornering effect

Introduction

This chapter investigates the polar questions and alternative questions in the two Eastern Indo-Aryan Languages, Bangla and Assamese, and it further explores the ways in which some of the polar question particles in these two languages are developing into interrogative disjunction particles. In a way, this chapter

A. Guha (✉)
Department of English Language and Literature, Adamas University, Kolkata, India
e-mail: ambalika1.guha@adamasuniversity.ac.in; guhaambalika64@gmail.com

Centre for Study of Contemporary Theory and Research, Adamas University, Kolkata, India contributes towards the research of language variation with respect to polar question particles. Language variation involves changes in category status, such as the emergence of a new grammatical category (article and auxiliary verb), loss of an existing grammatical category (inflectional case) or chain shifts (Grimm's law, the Great Vowel Shift), as mentioned in Brinton and Traugott (2005). The type of change that is crucially dealt in this chapter is *lexicalization*. Historically, it is defined as 'a process by which new linguistic entities be it simple or complex words or just new senses, become conventionalized on the level of lexicon' (Blank (2001)). Another interpretation of *lexicalization* refers to shifts from implied to coded (or conventional) meaning, i.e. from pragmatic to semantic polysemy (Brinton and Traugott (2005)). For example, the lexeme 'see' which usually refers to a visual experience can be interpreted as 'understanding' in certain contexts, such as 'I see that' (this example is borrowed from Brinton and Traugott (2005, p. 21). In the present chapter, we will adopt the second interpretation of *lexicalization* and observe how the polar question particles in Bangla and Assamese are interpreted as interrogative disjunction particles in certain contexts, such as alternative questions and embedded questions.

Both Assamese and Bangla belong to the Eastern group of Indo-Aryan Language family. Both are directly descended from Apabharmsa dialects developed from Maga Prakrit of the eastern group of Sanskrit language. Assamese which is the anglicized name of Asamiya is the principal language of the state of Assam and often regarded as Lingua Franca for the North-East of India (Goswami (1982)). Apart from Assam, it is widely spoken in the states of Arunachal Pradesh, Meghalaya, Mizoram and Nagaland. Bangla, on the other hand, is the official state language of West Bengal and Tripura. Bangla is the primary language spoken in Bangladesh and is the second most widely spoken language in India (Chetterji, 1970). Assamese and Bangla are both classifier languages, the nouns, numbers and quantifiers take inflection for classifiers. The nouns and pronouns in these two languages inflect for case, and the verbs inflect for tense and person but not for number and gender.

The chapter is divided into ten sections. The first section presents the two ways in which polar questions are formed in Bangla and Assamese. The second section explores the different semantic interpretations of the polar questions with and without polar question particles in these two languages. The third section presents empirical evidence of the occurrence of the Bangla polar question particle 'ki' and the Assamese polar question particle 'ne' as interrogative disjunction particles. The fourth section shows how polar questions, like alternative questions, in these languages indicate disjunction in the answer space. The fifth section interprets the new meaning of the polar question particles 'ki' and 'ne' in embedded questions in their respective languages. In the sixth section, we present our analysis of the lexicalization of the polar question particles in these two languages. The seventh section explores various types of interrogative disjunction markers in Bangla. The eighth and ninth sections demonstrate the syntactically restricted occurrence of some of the polar question particles in embedded polar questions in Bangla and Assamese. The tenth section concludes the chapter.

Polar Questions in Bangla and Assamese

In the two Indo-Aryan languages, Bangla and Assamese, the declarative sentence with a rising intonation at the clause final position indicates a polar question, as can be seen in (1) and (2).

1 Ram   ʧɑ: kha-b-e ↑   Bengali
   Ram   tea   eat-Fut-3P
   'Will Ram have tea?'

2 Ram-e   sah   kha-b-o ↑   Assamese
   Ram-AGN   tea   eat-Fut-3P
   'Will Ram have tea?'

The polar questions in these languages can also be formed by using P(olar) Q(uestion) P(articles) beside the prosody, cf. (3) and (4). The two ways in which polar questions are formed in these languages have already been noticed by Bhadra (2017) and Syed and Dash (2017) in Bengali, and Rajkhowa (2018) in Assamese.

3 Ram   ki   ʧɑ: kha-b-e ↑   Bengali
   Ram   PQP   tea   eat-Fut-3P
   'Will Ram have tea?'

4 Ram-e   sah   kha-b-o   ne ↑   Assamese
   Ram-AGN   tea   eat-Fut-3P   PQP
   'Will Ram have tea?'

The Bangla polar question particle 'ki' occurs in multiple positions in a clause; cf. (5). In Bangla, the occurrence of 'ki' in the clause initial position is not allowed (as noted by Bhadra (2017) and Syed and Dash (2017)). It requires some element to occur to its left position, cf. (5).

5 (*ki)   Ram   (ki)   ʧɑ   (ki)   kha-b-e   (ki) ↑
   PQP   Ram   PQP   tea   PQP   eat-Fut-3P   PQP
   'Will Ram have tea?'

In Assamese, the occurrence of the polar question particle 'ne' is restricted to the clause final position, as can be seen in (6) and has already been noted by

Barbora (2007) and Rajkhowa (2018). The particle 'ne' requires the entire sentence to get dislocated to its left.

6 (*ne) Ram-e   (*ne) sah (*ne) kha -b   -o   (ne)) ↑
   PQP   Ram-AGN   PQP   tea PQP   eat -future 3P   PQP
   'Will Ram have tea?'

Here, I should mention that the Bangla polar question particle 'ki' is homophonous to the thematic question word 'ki' (what), as can be seen in (7). This has already been noted by Bhadra (2017).

7 Ram   ki   kha-b-e ?
   Ram   what   eat-Fut-3P
   'What will Ram have?'

The syntactic position of the thematic 'ki' in Bangla is restricted only to the subject 2 position (8). But the PQP 'ki' can occur in multiple positions, as shown in (5).

8 Ram ki   ʧa   (*ki) kha-b-e   (*ki)?
   Ram what tea what   eat-Fut-3P what
   'What type of tea will Ram have?'

The multiple syntactic positions of the PQP 'ki' in Bangla affect the semantic interpretation of the polar questions. In fact, the meaning of polar question without PQP differs from the meaning of polar question with PQP in Bangla. Since the Assamese PQP occurs only in one position in the clause, i.e. clause finally, the meaning of polar questions with and without PQP in this language remains consistent.

The Semantics of Polar Questions with and Without Polar Question Particles in Bangla and Assamese

A polar question without PQP in Bangla and Assamese questions all the elements in the sentence. Let us start our observation with Bangla. Consider the polar question without PQP in (9A). The possible answers to the question in (9) are stated in (9B)–(9E). The addressee can either choose to answer by selecting the given alternative (9B), or by denying it (9C), or by denying it and choosing some other alternative, as in replacing the object in (9D) and replacing the subject in (9E).

9A	Ram	ʧa:	kha-b-e ↑
	Ram	tea	eat-Fut-3P
	'Will Ram have tea?'		
B	hyan,	ʧa	kha-b-e
	Yes	tea	eat-Fut-3P
	'Yes, he will have tea.'		
C	na:,	kha-b-e	na:
	No	eat-Fut-3P	no
	'No, he will not have tea.'		
D	na:,	coffee	khabe
	No	coffee	will have
	'No, he will have coffee.'		
E	na,	Shyam	khabe
	No,	Shyam	will have
	'No, Shyam will have tea.'		

Now, let us consider the polar questions with the PQP 'ki' and notice what difference it has with the polar question without 'ki.' The question with the PQP questions only the elements that occur to the right of the PQP and not to the left of it. Thus, in (10A) post 'ki' every constituent is questioned. In (10), an alternative question can be formed on any post 'ki' constituent, on the indirect object (10B), on the direct object (10C). But an alternative question cannot be formed on the subject (10D) as it occurs to the left of the PQP 'ki.'

10A	Ram	ki	Sita-ke	kalam	di-l-o ?
	Ram	KI	Sita-ACC	pen	give-PST-3P
	'Did Ram give a pen to Sita?'				
B	na		Ritu-ke	di-l-o ?	
	or		Ritu-Acc	give-PST-3P	
	'or gave it to Ritu?'				
C	na		Sari	di-l-o ?	
	or		sari	give-PST-3P	
	'or gave a sari?'				
D	#na		Raban	di-l-o ?	
	or		Ravan	give-PST-3P	
	'or Ravan gave it?'				

Similar behaviour of the Hindi PQP 'kya:' has been noticed by Beizam et al. (2018). They analyse PQP 'kya:' as a focus-sensitive operator, which further restricts the set of possible answers in a given context. They suggest that the element to the immediate right of 'kya:' is questioned. Later, Bhatt and Dayal (2020) show that in fact every element to the right of 'kya:' can be questioned. However, the element to the left of 'kya:' can also be questioned if that element bears stress (noted in Beizma et al. (2018)).

Like Hindi, the constituent to the left of the Bangla PQP 'ki' can be questioned if that constituent is stressed, as we can see in (11) where the alternative question is formed on the subject.

11A	*Ram*		ki	Sita-ke	kalam	di-l-o ?
	Ram		KI	Sita-ACC	pen	give-PST-3P
	'Did Ram give a pen to Sita?'					
B	na		*Raban*	di-l-o?		
	or		Ravan	give-PST-3P		
	'or Ravan gave it?'					

Unlike Bangla, in Assamese the polar questions without PQP and with PQP give rise to the same meaning. Whether or not the PQP 'ne' occurs, all the elements in the sentence are questioned. We can observe that in the set of possible answers in (12B)–(12F) for the question in (12A). To the question in (12A), the addressee can either say 'yes' (12B), or say 'no' (12C), or can replace the subject (12D), or can replace the indirect object (12E), or can replace the direct object (12F).

12A	Ram-e	Shyam-ok	kalam-tu	di-sil-e	(ne)?
	Ram-AGN	Shyam-DAT	pen-Cla	give-PST-3P	PQP
	'Did Ram give the pen to Shyam?'				
B	o				
	yes				
	yes				
C	nai				
	no				
	No				
D	nai,	maa-e	di-sil-e		
	no	mother-AGN	give-PST-3rd		
	'No, mother gave it.'				
E	nai,	Ram-e	Sita-k	kalam-tu	di-sil-e
	no	Ram-AGN	Sita-DAT	pen-Cla	give-PST-3rd
	'No, Ram gave the pen to Sita.'				
F	nai,	Ram-e	Shyam-ok	kitap	di-sil-e
	no	Ram-AGN	Shyam-DAT	book	give-PST-3P
	'No, Ram gave a book to Shyam.'				

Like Bangla, in Assamese if any element in the polar question is stressed (13A), then that element is questioned and nothing else, as evident from its response in (13B) where the subject is replaced is acceptable and (13C) where the indirect object is replaced is not acceptable.

13A	*Ram-e*	Shyam-ok	kalam-tu	di-sil-e	ne ?
	Ram-AGN	Shyam-DAT	pen-Cla	give-PST-3P	PQP
	'Did *Ram* give the pen to Shyam?				
B	nai,	*maa-e*	di-sil-e		
	no	mother-AGN	give-PST-3P		
	'No, mother gave it.'				
C	# nai,	Ram-e	Sita-k	kalam-tu	di-sil-e
	no	Ram-AGN	Sita-DAT	pen-Cla	give-PST-3P
	'No, Ram gave the pen to Sita.'				

So far we have noticed that in Bangla, there is difference in meaning of the polar questions with and without PQP. In Bangla, every element is questioned when a polar question is formed without PQP and when the PQP occurs, only the elements to the right of it are questioned and not the elements that occur to the left of it. However, in Assamese no such difference between polar questions with and without PQP is found.

Interestingly, in Bangla and Assamese it is found that there is an identity relation between the polar question particle and the interrogative disjunction marker. This will be explored in the next section.

Occurrence of the Bangla Polar Question Particle 'ki' and the Assamese Polar Question Particle 'ne' in Alternative Questions

The Bangla PQP 'ki' and the Assamese PQP 'ne' seem to surface as disjunction marker in alternative questions, as can be seen in (14) and (15), respectively, and noted in (Guha, 2022) for Bangla and Barbora (2007) for Assamese.

14	Ram	ʧa:	kha-b-e	ki	~~Ram~~	coffee	kha-b-e?
	Ram	tea	eat-Fut-3P	KI	~~Ram~~	coffee	eat-Fut-3P

15	Ram-e	sah	kha-b-o	ne	~~Ram-e~~	coffee	kha-b-o
	Ram-AGN	tea	eat-Fut-3P	NE	~~Ram-AGN~~	coffee	eat-Fut-3P
	'Will Ram have tea or coffee?'						

In both Bangla and Assamese, the declaratives are disjoined by the Boolean disjunction marker 'ba,' cf. (16) and (17), respectively. The [-Q] disjunction interpretation of (16) and (17) can become [+Q] disjunction when 'ba' is replaced by 'ki' in Bangla and 'ne' in Assamese, c.f. (18) and (19), respectively.

16 Ram   ʧa: khabe   ba   ~~Ram~~ coffee   khabe
    Ram   tea   will have   or   ~~Ram~~ coffee   will have
    'Ram will have tea or coffee'

17 Ram-e   sah   kha-b-o   ba   ~~Ram-e~~   coffee   kha-b-o
    Ram-AGN   tea   eat-Fut-3P   or   ~~Ram-AGN~~   coffee   eat-Fut-3P
    'Ram will have tea or coffee.'

18 Ram   ʧa: khabe   ki   ~~Ram~~ coffee   khabe
    Ram   tea   will have   KI   ~~Ram~~ coffee   will have
    'Will Ram have tea or coffee?'

19 Ram-e   sah   kha-b-o   ne   ~~Ram-e~~   coffee   kha-b-o
    Ram-AGN   tea   eat-Fut-3P NE   ~~Ram-AGN~~   coffee   eat-Fut-3P
    'Will Ram have tea or coffee?'

The Bangla PQP 'ki' and the Assamese PQP 'ne' can be used as interrogative disjunction morphemes in other alternative question constructions as well, like in polar alternative questions (20) and 'or something else' questions (21).

(20) i Ram   ʧa: kha-b-e   ki   ~~Ram~~   chaa   ~~kha-b-e~~   na
        Ram   tea   eat-Fut-3P KI   ~~Ram~~   ~~tea~~   ~~eat-Fut-3P~~   no
        'Will Ram have tea or not?'

    ii Ram-e   sah   kha-b-o   ne   ~~Ram-e~~   sah   na - ~~kha~~ –i
        Ram-AGN tea   eat-Fut-3rd NE ~~Ram-AGN~~ tea   neg –~~eat~~ -3rd
        'Will Ram have tea or not?'

(21) i Ram   ʧa: kha-b-e   ki   ~~Ram~~   ɔnjo   kichu   kha-b-e
        Ram   tea   eat-fut-3P KI   ~~Ram~~   different   some   eat-Fut-3P
        'Will Ram have tea or something else?'

ii	Ram-e	sah	kha-b-o	ne	Ram-e	ɔnjo	kiba	kha-b-o
	Ram-	tea	eat-Fut-3P	NE	~~Ram~~	some-	eat-	
	AGn				~~AGN~~	thing	Fut-3P	
						else		

'Will Ram have tea or something else?'

Following Bartels (1997) analysis of the properties of alternative questions and as also mentioned in Bhatt and Dayal (2020), I suggest that the alternative questions in (18), (19), (20) and (21) have the following features, a pitch accent on each disjunct, a prosodic break between the disjuncts, and a final fall.

In the Dravidian language Malayalam, the disjunction morpheme '−oo' as in (22) also appears to be a question particle in (23), as noted in (Jayaseelan (2008, p. 208, 209)).

22	John-oo	Bill-oo	Peter-oo	wannu
	John-DISJ	Bill-DISJ	Peter-DISJ	came

'John or Bill or Peter came.'

23	Mary	wannu-oo ?
	Mary	came- Q

'Did Mary come?'

This is also the case with Japanese and Sinhala. Following Hagstrom (1998) for Sinhala and Kuroda (1965) and Nishigauchi (1990) for Japanese, Jayseelan (2008) shows that the Sinhala and Japanese disjunctive morpheme also appears to be a question particle. Even Amritavalli (2003) shows that in another Dravidian language Kannada, the [+Q] disjunctive morpheme '-oo' also appears in yes/no question (though there is another yes/no question particle '-aa') and in constituent question.

Jayaseelan claims that in these languages, the question particle is not a clause typing (as assumed universally otherwise in Cheng 1991). He suggests that the question particle, in these languages, is the lexical realization of the disjunction operator. In the line of Baker's (1970) claim that 'question particle = question operator,' Jayaseelan proposes a 'three-way identification' (24) for the languages where QP and disjunction morpheme are identical.

24 question particle = question operator = disjunction operator

Jayaseelan (referring to Karttunen's (1977) semantics of questions) mentions that the relation between question and disjunction can be linked to the semantics of question words which are translated as existential quantifiers, like *who* and *what* are translated as *someone* or *something*. Following Vergnaud and Zubizarreta's (2006) analysis of the semantics of questions, as shown in (25) and (26), Jayaseelan suggests that question words indicate disjunction in the answer space. So, in (26), which is the possible answer of (25), '(OR someone else)^n' is 'recursive, generating an infinite disjunction' (Jayaseelan, 2008, p. 212).

25   Who did John see?

26   <(John saw someone), (someone = (someone (OR someone else)^n))>

Following Jayaseelan's account of disjunctive analysis of question words, in this chapter we will see that in Bangla and Assamese polar questions like alternative question indicates disjunction in the answer space, which further follows from Beizma and Rawlin's (2012) analysis of polar and alternative questions.

Disjunction in Polar and Alternative Questions in Bangla and Assamese

The meaning of a question can be understood from its range of possible answers. In this chapter, we will investigate the meaning of the Bangla and Assamese polar and alternative questions in the background of Beizma and Rawlin's (2012) question under discussion (QUD) approach. B&R presents a discourse-based analysis of polar and alternative questions. They state that polar questions involve one alternative semantically and the addressee must choose between the given alternative and some salient, unstated alternatives from the discourse. Whereas alternative questions present an exhaustive set of alternatives and the addressee has to choose from that closed set of alternatives. This analysis of polar and alternative questions follows from I(mmediate) Q(uestion) U(nder) D(iscussion)-based theory of discourse (Roberts, 1996; Buring, 2003; Beaver & Clark, 2008). This can be well-explained under the D(iscourse) tree, as shown in Beizma and Rawlin (2012, p. 30, ex. 60) and originally proposed by Buring (2003), cf. (27).

27.

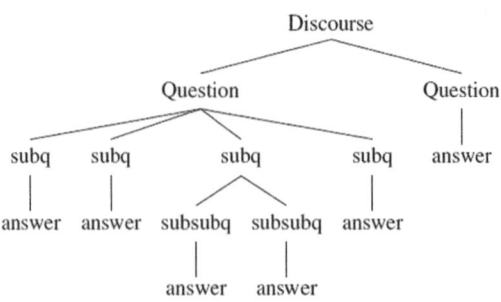

The D-tree in (27) shows that there is a 'Big Question' (termed by Roberts (1996)) and under which there are subquestions, which are either polar or alternative questions. The speaker utters a subquestion which could be answered by a discourse participant. The addressee must answer the IQUD, which is either a polar question or an alternative question and which is the most current question. To answer the IQUD, the addressee develops different strategies and the different strategies correspond to different subquestions which in turn will give answer to the 'Big Question.'

B&R states that the alternative presented by the polar question will have to be one of the many alternatives in the QUD for the move and alternative question in contrast will have to list all the alternatives in the QUD for the move. The QUD will be either an explicit or an implicit constituent question, and in order to get the answer for the QUD, the speaker will choose either to ask a polar question or an alternative question. Let us first consider the discourse structure of a polar question (28) and (29), as shown by B&R (2012, p. 33, ex. 71 and 72). In order to get the response for the Big Question 'what do you want to drink?' as shown in the D-tree in (29), the speaker chooses to ask a polar question, as in (28A). The addressee can either say 'yes' and choose the given alternative (28B), or he can say 'no' and then choose some other unstated alternative from the discourse (28B') and as shown in the D-tree in (29).

(28)A   Do you want coffee?

B   Yes, thank you

C   No, thank you, I would prefer tea

29.

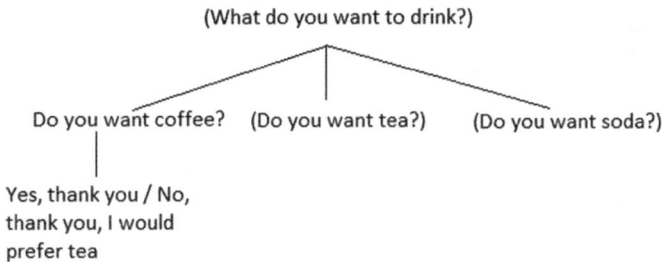

Alternatively, in order to get the response for the Big Question 'what do you want to drink?' in (29), the speaker can pose an alternative question. Let us now consider the discourse structure of an alternative questions (30) and (31), as shown by B&R (2012, p. 35, ex. 73 and 74). To the alternative question in (30A), the addressee has to choose between the stated alternatives (30B) and (30B') and cannot choose an unstated alternative, as evident from the unacceptability of (30B''). The corresponding D-tree of the alternative question in (30A) is in (31).

(30)A   Do you want coffee or tea?

B   I want coffee, please

B'   I want tea, please

B"   #I want soda, please

31.

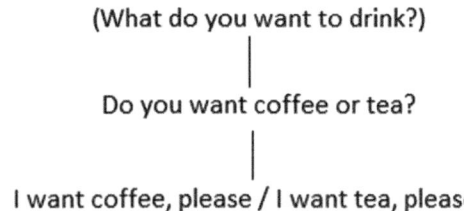

(What do you want to drink?)

Do you want coffee or tea?

I want coffee, please / I want tea, please

Following B&R's QUD approach of analysing polar and alternative questions, we can find that in Bangla and Assamese the polar questions, like the alternative questions, indicate disjunction in the answer space. Let us first consider the discourse structure of the polar question in Bangla, cf. (32) and its corresponding D-tree in (33). In order to get the response for the Big Question 'What will Ram have?' as shown in the D-tree in (33), the speaker adopts the strategy to ask a polar question (32A). The addressee can either say 'yes' (32B) and choose the given alternative, or he can say 'no' and choose some other unstated alternative available in the discourse (32B') and as shown in the D-tree in (33).

(32)A   Ram   ki   ʧa: kha-b-e

         Ram   PQP   tea   eat-fut-3P

         'Will Ram have tea?'

B   hyan, o   ʧa: kha-b-e

         Yes   he   tea   eat-fut-3P

         'Yes, he will have tea.'

B'   na:,   o   coffee   khe-te   chay

         no   he   coffee eat-INF   want

         'No, he wants to have coffee.'

33.

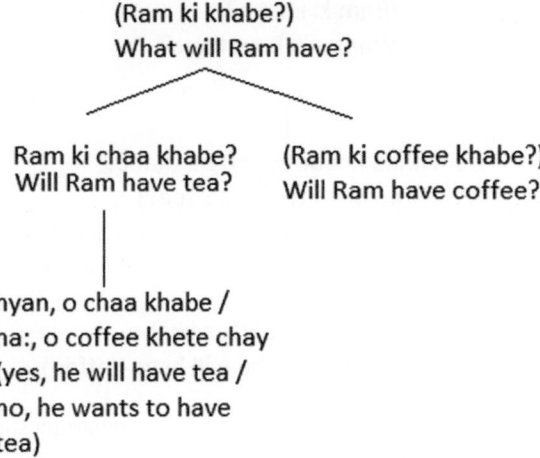

(Ram ki khabe?)
What will Ram have?

Ram ki chaa khabe?   (Ram ki coffee khabe?)
Will Ram have tea?   Will Ram have coffee?

hyan, o chaa khabe /
na:, o coffee khete chay
(yes, he will have tea /
no, he wants to have
tea)

The speaker can alternatively adopt the strategy of asking an alternative question (34A) in order to get the response for the Big Question 'what will Ram have?' In this case, the addressee has to choose between the given alternatives (34B) and (34B') and cannot choose any other unstated alternative (34B"). The corresponding D-tree of (34) is in (35).

(34)A   Ram   ʧa:a   kha-b-e   ki   coffee   kha-b-e

        Ram   tea   eat-Fut-3P   KI   coffee   eat-Fut-3P

        'Will ram have tea or coffee?'

B   o   ʧa: kha-b-e

        He   tea   eat-Fut-3P

        'He will have tea.'

B'   o   coffee   kha-b-e

        He   coffee   eat-Fut-3P

        'He will have coffee.'

C   #o   nimbu: dʒɔl   kha-b-e

        He   lemon   water eat-Fut-3P

        'He will have lemon water.'

35.

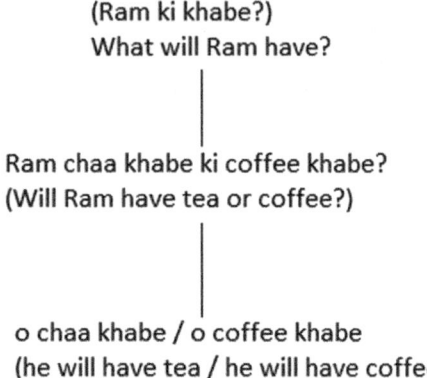

(Ram ki khabe?)
What will Ram have?

Ram chaa khabe ki coffee khabe?
(Will Ram have tea or coffee?)

o chaa khabe / o coffee khabe
(he will have tea / he will have coffee)

Let us now consider the discourse structure of the polar question in Assamese, cf. (36) and its corresponding D-tree in (37). In order to get the response for the Big Question 'What will Ram have?' as shown in the D-tree in (37), the speaker adopts the strategy to ask a polar question (36A). The addressee can either say 'yes' (36B) and choose the given alternative, or he can say 'no' and choose some other unstated alternative available in the discourse (36B') and as shown in the D-tree in (36B").

(36)A | Ram-e | sah | kha-b-o | ne |
| Ram-AGN | tea | eat-Fut-3P | PQP |

'Will Ram have tea?'

B | o, | Ram-e | sah | kha-b-o |
| Yes, | Ram-AGN | tea | eat-Fut-3P |

'Yes, Ram will have tea.'

B" | nai, | Ram-e | coffee | pɔchando | koribo |
| No | Ram-AGN | coffee | like | do-Fut-3P |

'No, Ram will prefer coffee.'

37.

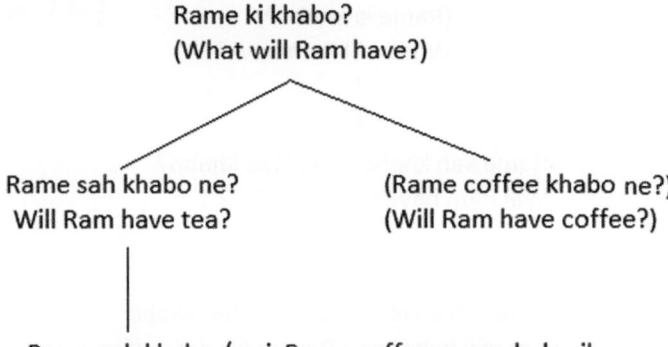

Rame ki khabo?
(What will Ram have?)

Rame sah khabo ne?   (Rame coffee khabo ne?)
Will Ram have tea?   (Will Ram have coffee?)

o, Rame sah khabo / nai, Rame coffee pasondo koribo
Yes, Ram will have tea / No, Ram will prefer coffee

The speaker can alternatively adopt the strategy of asking an alternative question (38A) in order to get the response for the Big Question 'what will Ram have?' In this case, the addressee has to choose between the given alternatives (38B) and (38B') and cannot choose any other unstated alternative (38B"). The corresponding D-tree of (38) is in (39).

(38)A   Ram-e   sah   kha-b-o   ne   coffee   kha-b-o
        Ram-AGN   tea   eat-Fut-3P   NE   coffee   eat-Fut-3P
        'Will Ram have tea or coffee?'

B   Ram-e   sah   kha-b-o
        Ram-AGN   tea   eat-Fut-3P
        'Ram will have tea.'

B'   Ram-e   coffee   kha-b-o
        Ram-AGN   coffee   eat-Fut-3P
        'Ram will have coffee.'

B"   #Ram-e   nemupani   kha-b-o
        Ram-AGN   lemon water eat-Fut-3P
        'Ram will have lemon water.'

39.

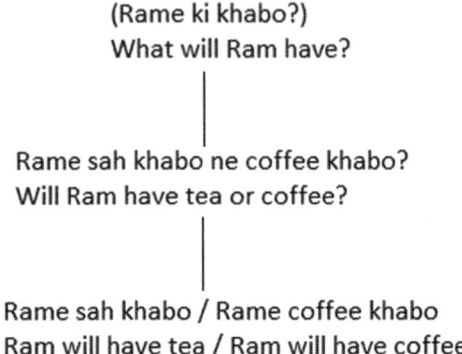

(Rame ki khabo?)
What will Ram have?

Rame sah khabo ne coffee khabo?
Will Ram have tea or coffee?

Rame sah khabo / Rame coffee khabo
Ram will have tea / Ram will have coffee

So far we have noticed that Bangla and Assamese polar questions, like alterna-tive questions, indicate disjunction in the answer space and the PQPs in these two languages occur both in the polar questions and alternative questions. Based on Jayaseelan's disjunctive analysis of question words, we can argue that in Bangla and Assamese there is a [+Q] disjunction operator, which occurs both in the alter-native questions and polar questions of these two languages and the Bangla PQP 'ki' and the Assamese PQP 'ne' are the lexical realizations of the [+Q] disjunction operator in their respective languages. Here, I will suggest that the development of the polar question operator to the interrogative disjunction operator in these two languages is a manifestation of *lexicalization*. The polar question operator in Bangla and Assamese can be reanalysed as interrogative disjunction operator. In this chapter, I will further propose that the Bangla PQP 'ki' and the Assamese PQP 'ne' receive the interpretation of interrogative disjunction particles in certain con-texts, such as embedded questions. In order to understand this claim, we need to explore embedded polar questions in Bangla and Assamese.

Occurrence of the Bangla Polar Question Particle 'ki' and the Assamese Polar Question Particle 'ne' in Embedded Polar Questions

Let us first consider an instance of embedded polar question in Bangla, cf. (40). The data in (40) indicate that 'ki' cannot occur in an embedded polar question, whether it is embedded under a responsive predicate (40A) or a rogative predicate (40B). These two types of predicates are chosen intentionally in (40) for a specific purpose, which will be discussed later in section (8).

(40) A   *maa   dʒan-e   [ram   ki   ʧa: kha-b-e]

       Mother   know-3P   Ram   PQP   tea   eat-Fut-3P

       Intended: 'Mother knows whether Ram will have tea.'

B   #maa   dʒiggeʃ   korch-il-o [ram ki   ʧa: kha-b-e]

       Mother   ask   do-Past-3P Ram PQP   tea   eat-Fut-3P

       Intended: 'Mother was asking whether Ram will drink tea.'

(40B) is marked infelicitous as the clause containing 'ki' gives a direct question interpretation and not an indirect one. So, the clause containing 'ki' in (40B) is a quotative structure and not the clause embedded under rogative predicate. This is evident from the ungrammatical data in (41), where the clause containing 'ki' cannot be preceded by the complementizer '**dʒe' (that), otherwise which had been possible in case of an indirect question construction.**

(41)A *maa   dʒiggeʃ   korch-il-o dʒe   [ram ki ʧa: kha-
                                                                b-e]

      Mother   ask   do-Past-3P that   Ram PQP tea eat-Fut-3P

      Intended: 'Mother was asking whether Ram will drink tea.'

The Assamese PQP 'ne' also cannot occur in an embedded clause, neither under responsive (42A) nor under rogative (42B).

(42)A *Maa-e   zane   [Ram-e   sah   khabo   ne]

       Mother-AGN   know   Ram-AGN   tea   will eat NE

       Intended: 'Mother knows whether Ram will drink tea.'

B   *Maa-e   xudʰ-isil-e [Ram-e   sah   khabo   ne]

       Mother-AGN   ask-Pst-3   Ram-AGN   tea   will eat NE

       Intended: 'Mother asked whether Ram will drink tea.'

The unacceptable derivations in (40) and (42) can be made acceptable if 'ki' occurs in the clause final position and is followed by a negation in Bangla (43A) and (43B), and 'ne' which already occurs in the clause final position in Assamese is followed by a negation (44A) and (44B).

(43) A maa   dʒan-e   [ram   tʃa: kha-b-e   ki-na]
        Mother know-3P   Ram   tea   eat-Fut-3P   KI-no
        'Mother knows whether Ram will have tea or not.'

    B   maa   dʒiggeʃ   korch-il-o   [ram   tʃa: kha-b-e   ki-na]
        Mother ask   do-Past-3P   Ram   tea   eat-Fut-3P   KI-no
        'Mother was asking whether Ram will drink tea or not.'

(44) A Maa-e   zane   [Ram-e   sah   kha-b-o   ne   nai]
        Mother-AGN   know   Ram-AGN   tea   eat-Fut-3P   NE   no
        'Mother knows whether Ram will drink tea or not.'

    B   Maa-e   xudʰ-isil-e [Ram-e   sah   kha-b-o   ne   nai]
        Mother-AGN   ask-Pst-3   Ram-AGN   tea   eat-Fut-3P   NE   no
        'Mother asked whether Ram will drink tea or not.'

In this chapter, I will argue that 'ki' and 'ne' can occur in embedded clauses in Bangla and Assamese, respectively, not as a question particle but as an interrogative disjunction particle. In (43A) and (43B), the 'ki-na' that occurs in the Bangla embedded clause has been considered in the literature (Bhadra 2017; Dasgupta 1980) to be equivalent to the English 'whether,' which I will deny and show that Bangla, like Hindi, has a null whether. I will further show that the acceptable structure in (43) does not indicate embedded polar question, but it gives an embedded alternative question interpretation. This will be discussed in a later section in section (6).

We will first start with the analysis of the occurrence of Assamese 'ne' followed by a negation in an embedded clause. Barbora (2007) proposes that 'ne' is not a polar question particle, but a disjunction marker. She shows that 'ne' can optionally take *wh* 'ki' (what) and neg 'nai' as complements, cf. (45) and (46). In these cases, 'ne' has a disjunctive reading. The examples in (45) and (46) are from Barbora ((2007), p. 200, e.x. 4a and 4b).

(45) Riju-e   kitap-khon   kin-il-e   ne   (ki)
      Riju-AGN   book-Cla   buy-PST-3P   NE   what
      'Did Riju buy the book (or what)?'

46	Riju-e	kitap-khon	kin-il-e		ne	(n-a-i)
	Riju-AGN	book-Cla	buy-PST-3P		NE	neg-be-3P
	'Did Riju buy the book (or did he not)?'					

Barbora, further, argues that in certain contexts 'ne' obligatorily takes *wh* 'ki' (what) and neg 'nai' as complements. In negative constructions, 'ne' obligatorily takes 'ki' as its complement, cf. (47), as evident from its ungrammatical counterpart in (48). The following examples are from Barbora ((2007), p.200, e.x. 5a and 5b).

47	Riju-e	kitap-khon	ni-kin-il-e	ne	ki
	Riju-AGN	book-Cla	neg-buy-PST-3P	NE	what
	'Didn't Riju buy the book or what?'				

48	*riju-e	kitap-khon	ni-kin-il-e	ne
	Riju-AGN	book-Cla	neg-buy-PST-3P	NE
	Intended: 'Didn't Riju buy the book?'			

Also, recall that 'ne' cannot be left stranded in an embedded clause, as shown in (42) and repeated below in (49). It has to be necessarily followed by a negation, as shown in (44) and repeated below in (50).

49 A	*Maa-e	zane	[Ram-e	sah	khabo	ne]
	Mother-AGN	know	Ram-AGN	tea	will eat	NE
	Intended: 'Mother knows whether Ram will drink tea.'					
B	*Maa-e	xudʰ-isil-e	[Ram-e	sah	khabo	ne]
	Mother-AGN	ask-Pst-3	Ram-AGN	tea	will eat	NE
	Intended: 'Mother asked whether Ram will drink tea.'					

50 A	Maa-e	zane	[Ram-e	sah	kha-b-o	ne	nai]
	Mother-AGN	know	Ram-AGN	tea	eat-Fut-3P	NE	no
	'Mother knows whether Ram will drink tea or not.'						
B	Maa-e	xudʰ-isil-e	[Ram-e	sah	kha-b-o	ne	nai]
	Mother-AGN	ask-Pst-3	Ram-AGN	tea	eat-Fut-3P	NE	no
	'Mother asked whether Ram will drink tea or not.'						

Brabora argues that in Assamese disjunction clause there is a null scope indicator, which has to be licensed either by a negation or a question word. Her argument follows from Amritavalli's (2000, 2003) analysis of disjunction in Kannada.

Amritavalli shows that in Kannada, the disjunctive particle '−oo' can disjoin phrases (51). But, it cannot disjoin declarative clauses (52).

51   bekk-oo   nay-oo

      cat-oo   dog-oo

      'cat or dog'

52 *avanu bar-utt-aan-oo,   naavu hoog-utt-iiv-oo

    He   come-NonPst-ARG-oo we   go-NonPST-ARG-oo

    'Either he comes or we go.'

She shows that the sentence in (52) is interpretable if it is understood as interrogative disjunction. Thus, '−oo' can disjoin two interrogative clauses, cf. (53).

53 avanu bar-utt-aan-oo,   naavu hoog-utt-iiv-oo

    He   come-NonPst-ARG-oo we   go-NonPST-ARG-oo

    'Does he come or do we go?'

Amritavalli further shows that the construction in (52) can be saved if we add neg 'illa.' So, a negative element is used to disjoin two declarative sentences, cf. (54).

54 .prati   shanivaara) illa avanu bar-utt-aane,   illa naavu

    Every Saturday   neg he   come-NONPST-ARG neg we

    hoog-utt-iivi

    go-NONPST-AGR

    '(Every Saturday) either he comes or we go.'

The 'illa' of the disjunction in (54) is not the same as the 'illa' of sentential negation. In Kannada, both kinds of 'illa' can co-occur. The disjunction 'illa' occurs in the clause initial adverbial position and the sentential negation 'illa' occurs in the clause final position (for details, see Amritavalli (2000)).

So, in Kannada in a [−Q] disjunction the neg 'illa' occurs as a disjunction marker, as shown in (54) and in an embedded [+Q] disjunction construction, the question word 'yelli' (where) occurs clause internally, cf. (55). Amritavalli claims that 'yelli' in (55) is a dummy word as it receives no interpretation, but its presence is required in the given [+Q] disjunction construction. The example in (55) is taken from Barbora (2007, p. 206, ex. 23), which is again taken from Amritavalli (2000).

55	nanage	[(naanu)	yelli	biLuttin-oo		anta	bhaya]
	I-dat	I	where	fall-I	SG-oo	that	fear

'I fear whether (lit. where) I will fall.' (= I am afraid that I will fall.)

In the lines of Giannakidou (1997) and Higginbotham (1991), Amritavalli proposes that the disjunctive connective in Kannada cannot be interpreted without certain environment. 'The interpretive environment for the disjunctive connective is provided by a Polarity Phrase, which hosts the licensors for the disjunctive morpheme. These licensors are principally Neg and Question operator …….' (Amritavalli, 2003; p.162).

In Assamese, in negative contexts where 'ne' is obligatorily followed by a question word 'ki' (what), cf. (56) and in embedded polar question contexts where 'ne' is obligatorily followed by negation 'nai,' cf. (57) and (58), Barbora, following Amritavalli's analysis of disjunction, proposes that the null scope operator requires 'ki' and 'nai' to act as licensors.

(56) A	*riju-e	kitap-khon	ni-kin-il-e	ne	
	Riju-AGN	book-Cla	neg-buy-PST-3P	NE	

Intended: 'Didn't Riju buy the book?'

B	Riju-e	kitap-khon	ni-kin-il-e	ne	ki
	Riju-AGN	book-Cla	neg-buy-PST-3P	NE	what

'Didn't Riju buy the book or what?'

(57) A	*Maa-e	zane	[Ram-e	sah	khabo	ne]
	Mother-AGN	know	Ram-AGN	tea	will eat	NE

Intended: 'Mother knows whether Ram will drink tea.'

B	*Maa-e	xud^h-isil-e	[Ram-e	sah	khabo	ne]
	Mother-AGN	ask-Pst-3	Ram-AGN	tea	will eat	NE

Intended: 'Mother asked whether Ram will drink tea.'

(58) A Maa-e   zane   [Ram-e   sah   kha-b-o   ne   nai]

       Mother-AGN   know   Ram-AGN tea   eat-Fut-3P   NE   no

       'Mother knows whether Ram will drink tea or not.'

     B Maa-e   xud^h-isil-e [Ram-e   sah   kha-b-o   ne   nai]

       Mother-AGN   ask-Pst-3   Ram-AGN tea   eat-Fut-3P   NE   no

       'Mother asked whether Ram will drink tea or not.'

Barbora's analysis differs from Amritavalli's analysis in one aspect. In Kannada, the disjunction negation 'illa' and the question word 'yelli' are the constituents of the disjunction phrase. But, in Assamese, the negation 'nai' and the *wh* 'ki' are not the constituents of the disjunction phrase. So, in (56B) the *wh* word 'ki' which follows 'ne' and in (58A) and (58B) where the neg 'nai' follows 'ne' have originated in a lower clause.

In fact, they are constituents of the lower clause. In (59), 'ne' disjoins two polar alternatives (P and negP), and in (60), 'ne' disjoins one polar question and a constituent question.

59 Ma-e   khud-is-e   [riju-e   kitap-khon kin-il-e]   ne

    Mother-AGN ask-PERF-3P Riju-AGN book-Cla   buy-PST-3P NE

    [~~riju-e~~   kitap-khon   ~~kin-a~~   n-a-i]

    Riju-AGN   ~~book-Cla~~   buy-NZR   neg-be-3P

    'Mother has asked whether Riju bought the book or not.'

60 [Riju-e   kitap-khon   ni-kin-il-e]   ne   [~~pro~~ ki   ~~kor-il-e~~]

    Riju-AGN   book-Cla   neg-buy-PST-3P   NE   what ~~do-PST-3P~~

    'Didn't Riju buy the book or what?'

As 'ne' disjoins two clauses in a negative context and an embedded context, Barbora claims that 'ne' is not a polar question particle but a disjunction marker. In this chapter, I will argue that 'ne' has originated as a polar question particle and gradually over time it is developing into an interrogative disjunction particle. However, it has not completely lost its meaning as a polar question particle.

Our Analysis of Assamese *ne* and Bangla *ki*

Lexicalization of Assamese Polar Question Particle 'ne'

In Assamese, it is not always the case that in negative contexts 'ne' has to be necessarily followed by the *wh* word 'ki,' and in embedded contexts, it has to be necessarily followed by the negation 'nai.' Let us observe the following data in (61) – (63) in negative contexts. In (61), 'ne' has a bias towards a positive answer. In (62), which has a counterfactual interpretation in a negative context, the occurrence of 'ne' is acceptable. 'Ne' can also occur in a negative tag question, as can be seen in (63).

61 tumi kam-tu   no-kor-a   ne
　　You   work-Cla   neg-do.Present-2P PQP
　　'Aren't you doing the work?'

62 .tumi kam-tu   no-kor-il-a-heten   ne
　　you   work-Cla   neg-do-Past-2P-CF   PQP
　　'Won't you have done the work?'

63 tumi sah khai-isil-a, no-hoi   ne
　　you   tea eat-Past-3P neg-be.Present PQP
　　'You had tea, didn't you?'

The data in (61)-(63) show that 'ne' can occur as a polar question particle in negative contexts. Let us now move towards the embedded context and find out if the lower clause always has to be the negation of the upper clause. The data in (64)-(66) indicate that the lower clause can be any other alternative and not necessarily the negation of the upper clause.

64 Ma-e   khud-is-e   [riju-e   kitap-khon kin-isil-e]   ne
　　Mother-AGN ask-PERF-3P Riju-AGN book-Cla   buy-PST-3P   NE
　　[~~riju-e~~   kalam-tu   kin-il-e]

65 Ma-e   khud-is-e   [riju-e   kitap-khon kin-isil-e]   ne
　　Mother-AGN ask-PERF-3P Riju-AGN book-Cla   buy-PST-3P   NE
　　[~~riju-e~~   ki   kor-isil-e]
　　~~Riju-AGN~~   what   do-Past-3P
　　'Mother asked whether Riju bought the book or what?'

66 Ma-e   khud-is-e   [riju-e   kitap-khon kin-isil-e]   ne

   Mother-AGN   ask-PERF-3P Riju-AGN book-Cla   buy-PST-3P NE

   [~~riju-e~~   aan   kiba   kin-isil-e]

   ~~Riju-AGN~~   something else   buy-Past-3P

'Mother asked whether Ram bought the book or something else.'

Based on the data set in (61)–(66), I propose that 'ne' in Assamese has originated as a polar question particle and it has developed its new meaning as an
interrogative disjunction particle. In the embedded question contexts, 'ne' cannot
be interpreted as a polar question particle but it is necessarily interpreted as an
interrogative disjunction particle. This is because in Assamese the null whether
requires the obligatory presence of [+Q] disjunction morpheme, followed by a
lower clause. Thus, we can further suggest that in Assamese there are embedded
alternative questions and no embedded polar question as the null whether gets
licensed by the presence of a [+Q] disjunction morpheme.

Lexicalization of the Bangla Polar Question Particle 'ki'

Let us recall that in Bangla, like Assamese, the PQP 'ki' cannot occur in an
embedded polar question, as shown in (40) and repeated below in (67). In the
embedded contexts, 'ki' has to occur in the post-verbal position and has to be
obligatorily followed by a negation, as shown in (43) and repeated below in (68).

67 A *maa   dʒan-e   [ram   ki   ʧa: kha-b-e]

      Mother know-3P   Ram   PQP   tea   eat-
                                                                    Fut-3P

   Intended: 'Mother knows whether Ram will have tea.'

   B   #maa   dʒiggeʃ   korch-il-o   [ram   ki   ʧa: kha-b-e]

      Mother ask   do-Past-3P Ram   PQP   tea   eat-
                                                                            Fut-3P

   Intended: 'Mother was asking whether Ram will drink tea.'

68 A maa   dʒan-e   [ram   ʧa: kha-b-e   ki-na]

      Mother know-3P   Ram   tea   eat-Fut-3P KI-no

   'Mother knows whether Ram will have tea or not.'

B	maa	dʒiggeʃ	korch-il-o	[ram	ʧa:	kha-b-e	ki-na]
	Mother	ask	do-Past-3P	Ram	tea	eat- Fut-3P	KI-no

'Mother was asking whether Ram will drink tea or not.'

Here, I will argue that the 'ki' which occurs in (68) cannot be interpreted as the polar question particle but it is obligatorily interpreted as an interrogative disjunction particle. Before I present my analysis of 'ki-na,' let us explore Bhadra's (2017) analysis of 'ki-na' in embedded polar questions in Bangla. Bhadra claims that 'ki-na' occurs both in a polar question and in an alternative question. This is how her analysis goes. When 'ki' and 'na' are concatenated together, as in (69), it is equivalent to English whether with and it gives a polar question interpretation. When 'ki' and 'na' are separated with a pause in between, as in (70), it still gives a polar question interpretation and the separated 'ki na' can be understood as 'whether or not' phrase. She further claims that 'kina' when it is used in an embedded alternative question, the particle 'ki' moves from its base position to the subject 2 position in order to mark scope for disjunction, as can be seen in (71).

69 Maa   jante   chaye   Ram   chaa   kheyeche   ki-na
     Mother   know   want   Ram   tea   had eaten   whether
    'Mother wants to know whether Ram had tea.'

70 Maa   jante   chaye Ram   chaa   kheyeche   ki na
     Mother   know   want   Ram   tea   had eaten   KINA
    'Mother wants to know whether or not Ram had tea.'

71 Maa   jante   chaye Ram ki   chaa kheyeche   na   coffee kheyeche
     Mother   know   want   Ram KI   tea had eaten   NA   coffee had eaten
    'Mother wants to know whether Ram had tea or coffee.'

So, as per Bhadra's analysis of 'ki-na' there is a single clause in the embedded clause in (69) and (70). In the present chapter, I will show that in (69) and (70) 'ki' appears an interrogative disjunction particle and it disjoins two clauses and 'na' belongs to the lower clause.

Let us consider the discourse structure of 'ki-na' in an embedded clause. The embedded question in (72) can derive either 'yes' or 'no' as responses, and nothing else, as can be seen in (73). The corresponding D-tree is given in (74). In order to get the response for the Big Question, 'Mother is going to Delhi. So, she wanted to know whether you will go somewhere or not,' the speaker chooses to ask the question in (72) where one alternative is stated explicitly. The addresses, in order to give response to the question in (72), say either 'yes' and thus choose the given alternative (73A), or he can say 'no' (73B), but he cannot choose any other unstated alternative from the discourse, as evident from the unacceptability of (73C).

72 Maa   dilli   ja-cch-e   tai   jan-te   chai-ch-e   je

    Mother   Delhi   go-proh-3   so   know-INF   want-perf-3P   that

    [tumi   dilli   ja-b-e   ki-na]

    you   Delhi   go-Fut-3P   KI-NA

'Mother is going to Delhi. So, she wanted to know whether you will go to Delhi or not.'

73 A   hyan,   ja-b-o

        yes,   go-Fut-3P

        'Yes, I will go.'

B   na:,   ja-b-o   na:

        No,   go-Fut-3P   no

        'No, I will not go.'

C   #na:,   Bombay   ja-b-o

        no   Bombay   go-Fut-3P

        'No, I will go to Bombay.'

74.

(maa dilli jacche tai jante chaiche je tumi kothao jabe kina)
(Mother is going to Delhi, so she wanted to know whether you will go
somewhere or not)

maa dilli jacche tai jante chaiche je tumi dilli jabe kina
Mother will go to Delhi, so she wanted to whether you will go to Delhi or not

hyan, jabo / na:, jabo na
Yes, I will go / No, I will not
go

Based on the responses to the given question in (72), I assume that 'ki' in (72) appears as an interrogative disjunction particle, which disjoins the upper clause 'Will Ram go to Delhi?' and its negation 'Will Ram not go to Delhi?' which is the lower clause, as can be seen in (75). So, the addressee is compelled to choose between the given alternatives, which is either P or negP, and nothing else, as evident from (73). In (72), except the negation all other elements remain implicit in the lower clause, as can be seen in (75).

75	Maa	dilli	ja-cch-e	tai	jan-te	chai-ch-e	je
	Mother	Delhi	go-proh-3	so	know-INF	want-perf-3P	that
	[tumi	dilli	ja-b-e	ki	tumi	dilli	ja-b-e	na]
	you	Delhi	go-Fut-3P	KI	you	Delhi	go-Fut-3P	no

'Mother is going to Delhi. So, she wanted to know whether you will go to Delhi or not.'

Thus, we can suggest that 'ki' in (72) does not appear as the polar question particle 'whether,' but it appears as an interrogative disjunction particle which disjoins polar alternative questions, as shown in (75). Like Assamese, in Bangla it is not always the case that in embedded contexts 'ki' can disjoin only polar alternatives. It can disjoin other alternatives, like 'P or Q' (76) and 'P or something else' (77).

76   Maa   jan-te   chaye   [Ram   dilli   ja-b-e   ki   Ram   Bombay
     Mother   know-   want   Ram   Delhi   go-Fut-3P   KI   ~~Ram~~   Bombay
                  INF

     ja-b-e]
     go-Fut-3P
     'Mother wants to know whether Ram will go to Delhi or Bombay.'

77   Maa   jan-te   chaye   [Ram   dilli   ja-b-e   ki   ɔnjo   kothao
     Mother   know-INF   want   Ram   Delhi   go-Fut-3P   KI   different   somewhere

     ja-b-e]
     go-Fut-3P
     'Mother wants to know whether Ram will go to Delhi or somewhere else.'

I further claim that both the embedded questions with the concatenated form of 'ki-na' in (69) and the separated form of 'ki na' in (70) are alternative questions and not polar questions. The difference between the concatenated form of 'ki-na' and the separated form of 'ki na' in an embedded clause is that of the cornering effect (Beizma (2009), and Beizma and Rawlins (2012)). Let us consider the discourse in (78). The speaker asks the question in (78A) by using the concatenated form of 'ki-na.' If the addressee remains silent to that question and makes dubitative faces (these words are borrowed from Beizma and Rawlins (2012)), then the speaker will adopt the strategy to repeat the question by separating 'ki' and 'na,' as shown in (78A') and this forces the addressee to choose between the given alternative and its negation, as can be seen in (78B').

78 A Maa   dilli   ja-cch-e   tai   jan-te   chai-ch-e   je
      Mother   Delhi   go-proh-3   so   know-INF   want-   that
                                                                  perf-3P

      [tumi   dilli   ja-b-e   ki-na]
      you   Delhi   go-Fut-3P   KI-no
      'Mother is going to Delhi. So, she wanted to know whether you will go to Delhi or not.'

78 A	Maa	dilli	ja-cch-e	tai	jan-te	chai-ch-e	je
B	(silence and dubitative faces)						
A'	Maa	dilli	ja-cch-e	tai	jan-te	chai-ch-e	je
	Mother	Delhi	go-proh-3	so	know-INF	want-perf-3P	that
	[tumi	dilli	ja-b-e	ki	na]		
	you	Delhi	go-Fut-3P	KI	no		

'Mother is going to Delhi. So, she wanted to know whether you will go to Delhi or not.'

B'	hyan,	ja-b-o/	na:,	ja-b-o	na:
	yes	go-Fut-3P	no	go-Fut-3P	no

'Yes, I will go / No, I will not go'

Based on the empirical evidence of 'ki' disjoining two clauses in an embedded context, like disjoining polar alternatives as in (75), disjoining two unrelated alternatives as in (76) and (77), we can make a claim that the 'ki' which occurs in the concatenated form of 'ki-na' and the separated form of 'ki na' is not a polar question particle, but an interrogative disjunction particle. I propose that 'ki' in Bangla (like the Assamese 'ne') has originated as a polar question particle, and it is lexicalized into an interrogative disjunction particle in certain contexts. Earlier we have seen that 'ki' occurs both in polar questions and alternative questions, and now in this section, we can see that in embedded questions 'ki' cannot surface; as a polar question particle, it has to obligatorily surface as an interrogative disjunction particle. This is because in Bangla, like Assamese, there is a null whether which requires the obligatory presence of [+Q] disjunction morpheme, followed by a lower clause. Thus, we can suggest that in Bangla there are embedded alternative questions and no embedded polar question as the null whether gets licensed by the presence of a [+Q] disjunction morpheme. Like Assamese 'ne,' the interpretation of the Bangla PQP 'ki' has become restricted in embedded questions, where it can only be interpreted as [+Q] disjunction particle.

Besides 'ki' there are two more interrogative disjunction particles in Bangla, which will be discussed in the next section. I should also briefly mention here that in an embedded alternative question, as in (71) and repeated below in (79), the 'ki' which occurs in the subject 2 position is not the moved 'ki' of the concatenated form 'ki-na,' but the PQP 'ki' which has originated in the subject 2 position. This will be explored in the next section.

79	Maa	jante	chaye	Ram ki	chaa	kheyeche	na	coffee	kheyeche
	Mother	know	want	Ram KI	tea	had eaten	NA	coffee	had eaten

'Mother wants to know whether Ram had tea or coffee.'

Other Interrogative Disjunction Particles in Bangla

Bengali speakers use another interrogative disjunction morpheme to form alternative questions, cf. (80). Also, the same morpheme can be used as a polar question particle, cf. (81).

80	Ram	chaa	kha-b-e	naki	coffee	kha-b-e
	Ram	tea	eat-fut-3p	NAKI	coffee	eat-fut-3p

'Will Ram have tea or coffee?

81	amra	chaa	kha-ch-i,	Ram	chaa	kha-b-e	naki
	we	tea	eat-prog-3p	Ram	tea	eat-fut-3p	NAKI

'We are having tea, will Ram have tea?'

Bhadra (2017) shows that the particle 'naki' is used as an evidential marker. She argues that *naki* gives a reportative evidential reading when it occurs clause internally (82) and inferential evidential polar question reading when it occurs clause finally (83).

82	Ram	naki	Delhi	ja-ch-e
	Ram	NAKI	Delhi	go-prog-3p

'Ram is going to Delhi (reportedly).'

83	Ram	Delhi	ja-ch-e	naki
	Ram	Delhi	go-prog-3p	NAKI

'Is ram going to Delhi (as I infer).'

Here, I suggest that the 'naki' used as the interrogative disjunction morpheme in (80) and used as a polar question particle in (81) is not the evidential 'naki.' It is just homophonous to the evidential one. The 'naki' used in (81) indicates a confirmation question without any strong evidence. This might lead us to suggest that in Bangla another polar question particle 'naki' also appears as an interrogative disjunction morpheme in alternative questions, as evident from (80).

The alternative questions formed by 'naki' and the one formed by the marker 'ki' cannot be used interchangeably. Let us consider the following discourse in (84) to understand the difference between 'ki' and 'naki' as [+Q] disjunction morphemes. In (84), speaker A wants to know whether the addressee will have tea or coffee and in order to know that the speaker adopts the strategy of asking an alternative question using 'naki' as the interrogative disjunction morpheme, cf. (84A). To this question, the addressee B doesn't give any direct response, as can in seen in (84B). In this situation, if the speaker A asks the same question using 'naki' as the disjunction morpheme then it will be infelicitous, as can be seen in (84A'). So, in order to force the addressee to choose one of the given alternatives and give a clear answera, the speaker has to pose the alternative question using the disjunction morpheme 'ki,' as can be seen in (84A"). This shows that 'ki' has a *cornering effect*, which 'naki' does not.

84 A	tumi	chaa	kha-b-e	naki	tumi	coffee	kha-b-e
	you	tea	eat-fut-3p	NAKI	~~you~~	coffee	eat-fut-3p

'Will you have tea or coffee?'

B	coffee-r	Sadh	khub	kora,	abar	chini	chara	chaa	o	kora	hoy

84 A tumi   chaa   kha-b-e naki   tumi   coffee   kha-b-e

Coffee-   taste   very   strong also   sugar   without tea   also   strong   be
Gen

'Coffee tastes strong. However, tea without sugar also tastes strong.'

A'   # tumi   chaa   kha-b-e naki   tumi   coffee   kha-b-e

you   tea   eat-   NAKI   you   coffee   eat-
                    fut-3p   fut-3p

'Will you have tea or coffee?'

A"   tumi   kha-b-e   ki   tumi   coffee kha-b-e
chaa

you tea   eat-   KI   you   coffee eat-
            fut-3p   fut-3p

'Will you have tea or coffee?'

Besides *cornering effect*, there are other differences between the interrogative disjunction morphemes 'ki' and 'naki.' Unlike 'naki,' 'ki' cannot disjoin noun phrases, cf. (85) and (86).

85 * Ram   chaa   ki   coffee   kha-b-e

Ram   tea   KI   coffee   eat-fut-3p

Intended: 'Will Ram have tea or coffee?'

86   Ram   chaa   naki   coffee   kha-b-e

Ram   tea   NAKI   coffee   eat-fut-3p

'Will Ram have tea or coffee?'

The disjunctive 'ki' cannot be used to disjoin non-finite clauses, cf. (87). But the disjunctive 'naki' can, cf. (88).

87 *Maa   Ram-ke   chaa   khe-te   ki coffee   khe-te   bol-l-o
   Mother   Ram-Acc   tea   eat-INF   KI coffee   eat-INF   say-past-3p
   Intended: 'Did mother ask Ram to have tea or coffee?'

88 Maa   Ram-ke   chaa   khe-te   naki   coffee   khe-te   bol-l-o
   Mother Ram-Acc   tea   eat-INF   NAKI   coffee   eat-INF   say-past-3p
   'Did mother ask Ram to have tea or coffee?'

There is a third interrogative disjunction marker in Bangla, i.e. 'na,' as can be seen in (89). The [+Q] disjunction marker 'na' is homophonous to the negation 'na:' in Bangla, cf. (90).

89 Ram   chaa   kha-b-e   na   coffee   kha-b-e
   Ram   tea   eat-fut-3p   NA   coffee   eat-fut-3p
   'Will Ram have tea or coffee?

90 Ram   chaa   kha-b-e   na:
   Ram   tea   eat-Fut-3P   no
   'Ram will not have tea.'

Let us now return to our data in (71) which is repeated below in (91) and where it is shown that 'ki' has moved from its base form 'ki-na' to the subject 2 position to mark the scope for disjunction in an embedded alternative question (as mentioned in Bhadra (2017)). What, I will suggest here is that the 'ki' in the subject 2 position in the embedded alternative question in (91) is not the moved 'ki,' but it has originated in that position and 'na' is the sole disjunction marker.

91 Maa   jante   chaye   Ram ki chaa kheyeche na   coffee kheyeche
   Mother know   want   Ram KI   tea   had eaten   NA   coffee had eaten
   'Mother wants to know whether Ram had tea or coffee.'

This claim is based on the data in (92) where 'ki' occurs in the subject 2 position and the interrogative disjunction morpheme 'naki' and not 'na' is used to disjoin two polar questions.

92 Maa   jante   chaye   Ram ki   chaa   kheyeche kheyeche

    Mother   know   want   Ram KI   tea   has eaten has eaten

    'Mother wants to know whether Ram had tea or coffee.'

If we consider Bhadra's analysis of 'ki' moving from the base position to the subject 2 position to mark scope for disjunction in an alternative question, then we cannot account for the data in (92) where 'naki' is used as the interrogative disjunction morpheme and 'ki' still appears in the subject 2 position. Thus, we can suggest that in (91) 'ki' has originated in the subject 2 position and 'na' is the interrogative disjunction morpheme disjoining two polar questions. In fact, the occurrence of 'ki' in the subject 2 position is optional, as can be seen in (93), also mentioned by Bhadra (2017).

93 Maa   jante   chaye   Ram (ki) chaa kheyeche   na   coffee   kheyeche

    Mother   know   want   Ram KI   tea had eaten   NA   coffee   had eaten

    'Mother wants to know whether Ram had tea or coffee.'

So, in Bangla we can have three interrogative disjunction morphemes. One is the PQP 'ki,' the other is another PQP 'naki,' and the last one is 'na,' which does not occur as a question particle and which is not the negative element (the negative element in Bangla is homophonous to the interrogative disjunction morpheme 'na'). The difference between 'ki' and 'na' and 'naki' and 'na' is not considered in the current chapter, and I leave that for future research.

Occurrence of the Polar Question Particle Naki in Polar Embedded Questions

The PQP 'naki,' unlike the PQP 'ki,' can occur in polar embedded questions. But there is a restriction on its occurrence. It can be embedded only under rogative predicates (94B), but not under responsive ones (94A).

94 A *maa   dʒan-e   [ram   ʧa: kha-b-e   naki]

Mother know-3P Ram   tea   eat-Fut-3P PQP

Intended: 'Mother knows whether Ram will have tea.'

B   maa   dʒiggeʃ   korch-il-o [ram ʧa: kha-b-e   naki]

Mother ask   do-Past-3P Ram tea   eat-Fut-3P PQP

'Mother was asking whether Ram will drink tea.'

This behaviour of the Bangla PQP 'naki' can be linked to Bhatt and Dayal's ((2014), (2016), (2020)) account for the restricted occurrence of the Hindi PQP 'kya:' in polar embedded questions. B&D show that in Hindi the QP 'kya:' cannot be embedded under a responsive predicate (95), but it can be embedded under a rogative predicate (96).

95 *Maa   jan-t-ii   hai ki   kya: Ram cai piye-g-aa cai   piye-g-aa

Mother know-   be   that PQP Ram tea drink-Fut- drink-Fut-
Hab-Fut   3MSg   3MSg

Intended: 'Mother knows whether Ram will drink tea.'

96 Maa   puunch rahii   thii   ki   kya: Ram cai piye-g-aa

Mother ask   Prog.FSg be.Pst.Fsg that PQP Ram tea drink-Fut-3Msg

'Mother was asking whether Ram will drink tea.'

Bhatt and Dayal draw an explanation for this syntactically restricted occurrence of 'kya:' from McCloskey's (2006) account for the syntactic distribution of embedded inversion in English. In English, responsive predicates are not compatible with embedded inversion clause (97); but rogative predicates are (98). The following examples are from Bhatt and Dayal (2020, e.g. (11a) and (11b)).

97 Responsive: ......[CP1 ......

I found out how they got into the building

*I found out how did they get into the building

98   Rogative: …..[CP2……[CP1….

> I asked him from what source the reprisals could come

> I asked him from what source could the reprisals come

Since responsive predicates do not occur with an embedded inversion clause, but rogatives do, McCloskey suggests that responsive predicates take regular CP complements that denote questions (99) and rogative predicates take ForceP complements that denote the question speech act (100), as shown by Bhatt and Dayal (2020, e.g. (21a) and (21b)).

99   Responsive (know): [CP C$^0_{+Q}$ [TP]]

100   Rogatives (wonder): [ForceP [CP C$^0_{+Q}$ [TP]]]

Following McCloskey's analysis of embedded inversion clause, in the line of the restricted syntactic distribution of Hindi PQP 'kya:' in embedded clause, Bhatt and Dayal (2020) propose that 'kya:' occurs in a position above CP, i.e. in ForceP. They claim that 'kya:' is only acceptable in the complement of predicates that take ForceP; and rogatives are those kinds of predicates. But responsive predicate takes CP as complement. Thus, 'kya:' cannot occur in the clause that is the complement of responsive predicate, as the position of 'kya:' is higher than CP in the clause.

Thus, a similar analysis can be drawn for the syntactically restricted occurrence of the Bangla polar question particle 'naki.' So, here I should modify my earlier argument that in Bangla there exist no embedded polar questions (as mentioned in sec.) since the PQP 'ki' occurred only as an interrogative disjunction morpheme in embedded questions. But, based on our observation of the syntactically restricted occurrence of the PQP 'naki' in embedded polar question, we can suggest that embedded polar question do occur in Bangla and in that case the speaker uses the PQP 'naki' to give an embedded polar question interpretation. But 'ki' cannot be used as a polar question particle in an embedded question. It has to be always used as a [+Q] disjunction particle in an embedded question.

Assamese Polar Question Particle *neki*

In Assamese, there is another polar question particle 'neki' which is used to give yes/no question interpretation. 'Neki' like 'ne' occurs only in the clause final position, cf. (102). But unlike 'ne,' 'neki' does not appear as interrogative disjunction morpheme in alternative questions, cf. (103).

101   Ram-e   sah   kha-b-o   neki ↑
      Ram-AGN   tea   eat-Fut-3P   NEKI
      'Will Ram have tea?'

102   (*neki) Ram-e   (*neki) sah (*neki) kha-b-o   (neki) ↑
      NEKI   Ram-AGN   NEKI   tea   NEKI   eat-future-3P   NEKI
      'Will Ram have tea?'

103   *Ram-e   sah   kha-b-o   neki   coffee   kha-b-o
      Ram-AGN   tea   eat-Fut-3P   NEKI   coffee   eat-Fut-3P
      Intended: 'Will ram have tea or coffee?'

The Assamese PQP 'neki,' like the Bangla PQP 'naki,' can be embedded under rogative predicates (105) but not under responsive ones (104).

104   *maa-e   zane   ram-e   sah   khabo   neki   neki
      Mother-AGN   know   Ram-AGN   tea   will eat NEKI   NEKI
      'Mother knows if Ram will have tea.'

105   Maa-e   xudh-isil-e   Ram-e   sah   khabo   neki
      Mother-AGN   ask-PST-3   Ram-AGN   tea   will eat   NEKI
      'Mother asked if Ram will have tea.'

So, in the case of the occurrence of the Assamese PQP 'neki' embedded under rogatives and not responsives, the argument can be followed from B&D's argument for responsive and rogative predicates and the syntactic position of the PQP with respect to these two types of predicates. Here, also we should modify our previous argument for the non-existence of embedded polar questions in Assamese (as mentioned in sec). We can suggest that embedded polar question do occur in Assamese, like Bangla, and in that case the speaker uses the PQP 'neki' to give an embedded polar question interpretation. But 'ne' cannot be used as a polar question particle in an embedded question. It has to be always used as a [+Q] disjunction particle in an embedded question. The difference between the PQP 'ne' and 'neki' is not explored in this chapter and is left for future research.

Conclusion

In this chapter, we have found that in Bangla and Assamese the polar questions like alternative questions indicate disjunction. This has led to the proposal that the polar question operator in these two languages has been lexicalized into disjunction operator. We have also noticed that the particle 'ki' in Bangla and the particle 'ne' in Assamese occur both as polar question particles and interrogative disjunction particles. In fact, these two particles cannot be interpreted as polar question particles in embedded question contexts, but can only be interpreted as interrogative disjunction particles. This has further led to the argument for the lexicalization process of these two question particles in their respective languages.

References

Amritivalli, R. (2003). Question and negative polarity in the disjunction phrase. *Syntax* 6(1), 1–18. https://doi.org/10.1111/1467-9612.00054

Baker, C. L. (1970). Notes on the description of English questions: The role of an abstract question morpheme. *Foundations of Language, 6*, 197–219.

Barbora, M. (2007). The particle ne in direct yes-no questions. Linguistic Theory and South-Asian Languages, Essay in Honor of K. A. Jayaseelan, 199–214.

Bartels, C. (1997). *Towards a compositional interpretation of English statement and question intonation.* Ph.D. thesis, University of Massachusetts, Amherst.

Beaver, D. I., & Clark, B. Z. (2008). *Sense and sensitivity: How focus determines meaning.* Wiley-Blackwell.

Biezma, M. (2009). Alternative vs polar questions: The cornering effect. *Semantics and Linguistic Theory, 19*, 37. https://doi.org/10.3765/salt.v19i0.2519

Biezma, M., & Rawlins, K. (2012). Responding to alternative and polar questions. *Linguistics and Philosophy, 35*(5), 361–406. https://doi.org/10.1007/s10988-012-9123-z

Beizam, M., Butt, M., & Jabeen, F. (2018). Polar Questions vs. kya: Questions in Hindi/Urdu. GLOW 41.

Bhadra, D. (2017). *Evidentiality and questions: Bangla at the interfaces.* Rutgers University.

Bhatt, R., & Dayal, V. (2014). Polar-kyaa: Y/N or Speech Act Operator? Presented at the Workshop on Non-Canonical Questions and Interface Issues, Hegne. https://cpb-us-w2.wpmucdn.com/campuspress.yale.edu/dist/6/2964/files/2020/01/polar-kyaa.pdf

Bhatt, R., & Dayal, V. (2020). "Polar Question Particles: Hindi-Urdu Kya:" *Natural Language & Linguistic Theory.* https://doi.org/10.1007/s11049-020-09464-0

Buring, D. (2003). On D-trees, beans, and B-accents. *Linguistics & Philosophy, 26*, 511–545.

Blank, A. (2001). Pathways of lexicalization. In: M. Haspelmath, E. Ko¨nig, W. Oesterreicher, & W. Raible (eds.), *Language Typology and Language Universals*, vol. II, 1596–1608. (Handbu¨cher zur Sprach- und Kommunikationswissenschaft, 20.2.) Berlin and New York: Walter de Gruyter.

Brinton, L. J., & Traugott, E. C. (2005). *Lexicalization and language change.* Cambridge University Press.

Chetterji, S. K. (1970). *The origin and development of Bengali language.* London: George Allen 8 Unwin, Rupa & Co.

Cheng, L. L. S. (1991). On the Typology of Wh-questions. MIT doctoral dissertation.

Dasgupta, P. (1980). *Questions and relative and complement clauses in a Bangla grammar.* Ph.D. thesis, New York University Doctoral dissertation.

Dayal, V. (2016). *Questions*. Oxford University Press.

Giannakidou, A. (1997). *The landscape of polarity items*."Ph.D. dissertation, University of Groningen, the Netherlands.

Goswami, G. (1982). *Structure of assamese*. Gauhati University.

Hagstrom, P. (1998). Decomposing questions. MIT doctoral dissertation.

Higginbotham, J. (1991). Either/ or. In: Proceedings of NELS 21, ed. T. Sherer. Amherst, Mass.: GLSA Publications, pp. 143–155.

Jayaseelan, K. A. (2008). Question particles and disjunction. *Linguistic Analysis, 38*(1), 208–221.

Karttunen, L. (1997). Syntax and semantics of questions. *Questions*, 165–210. https://doi.org/10.1007/978-94-009-9509-3_6

Kuroda, S.-Y. (1965). *Generative grammatical studies in the Japanese language*. MIT Doctoral Dissertation.

McCloskey, J. (2006). Questions and questioning in a local English. In: R. Zanuttini, H. Campos, E. Herburger, & P. H. Portner (eds.), *Crosslinguistic Research in Syntax and Semantics: Negation, Tense, and Clausal Architecture*. Washington, DC: Georgetown University Press, pp. 87–126.

Nishigauchi, T. (1990). Quantification in the theory of Grammar. *Studies in Linguistics and Philosophy*. https://doi.org/10.1007/978-94-009-1972-3

Rajkhowa, S. (2018). On the disjunction particle *ne* in assamese. *Presented in 40th International Conference of the Linguistic Society of India*.

Roberts, C. (1996). Information structure in discourse: Towards an integrated formal theory of pragmatics. In: *OSU Working Papers in Linguistics 49: Papers in Semantics*, pp. 91–136.

Syed, S., & Dash, B. (2017). A unified account of the yes/no particle in Hindi, Bangla and Odia. In: M. Y. Erlewine (eds.), *Generative Linguistics in the Old World (GLOW) in Asia 11, volume 1*, Vol. 84. Cambridge: MITWPL, pp. 201–212.

Vergnaud, J. R., & Zubizarreta, M. L. (2006). The representation of focus and its implications: Towards an alternative account of some "Intervention Effects". In: H. Broekhuis, N. Corver, & R. Huybregts (eds.), *Organizing Grammar*. Berlin: Mouton de Gruyter, pp. 641–660.

Ambalika Guha is Assistant Professor in the Department of English at Adamas University (Kolkata). Her research interests are in Generative Syntax and Semantics. Particularly, she investigates the uniformity between nominal and clausal left periphery. Recently, she has also been intrigued by the semantics of questions, showing how a language speaker uses a question particle as a disjunction marker.

observed in Indo—Aryan Languages like Hindi—Urdu. Some languages use polite/ honorific addressee pronouns for formal situations, like French, German and Italian, whereas some languages grammaticalize politeness using both polite/honorific pronouns as well as honorific verbal inflection. The focus of this paper is languages of this last kind, which capture politeness through honorific pronouns as well as verbal inflection. Agreement between an honorific pronoun/noun and the verb/auxiliary is termed as honorification by Harada (1976). Languages like Japanese, Korean, Hindi, Tamil, etc., have the system of honorification (Harada, 1976; Shibatani, 1977; Toribio, 1990; Subbarao et al., 1991; Boeckx & Niinuma, 2004; Pak, 2017). Honorification can be of two kinds: the first kind is called referent honorification, which stands for the subject/object of a sentence triggering honorific inflection on the verb (Brown & Levinson, 1978; Harada, 1976). Consider the following Japanese example where (1a) is a case of object honorification, and (1b) is its non—honorific counterpart. Object honorification on the verb has an Honorific Prefix (HP) —*o*, followed by the verb, which is then followed by the object honorificity (OH) marker —*si*.

(1) a   *Taroo—ga Tanaka sensei—o*   ***o—tasuke—si—ta***   Boeckx & Niinuma, (2004: (6))

Taro—nom Tanaka   HP—help—OH—past
Professor—acc

'Taro helped Prof. Tanaka'

   b   *Taroo—ga Tanaka—o*   *tasuke—ta*

Taro—nom Tanaka—acc   help—past

'Taro helped Tanaka'

The second kind of honorificity agreement is called performative honorification (Harada, 1976) or allocutive honorification. It stands for agreement with a null hearer/addressee/interlocutor DP, which present in the discourse but not part of the argument structure of the verb. For example, consider the following sentence from Korean, which can be spoken in six different ways, depending on who the addressee of the sentence is. The sentence final particles in (2a—f), i.e. —*sup-nita*, —*eyo*, —*so*, —*ney*, —*e* and —*ta* denote whether the relationship between the speaker and the addressee is formal (FRM), polite (POL), semiformal (SMFRM), blunt (BLT), intimate (INM) or plain (PLN), respectively (Pak, 2017).

(2)   a.   *Ecey—ka nay sayngil—i—ess—**supnita***   (Pak, 2017: (5)).

yesterday—nom my birthday—cpl—pst—dc.frm

         b.   *Ecey—ka nay sayngil—i—ess—**eyo***

yesterday—nom my birthday—cpl—pst—dc.pol

         c.   *Ecey—ka nay sayngil—i—ess—**so***

yesterday—nom my birthday—cpl—pst—dc.smfrm

d.   *Ecey−ka nay sayngil−i−ess−**ney***
        yesterday−nom my birthday−cpl−pst−dc.blt

e.   *Ecey−ka nay sayngil−i−ess−**e***
        yesterday−nom my birthday−cpl−pst−dc.inm

f.   *Ecey−ka nay sayngil−i−ess−**ta***
        yesterday−nom my birthday−cpl−pst−dc.pln
        'Yesterday was my birthday.'

These inflectional cases of honorification have been treated to be at par with phi−feature inflection, leading to the understanding that honorificity is an interpretable feature on the noun and an uninterpretable feature on the agreeing functional head. Boeckx and Niinuma (2004) show that honorification follows defective intervention effect, which is a restriction on Agree, like other phi−features. This treatment of honorification establishes honorificity as a syntactic feature.

The examples above establish that honorificity is inflectional in nature. In the literature, the inflectional phi−features have been claimed to project a separate functional layer in the DP, at par with the clausal structure (Ritter, 1991 & Picallo, 1991). In these accounts, number projects to NumP, headed by Num, while in some languages gender also projects to GenP, headed by Gen. I assume, following Abney (1987) that all languages have a DP layer at the edge of the nominal structure. Therefore, I propose that honorificity, just like person, number and gender (in some languages), projects to a functional layer HonP headed by Hon. This proposed DP structure is given in (3). I leave out gender and number here for simplicity's sake.

(3)   [DP D [HonP Hon [NP N]]]

The question now arises, if honorificity is a syntactic feature, how is it encoded in the system? Is it specified on the lexical items in the lexicon? I claim that despite all these similarities with phi−features, honorificity is fundamentally different from other phi−features in being an 'interpretable unvalued' (on lines of Pesetsky & Torrego, 2007) feature in the DP. It is not specified in the lexicon because nouns do not come in the computation with a fixed honorificity value. The rationale behind this claim lies in the fact that honorificity feature involves the discourse knowledge of the relationship between two entities. For example, let's look at number feature. Number is not dependent on anyone's perception of what plural or singular is, whereas honorificity is. Similarly, unlike biological gender honorificity is not part of the fundamental meaning of a noun as the same noun can have different honorificity values, depending on the speaker's perception. Therefore, in order to encode the right discourse knowledge, it must get licensed by a functional head in the discourse domain. I turn to Portner & Zanuttini (2019), henceforth

PPZ, who present a similar account for addressee honorification. In their account, the addressee pronouns get values for the honorificity feature from the c head, which projects to the c(ontext) Phrase/cP and encodes the 'status' feature. I extend PPZ's approach to non−addressee referents as well. This extension of the discourse domain to referents other than the addressee is based on the assumption that the cP domain is different from other discourse domains such as the Speech Act Phrase, which is only speaker and addressee oriented. The cP domain is meant for politeness only, and hence, it can capture the relation of the speaker with both the addressee as well as the non−addressee referent.

Finally, I look at cross−linguistic variation that emerges from honorificity feature, following the Borer–Chomsky Conjecture, in two EIA languages—Maithili and Bangla. I place the differences found in the honorificity agreement pattern of these two languages in a parameter hierarchy, based on Roberts and Holmberg (2010) & Roberts (2012) and claim that honorificity differences are partly dependent on animacy differences in the two languages.

This paper has been organized in the following ways: Sect. 2 presents existing evidence for placing honorificity at par with phi−features. This section also proposes the internal structure of the DP, with respect to the honorificity feature. Section 3 points out the fundamental difference between phi−features and the honorificity feature which explains the need for a licensing mechanism for the latter. Section 4 presents cross−linguistic differences found between Maithili and Bangla honorificity agreement. Section 5 explains the cross−linguistic differences from a minimalist perspective. Section 6 concludes the paper.

Honorificity: A Syntactic Feature

Boeckx and Niinuma (2004), considers honorification to be a syntactic phenomenon. The reason behind this claim is that the phenomenon of honorification, as shown in (1), follows Agree restrictions that are followed by other phi−features too. This is an evidence for the claim that honorification is triggered by the honorificity feature on the noun. This parallel between honorificity and other syntactic features, i.e. the phi−features, becomes evident due to the way syntactic features and the agreement mechanism are understood in the minimalist framework.

Agree Restriction on Honorificity

Chomsky (1995, 2000) notes that lexical items such as nouns have a set of interpretable phi−features, i.e. person, number and gender (PNG), as part of their feature matrix, while the core functional categories (CFCs) such as C, T and v have an uninterpretable set of phi−features on them. The interpretable phi−features are valued (+PNG), and the uninterpretable phi−features are unvalued (−PNG). The

CFCs act as probes that look for goals with valued features, so that the unvalued features on the probes can be cancelled out. This mechanism of feature saturation on CFCs is termed as Agree. Agree requires the Probe and the Goal to Match in their features, meaning that the set of uninterpretable unvalued features on the CFCs and the interpretable valued features on the substantive LIs should have identical features differing in their values. Once the matching takes place, Agree establishes featural agreement between the two categories.

Since we see honorification as a kind of featural agreement between a noun and a verb/auxiliary, it can be claimed that honorificity, like other phi−features is an interpretable feature on the noun and an uninterpretable feature on the verb/auxiliary. However, this claim would gain more ground if honorification agreement also follows Agree restrictions that are followed by other phi−features. Agree has some restrictions, which are defined in Chomsky (2000) and summarized by Baker (2008) as.

(4) A functional head F agrees with XP, XP a maximal projection, only if[1]:

- F c−commands XP (the *c−command condition*,[2] *MI*:122)

- There is no YP such that F c−commands YP, YP c−commands XP, and YP has φ−features (the *intervention condition, MI*:122)

- F and XP are contained in all the same phases (e.g. full CPs) (the *phase condition*,[3] *MI*:108)

- XP is made active for agreement by having an unchecked case feature (the *activity condition, MI*:123)

Boeckx and Niinuma (2004) have shown that object honorification in Japanese displays special intervention effects, called 'Defective Intervention Effect' (DIE). 'Defective intervention arises when an element A matches the featural requirements of a probe P, but fails to agree with it'.[4] For example, take a look at (5) and (6):

(5) *Hanako−ga   Tanaka sensei−ni Mary−o   go−syookai−*
                                       si−ta

Hanako−Nom Prof. Tanaka−Dat Mary−Acc introduce−OH−past

Hanako introduced Mary to Prof. Tanaka   Boeckx and Niinuma
                                                          (2004:456, (7))

---

[1] Baker (2008: 40 (62)).

[2] An expression X c-commands another expression Y if and only if X does not dominate Y and every phrase that dominates X dominates Y (Chomsky 1986:8).

[3] Phase-Impenetrability Condition: In phase α with head H, the domain of H is not accessible to operations outside a, only H and its edge are accessible to such operations (Chomsky, 2000: 108 (21)).

[4] Boeckx and Niinuma (2004).

(6)   *Hanako−ga   Mary−ni   Tanaka sensei−o   go−syookai−
                                                       si−ta

Hanako−Nom Mary−Dat Prof. Tanaka−Acc introduce−OH−past

Hanako introduced Prof Tanaka to Mary   Boeckx and Niinuma
                                                           (2004:456, (8))

(5) illustrates honorification agreement between the indirect object and the
verb. (6) illustrates how an honorific direct object fails to trigger honorification
agreement in the presence of an indirect object. This shows that honorification
agreement of the direct object is blocked by an indirect object, even when it is
not honorific. Boeckx and Niinuma (2004) claim that (6) is a case of defective
intervention because even though the indirect object does not have the matching
feature, i.e. the honorificity feature, it still acts as an intervenor.

Honorificity in the DP

Since honorificity is a syntactic feature, the obvious question to ask is—what does
the structure of an honorific DP look like? In order to answer this question, I follow the line of research that draws parallels between the nominal structure and the
clausal structure and claims that inflectional features in the noun project a separate
functional layer. These functional layers have mostly been considered to be DP,
NumP and GenP (in some languages). Since Abney (1987), all NPs are claimed to
be headed by a DP which encodes discourse properties related to a noun such as
proximate and obviate distinctions. I also follow Dechaine and Wiltishchko (2000)
in assuming that the DP layer also hosts person feature. Ritter (1990) presents
argument in favour of proposing a number projection NumP, as an intermediate
projection between DP and NP. Similarly, Picallo (1991) claims that some languages also have GenP, for gender feature, as an intermediate projection, in addition to the NumP. This elaborate DP structure is given in (7).

(7)   [DP D [NumP Num [GenP Gen [NP N]]]]

The key motivation behind proposing an elaborate structure for the nominal
domain is the fact that nouns acquire these features in the syntax. These inflectional features are not predefined on the nouns in the lexicon. For example, consider the number feature—any noun can have different number values attached
to it, thus, a noun cannot be specified for its number value in the lexicon. If it
is not specified for number value in the lexicon, the noun must get the value in
the computational workspace. It is only the inflectional phi−features that project
a separate functional layer in the nominal domain. This contrast becomes very
clear when we look at the difference between the Hebrew number and grammatical gender features, as presented in Ritter (1991). Ritter explains that number is an
inflectional property of Hebrew nouns, and hence, need not be learned by children
during language acquisition, whereas, grammatical gender, especially feminine

gender, is a derivational feature and must be learned by children as attaching the feminine marker results in a new noun. Consider (8), an example from Hebrew, which shows that gender switching on inanimate nouns results in a productive strategy for deriving new nouns.

(8)	Masculine nouns		Feminine nouns	
a.	*magav*	'wiper'	*magav−et*	'towel'
	magav−im	'wipers'	*magav−ot*	'towels'
b.	*maxsan*	'warehouse'	*maxsan−it*	'magazine'
	maxsan−im	'warehouses'	*maxsani−ot*	'magazines'
c.	*amud*	'page'	*amud−a*	'column'
	amud−im	'pages'	*amud−ot*	'columns'

In the examples in (8a−c), note that the addition of the feminine suffixes −*et*, −*it* and −*a* to masculine nouns derives new feminine nouns. In order to understand this derivational method better, contrast this with the number suffix −*im*. The number morpheme only gives the plural of the noun that it attaches to and not a new noun. Therefore, in Hebrew, Ritter proposes that only NumP is an intermediate projection between DP and NP and gender is specified on the N. This reason for proposing a separate functional layer for inflectional features predicts that for those languages where gender is an inflectional property, GenP should also be a projection in the DP. This is indeed the case with the Catalan nominals presented by Picallo (1991). Catalan number and gender feature only result in different number and gender values of the same noun, as shown in (9). Therefore, Picallo proposes that Catalan nominals have a GenP, in addition to a NumP.

(9) *el gos, la gossa, els gossos, les gosses*
     'the dog(s) M/Sg, F/Sg, M/Pl, F/Pl

Going by this logic, we are clear that functional projections can only be suggested for those phi−features, which are inflectional in nature. This also seems to be the case for the honorificity feature, as adding it to a noun does not result in a separate noun. All nouns are capable of being both honorific and non−honorific depending on the social context that changes the speaker's perception. This means that different values of honorificity feature don't change anything in the fundamental meaning of the noun, but just add more meaning on top of it. Therefore, I propose that honorificity, just like inflectional person, number and gender features, also projects a separate functional layer—HonP—in the DP structure. I consider HonP to be the universal form of the honorificity feature in DPs. Since DPs are at the edge of a nominal structure, I place HonP as an intermediate projection between DP and NP (10). I do not elaborate on what will be the order of the functional heads NumP and GenP with respect to HonP, for keeping the structure simple and focusing only on HonP.

(10)   [DP D [HonP Hon [NP N]]]

I also claim honorificity is an 'interpretable unvalued' feature on the noun. In claiming so, I follow the four−way combination of interpretability and valuabil- ity of features, as proposed by Pesetsky & Torrego (2007). I argue that honori- ficity is an unvalued feature in the DP because it is dependent on the discourse relation between two entities—a speaker and an addressee/non−addressee. As noted briefly in the introduction to this paper, when we compare honorificity to something like a number feature, we realize that unlike the former, the latter is not dependent on any discourse relation. This stark difference between other inflectional features and honorificity feature leads to the proposal that honori- ficity cannot be a valued feature in the DP. This property of the honorificity fea- ture immediately leads to the next question− how does honorificity get valued? I answer this in the next section.

Honorificity Licensing

In this section, I follow PPZ (2019) to highlight the mechanism of how the prag- matic notion of politeness is licensed in the syntax in the form of honorificity fea- ture on the nouns/pronouns. Their mechanism deals only with cases of addressee agreement, i.e. 2nd person. I propose a modification to PPZ's mechanism to incor- porate third person argument as well (see Chandra et al. (in prep) for a recent proposal).

Honorificity in the cP Layer

Languages often grammaticalize discourse information that is related to the speaker and/or the addressee/hearer through various ways. This discourse infor- mation has been claimed to have a syntactic representation (Tenny 2000, Speas and Tenny, 2003, Speas 2006, Haegeman & Hill, 2013, Pak 2006, Pak et al. 2008, Zanuttini et al., 2012, a.o.).

For example, grammaticalization of the addressee is noticed for Basque in the form of addressee/allocutive agreement (Oyharçabal, 1993 & Miyagawa, 2012). Consider the example given in (11), where the auxiliary forms differ according to the different addressees of the sentences.

(11)   a.   *Pettek lan egin dik*

Peter.erg work.abs do.prf aux−3 s.abs.2 s.c.m.alloc−3 s. erg

'Peter worked.' (spoken to a male friend)   (Oyharçabal, 1993)

b. *Pettek lan egin din*

Peter.erg work.abs do.prf aux−3 s.abs.2 s.c. f.alloc−3 s.
erg

'Peter worked.' (spoken to a female friend)

c. *Pettek lan egin dizü*

Peter.erg work.abs do.prf aux−3 s.abs.2 s.f.alloc−3 s.erg

'Peter worked.' (spoken to someone of a higher status)

There are multiple accounts that propose that these kinds of discourse information that give the relation between the speaker and the hearer are encoded via functional projections for the speaker and the hearer. For example, Miyagawa (2012)
follows Speas and Tenny (2003); Haegeman & Hill (2013) in positing functional
projection SAP for the speaker and saP for the hearer for addressee agreement
case given in (12). He proposes a CP domain above TP that hosts these functional
projections and encodes their discourse information. The schematic representation
is given in (12).

(12)

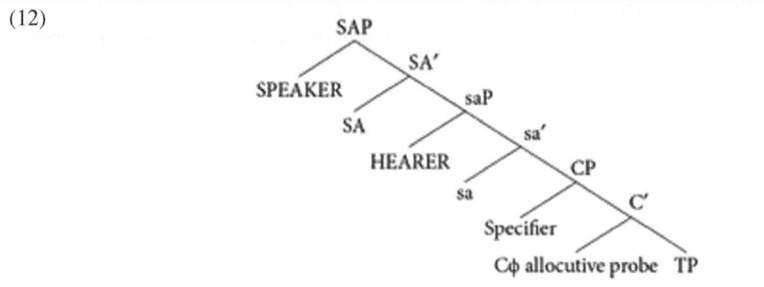

PPZ (2019) note that although both subject/object honorification and addressee
honorification capture politeness, there is a key difference between the two.
Subject/object honorification can be embedded in a sentence while addressee honorification cannot be embedded. They note this difference for Korean, Japanese
and Basque. Consider the Korean example in (13) and (14). (13) is a case of subject honorification and (14) is the embedded context and both of them are grammatical. The honorific particle −*kkeyse* indicates the honorific subject and the
verbal honorific affix −*si* indicates honorification agreement with the verb.

(13) *Wuli pwumonim−**kkeyse** ecey o−**si**−ess−ta*

Our parents−nom.hon yesterday come−hon−past−dec

'My parents came yesterday.'   Portner et al. (2019:3, (3))

(14) *Inho−ka pwumonim−**kkeyse** ecey o−**si**−ess−ta−ko
      malhayss−ta*

      Inho−nom parents−nom.hon yesterday come−hon−
      past−dec−comp said−dec

      'Inho said his parents came yesterday.'   Portner et al. (2019:3, (4))

(15a) is a case of addressee honorification and (15b) is the embedded context,
and it is ungrammatical because addressee agreement cases cannot be embedded.
Korean indicates addressee agreement with sentence final particles that are called
speech style particles.

(15) a. *Ecey pi−ka o−ass−**supnita***

          yesterday rain−nom come−past−dec.formal

          'It rained yesterday.'   Portner et al. (2019:4, (5))

      b. **Inho−ka [ecey pi−ka o−ass−**supnita**−ko]*
          *malhayss−**supnita***

          Inho−nom [yesterday rain−nom come past−dec.
          formal−comp] said−dec.formal

          'Inho said that it rained yesterday.'   Portner et al. (2019:4, (6))

To capture the discourse information of politeness, PPZ propose a discourse
layer that acts as an interface between the syntax and the pragmatic component.
This discourse layer captures politeness in the form of the 'status' feature that has
values that decide the hierarchy between the speaker and the addressee. They call
this discourse layer, the cP (context phrase) domain and the c head carries the 'status' feature. In order to account for the difference between the embeddability of
subject/object honorification and addressee honorification, they propose that:

- The addressee agreement markers are overt realization of c.
- The subject/object markers of honorificity are bound by c.

The structure proposed by them is given in (16).

(16)

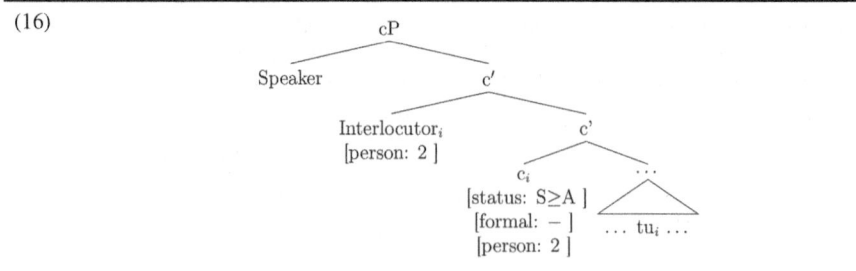

The mechanism given in (16) accounts for addressee agreement as a realization of c and subject/object agreement is explained in an operator−variable kind

of relationship, following Baker (2008) and Kratzer (2009). The interlocutor/ addressee operator binds the subject DP and it gets the status/honorificity feature value from c, where c acts as a mediator. When a DP of a sentence is bound by the addressee and the c in the cP layer, the status feature on c reflects on the DP, making it an honorific entity. Therefore, the resulting DP has 2nd person honorific features. Thus, subject/object agreement for 2nd person is also explained under this mechanism. I use this idea and extend it to capture 3rd person as well.

Extending c−binding to Non−Addressees

The claim here is that the cP layer also hosts a referent phrase that represents all 3rd person arguments. The simple reason for claiming this is that the social hierarchy between the speaker and the 2nd person addressee, 2nd person referent and 3rd person referent has to be captured in the discourse layer. Since all these three relations, i.e. speaker–addressee, speaker–2nd person referent and speaker–3rd person referent, fundamentally capture the pragmatic notion of politeness, it only makes sense that they are all incorporated in the syntax through the cP layer. This cP layer acts as an interface between pragmatics and syntax. Therefore, the structure that this paper proposes is given in (17). The mechanism for 2nd person addressee and referent remains as given in Portner et al., (16). As for the 3rd person, similarly, when a DP is bound by the referent and the c head in the cP layer, it reflects 3rd person feature and the honorificity value of c. This modification in the structure proposed by Portner et al., includes both the 2nd and 3rd person DPs that are overt arguments of a sentence, as well as the addressee.

(17)

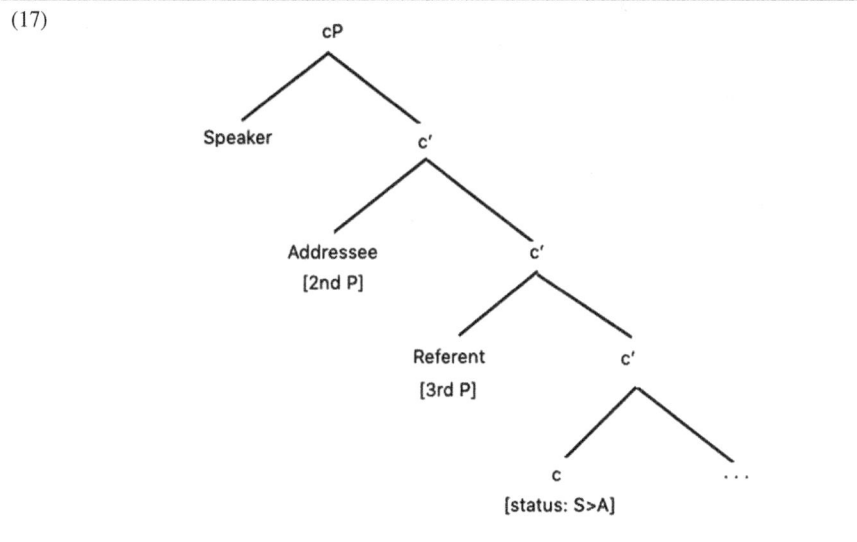

Table 7.1 Comparison between Maithili and Bangla Honorification

	Maithili	Bangla
Subject honorification:	Yes	Yes
Multiple argument honorification:	Yes	No
Addressee honorification:	Yes	No

Now that the mechanism of how the cP interface layer encodes politeness in the form of honorificity feature is clear, I turn to explain the honorification variation found between Maithili and Bangla.

Honorification Variation Between Maithili and Bangla

Maithili and Bangla are Eastern Indo–Aryan languages spoken mainly in India in the states of Bihar and West Bengal, respectively. Both are SOV languages, which inflect only for person and honorificity feature. Number and gender[5] inflection is absent in both the languages. As for a comparison of honorification agreement, this paper looks at three construction types: subject or object honorification agreement, double argument agreement (both subject and object agreement at the same time) and addressee agreement. Table 7.1 summarizes the honorification agreement pattern in the two languages in these three construction types.

Let's look at these cases in detail for both Maithili and Bangla.

Maithili Subject/Object Honorification

Maithili has an honorification system which distinguishes between four levels of honorificity in the second person and two levels of honorificity in the third person (given in Table 7.2).

Maithili has subject honorification inflection for both second and third person pronouns. It also shows object honorification for the second and third person. The following examples show subject honorification for 2nd person high honorific (18a), mid–honorific (18b) and non–honorific (18c).

---

[5] Maithili has minimal presence of gender where subjects trigger gender agreement on intransitive verbs in the past and future tense. However, it is not relevant for the discussion here, so I leave it out of this paper.

Table 7.2 Maithili pronouns

	Singular	Plural
1st P	həm	həm səb/lokəin
2nd P		
High Honorific	əpne	əpne səb/lokəin
Honorific	əhã	əhã səb/lokəin
Mid−honorific	tõ	tõ səb/lokəin
Non−honorific	tõ	tõ səb
3rd P		
Honorific	o	o səb/lokəin
Non−honorific	u/o	u/o səb

(18) a *əhã əe−**nu***

　　　　you(2H) come−(2H)

　　　　'You came'

　　b *tõ əe−l−**əh***

　　　　you(MH) come−Past−(2MH)

　　　　'You came'

　　c *tõ əe−l−**e***

　　　　you(NH) come−Past−(2NH)

　　　　'You came'

Maithili also shows the phenomenon of multiple argument agreement, where the subject and the object trigger agreement at the same time. For example, (19a) and (19b) have the same subject, while the object changes from being honorific in the former to non−honorific in the latter. The verbal agreement accordingly changes, showing the presence of multiple argument agreement.

(19) a *tõ hun−ka dekh−əl−**hunh***

　　　　you(NH) he(H)−ACC/DAT see−PST−(2NH+3H)

　　　　'You(NH) saw him(H).'

　　b *tõ ok−ra dekh−əl−**hin***

　　　　you(NH) he(NH)−ACC/DAT see−PST−(2NH+3NH)

　　　　'You(NH) saw him(NH).'

Finally, Maithili also has the phenomenon of addressee honorification, which stands for addressee agreement on the verb, when the addressee is not an argument of the verb. For example, (20a) is uttered to an addressee who is not an argument of the verb but its social relationship of being inferior to the speaker is captured in the form of the marker **−əu** on the verb. This marker changes to **−nəuh** in (20b) because the addressee in this case (also not an argument) is superior to the speaker.

Table 7.3 Bangla pronouns

	Singular	Plural
1stP	*aami*	*aam—ra*
2ndP		
Non—honorific	*Tui*	*to—ra*
Mid—honorific	*tumi*	*tom—ra*
High—honorific	*aapni*	*aapna—ra*
3rdP		
Non—honorific	*se/o*	*ta—ra/ o—ra*
Honorific	*tini/uni*	*ona—ra*

(20) a *həm khana kha le—li—əu* (addressal to a —Hon entity)

         I food eat do—PERF—(Add(—Hon))

         'I have eaten'

      b *həm khana kha le—nəuh* (addressal to an + Hon entity)

         I food eat do—PERF—(Add(+Hon))

         'I have eaten'

Bangla Honorification

Bangla honorification system distinguishes between three levels of honorificity in the second person and two in the third (given in Table 7.3).

Bangla also has subject honorification agreement. Consider (21b) and (21d), which are honorific counterparts of (21a) and (21c), respectively.

(21) a *tumi kha**chho***

         You eat(2p)

         'You eat'

      b *aapni kha**chhen***

         You(+ Hon) eat(2p + Hon)

         'You (+Hon) eat'

      c *tomra kha**chho***

         You (Pl) eat(2p)

         'You all eat'

      d *aapnara kha**chhen***

         You(PL)(+ Hon) eat(2p + Hon)

         'You all (+ Hon) eat'

Bangla does not have object agreement. Consider (22a) and (22b) where in both the cases, it is only the subject that triggers agreement.

(22) a   *tumi oke **dekhle***

           You(−Hon) he(−Hon) see(−Hon)

           'You saw him (−Hon)'

      b   *tumi onake **dekhle***

           You(−Hon) he(+ Hon) see(−Hon)

           'You saw him (+ Hon)'

Another point of variation between Maithili and Bangla is that Bangla does not have addressee agreement either. Consider (23a) and (23b), where the address to an honorific or a non−honorific entity does not change the agreement on the verb.

(23) a.   *aami **kheyechi*** (addressal to a −Hon entity)

           I eat.perf

           'I have eaten'

      b.   *aami **kheyechi*** (addressal to a + Hon entity)

           I eat.perf

           'I have eaten'

Since the data is now clear to us, let's look at the syntactic analysis of this variation in the next subsection. Given the Borer–Chomsky Conjecture, the idea is that parametric variation depends on features and therefore, I propose that in the case of honorificity feature, this variation is in the cP layer. The cP layer is where honorificity gets incorporated and the difference between how various features are valued in this layer, results into honorification variation.

Honorificity Parameter

In order to understand how the variation between Maithili and Bangla honorification comes about, let's understand how different honorification agreement is licensed in the syntax.

Subject Honorification

In both Maithili and Bangla, the mechanism for subject honorification remains the same. Since in both the languages, the 1st person subject does not trigger honorificity, there is no question about how it gets licensed in the syntax. As for the 2nd and 3rd person in both languages, the subject gets its honorificity feature via the mechanism given in (17). Therefore, Maithili and Bangla subjects get their honorificity feature via binding by the addressee in case of 2nd person and via Referent in case of 3rd person. The structure is shown in (24).

(24)

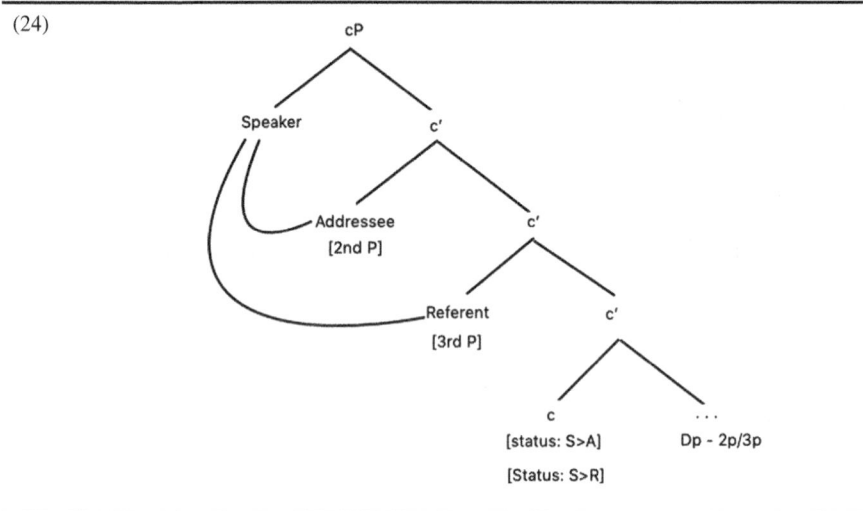

Simultaneous Subject and Object Honorification

As explained already, Maithili has multiple argument honorification where both the subject and the object agree with the v/T. In order to explain this phenomenon using the given mechanism, I propose that multiple argument honorification in Maithili involves more than just the cP layer. The claim that the addressee and the referent heads host 2nd and 3rd person feature, respectively, gives us only the possibility of two DPs being honorific. It does not say anything about how these two arguments agree with the verb/T at the same time. In this case, the intuitive idea is that the object in Maithili uses an escape hatch to move out of the vP layer and by being equidistant with the subject DP, it agrees with the T head. This is shown in the structure given in (25).

(25)

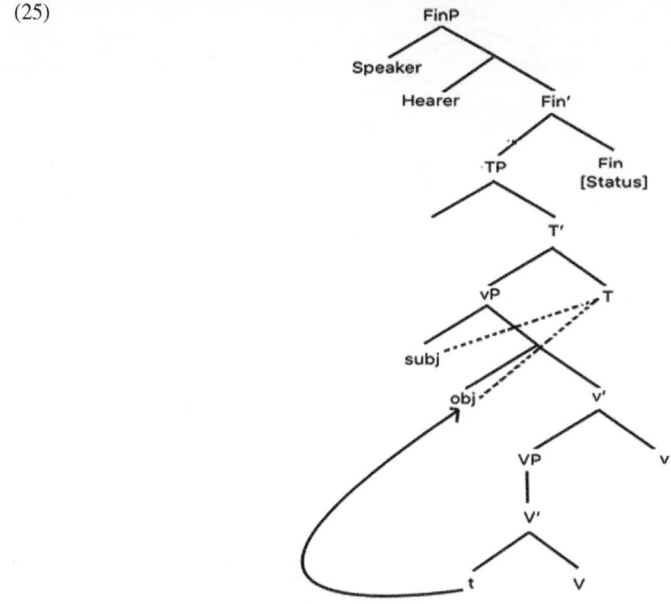

In order to support the claim that the object moves out of the vP domain, we need to pay attention to the details of object agreement in Maithili. In this language, only the 'human' and 'non−human specific' objects trigger agreement and not the non−specific animate or inanimate ones. We follow Wiltschko & Ritter (2015) in claiming that+animate nouns, restricted to+human and non−human specific animals, must occupy the specifier position of a functional head. Such an account of animacy is separately supported by Woolford (1999), who follows an OT analysis to suggest the same. Woolford says that+animacy is a feature that VP internal objects cannot get checked and hence, they must raise to the specifier of a higher functional projection for agreement. The theoretical assumption that I make here is that these objects are able to get accusative case from v but unable to trigger agreement because of their animacy feature. Thus, case and agreement are separated in this analysis.

On the other hand, in the case of Bangla, only subjects trigger agreement and objects do not get their animacy feature checked. This difference in Bangla does not let the object escape the vP domain and it gets spelt out along with the vP phase. Therefore, only subjects trigger agreement in Bangla with the T head. This is shown in the structure given in (26).

(26)

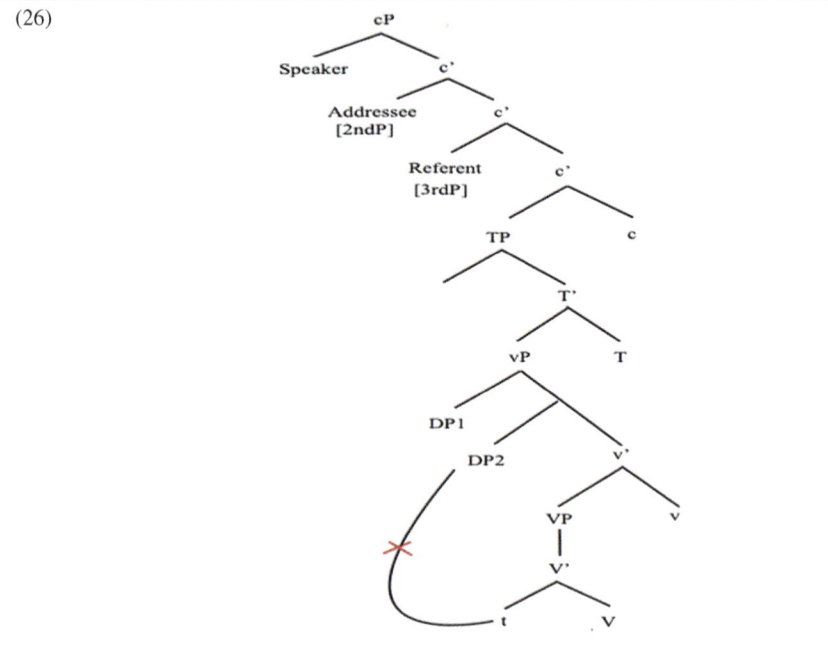

Addressee Honorification

The structure proposed for addressee honorification in Sect. 3, says that it is borne when the c head, carrying the status feature, agrees with the null addressee DP in its specifier position. As per the claim in this paper, both Maithili and Bangla will have the c head. This can be attested by the fact that both languages have honorificity agreement. However, the presence of honorificity agreement in Maithili and its absence in Bangla can only be explained by assuming that Bangla null addressees are incapable of agreeing with the c head. The other way of explaining this difference can be that the allocutive agreement on the c head in Maithili is realized, like other languages such as Korean and Basque, whereas it does not get realized in Bangla.

Tying Honorification Differences as a Parameter

As mentioned briefly in the beginning of this section, under the minimalist framework, cross−linguistic differences are understood as differences emerging from the features on the functional head. This idea comes from the Borer–Chomsky

Conjecture (Borer 1984) and Chomsky (1995) which places all cross−linguistic variation in the lexicon:

All parameters of variation are attributable to differences in features of particular items (e.g. the functional heads) in the lexicon.

Following the Borer–Chomsky Conjecture, Biberauer & Roberts (2015) reanalyse various macro− and micro−differences in languages in the form of a parameter hierarchy. According to them, cross−linguistic differences, for a value v_i of a feature F, can be understood at the following levels:

(27)   • For a given value v_i of a parametrically variant feature F:

    • Macro−parameters: all heads of the relevant type, e.g. all probes, all phase heads, etc., share v_i;

    • Meso−parameters: all heads of a given natural class, e.g. [+V] or a core functional category, share v_i;

    • Micro−parameters: a small, lexically definable subclass of functional heads (e.g. modal auxiliaries, subject clitics) shows v_i;

    • Nano−parameters: one or more individual lexical items is/are specified for v_i

I explain the differences between Maithili and Bangla honorificity agreement as per the parameter hierarchy given above. Since honorificity feature is present in both the languages, the differences cannot be a macro−level difference. Since these languages differ in the kinds of honorification that they have, this can be categorized as a meso−level difference. The first such difference between these two languages is the presence of addressee agreement in Maithili and the absence of the same in Bangla. The second difference between the two languages is the presence of object honorificity agreement Maithili and its absence in Bangla. As explained already, I claim that object honorificity agreement difference is tied to animacy difference between the two languages. Therefore, I follow Roberts and Holmberg (2010) & Roberts (2012) in explaining these differences as a dependent parameter hierarchy. According to them, one parametric difference between languages can be dependent on some other parametric difference. Therefore, honorificity parameter in Maithili and Bangla is dependent on animacy parameter.

Conclusion

Honorificity is a syntactic feature. It is similar to the phi−features in its inflectional nature. However, it also differs from the phi−features by being discourse dependent. Therefore, it needs to be valued by a functional head in the discourse domain. Since it is a feature, it gives rise to cross−linguistic differences. In the case of Maithili and Bangla, these differences are meso−level and also dependent on the animacy feature.

References

Abney, S. (1987). *The English NP in its Sentential Aspect*. Doctoral dissertation, MIT.

Baker, M. (2008). The macroparameter in a microparametric world. In T. Biberauer (Ed.), *The limits of syntactic variation* (pp. 351−74). Amsterdam: Benjamins.

Biberauer, T., & Roberts, I. (2015). Rethinking formal hierarchies: A proposed unification. In J. Chancharu, X. Hu & M. Mitrović (Eds.). *Cambridge Occasional Papers in Linguistics* (Vol. 7, pp. 1–31).

Boeckx, C., & Niinuma, F. (2004). Conditions on agreement in Japanese. *Natural Language and Linguistic Theory, 22*, 453–480.

Brown, P., & Levinson, S. (1978). Universals in language usage: Politeness phenomena. In E. Goody (Ed.), *Questions and politeness* (pp. 56−289). Cambridge: University of Cambridge Press.

Chomsky, N. (1995). *The Minimalist Program*. MIT Press.

Haegeman, L., & Hill, V. (2013). The syntactization of discourse. In R. Folli, C. Sevdali & R. Truswell (Eds.), *Syntax and its limits* (pp. 370−390). Oxford: Oxford University Press.

Harada, S. I. (1976). 'Honorifics'. In M. Shibatani (Ed.), *Syntax and Semantics 5* (pp. 499–561). New York: Academic Press.

Holmberg A. (2010). Null subject parameters. In T. Biberauer, A. Holmberg, I. Roberts & M. Sheehan (Ed.), *Parametric variation: Null subjects in minimalist theory* (pp.88−124). Cambridge: Cambridge University Press.

Kratzer, A. (2009). Making a pronoun: Fake indexicals as windows into the properties of pronouns. *Linguistic Inquiry, 40*, 187–237.

Miyagawa, S. (2012). Agreements that occur mainly in the main clause. In L. Aelbrecht, L. Haegeman & R. Nye (Ed.), *Main clause phenomena: New horizons* (pp. 79–112). Amsterdam/ Philadelphia: John Benjamins.

Noam, C. (2000). Minimalist inquiries: The framework. In R. Martin, D. Michaels & J. Uriagereka (Eds.), *Step by step: Essays on minimalist syntax in honor of Howard Lasnik* (pp. 89−156). Cambridge, Mass: MIT Press.

Oyharçabal, B. (1993). Verb agreement with non−arguments: On allocutive agreement. In J. I. Hualde & J. O. de Urbina (Ed.), *Generative studies in Basque linguistics* (pp. 89–114). Amsterdam/Philadelphia: John Benjamins.

Pak, M. (2017). Towards understanding the syntactic representation of honorifics in Korean. In J. Whitman & L. Brown (Eds.), *Honorific language and linguistic politeness in Korean, Korean Linguistics* (Vol. 17, No. 2, pp. 132−166). John Benjamins.

Pesetsky, D. & Torrego, E. (2007). The syntax of valuation and the interpretability of features. In S. Karimi, V. Samiian & W. Wilkins (Eds.), *Phrasal and Clausal Architecture: Syntactic Derivation and Interpretation*. Amsterdam: Benjamins.

Picallo, M. C. (1991). Nominals and nominalizations in catalan. *Probus, 3*, 279–316.

Portner, P., Pak M., & R. Zanuttini. (2019). "The speaker−addressee relation at the syntax− semantics interface." Language.

Ritter, E. (1993). Where's gender? *Linguistic Inquiry, 24*, 795–803.

Roberts, I. (2012). Macroparameters and minimalism: A programme for comparative research. In C. Galves, S. Cyrino, R. Lopes, F. Sândalo & J. Avelar (Eds.), *Parameter Theory and Linguistic Change* (pp. 320−335). Oxford: Oxford University Press.

Speas, M., & Tenny, C. L. (2003). Configurational properties of point of view roles. In A. M. Di Sciullo (Ed.), *Asymmetry in grammar* (pp. 315–344). Amsterdam/Philadelphia: John Benjamins.

Subbarao, K. V., Agnihotri, R. K., & Mukherjee, A. (1991). Syntactic strategies and politeness phenomena. *International Journal of the Sociology of Language, 92*, 35–53.

The World Atlas of Language Structures (WALS): https://wals.info

Toribio, A. (1990). 'Specifier−head agreement in Japanese', In *Proceedings of WCCFL 9* (pp. 535–548). CSLI, Stanford.

Wiltschko, M., & Ritter, E. (2015). Animating the narrow syntax. *The Linguistic Review, 32*, 869–908. https://doi.org/10.1515/tlr-2015-0011

Zanuttini, R., Pak M., & Portner P. (2012). A syntactic analysis of interpretive restrictions on imperative, promissive and exhortative subjects. *Natural Language and Linguistic Theory, 30*, 1231-1274.

Preeti Kumari is Assistant Professor at the Institute of Technical Education and Research, Siksha O Anusandhan University in Bhubaneswar. Her Ph.D. thesis from the Indian Institute of Technology Delhi investigates the syntax of honorificity in the Eastern Indo-Aryan languages such as Maithili, Magahi and Bangla. Specifically, she looks at the phenomenon of referent honorifics and its interaction with allocutive honorifics in these languages.

Chapter 8
Towards an Understanding of Micro-variations: Decoding the Hierarchical Module of Variation and the Correlates of Mappila Malayalam

Thapasya Jayaraj and Rajesh Kumar

Abstract Language variation always indicates a social meaning attached to it, and this indexical process eventually contributes to the progression of linguistic change in progress. This paper provides a perspective of the underlying process of such micro-variations in languages by modelling the hierarchy of variation in Mappila Malayalam, one of the distinguishable sociolects of Malayalam. It describes how the process of language variation is affected in response to the linguistic and extralinguistic factors. The current study identifies two dominant phases of variation in Mappila Malayalam, denoted as first wave variation and second wave variation, and explores variations at different levels of linguistic expressions such as phonology and morphosyntax. The first wave variations are traced back from the literature and documented by tracing them from the most older generation speech samples available. The paper advances with the analysis of supportive empirical data that substantiates the second wave variation in Mappila Malayalam, which is in progress and derives a hierarchical order of variation. The paper identifies three significant domains influencing the hierarchy of language variation in its contexts and describes the interweaved system of layered hierarchy influenced by the level of linguistic expression, visibility of the variant and the progressive transition of variants. It also suggests a variation modelling based on the hierarchy that can be further extended to variations in other languages with similar contexts.

Keywords Hierarchy of variation · Mappila Malayalam · Sociolect · Change in progress · Second wave variation

T. Jayaraj (✉)
Indian Institute of Technology Indore, Indore, India
e-mail: thapasya@iiti.ac.in

R. Kumar
Indian Institute of Technology Madras, Chennai, India
e-mail: rajesh@iitm.ac.in

© The Author(s), under exclusive license to Springer Nature Singapore Pte Ltd. 2023
P. Chandra (ed.), *Variation in South Asian Languages*,
https://doi.org/10.1007/978-981-99-1149-3_8

179

Abbreviations

CONJ	Conjunctive
FUT	Future
INF	Infinitive
LOC	Locative
PERF	Perfect
PP	Postposition
PRES	Present
PROG	Progressive
PST	Past

Introduction

The field of sociolinguistics is enthralled by language variations at micro- and macro-levels concerning its existence in the society ever since its birth. The studies in variation linguistics indicate the fact that language universally encompasses various forms and structures that grapple with each other in their usage in different contexts. A micro-analysis of variations within a living language as well as a comparative analysis of variations in multiple languages benefits to establish the relationship between linguistic structures with the social factors. However, an attempt for an acceptable cohesive pattern of language variation as a process has left a room in the area of analysis in its social context since such studies largely focused on the diachronic variation and reconstructing languages or in the context of language contact (Bailey, 1973; Labov, 2007). Though the idea of dynamic nature universally distributed among all the languages with specific parameters is a widely accepted fact, an explanatorily adequate model of language variation in its social context with predictive capacity creates a broad aperture in the literature. Therefore, this paper attempts to draw a basic pattern of language variation concerning the aspect of its hierarchy related to the levels of linguistic expressions. It takes primary data from real speech samples of the Central Malabar[1] Mappila Malayalam (henceforth Mappila Malayalam) speakers, focusing on the different aspects of variations in their speech to reach a general explanatory pattern of variation in Mappila Malayalam. Mappila Malayalam is the sociolect of Malayalam spoken by the Muslim community of Malabar, namely Mappilas. Among the diverse manifestations of Malayalam in the form of various dialects, Mappila Malayalam is recognized as the most divergent sociolect in many aspects (Asher & Kumari, 1997; Devy, 2015; Namboothirippadu, 1994; Panikkar, 2017).

---

[1] Adopted from the dialect mapping of Malayalam carried out by V.I Subramoniam in his work 'Dialect Survey of Malayalam' ('Ezhava-Tiyya').

Chapter 7
Comparing Honorificity Agreement in Maithili and Bangla

Preeti Kumari

Abstract This paper aims (i) to explain honorificity as a syntactic feature and its licensing in the computational workspace; (ii) to account for cross−linguistic variation emerging from the honorificity feature, using data from two Eastern Indo−Aryan languages—Maithili and Bangla. I claim that honorificity is an interpretable unvalued feature in the DP, and hence, it needs to get valued by a functional head. Adopting (Portner and Zanuttini, (Portner et al. (2019). "The speaker−addressee relation at the syntax−semantics interface." Language.), this paper suggests that the valuation of honorificity is done by the c(ontext) head in the discourse domain, which encodes the status feature. With this understanding of the honorificity feature, cross-linguistic differences between two Eastern Indo-Aryan languages—Maithili and Bangla—are explained as per the Borer–Chomsky Conjecture.

Keywords Honorificity · Feature · Variation · Maithili · Bangla

Introduction

Politeness is a socio−pragmatic notion that reflects the hierarchical relationship between the speaker and the addressee, i.e. 2nd person, or the speaker and a non−addressee, i.e. 3rd person (Brown & Levinson, 1978; Harada, 1976). Such a hierarchy is dependent on multiple factors such as age, superior position in the society and formal relationship. This social convention is grammaticalized in natural languages in various ways (Subbarao et al., (1991), World Atlas of Language Structures). For example, the use of causatives, passives, intransitive verb forms, etc., are some politeness strategies, among many others, that are

P. Kumari (✉)
Institute of Technical Education and Research, Siksha O Anusandhan University, Bhubaneswar, India
e-mail: kumaripreeti.2293@gmail.com

The study identifies two phases of variations in Mappila Malayalam and denotes them as first wave variation and second wave variation. The analysis considers the pattern of second wave variations of Mappila Malayalam compared to the first wave variants. The analysis specifically looks at the phonological and morphosyntactic variations to identify the pattern and reach a conclusive remark on the hierarchy of variations according to the level of linguistic expression by empirically examining the variations of the second wave in comparison with the variants of the first wave preserved in the older generation of Mappila Malayalam speakers. We also look at how the speakers receive these variations and reflect them according to the speech. Therefore, the study advances by looking at the variations in the speech patterns of different age groups and contexts, such as casual and formal utterances. It further tries to deduce them at a framework of the hierarchical pattern in the process of variation in progress as part of the second wave in Mappila Malayalam based on the qualitative and quantitative data elicited from the speech patterns of Mappila Malayalam speakers. The analysis shows significant involvement of a hierarchy in the second wave variation, manifested by the influence of linguistic and extralinguistic correlations. Thus, the analysis leads to a better understanding of language variations as the process and tries to provide adequate explanations of such linguistic phenomena by imparting the notion of a hierarchical order of linguistic variation and its depending factors to the existing conception of micro-variations in languages that would benefit future research.

The paper is organized in a fashion where section "Language Variations in the Contemporary Society and Studying Language Variations" provides the background of the present study by describing the literature on language variations in contemporary society and how essential to study such variation. It also provides the aspects of micro-variations adopted in the present analysis, such as the transformation of variants from indicators to markers and then stereotypes and the concepts of hierarchy and waves in variation analysis. Section "Malabar, Mappilas and Mappila Malayalam" details the speech community, their language and the space they are located in, which are crucial to understanding the current analysis. The detailed research design is explained in section "Research Design", followed by a description of Mappila Malayalam variations identified to have two waves. Section "First Wave Variation of Mappila Malayalam" documents the first wave variations of Mappila Malayalam at the level of phonology and morphosyntax by providing specific instances. Section "Second Wave Variation of Mappila Malayalam" provides a detailed description of variations in the second wave and shows how the first wave variants are transforming in the second wave with empirical evidence. The paper further advances by analysing the linguistic and extralinguistic correlations for such transformations and formulating the hierarchy associated with language variation. It seeks to provide a generic approach that can be adopted to analyse language variation as a process.

Language Variations in the Contemporary Society and Studying Language Variations

Language variation is a fascinating phenomenon that gained attention for a long. Linguistics always observed the phenomenon through various lenses, beginning from historical linguistics to cognitive linguistics (Eckert, 2012). Between the speakers of any language, there can be a variation in the way they use their language. Such variations are explained by linguistic differences regarding phonological to structural variations. By the emergence of sociolinguistics as a significant discipline, language variation analyses gained much attention and explored multiple aspects of its realizations. The perspective on language variation and its analysis has changed from time to time. Sociolinguistics and the sociology of language try to establish the relationships between language choice and language status in a speech community. Such analysis of a language variation at various levels such as phonology, morphology, syntactic, semantic, lexical and so on showed its correlation with social factors such as region, caste, community, social stratum, age, sex, education, profession, economic status and the such. There are substantial attempts advanced to theorize variations in languages and methodologies to elicit and document its implications in the field of sociolinguistics (Fischer, 1964; Hymes, 1964; Kroch, 1978; Labov, 1966, 1972, 2001, 2007; Labov et al., 1972).

Eckert (2012) notes three different waves in variation studies. These are called waves since there is no definite distinction between these approaches. The first wave focused on language variation and its social correlation and how social factors affect language use. It includes Labov's framework of analysing language variation, which employs an empirical approach to sociolinguistic analysis. The second wave in variation studies had an ethnographical approach, whereas the third wave of variation studies focuses on stylistic perspective. Language variation in the context of identity came into the locus during this wave. People started analysing how people use language variation to project their identity, i.e. how they wanted to express their identity or depict themselves (Le Page, 1998). The third wave locates ideology in the language itself in constructing meaning, with potentially significant consequences for linguistic theory more generally (Eckert, 2012). However, these waves do not overlook the interaction of language and society, though the focus of analysing language variation is also varying.

There has been an emphasis on interdisciplinarity in sociolinguistics, especially in integrating variation studies with sociological and anthropological theory. However, the importance of variation started to pervade in own fields such as phonetics, phonology, syntax, semantics, psycholinguistics, computational linguistics, among others (Labov, 2001, 2010). Similar to the shift in focus, the approach to analysing language variation also changed its perspective regarding its occurrence. It has moved from the restrictions to look at variations in progress as language began to change according to the rapid changes in society. The availability of speech recognition and analysis technology elevated the study of variation onto new dimensions. The technological revolution provides access to different linguistic samples. Simultaneously, the pace of language variation has also increased. These advancements allow us to dive even more deeply into the kinds of analyses on variation and expand our focus to multiple aspects of variation. Modelling the hierarchy of variation in the analysis of language variation in progress would provide a clearer picture of what all variants can undergo variations in a language or a variety of a language over the other variants with empirical evidence. The present study on Mappila Malayalam variation would provide a new perspective on observing language variation in progress in terms of its order. It emancipates new directions in analysing language variation with an empirical perspective.

Variants as Indicators, Markers and Stereotypes

Labovian framework of variation analysis has become unavoidable in the field of sociolinguistics by the plethora of his contributions in the field. The current study absorbs the idea of classification of phonetic variants put forward by Labov (2001) in his pivotal work *Principles of Linguistic Change: Social Factors*. He categorizes the phonetic variants into three types: a phonetic 'variant with little or no social meaning and significance' is denoted as an 'indicator'; if a 'variant conveys social information about the speaker or when people are aware of the markers which are related to social categories and speech styles,' it is called a 'marker'; the third variant is labelled as 'stereotype,' wherein there is a popular and conscious characterization of particular social groups; in other words, 'the social values of a variant are raised to the level of social consciousness' (Labov, 2001).

Though the description is about phonetic variants, a similar to kind of categorization can be done in the case of variants of different levels of expressions in any language and in Mappila Malayalam as well. Rather than independent entities, we consider these three types of variants in a linear order of progression. That is, a variant can progress through all the three stages in the given order as indicator, marker and stereotype over a period of time according to its popularity and social significance. The popularity is decided by how familiar the variant is. In other words, it is the visibility of the variant to the speakers as well as the other dialect speakers around the speech community. The current paper will analyse the variants based on this classification in different periods and try to map the hierarchical order of variation. The study also analyses how the internal and external factors affect the language variation of Mappila Malayalam.

Hierarchy and Variations in Waves

The universal phenomenon of covariation of language and social context has been under inquiry to reach a combined theory for better knowledge about the pattern of variation with a predictive capacity. The analysis mostly focused on the social aspects of language variation in this context rather than the structural elements based on the order and direction of the variation. One of the significant contributions in this aspect was made by Bailey (1973) in which he notes about the directionality of variation. According to him, the directionality of natural change is from what is more marked to what is less marked. Bailey (1973) notes that;

> Patterns of a language are the cumulative result of natural, unidirectional changes, which begins variably and spread across the social barriers of age, sex, class, space, and the like in waves. (Bailey, 1973, pp. 36)

By creating a classification among the variables based on the levels of markedness, he mentions about a hierarchy among the variables. In this paper, we try to find out the hierarchy of variation in Mappila Malayalam based on the level of linguistic expression and the reason behind the hierarchy. The study does not accurately replicate the idea put forward by Bailey (1973), rather than creating a hierarchy among the variables, the current analysis looks at the hierarchy of variations existing in line with the phonological variants and morphosyntactic variants. It advances by analysing which variant undergoes through the progressive variation of indicator to the marker and then to stereotype. Here hierarchy indicates the priority order of variations that occurs within different levels of linguistic expression and in the transition from an indicator to the stereotype in Mappila Malayalam which is due to some of the variants getting more attention and visibility and thereby influences the process of further variations. In this scenario, the paper looks at how the linguistic features influence the process of variation with respect to the hierarchy.

Malabar, Mappilas and Mappila Malayalam

Malabar refers to the geographic and historical region situated in the southwest of India, comprising the northern region of the state of Kerala. It is situated between the Arabian Sea and the Western Ghats. The region is of great historical importance for many reasons that are not only limited to the context of India or Kerala, but expands to the broader prospect of world history. The region has undergone and witnessed major historical and sociopolitical transitions in multiple aspects, such as geography, economy, administration, social movements, conflicts and its people. Associating Malabar with the northern districts of Kerala began with the advent of colonialism in India. The British established the region as one of the districts under the Madras Presidency after they assumed control over the region in 1792 (Fig. 8.1).

The present districts of Kerala such as Kannur, Kozhikode, Wayanad, Malappuram, most of the areas in Palakkad (excluding Alathur and Chittur taluks) and some parts of Thrissur (Chavakkad Taluk) together constituted the British district of Malabar. Malabar witnessed and actively involved in diversified

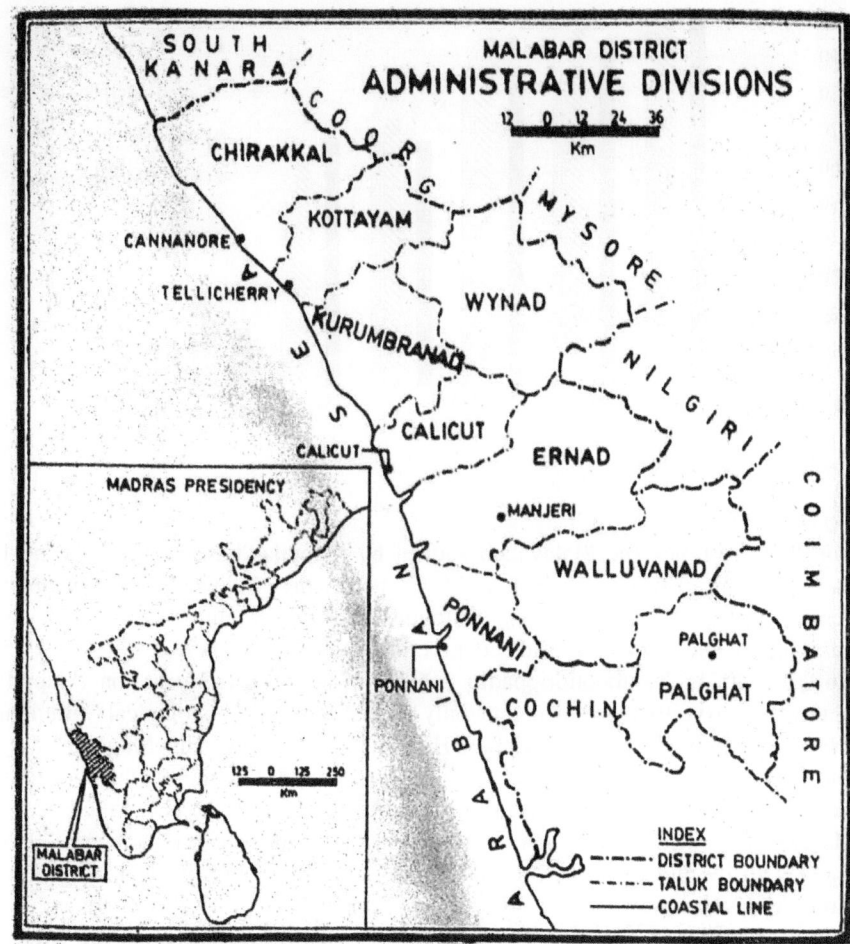

Fig. 8.1 Malabar. *Source* Panikkar (1989) *Against Lord and State*

historical experiences, which makes this region significant in the history of the modern world (Nair, 1986; Panikkar, 1989). It is one of the significant regions for socio-historical and political research and discussions in academia. The existing dialect surveys of Malayalam also mark this area as having a distinct linguistic identity. Central Malabar is one of the dialect areas within that geographic region that comprises parts of present-day Kozhikode and Malappuram districts of Kerala, where a significant population of Malabar Mappilas inhabits (Subramoniam, 1974).

The socio-historical background of Mappila Malayalam points towards its development during the spread of Islamism in the region. Subsequently, it underwent significant variations following the sociopolitical changes that happened

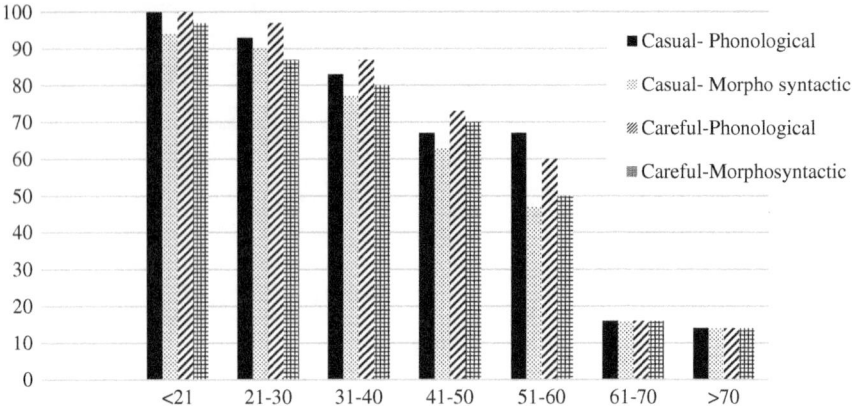

Fig. 8.2 Pattern of second wave variation

from time to time. The Malayalam spoken by Mappilas has absorbed a considerable amount of Arabic, Persian and Urdu borrowings followed by various phonemes; hence, they can be easily distinguished from the other sociolects (based on religion and caste) of Malayalam (Asher & Kumari, 1997; Girish, 2015; Hussain, 2005; Namboothirippadu, 1994). Most of the works on Mappila Malayalam have tried to document only the lexical and phonological variations (Namboothirippadu, 1994; Joseph, 2015; Panikkar, 2017). The Mappilas were known for their literary interest and to express their literature which encompassed their community identity; they developed a literary tradition called Arabi-Malayalam in which Malayalam is written in the Arabic script (Karassery, 1995) along with the inclusion of some lexical items from Arabic, Persian, and Urdu. Arabi-Malayalam had become an essential segment of the Mappila culture and tradition, and it has even extended to be their spoken language. 'Until the twentieth century, the script was widely taught to all Muslims in the primary education madrasas of Kerala' (Menon, 2002).

The Mappilas put a very conscious effort into making changes in the language they speak during the period of conversion, so that they could project their identity as members of the newly formed Mappila community and claim a better social space. This stage of variation is identified as a founding landmark that led to the development of a sociolect, Mappila Malayalam, to have an individuality and uniqueness among the varieties of Malayalam (Jayaraj & Kumar, 2020). Variations spread to various levels of linguistic expressions such as phonology, morphology, lexis, tone and so on. Most of the variations, especially the phonological and lexical ones, gained a lot of visibility among the speakers of Malayalam and thereby identified Mappila Malayalam as different from the others.

Research Design

The paper employs the qualitative and quantitative analysis of variations in Mappila Malayalam. The fieldwork is structured to capture the variation between careful and casual speech, variably supplemented by consciousness projecting identity through linguistic choices. The data from the speech patterns obtained through semi-structured interviews supplement to map the variation across generations in apparent time. The first wave variations are retrieved from the existing literature on Mappila Malayalam and verified with the speech patterns of the older generations. The second wave variations are documented from the field supported by empirical evidence. The speech samples of speakers from different age groups such as below 21, 21–30, 31–40, 41–50, 51–60, 61–70 and above 70 have been elicited from different regions of Central Malabar. The study assimilated speech samples of different degrees of formality from each speaker under the analysis and tested the familiarity and relatability factor to identify the visibility of the variants and the attitudes of the speakers towards these variations. The familiarity and relatability factor is a casual speech test that allows identifying whether a variant is familiar to the person, does he/she identify it as a dialect property. Therefore, the same test is employed on other dialect speakers from the same region to determine the visibility of the variant and thereby map its transformation from an indicator to a stereotype.

Mappila Malayalam Variations

Variations in Mappila Malayalam have multiple dimensions including linguistic and non-linguistic factors. Both religion and language play a major role in informing and structuring social practice. Fasold (1984) notes the importance of language in recognizing social identity. He proposes the conventional tools for 'measuring' individual and group attitudes to other individuals/groups or an established social characteristic of such groups by the matched guise and the semantic differential scale (Fasold, 1984). In line with this, we are analysing the phonological and morphosyntactic variations prevailed during the development of Mappila Malayalam as a dialect of unique features under the notion of first wave variation and its transformations to its current state of variations in progress under the notion of second wave variation. Basically, this analysis would give a comparative picture of the historical variation in Mappila Malayalam under the influence of different social factors. The second wave variations are explained based on the empirical evidence that eventually led to the understanding on the hierarchy of variations in Mappila Malayalam. Apart from this, the Labovian classification of phonetic variants (Labov, 2001) has been extended and adopted to the current analysis to develop a conceptual model of variation.

Two Waves of Variations in Mappila Malayalam

Mappila Malayalam has undergone several changes at different points of time in line with the social changes that influenced the community. We identified two phases of variations in Mappila Malayalam that significantly shaped the sociodialect and contributed to its characteristics and identity. Why these phases are represented with the term 'wave' is an essential factor to have a note. As pointed in the onset, the current analysis driven from the idea of wave nature of variation has been discussed mostly in the field of historical linguistics and specifically in the context of variation studies by Bailey (1973). Along with that, the variations are not distinguishable with precise edges in the timeline. Finding where and when it began exactly and until when it continued to exist is difficult as in the case of waves which moves as overlapping continuums having difficulty in distinguishing each wave separately. Likewise, the variations in Mappila Malayalam spread to different levels of linguistic expressions starting from phonology to pragmatics and show a steady spread of variation over a period. This variation creates a movement in the whole system of Mappila Malayalam, affecting its balance.

Religion and language perform a significant part in acquainting and structuring social practices. Accordingly, they influence the attitudes and social practices of individuals and groups which mark them apart from another (Omoniyi, 2006). Variations occur when a new religious code is introduced to carry out the function of the earlier code. Those variations can be in the following levels as Pandharipande (2006) observes; (a) the patterns of language choice, (b) the variation in the power hierarchies of religious languages across time and space, (c) the ideologies (about the form, content and function of religious language) which determine those hierarchies, (d) the sociocultural history which gives rise to the ideologies and (e) the 'authority' which authenticates those ideologies. Religion is one of the major symbols of social identities in the South Asian scenario (Pandharipande, 2006). In a similar scenario, Mappila Malayalam emerged with a variation from others' Malayalam after people started to convert to Islamism and spread the belief system in the region (Devy, 2015; Panikkar, 2017).

The variety developed by commencing changes at different levels of linguistic expressions such as phonology, morphology, morphosyntax, and lexis, and we denote these variations at the initial stage of Mappila Malayalam as the first wave variation. The phonological and lexical variations are easily perceptible at the surface by the people, and the other levels of variations such as morphological, morphosyntactic are not. These variations helped in composing a distinctiveness to Mappila Malayalam as compared to the other dialects of Malayalam spoken in the region, which in turn contributed to founding a discrete Mappila identity to the community. This language attitude for creating a difference from others was a result of the sociopolitical condition of the time when Mappila community members as the newly converted population based on the egalitarian principle proclaimed by Islam. They gained more acceptance in the society than their previous caste (Girish, 2015; Hardgrave, 1964). Likewise, language variation was used as an effective tool for identity creation according to the social condition that existed during that period.

Similar to any other living language, Mappila Malayalam has also not remained stagnant and exposed to further variations in line with the flow of social changes. In the light of this, the paper attempts to analyse the patterns of some of the variations in Mappila Malayalam that has happened afterwards in accordance with the change in social factors, which are dealt under the second wave variation. This phase of variation in Mappila Malayalam gains importance primarily because of the significant deviation from Mappila Malayalam's variation pattern existed till then and secondly because it can be qualitatively and empirically analysed since the process is in progress. When it comes to the second wave variation, Mappila Malayalam again shows variations at the levels of phonology, morphology, morphosyntax and lexis.

First Wave Variation of Mappila Malayalam

The first wave variation of Mappila Malayalam can be denoted as the birth phase of the sociolect with its own characteristics. First wave variation initiated a flux in all the levels of linguistic expression in Mappila Malayalam that made the sociolect with unique identity. Mappila Malayalam flourished as having an independent identity along with the foundation of Arabi-Malayalam among the Mappila community. Arabi-Malayalam is a mixed language used for literary activities by the Mappilas in the form of both prose and poetry. It is a composition of various languages as it adopted the grammar and syntax of Malayalam and lexis included vocabulary from Arabic, Urdu, Persian, Malayalam and Tamil (Ilias & Hussain, 2017; Saidalavi, 2013). Arabi-Malayalam had become an essential segment of Mappila culture, tradition and their spoken language. Until the twentieth century, the script was widely taught to all Muslims in the primary education *madrasas*[2] of Kerala (Menon, 2002). Mappila Malayalam shows an inclination towards Arabi-Malayalam in many aspects precisely because of this enrooted connection with the community that eventually influenced their spoken language also. Mappila Malayalam has thus adopted number of features from Arabi-Malayalam which helped in expressing their identity through language variation. The current analysis would consider these variations under the first wave variation of Mappila Malayalam. During the first wave variation, the variants of Mappila Malayalam elevated from its status as indicators and appeared as markers loaded with the social meaning and indexical to the community identity. Particularly, among these variations, as some of the variants are observed to get more visibility than the others, we analyse the further implications and effects of this phenomenon as well.

---

[2] The word *madrasa* from Arabic denotes any educational institution. However, in the Indian context, the word is used for representing institutions established by Muslim communities primarily aiming for religious education.

Phonological Variations

Phonological variations along with the lexical variations are the most observable variations in any language variety since the speakers are aware of the variations (Field, 2012). Mappila Malayalam is one of the most deviated sociolects of Malayalam from the existing system of Malayalam language in terms of phonology and lexis. In this section, we look at two important phonological variations in Mappila Malayalam developed during the first wave of variations. One of the most significant variations identified as a characteristic feature of Mappila Malayalam is the absence of the voiced palatal retroflex phoneme /ɻ/. The phoneme /ɻ/ is one of the significant elements that defines Malayalam phonology because of the unfamiliarity of the other language speakers in the neighbourhood as well as the Indian subcontinent. This liquid sound /ɻ/ occurs intervocalically; as the first element of in some medial consonant clusters and in the word final position (in careful and formal speech and in which there is an alternative with vocalic release) (Asher& Kumari, 1997). However, Mappila Malayalam is the only prominent variety of Malayalam that is marked for the feature of the absence of the phoneme /ɻ/. Various studies on Mappila Malayalam note this feature as one of the identifying characteristics of Mappila Malayalam (Namboothirippadu, 1994; Panikkar, 2017).

One of them is the speakers of Mappila Malayalam replacing the phoneme /ɻ/ with /j/ (voiced palatal approximant) in every occurrence as seen in the following example (1). It shows how Mappila Malayalam is varied from other varieties of Malayalam.

(1)   *Mappila Malayalam*

     a) puɻa   →*puja*   'river'

     b) ʋa:ɻa   →*ʋa:ja*   'plantain'

     c) maɻa   →*maja*   'rain'

Similar feature can be seen in the Arabi-Malayalam tradition. The absence of /ɻ/ in Arabic writing system is approximated with /j/ in Arabi-Malayalam since it uses Arabic script and Malayalam lexical items and structures. Later, this feature extended to the spoken system of Mappila Malayalam under the influence of Arabi-Malayalam. Therefore, the absence of the phoneme /ɻ/ is a feature carried from the Arabi-Malayalam to Mappila Malayalam. This variation created a homonymous condition in some contexts in Mappila Malayalam. For instance, the word *ʋa:ja* means 'mouth' in Malayalam, whereas in Mappila Malayalam, it means both 'plantain' (as seen in example 1b) and 'mouth.' The contextual decoding of the information helps the speakers and listeners in real speech events to make a distinction between the two meanings. This kind of variation in Mappila Malayalam results in the loss of a phoneme in its phonemic inventory when compared with the other dialects of Malayalam and thereby affects the total economy of the phonological system of Mappila Malayalam. /ɻ/ is one of the frequently used phoneme in Malayalam and most of the people who at least have listened to Malayalam recollect the existence of this phoneme. Thus, the absence of /ɻ/ from one of the sociolects of Malayalam is very visible and gains attention among the speech community. Therefore, Mappila Malayalam is characterized by the absence of /ɻ/ even among the common people. Hence, the transition from the status of an indicator to a marker is very spontaneous in the case of this variant in the first wave of variation in Mappila Malayalam.

Another variation in Mappila Malayalam during the first wave is the free variation between the phonemes /ʋ/ (voiced labiodental approximant) and /b/ (voiced bilabial plosive) when /ʋ/ is at the initial position as seen in the following example (2). These phonemes are two distinctive phonemes in Malayalam and can occur at the initial and medial positions, and in medial positions, it can exist as geminated forms. /b/ can also be a part of a consonant cluster while it is following the voiced bilabial nasal /m/ (Asher & Kumari, 1997).

(2)   ***Mappila Malayalam***

   a) vima:nam   *- bima:nam*   'aeroplane'

   b) vannu   *- bannu*   'came'

   c) vi:ɳu   *- bi:ɳu*   'fell'

Contrasting the previously discussed phonological variation, absence of /ɻ/ in Mappila Malayalam, free variation between the phonemes /ʋ/ and /b/ does not create significant change in the total economy of phonemic inventory of Mappila Malayalam. The feature gain seen in *Arabi-Malayalam* in words such as *ʋ:anam* 'sky' changes to *ba:nam* when it comes to *Arabi-Malayalam* and *ʋe:ɖam* 'sacred text' becomes *be:ɖam* (Ilias& Hussain, 2017). Unlike the absence of /ɻ/, the free variation between /ʋ/ and /b/ was identified or recognized by most of the speakers themselves as a variation in their speech. Therefore, as compared to the previous variation, the free variation of /ʋ/ and /b/ was slightly lower in the hierarchy of popularity.

However, both of these phonological variations turn out to be as markers from indicators during the first wave of variations in Mappila Malayalam. Both of the above phonemes under free variation exist in their phonological inventory causing no loss or split of phonemes to the overall phonological system and thereby not affecting the overall stability of the phonological economy. Thus, the absence of the phoneme /ɻ/ gets more significance in terms of attention when compared to the free variation between /ʋ/ and /b/ in Mappila Malayalam. The loss of a phoneme in the system creates more divergence and gains attention than the free variation between two phonemes that does not create a significant change in the phonemic economy the variety. More visible features get stereotyped with a priority by creating a hierarchy among the stereotyping of the variants. The second wave variation was triggered at a point where the markers were redefined as stereotype after the first wave variation.

Morphosyntactic Variations

Morphosyntax is used to capture that morphemes often have sentence level functions. The variations by the interaction of morphology and syntax can be identified as morphosyntactic variations. Such variants have both morphological and syntactic functions in a language. As Kroch (1994) points out, all syntactic variability reflects changes in the properties of vocabulary, including both lexical items and grammatical formatives. Syntactic variation should be governed by the same principles as the variation in morphology since the locus of the variation in the two cases is the same. However, morphosyntactic variations in languages are realized in a way that the speakers and the other speech communities familiar with the variety have very little awareness about it (Fischer, 2007; Kroch, 1994).

This paper takes primarily three variations (present perfective marking, serial verb constructions and semantic selection in locative case marking) from Mappila Malayalam for the analysis. Among these three variations, two of the variants (present perfective marker and serial verb construction) are identified as a marker by the people. The variation in semantic selection in locative case marking is not recognized as markers by the speech community or the immediately surrounded speech communities in any stage of variation in Mappila Malayalam. It is precisely because the variants are not foreign to the existing linguistic system. They have been normalized and submerged due to the familiarity of the forms to the speakers of Malayalam. However, the lack of recognition of a variant as marker does not deny its existence as a variant in the language system. Such a variation is seen in the instance of variation semantic selection in locative case marking in Malayalam and Mappila Malayalam.

Nonetheless, the notion of morphosyntactic variations having less visibility, there are other variations which show an inconsistency in this regard. A variation which obtains a visibility is the present perfect marking in Mappila Malayalam. The perfect aspect in Malayalam is a combination of –ṭṭǝ[3] (postposition to mark

---

[3] The postposition –ṭṭǝ can be seen in the serial verb construction with an emphasis on the sequential order discussed in the following section on variation of serial verb constructions in Mappila Malayalam.

the completion of an event) immediately followed by *uɳɖə*[4] and added to the verb as the suffix as seen in the examples 3 (a) and (b).[5]

(3) (a) *avan* *pi:ɖikajil* *vaɳɳittuɳɖə*

He   shop-LOC   come-PERF-PRES

'He has come to the shop'

  b) *avan* *paḷḷi:l* *vaɳɳittuɳɖə*

He   mosque/church-LOC   come-PERF-PRES

'He has come to the mosque/church'

When most of the dialects in Malayalam has this structure seen in example 3, Mappila Malayalam displays a variation in this kind of constructions marking present perfect. The perfective aspect in Mappila Malayalam is marked with a different form; at the same time, the copular constructions remain the same as *uɳɖə*. This variation makes a definite distinction of structures with *uɳɖə*—copular constructions and structures with present perfective in Mappila Malayalam. Unlike the other dialects of Malayalam, Mappila Malayalam has a structure with the marker –*kkənə* (an assimilated form of the present perfective marker -*ttuɳɖə*) as seen in example (4).

---

[4] *uɳɖə* is also used in copular constructions with adverbial complements. The existential sentences with absolutely clear position are usually produced with the copular form *uɳɖə* (Asher & Kumari, 1997) as seen in the following example. *uɳɖə* is used as the verb for 'exist' or 'be at a place' (i).

ke:raḷattil *te:ŋŋukaḷ* *uɳɖə*

Keralam-LOC   coconut tree-PL   be-PRES

'There are coconut trees in Kerala'

[5] Malayalam has another structure for present perfect with *irikkuɳɳu* as seen in the following example.

avan *paḷḷi:l* *vaɳɳirikkuɳɳu.*

he   mosque/church   come-PERF-PRES

'He has come to the mosque or church'

The marker *irikkuɳɳu* is derived from the word *irikkuka*, a lexical verb occurs with the meaning 'to sit'. However, it also has the status as a 'being' verb (Asher& Kumari, 1997).

(4) o:n   paḷḷikkal   vaṇṇə-kkəṇə
     He   mosque-LOC   come-PERF-PRES
     'He has come to the mosque'

The marker *-kkəṇə* is absolutely a form not used in other dialects of Malayalam. This uniqueness of the form in the phonological appearance gives the variant more attention as compared to the different morphosyntactic variations of Mappila Malayalam. The phonological unfamiliarity of a recurrently used structure provides noticeability to the structure than the other morphosyntactic variants in Mappila Malayalam even though people are not identifying it as a structural variation.

Another variation in Mappila Malayalam is regarding serial verb constructions. Serial verbs in Malayalam are one of the disputable areas in Dravidian linguistics because some of the studies consider them as conjunctive constructions, whereas some others do not (Steever, 1988; Jayaseelan, 2004; Aikhenvald & Dixon, 2006). In Malayalam, the serial verb constructions comprise one finite verb preceded by other verbal participles, which do not distinguish tense. Asher and Kumari (1997) describe these kinds of constructions as verb clusters with adverbial participles conjoined to them, whereas Jayaseelan (2004) accounts them as serial verb constructions and not conjunctive constructions. Jayaseelan refuses the possibility of having these kinds of constructions as conjunctive constructions because of the absence of a conjunctive particle in these constructions (Jayaseelan, 2004). But the literature with various arguments on serial verb constructions in Malayalam agrees to the point that only the last verb is finite and marks for tense (Asher& Kumari, 1997; Jayaseelan, 2004). Consider the following construction in (5) as an example of serial verb construction in Malayalam.

(5) avaḷ   oru   ma:ŋŋa   pariɕɕə   t̪iṉṉu
     she   one   mango   pluck-INF   eat-PST
     'She plucked a mango (and) ate'

The sentence can be added with more verbal phrases as a serial construction as seen in example (6).

(6) avaḷ   oru   ma:ŋŋa   pariɕɕə   kaɻuki   muriɕɕə   t̪iṉṉu
     she   one   mango   pluck   wash   cut   eat-PST
     'She plucked a mango, washed, cut (and) eat'

The tense is marked only on the final verb as seen in the above examples. To denote the other tenses also, the marking alters at the final verb as seen in example 7 (a) and 7 (b).

(7) *(a)* *aʋaɭ   oru   ma:ŋŋa   pariɕɕə   ṯiŋŋum*
       she   one   mango   pluck   eat-FUT
       'She will pluck a mango (and) eat'

  (b) *aʋaɭ   oru   ma:ŋŋa   pariɕɕə   ṯiŋŋuŋŋu*
       she   one   mango   pluck   eat-PRES
       'She plucks a mango (and) eats'

However, Malayalam uses distinctive structures to indicate the order of occurrence of the events in the serial verb constructions. The above denoted instance of example (5) does not have any emphasis on the order of events in the serial verb construction. On the other hand, Malayalam has two variants of serial verb constructions, which emphasize the time reference of the participle forms in a serial verb construction. The first one among these is by suffixing the participle verb with the postposition -*ṭṭə*, a contracted form of *eɲɲiṭṭə*, meaning *something is over* or *after something* to indicate the sequential order of events in a serial verb construction as seen in the example (8).

(8) *(a)* *aʋan   oru   ma:ŋŋa   pariɕɕiṭṭə   ṯiŋŋu*
       he   one   mango   pluck-PP   eat-PST
       'He plucked a mango and ate'

  (b) *aʋan   ɟanal   aɖaɕɕiṭṭə   po:ji*
       he   window   close-PP   go-PST
       'He closed the window and went'

In the above example, 8 (a) indicates that the act of plucking the mango is followed by the act of eating it.[6] Similarly, in the example 8 (b) 'he' went after closing the door.

Another kind of construction, which emphasizes the order of events in serial construction, is to show the simultaneity of the events by adding the postposition -*koɳɖə* to the participle form of the verb. -*koɳɖə* denotes a progressive aspect, and

---

[6]A similar construction is used with more longer serial verb constructions with more number of events. However, it is not likely to add the -*ṭṭə* marking at the end of each verb phrase though it does not seem like an error to the speakers, rather they prefer to add the marker at the second last verb while speaking.

aʋan   oru   pe:rajkka   pariɕɕə   kaɻuki   muriɕɕiṭṭə   ṯiŋŋu
he   one   guava   pluck   wash   cut-PP   eat-PST
'He plucked a guava, washed, cut and eat'

together with the following verb with tense marking in the serial verb construction,[7] it acts as a marker of simultaneity of two events as seen in example (9).

(9) (a) avan   karaɲɲəkonɖə   kuʎiɕɕu
         he   cry- PROG-PP   bath-PST
         'He took bath crying'

    (b) kuʈʈi   karaɲɲəkonɖə   uraŋŋi
         child   cry-INF-PP   sleep-PST
         'The child slept crying'

The events in both the examples given in (9) are simultaneously taking place and marked by the postposition -konɖə in the serial verb construction. Likewise, there are three different ways of representing the serial verbs with different aspectual senses (Asher & Kumari, 1997; Jayaseelan, 2004) in various dialects of Malayalam.

However, the serial verb construction in Mappila Malayalam has only one structure. It is expressed only by suffixing the first infinite verb with the conjunctive marker –um followed by the postposition –ka:nɖə, which is the contracted form of kaɹiɲɲiʈʈə meaning 'having finished' (nominalized verb form indicates an action that is immediately subsequent to another) in the series as seen in (10).

(10) (a) kuʈʈi   karaɲɲumka:nɖə   uraŋŋi
          child   cry-CNJP-PP   sleep-PST
          'Child slept crying'

     (b) kuʈʈi   ma:ŋŋa   pariɕɕumka:nɖə   ʈiɳɳu
          child   mango   pluck-CNJP-PP   eat-PST
          'Child plucked the mango and ate it'

     (c) kuʈʈi   ɟanal   aɖaɕɕumka:nɖə   po:ji
          child   window   close-CNJP-PP   go-PST
          'Child went closing the door'

Mappila Malayalam does not have such variations in the structure of serial verb construction according to the aspect as seen in the above examples (10) in Malayalam. However, the sense is conveyed through the context of the speech. At the same time, the idea that serial verbs in Malayalam having no conjunctive

---

[7] It is also a marker of instrumental case as well as progressive aspect in some other contexts.

Table 8.1 Case markers

Case	Malayalam	Mappila Malayalam
Nominative	Ø	Ø
Accusative	-e	-e
Dative	-kkə/-(n)ə	-kkə/-(nə)kkə
Sociative	-o:ɖə	-o:ɖə
Locative	-il/ -ʈʈil/ ʈʈə/ -kkal/-inme:l	-il/ -ʈʈə/ -kkal/-mmal
Instrumental	-a:l/ koṇɖə/ ACC koṇɖə	-jo:nɖə/ACC koṇɖə
Genitive	-uɖe/ -nte	-nte/ -uɖe

marker is under question in the case of Mappila Malayalam since it has the conjunctive marker *–um* in the serial verb structure. *–um* can be observed as a conjunctive marker in Malayalam where the constituents within sentences and clauses coordinated if they belong the same category such as two or more nouns in the same case, or two or more adverbs. Moreover, the sentence structures using the verb *ɕejjuka* 'do' also allow to produce sentences to be conjoined using the suffix *–um* (Asher & Kumari, 1997).

However, *–um* as an unavoidable element that acts as a conjunction in the serial verb construction is unique to Mappila Malayalam. The conjunctive marker *–um* could be seen in some of the instances from Arabi-Malayalam literature, and the feature must have been carried to the speech of Mappila Malayalam during the first wave variation. Although the variation of serial verb construction is primarily lacking the capacity of marking the order of events in the construction, the speakers or the other dialect speakers of the variety do not identify this aspect as a marker of Mappila Malayalam. Similarly, there is not much attention given about the inclusion of conjunctive marker *–um* in the construction of Mappila Malayalam. Instead, people notice the variation only as phonological variation, a difference from the existing form and the variation serial verb constructions in Mappila Malayalam become a marker at this juncture. The variation of case marking in Mappila Malayalam also shows a spectrum of deviations in many aspects as provided in Table 8.1.

Apart from these, there are various realizations that show a deviation in Mappila Malayalam from the case marking of Malayalam. In this paper, we discuss the variation in the locative case marking through semantic selection[8] in Mappila Malayalam. Malayalam has a specific set of locative case markers with specific senses attached to them. The generic form of locative case marker in Malayalam is the suffix *-il*. It gives the sense of containment most of the time and also gives a sense of 'among.' *-kkal* is another locative marker for locations with proximity. Since *-kkal* lacks the sense of containment, it is considered different

---

[8] The semantics/meaning of the word selects which marker should be taken among different markers to convey the intended sense.

from *-il*. One of the variations regarding the locative case marking in Mappila Malayalam lies in the marking of *–il* where it replaces *-il* with *–kkal* in some of the semantic contexts. The prominently observed instance among them is the word *paḷḷi*, which used to represent both church and mosque in Malayalam. When referring to the mosque, a Mappila Malayalam speaker uses *–kkal* instead of the case marker *–il*, as seen in the following example (11).

(11) *avan*   *paḷḷikkal / *paḷḷijil*   *pɔːji*

      he   mosque-LOC   go-PST

      'He went to the mosque'

Conversely, Mappila Malayalam speakers use *–il* as the locative marker in contexts where they talk specifically about a church, for example:

(12) *avan*   *paḷḷijil/*paḷḷikkal*   *pɔːji*

      he   church-LOC   go-PST

      'He went to the church'

However, other dialects of Malayalam do not have a similar kind of semantic selection in locative case marking as seen in Mappila Malayalam. Instead, they use *–il* as the locative case marker in the above-mentioned contexts, for both mosque and church and certainly not use *-kkal* as the locative marker as seen in the following example (13).

(13) *avan*   *paḷḷijil*   *pɔːji*

      he   mosque/church-LOC   go-PST

      'He went to the mosque/church'

Hence, the semantic selection of locative case marker in the case of *paḷḷi* in Mappila Malayalam does not exist in other dialects of Malayalam. This variation by making a distinction between the mosque and the church could possibly be an attempt to create a different identity associated with their religious symbols. This variation is neither identified as a marker by the speech communities in the encircled areas nor by the Mappila Malayalam speakers themselves. This is due to the familiarity of the suffixes *–il* and *–kkal* as the locative case markers in Malayalam. However, the structural pattern makes the variation significant while analysing the variations of Mappila Malayalam.

Morphosyntactic variations have lesser visibility as markers when compared with the phonological variations. However, the variation such as in present perfect marking and serial verb constructions gains more visibility than the other morphosyntactic variations such as semantic selection in locative case marking. It is due to the unfamiliarity of forms based on the divergence from the existing forms (predominantly in phonological forms) in Malayalam. Such a phenomenon leads the variants to become a marker of Mappila Malayalam from the first wave variation. As the visibility and popularity of markers of a speech variety intensify, the likelihoods to become a stereotype by indexing them to the community also rise. Some of the markers of Mappila Malayalam discussed above have undergone similar kind of variation over a period. These variations originated at the first wave variation of Mappila Malayalam as a part of creating distinct identity during the spread of the Mappila religion in the Malabar region. The influence of Arabi-Malayalam in the speech is a remarkable feature that supplemented the first wave variations. It helped to create a uniqueness to Mappila Malayalam as compared to the other dialects of Malayalam also. The markers as becoming noticeable and gain visibility tend to become stereotypes. The process of stereotyping after the visibility of these markers has become an external factor for further variation in Mappila Malayalam along with the internal factors in the community in a changed sociopolitical scenario. These triggered the process of second wave variation in Mappila Malayalam. The second wave variation in Mappila Malayalam is a result of joined variations inducted by the internal and external factors and restructured linguistic attitude.

Second Wave Variation of Mappila Malayalam

Second wave variation in Mappila Malayalam gains importance in modern variation linguistics as it is an observable variation currently in progress. The analysis of variations in progress provides the subtle movements, and the direction of variation and ultimately leads towards understanding the hierarchy and priority of existing variants, and its characteristics under the process of variation. The variants obtained more visibility have become stereotypes in a later stage and eventually initiated the second wave variation in Mappila Malayalam. The second wave variation occurring at present in Mappila Malayalam is an outcome of concurrent action of internal and external factors coextending with Mappila Malayalam tradition. The stereotyping of the markers beside created a denounced public notion that the markers of Mappila Malayalam are from the non-educated and less prestigious variety. The history of Mappila community indications is that, during its earlier days, Mappila community members did not give importance to the public modern education system. Instead, the emphasis is given to madrasa education (Abraham, 2014; Ali, 1990; Engineer, 1995; Mohammed, 2007). This scenario ultimately resulted in associating their speech as the non-educated variety by the mainstream society.

However, after the reformation movement in the community, the attitude towards modern public education had changed (Abraham, 2014) and also a change in linguistic attitude developed as a part of stereotyping within the speech community also. During the current study, the younger generations of Mappila Malayalam speakers themselves expressed the concern about some of the markers as less prestigious. That is, Mappila Malayalam speakers themselves started identifying some of their linguistic forms as less prestigious. The external factor of social pressure along with the internal factor of consciousness among the speech community based on the changing linguistic attitudes elicited the second wave variation in Mappila Malayalam in which most of the variants in the first wave are undergoing the process of dialect levelling through a conscious effort by the speakers of Mappila Malayalam. The paper looks at the process of variation at this juncture as part of the second wave variation in Mappila Malayalam to generate an idea about a cohesive pattern of language variation as a process.

Analysis

Figure 8.2 shows the pattern of second wave variation in Mappila Malayalam by plotting various age groups of the Mappila Malayalam speakers on the x-axis and the percentage of using non-variants (i.e. variant markers of the first wave variation) in their speech on the y-axis. Different patterned designs on the chart depict phonological and morphosyntactic variations in casual and careful speech contexts.

When we look at the casual speech patterns of the speakers, the older generations of the age group 51–60 and above recurrently use the variant markers of the first wave in their speech, whereas the younger generations incline towards dialect levelling. An analogous pattern is existing in the careful speech also. However, the age group using the variant markers of first wave variation moved to 61–70 and above. Thus, 61–70 and 70 above age groups do not show substantial fluctuations in the variants while comparing the casual and careful speech, whereas the age group 51–60 shows a significant shift in the careful speech denoting that they tend to move towards dialect levelling, but not in the casual speech. The younger generation of the age group 21–30 and below showed a stable output without many instabilities according to the context. The rest of the age groups are in a transition process. Thus, the variation is found to be progressive over time and realized through different generations. The linguistic attitudes of the speakers imply that the initiating force of a conscious effort for dialect levelling in the second wave variation of Mappila Malayalam is the process of markers becoming stereotypes.

Analysis of the variations during the second wave—it has been perceived that the more visible variants such as the absence of the phoneme /ɻ/ at the phonological level, the present perfective marking with –kkəɳə at the morphosyntactic level attained more visibility and prominence in the development process to become a stereotype owing to the unfamiliarity and deviation of form (predominantly phonological) from the existing linguistic forms in Malayalam. Hence, dialect levelling caused in the inclusion the phoneme /ɻ/ and marking the present perfective by –ʈʈuɳɖə in their speech got prioritized when compared to the other variations. Likewise, the phonological variations are more visible while compared with the morphosyntactic variations, and eventually the stereotyping focused on phonological variations rather than morphosyntactic variations. Dialect levelling in the second wave also followed the same pattern. The tendency of dialect levelling is further extended to the other markers of Mappila Malayalam over a period in a discernible fashion when we analyse the speech patterns of various age groups in different contexts. The variations in different contexts of communication display that speakers make a conscious effort for dialect levelling. This echoes the change in linguistic attitudes of the speakers when moving from the first wave to the second wave, tendency to move from difference to unity in terms of language due to the sociopolitical changes.

Towards an Understanding of the Hierarchy and Levels of Variations

The two phases of variation in Mappila Malayalam denoted as the first and second wave variations, respectively, suggest a hierarchical order of variation with multiple layers intertwined within the process. The hierarchy of variation is based on various factors influencing and complementing each other. They are the following:

i.   Level of linguistic expression that the variant belongs to (phonological, morphological, morphosyntactic, lexical and so on)
ii. Visibility of the variant

   a. Degree of the unfamiliarity of the variant form
   b. Frequency of the variant structure

iii. The transition of variants: indicators–markers–stereotype

   a. Internal factors
   b. External factors.

The level of linguistic expression of the variant is essential in the variation process. The variations gain more visibility in levels such as phonology and lexical as the ordinary people easily identify the variations among these levels. However, the analysis of variation of Mappila Malayalam shows that there is a hierarchy existing within each level as well. When compared with the phonological and morphosyntactic variations of the two waves of Mappila Malayalam variations, phonological variations show a higher tendency of dialect levelling than the morphosyntactic variations in the second wave variation. The phonological variations get noticed by the people, and this attention drives the variants to the transition from indicators to markers and then to stereotypes. Among the phonological variants also, there is a hierarchy in play. The frequent variant and also the one which creates a change in the economy of the language system by affecting the phonemic inventory as in the case of absence of /ɻ/ dominating the free variation between /v/ and /b/ in Mappila Malayalam gets higher position in the hierarchy of further variations due to its visibility. The traditional notion that language gets visibility to the speakers from the level of lexis has been relooked here and observed to have substantial occurrences of visibility in terms of phonemes also.

Among the morphosyntactic variations also, there is a hierarchy in further variations. The present perfect marker gains the most higher position in the order followed by the serial verb construction and finally the semantic selection in locative case marking among the variations considered in the current analysis. This scenario also depended on the familiarity of forms and frequency of structures. As a variant gains more visibility based on the features mentioned in ii(a) and ii(b), it is placed at the initial position in the hierarchy of the transition process from indicators to markers and then to a stereotype. Both internal and external factors influence the process. Internal factors mentioned here are the force for variation initiated within the speech community due to the process of variants becoming stereotypes, and external factors are the influence from the society outside the speech community by the process of stereotyping a variant itself and also the sociopolitical changes. Likewise, the analysis of variations in Mappila Malayalam provides with a hierarchical order of variations in languages by reiterating the influence of both linguistic and extralinguistic factors connected to each other and thereby involved in the process of variation.

Conclusion

The variation patterns of Mappila Malayalam show a multi-layered hierarchy of variation as a collective effect of various factors. The analysis of variation based on the Labovian framework suggests a progression of the variant from an indicator to a marker and then to a stereotype has significant implications on variations as it has the power to impart further variations in languages. The evaluation further illustrates that the stereotypes progress to further variations in simultaneously with the internal and external factors affecting the language, including the change in linguistic attitudes due to sociopolitical changes. The more divergent the variant from the existing form, the more enhanced the pace of the variation process is. Among the internally or externally driven variations, the most visible ones are the phonological and lexical variations, and it is not prospective for these variants to be a stable variant. The phonological and lexical variants have a high chance of becoming a marker and ultimately a stereotype when compared to the morphosyntactic variants (also, variants at other levels of linguistic expression). And within each level, there is a hierarchy existing in the process of further variation. The reaction to the transformation of markers to stereotypes initiates further variations. The analysis shows that the most dominant variation in the second wave variation is phonological. The combination of the line between markers and stereotypes, social factors and the linguistic attitudes of the speakers opts the developments and presence of transformations within any language. Variations in languages as a process can be analysed and described based on its hierarchical implications for deeper understandings and descriptions of languages. Likewise, studies of similar kind and generalizations would contribute to further analysis that led to an appropriate description of language as a dynamic system by organizing different aspects of variation starting from the wave nature and directionality of variation and how it is contributing the hierarchy of variations to develop a cohesive description of variation in languages.

References

Abraham, J. (2014). *Islamic reform and colonial discourse on modernity in India: Socio-political and religious thought of Vakkom Moulavi*. Palgrave Macmillan.

Aikhenvald, A. Y., & Dixon, R. M. W. (2006). *Serial verb constructions: A cross-linguistic typology* (Vol. 2). Oxford University Press.

Ali, K. M. (1990). *The development of education among the Mappilas of Malabar, 1800 to 1965*. Nunes Publishers.

Asher, R. E., & Kumari, T. C. (1997). *Malayalam*. Routledge.

Bailey, C. J. N. (1973). *Variation and linguistic theory*. Arlington: Centre for Applied Linguistics.

Devy, G. N. (2015). *People's linguistic survey of India volume fifteen: The languages of kerala and lakshadweep*. New Delhi, India: Orient Blackswan.

Eckert, P. (2012). Three waves of variation study: The emergence of meaning in the study of sociolinguistic variation. *Annual Review of Anthropology, 41*, 87–100.

Engineer, A. (1995). *Kerala muslims: A historical perspective*. Ajanta Publications.

Fasold, R. W. (1984). *The sociolinguistics of society*. Basil Blackwell.

Field, M. (2012). Kumeyaay language variation, group identity, and the land. *International Journal of American Linguistics, 78*(4), 557–573.

Fischer, J. L. (1964). Social influence in the choice of a linguistic variant. In D. Hymes (Ed.), *Language in Culture and Society* (pp. 483–488). Harper & Row.

Fischer, O. (2007). *Morphosyntactic change: Functional and formal perspectives* (Vol. 2). Oxford University Press on Demand.

Girish, P. M. (2015). *Adhikaaravum Bhashayum* (Malayalam). Calicut, Kerala: Eye Books Kerala.

Hardgrave, R. L., Jr. (1964). Caste in Kerala: A preface to the elections. *Economic and Political Weekly, 16*(47), 1841–1847.

Hussain, S. K. T. (2005). Malabar kalapathinte vaamozhiparambaryam (Oral traditions of Malabar rebellion), (Doctoral thesis, Department of Malayalam, Sree Sankaracharya University of Sanskrit, Kalady, India).

Hymes, D. (1964). *Language in culture and society: A reader in linguistics and anthropology*. Harper & Row.

Ilias, M. H., & Hussain, S. K. T. (2017). *Arabi-Malayalam: Linguistic and cultural traditions of Mappila Muslims of Kerala*. Gyan Publishing House.

Jayaraj, T., & Kumar, R. (2020). Variation of lexical items and the changing need of identity projection: a study on Mappila Malayalam. *Dialectologia: revista electrònica, 157*–176.

Jayaseelan, K. A. (2004). The serial verb construction in Malayalam. In A. Mahajan & V. Dayal (Eds.), *Clause structure in South Asian languages* (pp. 67–91). Springer.

Joseph, P. M. (2015). *Malayalathile Parakeeya Padangal* (Malayalam). Thiruvananthapuram: Kerala Bhasha Institute.

Karassery, M. N. (1995). Arabi-Malayalam. In Asghar Ali Engineer (Ed.), *Kerala Muslims: A historical perspective*. New Delhi: Ajanta Publishers.

Kroch, A. (1994). Morphosyntactic variation. In *Papers from the 30th regional meeting of the Chicago Linguistics Society: Parasession on variation and linguistic theory* (Vol. 2, pp. 180–201). Chicago, IL: Chicago Linguistic Society.

Kroch, A. S. (1978). Toward a theory of social dialect variation. *Language in Society, 7*(1), 17–36.

Labov, W. (1966). *The social stratification of english in New York city.* Center for Applied Linguistics.

Labov, W. (1972). *Sociolinguistic patterns.* University of Pennsylvania Press.

Labov, W. (2001). *Principles of linguistic change. Volume 2: Social factors.* Malden, MA: Wiley-Blackwell.

Labov, W. (2007). Transmission and diffusion. *Language, 83*(2), 344–387.

Labov, W. (2010). *Principles of linguistic change.* (Vol. 3): *Cognitive factors.* Oxford, UK: Blackwell.

Labov, W., Yaeger, M., & Steiner, R. (1972). *A quantitative study of sound change in progress (Vol. 1).* US Regional Survey.

Le Page, R. B. (1998). The evolution of a sociolinguistic theory of language. In F. Coulmas (Ed.), *The handbook of sociolinguistics* (pp. 13–32). Blackwell.

Menon, T. M. (2002). *A Handbook of Kerala.* (Vol. 2). Trivandrum: International School of Dravidian Linguistics.

Mohammed, U. (2007). *Educational empowerment of Kerala Muslims: A socio-historical perspective.* Other Books.

Nair, A. K. K. R. (1986). *Gazetteer of India- Kerala- Malappuram.* Government Press.

Namboothiripadu, U. (1994). *Saamoohika bhasha vijnanam* (Malayalam). Thiruvananthapuram: Kerala Bhasha Institute.

Omoniyi, T. (2006). Societal multilingualism and multifaithism. In T. Omoniyi & J. A. Fishman (Eds.), *Explorations in the Sociology of Language and Religion* (pp. 121–140). John Benjamins Publishing Company.

Pandharipande, R. V. (2006). Ideology, authority, and language choice. In T. Omoniyi & J. A. Fishman (Eds.), *Explorations in the Sociology of Language and Religion* (pp. 141–164). John Benjamins Publishing.

Panikkar, G. K. (2017). *Mappila Dialect of Malabar.* Thiruvananthapuram: International School of Dravidian Linguistics.

Panikkar, K. N. (1989). *Against lord and state: Religion and peasant uprisings in Malabar, 1836–1921.* Oxford University Press.

Saidalavi, C. (2013). *A sociolinguistic evaluation of Arabi Malayalam* (Unpublished Doctoral Thesis). Department of Studies in Linguistics, University of Mysore, Mysore, India.

Steever, S. B. (1988). *The serial verb formation in the dravidian languages* (Vol. 4). Motilal Banarsidass Publications.

Subramoniam, V. I. (1974). *Dialect Survey of Malayalam (Ezhava-Tiiya).* Department of Linguistics, University of Kerala.

Thapasya Jayaraj is currently Assistant Professor in the Indian Institute of Technology Indore. She completed her doctoral degree from the Department of Humanities and Social Sciences, Indian Institute of Technology Madras in 2020. Her dissertation was on 'Dynamics of Malabar Mappila Malayalam and Projecting Identity: A Sociolinguistic Analysis'. She did her Masters in Applied Linguistics from the Centre for Applied Linguistics and Translation Studies, University of Hyderabad in 2015. She has formerly completed her Bachelors in Functional English from University of Calicut in 2013 with first position in the university. Her areas of research interest inclined towards sociolinguistic perspectives of language variation and identity.

Chapter 9
Variation and Change in Dialects of Marathi: A Social-Dialectological Approach

Sonal Kulkarni-Joshi

Abstract This paper provides a social-dialectological slant on variation and change in language. The particular analytical framework used here brings together language synchrony and diachrony for examining dialect change in the Marathi region. First a brief overview of the central theoretical and methodological tenets of this approach to variation and change in language is presented. Drawing on data collected in an on-going dialectological survey of Marathi, the paper provides a description of synchronic variation in case marking and agreement in the transitive-perfective clause in regional varieties of Marathi. It is suggested that the variation is the result of both language-internal and language-external factors. The contemporary dialectal data are compared with data from historical sources (Grierson, G. (1905). Linguistic Survey of India. Vol. 7. Indo-Aran family. Southern group. Specimens of the Marathi Language. Calcutta. Reprinted 1968. Delhi: Motilal Banarsidass.). An expansion in the pool of linguistic feature variants and a broad tendency towards dialect levelling (i.e. reduction in inter-dialectal differences) through standardization are noted for the regional varieties. However, the rates of standardization across linguistic features and across social groups and regions are shown to vary. The paper concludes by highlighting the benefits of a dialect survey/database for examining language variation and change.

Keywords Dialectology · Social dialectology · Variationism · Dialect change · Standardization · Marathi

S. Kulkarni-Joshi (✉)
Deccan College, Pune, Maharashtra, India
e-mail: sonal.kulkarni@dcpune.ac.in

© The Author(s), under exclusive license to Springer Nature Singapore Pte Ltd. 2023   207
P. Chandra (ed.), *Variation in South Asian Languages*,
https://doi.org/10.1007/978-981-99-1149-3_9

Introduction

The study of variation in language is at the heart of the linguistic enterprise named *social dialectology*. Variation in pronunciation or in the use of grammatical features is understood in terms of the social structure (measured in terms of age, social class, caste, etc.) of the community of speakers. Change in language too is correlated with sociological attributes of the community, e.g. change in social networks, social mobility and so on. Social dialectology differs from traditional dialectology in shifting the focus from invariant, archaic, rural forms of language used by settled communities to incorporating variationist/sociolinguistic methods of sampling as well as the quantitative methods of analysis based on data from large corpora (e.g. Siewierska & Bakker, 2006).

Dialectology, a precursor of sociolinguistics, examines divergence of two local dialects[1] from a common ancestor and synchronic variation in the regional varieties. Sociolinguists, on the other hand, are interested in the full range of forms in a community (and their social evaluation). Sociolinguists use information about social structure, people movements, extralinguistic situation, contextual factors and social evaluation of structural options in explaining mechanisms of language change/evolution. Modern social dialectology integrates a discussion of these social factors as also historical facts in the interpretation of dialectal variation and change. It not only identifies the areal distribution of particular linguistic features but also takes interest in the effect of mobility and contact with speakers on the speech variety/varieties of a region. The sociolinguistic nature of language variation, the processes of language change, the effect of standard varieties and of standardization, dialect contact and dialect formation are some of the issues examined by a social dialectologist.

Social dialectologists believe that languages are inherently variable. Such variation is not 'free' but is 'structured heterogeneity' (Weinreich et al., 1968:188). Further, language evolution is variational (like biological evolution), proceeding by competition and selection among competing linguistic alternatives: A and B (and C), with A or B (or C, or A and C, or B and C) prevailing because they were favoured by particular ecological factors (Mufwene, 2001). The research agenda for studies of dialect/language variation and change was charted by Weinreich et al. (1968) in their seminal paper, 'Empirical Foundations for a Theory of Language Change.' This agenda can be summarized in the form of five 'problems' or aspects of language change (also see Walkden 2017):

---

[1] 'Dialect' here refers to a language variety which is used in a geographically limited part of a language area in which it is 'roofed' by a structurally related standard variety; a dialect typically displays structural peculiarities in several language components (cf. Chambers & Trudgill, 1998: 5; Auer et al. (2005)). Usually dialects have relatively little overt prestige and are mainly used orally.

(i) The constraints problem: This involves formulating 'constraints on the transition from one state of a language to an immediately succeeding state' (Weinreich et al., 1968:100).

(ii) The transition problem: This is the question of what intervening stages can (or must) be posited between any two forms of a language separated by time. (Weinreich et al., 1968:184).

(iii) The actuation problem: Here, the interest is in understanding why the change was not actuated sooner, or why it was not simultaneously activated wherever identical functional conditions prevailed. This is paraphrased by Walkden in the Handbook of Historical Syntax as follows: 'What factors can account for the actuation of changes? Why do changes in a structural feature take place in a particular language at a particular time, but not in other languages with the same feature, or in the same language at other times?'

(iv) The embedding problem: 'How are the observed changes embedded in the matrix of linguistic and extralinguistic concomitants of the forms in question? (That is, what other changes are associated with the given changes in a manner that cannot be attributed to chance?)' (Weinreich et al., 1968:185).

(v) The evaluation problem: How do members of the speech community evaluate the change in progress?

Of the five, Weinreich et al. recognized the actuation problem, 'why did a particular change occur at a particular place at a particular time' to be at the heart of a theory of language change.

Social Dialectology/Sociolinguistics

An exploration of constraints on the diffusion of dialectal features/linguistic innovations has engaged social dialectologists. Theories of language change differ in that they deal either with language-internal factors (e.g. language acquisition, cognition, language use) or with language-external factors, which concern population dynamics (e.g. migration/population movements, contact, network ties, imperfect learning). The latter are examined by social dialectologists (i.e. sociolinguists). The sociolinguistic approach to language variation and change (which developed largely from the pioneering work of William Labov) includes consideration of both linguistic constraints (e.g. the conditioning environment) as well as sociological and contextual constraints (e.g. speaker's age, sex, education, formality, etc.).

Sociolinguistic sampling methods are used to examine both urban and rural dialects; data are collected from a wide spread of speakers in the local speech community, including speakers who are mobile and have come in contact with other regional speech varieties. Speakers belonging to diverse age-groups, educational and professional backgrounds and both sexes are sampled. (For an overview of applications of this method see Trudgill et al., 2003.) The particular methodology helps to examine the mechanisms of diffusion of language/dialect change which can then be modelled (e.g. the cascade model or the gravity model, Trudgill et al., 2003; reviewed by Labov, 2003).

Besides addressing traditional areas of sociolinguistic variation and change, social dialectology is also concerned with newer areas of research such as dialect formation, dialect diffusion and dialect levelling. Language change is the diffusion of change (Labov, 2003:9); an understanding of language change therefore necessitates an understanding of the mechanisms of diffusion. The mechanisms by which language change is effected encompass dialect levelling, dialect mixture, koineization, accommodation, supralocalization, dedialectalization, etc. (see Auer et al., 2005:2). Dialect contact can result in the reduction of variation within and between dialects thereby making the diasystems more homogenous (i.e. dialect convergence); alternatively, dialect contact can result in linguistic diversification, growing diffuseness and heterogenization (i.e. dialect divergence). As observed by Hinskens (2021), the object of dialectology is changing rapidly in the Old World, giving rise to the erosion of traditional dialect landscapes and the emergence of supra-local koinai as well as dialect/standard continua. Such dialect-standard continua among contemporary Indic languages have rarely received close examination.

Social dialectology has developed methodological offshoots. Socio-historical linguistics uses the quantitative, variationist methods of sociolinguistics to examine diachronic development of social/regional dialects. A central assumption of the approach is that the linguistic forces which operate today are not unlike those of the past (Romaine, 1982), i.e. there is no reason for assuming that language did not vary in the same patterned way in the past as it does today (cf. the uniformitarian principle). Current variation and its correlation with social structure and patterns of human interaction may be used in constructing a social model. The approach helps the researcher to investigate whether and to what extent synchronic variation in contemporary regional varieties of a language reflects diachronic developments. (See Romaine, 1982 for a case study of syntactic variation in Scots English using the socio-historical approach. Also see Kulkarni-Joshi and Kelkar (2020) for a discussion using Marathi data.) Methods such as age-grading or apparent time are employed in making use of synchronic data to reconstruct language change within a speech community (see, e.g. Sankoff, 2006). However, the social–historical method has inherent limitations. Reconstruction of diachronic changes in language using synchronic data within the socio-historical approach relies significantly on having access to comparable data from different points in time. Typically, these are written texts. Very often the varying genres of the available texts make it difficult to compare and draw reliable inferences about language change. At times it is the formal nature of written language which renders texts a less than satisfactory source of information.

Probably a special case of socio-historical linguistics is Trudgill's (2002, 2011, 2020) approach which is named 'sociolinguistic typology.' He suggests interdependence between linguistic structural simplification or complexification on the one hand and prehistoric population movements and language contact on the other (e.g. see Peterson, 2022 for application of this approach to two Indic languages, Konkani and Sadri).

Dialectology has forged interfaces with subdisciplines other than sociolinguistics too. In recent times, there has been a growing realization of the need for collaboration among syntacticians and typologists on the one hand (who deal with cross-linguistic data drawn from standard varieties; e.g. data presented in the *World Atlas of Language Structures* see www.wals.info) and dialectologists/sociolinguists (who deal with non-standard, spoken varieties; e.g. *Linguistic Survey of India* https://dsal.uchicago.edu/books/lsi/, Survey of Dialects of the Marathi Language www.sdml.ac.in and Romani Project https://romani.humanities.manchester. ac.uk//, https://www.dialectsarchive.com/InternationalDialectsofEnglishArchive). Subdisciplines such as syntax and typology are now turning attention to variation in language. Dialectology is seen as complementing the typological interest in cross-linguistic variation by making available a larger number of attested grammatical systems. A further advantage is seen in the dialects as non-standardized grammatical systems (unlike the languages that typology generally deals with). The advantage is that dialectal data gives typologists and syntacticians a larger number of attested grammatical systems to explain within their theoretical frameworks. Dialectology (whether regional or social) has focused attention on non-standard speech varieties; typological linguistics and syntax, on the other hand, have tended to focus attention on standard languages. We are witnessing today a cross-fertilization of methods from subdisciplines of linguistics—dialectology, historical linguistics, typology and contact linguistics—in mutually beneficial ways (e.g. Bisang, 2004; Chamoreau & Léglise, 2012). This development has led to fresh opportunities for explaining language change using dialectological data. Studies of dialect/ language change too are exploring explanatory connections between linguistic variation, language acquisition, language use and the grammatical organization of language (cf. Kiparsky, 2008).

However, the role of dialectology is often that of a hand-maiden (one which provides rich dialectal data) just as it was in the nineteenth century for historical linguistics. A truly fruitful integrated approach to language variation and change must accommodate the goals of dialectology. Having identified the areal spread of a given structural feature, social dialectologists seek answers to questions such as the following:

i.   How did a particular regional variety come to have the linguistic features that it has?
ii. Do the optional structures x and y co-exist in an idiolect/dialect or is only one of the structures possible in an idiolect? (i.e. is the variation inter-speaker or intra-speaker?)
iii. Are there systematic linguistic and social contexts in which either option/variant is preferred by the speaker?

The remaining sections of the paper are organized as follows. Section "Regional Variation in Marathi" presents an overview of regional variation in the Marathi-speaking region. Fresh dialectal data from regional varieties of Marathi is presented and compared with specimens from the *Linguistic Survey of India* (1905) in Sect. "The Ergative Construction in Marathi". Section "Intra-Dialectal Variation in the Transitive-Perfective Clause" picks up a discussion on mechanisms and motivations underlying language/dialect change. Optionality in regional, social as well as in idiolectal usage is described within the framework of social dialectology. Some interim conclusions and suggestions for future research are presented in the final Sect. "Sources and Pathways of Asymmetry in the Ergative Construction in Dialectal Marathi: Motivations for Change".

Regional Variation in Marathi

The Marathi-speaking region (i.e. the modern state of Maharashtra) is flanked by at least five other language regions: Gujarati-speaking regions to the northwest, Hindi-speaking in Madhya Pradesh and Chattisgarh to the north and northeast, Telugu and Kannada-speaking areas to the south-east and the south and the Konkani-speaking region to the south-west. Of these Gujarati, Hindi and Konkani are classified as New Indo-Aryan (NIA) languages along with Marathi while Telugu and Kannada are Dravidian languages. Each of these languages is the state official language of a modern state in India. Geographically, linguistically and culturally the Marathi-speaking region occupies a vantage position: it is transient between the Indo-Aryan north and the Dravidian south. This position of Maharashtra/Marathi is significant in order to understand the dialectal variation in Marathi too. Influence of neighbouring languages on regional linguistic practices is evident in one of at least two forms: either in the form of widespread local bilingualism as is seen in the case of the urban Vidarbh/Nagpur region (bilingualism in Hindi in north-east Maharashtra); or the influence is seen in the grammatical system of the local variety as is seen in the southern and south-eastern tehsils (villages in these tehsils are inhabited by speakers of Kannada or Telugu in addition to those of Marathi). In addition to these major literary languages, the Marathi-speaking region has historically been inhabited by a number of 'smaller' languages including Bhili in Khandesh, Gondi and Kolami in Vidarbha, Korku in Marathwada, etc. This geographical distribution of languages is criss-crossed by sociological factors such as religion (e.g. Hindu-Muslim in Ratnagiri; Hindu-Muslim-Christian in Sindhudurg; Hindu-Christian in Palghar), sect (e.g. Lingayat–non-Lingayat in southern Maharashtra), tribal–non-tribal (e.g. Bhil and others in Nandurbar; Katkari/Agri/Warli and others in Thane-Palghar), migrant–non-migrant (Telugu speaking Padmashalis and others in Solapur) as well as education, age, occupation, etc., creating a complex mosaic of linguistic varieties.

Traditionally, the following six dialects have been identified for Marathi: Deshi, Khandeshi, Nagpuri, Varhadi (Vidarbh region), Konkan-Deshi and Konkani (e.g. Pandharipande, 1997; Kalelkar, 1960). Of these, the standard dialect is a historical development of the speech variety of the educated Brahmins in Pune (Poona). Grierson (1905) recognized Konkani to be the only true dialect of Marathi; he also noted that there were transient varieties of Marathi at the Dravidian border which he refers to as 'broken dialects' of Marathi. Ahirani/Khandeshi spoken to the north-west of Maharashtra today is a transient speech variety between Gujarati/Bhili and Marathi. Ahirani (Khandeshi) is not classified as a dialect of Marathi by Grierson, but as belonging to the central NIA group along with Bhili, Banjārī or Labhānī, Bahrūpiā, etc.

The dialect regions: Dhule, Nagpur, (Gadahinglaj) Kolhapur and Malwan

A note must be added about the four peripheries of the contiguous Marathi-speaking region today which will be referred to in 4.1 below.

(i)   Dhule-Nandurbar (no. 6 in Fig. 9.1) region is flanked by the Hindi-speaking state of Madhya Pradesh and the Gujarati-speaking state of Gujarat. This region is the heartland of Ahirani (Khandeshi), a New Indo-Aryan (NIA) speech variety which has variously been classified as a dialect of Marathi/dialect of Gujarati/a speech variety intermediate between Marathi and Gujarati. In colonial India, this region was included in the Bombay Presidency. The Dhule-Nandurbar region is predominantly inhabited by tribals who speak a variety of Bhil speech varieties. Ahirani, the home variety of the non-tribals in the region, is an important lingua franca for all rural communities in the region. Marathi is almost exclusively the language of school education in the region and is used as a contact language in urban centres such as Taloda, Nandurbar and in Dhule. Local communities have both familial and market ties in neighbouring villages and towns in the two adjacent states.

(ii) Nagpur region (nos. 26–30 in Fig. 9.1) marks the north-eastern periphery of Maharashtra and is adjacent to the Hindi-speaking state of Madhya Pradesh. In colonial India, Nagpur was the capital of the British colonial province of Central Province and Berar. Today the region is a part of the Marathi-speaking state of Maharashtra. However, bilingualism in Hindi is widespread in the region, especially in the urban centres. The local variety of Hindi is the Bundeli dialect of western Hindi and Chattisgarhi which are considerably influenced by Marathi grammatical structure. The Gonds (speakers of Dravidian Gondi) also have a considerable presence in the region. Both Marathi and Hind are used as contact languages in the region. Social and economic ties of the local communities are strong within the Nagpur region and in neighbouring Madhya Pradesh.

(iii) Sindhudurg (no. 5 in Fig. 9.1) on the western coast of India is the southern-most district of Maharashtra neighbouring the Konkani-speaking state of Goa. The local speech variety (referred to as Malwani) has affinity with both Goan Konkani and Marathi (Satam, 2020). Schooling in rural Sindhudurg is almost exclusively in Marathi; however, Malwani is the primary linguistic means of daily interaction; it is an important index of local identity. Locals regularly travel to neighbouring villages and towns in Goa for employment and to the neighbouring district of Kolhapur for higher education. The discussion of dialect change in this chapter relies on a comparison with Grierson's LSI data. The Konkan speech varieties closest to Sindhudurg which are sampled in the LSI include Sangameshwari (LSI 1905: 122)

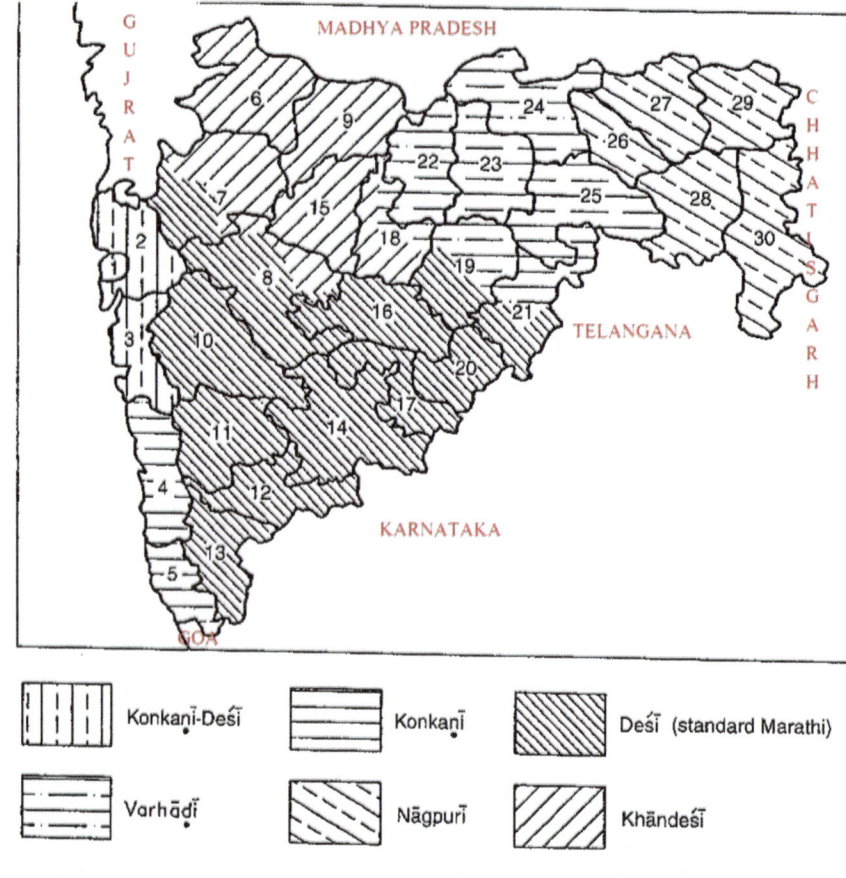

Fig. 9.1 Dialect regions of Marathi (based on Pandharipande, 1997:xxxiv)

and Bankoti (p. 128); both Sangameshwar and Bankot are in southern
Ratnagiri district (no. 4 in Fig. 9.1). (Sindhudurg district was carved out
of Ratnagiri district in 1981.) Hence, SDML data for both Sindhudurg and
Sangameshwar are discussed in this chapter.

(iv) Kolhapur district (no. 13 in Fig. 9.1) in southern Maharashtra shares bor-
      ders with the Kannada-speaking (Dravidian language) state of Karnataka
      to the east and the south and with Sindhudurg and Ratnagiri in the Konkan

region to the west and north-west. The influence of Kannada and the Konkan speech varieties are observed in the respective regions of Kolhapur Marathi. Kolhapur district has strong economic ties with Belgaum and Khanapur region in north Karnataka. Kolhapur-Belgaum districts were a part of the Bombay Presidency in colonial India. School education in Kolhapur district is almost exclusively in Marathi. (Kannada and Urdu are the two other languages of school instruction.)

The Data

The focus of this chapter is on variability in a single morphosyntactic feature—ergativity—across geographically representative varieties of Marathi.

The synchronic data presented in the section were collected in the course of an on-going project at the Deccan College, Pune: The Survey of the Dialects of the Marathi Language (SDML).[2] The primary goal of the project is to create a digital archive of geographical and social variation in contemporary Marathi. The focus of this project is on capturing morphosyntactic variability.

Data Collection Methods

Data presented in this chapter are gleaned from personal narrations, narrations of traditional stories and responses to a semi-structured questionnaire based on videos developed by the project team at the Deccan College.[3] The limitations of relying on elicitation and translation (used, for instance, by Grierson in the LSI) as methods of data collection were realized very early in the project. It was observed that, with the spread of formal education and the media, better means of transport and connectivity, etc., a large proportion of speakers of regional rural varieties of Marathi have become bidialectal—their repertoire includes the standard variety of Marathi in addition to the local/regional variants. It was observed that the villagers often construed this interaction as an 'interview with educated people from Pune city' and switched to a more formal style of speaking. The relatively infrequent occurrence of morphosyntactic variables in natural speech was also a consideration in chalking out the methodology. In response to these considerations, the project team developed and filmed a set of about seventy videos depicting several situations to elicit particular agreement patterns, case-markers, verb forms,

---

[2] The project is funded by the Rajya Marathi Vikas Sanstha, Govt. of Maharashtra (2017-).

[3] The videos ('The Deccan College Stimulus Kit') can be accessed be accessed on the project website www.sdml.ac.in.

etc. These responses were cross-checked with data from narrations. Narrations are seen as advantageous for employing the social-dialectological approach. Narration is a cultural universal; narrations have ready accessibility, the length of discourse specimens facilitates statistical counts (cf. quantitative analyses in social dialectology), and they guarantee availability of a number of examples of given construction-types in the text (Hopper Thompson, 1980:282).

In all, data were collected from 2535 speakers (male and female) in 263 villages in 32 districts of Maharashtra. (Data are still to be collected two of the 34 target districts, Gadchiroli and Chandrapur.) Eight to twelve speakers who were born in the village, who had an uninterrupted stay in the same village for at least fifteen years and who reported to be mother tongue speakers of Marathi or used Marathi as the dominant link language were interviewed for the survey. Each interview lasted between 40 and 60 minutes. The speakers represent all the numerically dominant communities in the village. The data collection using videos was customized to obtain tokens of morphological and morphosyntactic features including possession, negation and ergativity.

The Linguistic Feature: Ergativity

Ergative is a case assigned to subjects of transitive verbs but not to subjects of intransitive verbs. Intransitive subject (S) and transitive object (O) are treated in the same manner and differently from transitive subject in ergative languages (Dixon, 1979:60–61). Ergativity occurs exclusively at the level of morphology in a majority of languages; relatively fewer languages behave ergatively at the level of syntax. This is also true of Indic languages (Klaiman, 1987:61). Split-ergative systems have ergative case marking under restricted conditions, most commonly depending either on the nature of the NP (e.g. noun or pronoun) or on the tense/aspect of the verb (Kiparsky, 2008). Ergativity in Indo-Aryan languages is a well-studied phenomenon and has been examined using various approaches in linguistics—historical, typological, syntactic and sociolinguistic. Previous studies of the ergative construction in western NIA include Bhatt (2007), Davison (2004), Kachru (1987), Kachru and Pandharipande (1978) Mahajan (1990, 1997, 2012), Mohanan (1994), Subbarao (2012) and others for Hindi-Urdu; Deo and Sharma (2002), Pandharipande (1997) for Marathi; Patel (2007) for Kutchi Gujarati; Khokhlova (2000, 2002) for Marwari; Bickel and Yadava (2000) for Nepali; and Bhatia (1993), Bhatt (2007), Butt and Deo (2001), Chandra et al., (2014) for Punjabi.

The focus of this paper will be on an examination of spatial and temporal variation in the morpho-syntax of the transitive-perfective clause in Marathi. Both morphological case marking on the subject of the transitive-perfective clause and verb agreement across regional varieties of Marathi will be examined.

The Ergative Construction in Marathi

Present-day standard Marathi is a split-ergative language (split for person and aspect). Only third person nominal expressions in transitive-perfective clauses (= perf) are marked for the ergative case and the verb in such clauses agrees with the nominative object NP. Overt ergative marking is absent in the first and second persons though the rule for agreement remains the same (this is the case for first and second person pronouns in a number of Indo-Aryan languages, including Punjabi, Eastern Rajasthani, Assamese and Siraiki; Masica (1991:252). Old Marathi (which is accessible in literary and inscriptional texts) reveals that Old Marathi (c.1000 AD to 1390 AD) overtly case-marked the agent in all three persons and the verb agreement was with the nominative object (or the verb took default neuter agreement if the object was case-marked).

Nominal marking and the verbal agreement in the ergative construction in regional varieties of present-day Marathi reveal a spectrum of possibilities ranging from preservation of Old-Marathi-like pattern to a standard-Marathi-like pattern, a regional innovation in the domain of verbal agreement and reduced ergativity. The variability is most evident in the speech varieties at the borders of the Marathi-speaking region today. Importantly, we observe *dialect levelling* (i.e. an overall reduction of inter-dialectal variability) presumably due to standardization and bidialectalism across the Marathi-speaking region. Dialect levelling has not, however, led to a complete loss of traditional dialects but to the creation of an intermediate space of structural variants constituting a continuum between the traditional variety and the standard speech variety (see further Sect. "The Ergative Construction in Marathi").

We will now proceed to a description of the synchronic ergative systems and a comparison of each with the historically attested prior system. We will present four broad patterns in the ergative construction in regional dialects of Marathi: (i) preservation of Old-Marathi-like ergativity, (ii) standard-Marathi-like ergativity, (iii) local innovation (subject agreement) and (iv) loss/reduction of ergativity. The diachronic data used for comparison are mainly drawn from the Linguistic Survey of India (volumes VII and IX).

Synchronic and Diachronic Variation in the Regional Vernaculars of Marathi

Preservation of Old-Marathi-Like Ergativity

Old Marathi
The transitive-perfective construction in Old Marathi had overt morphological marking on personal pronouns in all three persons. The first and second person plural pronouns in Old Marathi show syncretism. Agreement was with the nominative object. The available written records for Old Marathi suggest a homogenous, non-variable ergative system in Old Marathi.

Examples of the transitive-perfective construction in Old Marathi

1   *mīya ramatē mhəṇitlē*   [Līḷācəritrə: Līḷā 317]
    I.ERG ram.ACC say.PFV.3SN
    'I said to Ram.'

2   *tēhĩ gosawīyātē dekhilē*   [Līḷācəritrə: Līḷā 315]
    he.ERG sage.ACC see.PFV.3SN
    'He saw the sage.'

Regional varieties with Old-Marathi-like ergativity

Overt ergative case marking on first, second as well as third person pronouns and verbal agreement with the non-case-marked object noun phrase is observed in the region stretching from the Nagpur region in the north-east via Amravati, Buldhana Jalgao districts, across the Khandeshi/Ahirani belt up to Thane-Palghar and Raigad districts in the north Konkan region.

An example: The Nagpur/Vidarbh speech variety
The ergative system attested in the LSI is as shown in Table 9.2A.
Example of Nagpur Marathi of the late nineteenth century (Grierson, 1905: Specimen no. 1) (Table 9.2B).

3. **mya** *apəlya mitra-bərobər čəin kəray-saṭhi* **twa** *mə-la kokəru dekhil dellə nahi*
1S.ERG self.OBL. friend.3SGM-with fun.3SGF do.NON.FIN.-for you.ERG 1S-DAT young goat.SN
even give.PFV.3SN NEG
'You didn't even give me a young goat for me and my friends to play with.'

Example of Nagpur Marathi of the present times (SDML, 2019)
4. *mi-nə khal-un pay-l-ə*
I-ERG below-ABL see-PFV-3SN
'I saw (something) from below.'

The most frequently used first and second person pronominal forms in the transitive-perfective clause in Nagpur/Vidarbh Marathi in the SDML database

Table 9.1 Pronominal paradigm of Old Marathi (based on Tulpule 1960)

Aspect	Person	Number	
		Singular	Plural
Non-perf	1	mi	amʰi
Perf	1	miya	am ʰi
Non-perf	2	tu	tumʰi
Perf	2	tuwa	tumʰi
Non-perf	3	to	tyani
Perf	3	tene	tyani

Table 9.2 A: Pronominal paradigm of the Nagpur dialect (based on LSI data); NA = not available. B: Pronominal paradigm of the Ahirani dialect (based on SDML data)

Aspect	Person	Number	
		Singular	Plural
A: Pronominal paradigm of the Nagpur dialect (based on LSI data); NA = not available			
Non-perf	1	mi	ami
Perf	1	mya, mi	ami
Non-perf	2	tu	tumi
Perf	2	twa	tumi
Non-perf	3	to/ti/te	NA
Perf	3	tyanə (M.)	tyani
B: Pronominal paradigm of the Nagpur dialect (based on SDML data)			
Non-perf	1	mi	ami
Perf	1	mi/ minə* /miya	ami / aminə
Non-perf	2	tu	tumi
Perf	2	tu/ tunə* / tya	tumi / / tuminə
Non-perf	3	to/ti/te	te
Perf	3	tyani (M.)/ tini (F.) / tyanə/i (N.)	tyasni

are 'minə' and 'tunə,' respectively. Interestingly, these are not attested in the LSI Nagpur specimens. (Hindi-like ergative pronominal forms case-marked by −ne are attested in the LSI further to the east in the Chhindwara speech variety (see Grierson, 1905: 319–329). Further research would reveal the developments which led to the present-day first and second person pronominal forms in the Nagpur variety. (It is relevant to note that Nagpur and Chhindwara were a part of the Central province under British rule.) Was a non-local morphological marker adopted to mark the ergative first and second person pronouns in the Nagpur variety? If yes, how do we account for it? Or, could the −ni marking in the first and second persons have resulted from an analogical change modelled on the third person pronouns? Answering these questions requires further examination of the data. The pronominal forms 'mi' and 'tu' occur more frequently in the ergative construction in educated speech. (See further the discussion in Sect. "The Ergative Construction in Marathi".)

Standard-Marathi-Like Ergativity

Overt ergative case marking only on the third person pronoun and verbal agreement with the non-case-marked object noun phrase is variably present in the entire Marathi-speaking region included in the survey. This is also the predominant pattern observed in the 'deshi' (= belonging to the *desh*) speech varieties (i.e. Pune,

Ahmednagar, Satara, Sangli, Solapur districts), in Marathwada (i.e. Aurangabad, Jalna, Nanded, etc.) and among the Hindu speech communities in Ratnagiri district in the Konkan.

As was noted above, split-ergativity, where the ergative case marking occurs only in the perfective aspect, is reported for the western NIA (New Indo-Aryan) languages such as Hindi-Urdu, Gujarati, Punjabi, Sindhi, but not for Bangla, Oriya and Bhojpuri. In the standard dialect of Marathi, only the third person subject NP of a finite transitive clause in the perfective aspect bears ergative marker (i.e. the case-marker -ne/-ni/-nə); direct objects and subjects of intransitive clauses are nominative and the verb agrees with the non-case-marked NP (5a); if both subject and object NPs are case-marked, the verb shows default, neuter agreement (5b). Overt morphological marking on the first and second person pronouns in the ergative construction of Old Marathi is lost in present-day standard Marathi. Further, the first and second person pronominal forms (*mi* and *tu,* respectively) are identical to the corresponding non-perfective pronominal forms in OM (see Table 9.1). Syncretism in the first and second person plural pronouns of OM persists in today's standard variety.

5a *ti-nə/e/i*   *kagəd*   *phaḍ-l-a*

she-ERG   paper.3SM   tear-PERF-3SM

'She tore the paper.'

5b *tyanə/i/e*   *muli-la*   *mar-l-ə/e*

he-ERG   girl.3SF-ACC   hit-PERF-3SN

'He hit the girl.'

An example: Ahirani/Khandeshi.

Ahirani (also referred to in the literature as Khandeshi or Dhed Gujarai) instantiates this type of ergativity among the regional varieties of Marathi. Ahirani (Khandeshi) was not classified as a dialect of Marathi by Grierson, but as belonging to the central NIA group along with Bhili, Banjārī or Labhānī, Bahrūpiā, etc. Grierson provides two specimens of the speech variety sampled in Khandesh, Nandurbar taluka (Grierson, 1905, Vol IX.3. specimen nos. 65 and 66). The pronominal paradigms for Ahirani of the late nineteenth century (LSI data) and that of the present day are presented in Table 9.3A and B, respectively. (The LSI specimen was collected in Nandurbar district, and the SDML specimen cited below was collected in the neighbouring Dhule district.)

On comparing the two paradigms, we note complete syncretism in the first and second person singular forms in present-day Ahirani; the forms *mi* and *tu* are used both in non-perfective and in perfective constructions.

Rajesh Kumar is Professor of linguistics in the Department of Humanities and Social Sciences at the Indian Institute of Technology Madras, Chennai. He serves as the associate editor of the journal Language and Language Teaching. The broad goal of his research is uncovering regularities underlying both the structural form (what language is) and sociolinguistic functions (what language does) of natural language. He works on the structure of South Asian Languages. He is also interested in issues related to language (multilingualism) in education; politics; human cognition; and landscape.

Table 9.3 A: Pronominal paradigm of the Khandeshi/Ahirani dialect (based on LSI Vol. IX.3, p. 209). B: Pronominal paradigm of the Ahirani dialect (based on SDML data)

Aspect	Person	Number	
		Singular	Plural
A: Pronominal paradigm of the Khandeshi/Ahirani dialect (based on LSI Vol. IX.3, p. 209)			
Non-perf	1	mi, məi	ham, am, apən
Perf	1	mi, me	ami, amhu
Non-perf	2	tu	tum
Perf	2	tu, tunə	tumi, tumhi
Non-perf	3	to, ti, te	te, tya
Perf	3	tyane	NA
B: Pronominal paradigm of the Ahirani dialect (based on SDML data)			
Non-perf	1	mi	am(h)i
Perf	1	mi	am(h)i, amin
Non-perf	2	tu	tumi
Perf	2	tu	tumi, tumin
Non-perf	3	to, ti, te	tya
Perf	3	tyani	tyasni

Ahirani is said to represent a grammatical system having a mix of characteristics of neighbouring NIA languages, Gujarati and Marathi. But we observe that the plural forms in the pronominal paradigm of Ahirani are more differentiated than those of either Marathi or Gujarati (cf. Sect. "An example: Ahirani/Khandeshi" above for standard Marathi and in the notes for Gujarati).[1] While the nominative and agentive first and second person plural pronouns in both Marathi and Gujarati show syncretism, the equivalent pronominal forms in Ahirani (LSI Vol. IX.3, p. 209 as well as SDML data) show absence of syncretism. However, the SDML Ahirani data shows overlap among the pronominal forms used in non-perfective and in perfective constructions. This variability reflects reflexes of diachronic change and indicates a period of fluctuation and potential language change. It will be interesting to note the projected direction of this on-going change. The –n marking on first and second person plural pronouns in the perfective (*amin* we.ERG, *tumin* you.PL.ERG) may also have resulted from analogy with the third person pronominal forms. Educated Ahirani speakers optionally used standard-Marathi-like pronominal forms.

Verbal agreement in the LSI specimen of Khandeshi/Ahirani and that in the present-day Dhule Ahirani (SDML) is like that in Old Marathi and in Standard Marathi.

6 tya-ni   tyas-le   apᵊli   jinᵊgi   waṭ-ī   did-ī
   he-ERG   he-DAT   self.3SF   property.SF   distribute-CP   give.PFV.3SF
   'He divided his property (among his sons).'
   (LSI Vol IX.3, Specimen No. 65 collected in Nandurbar district)

7 *te por-ni*   *tya*   *manus-le*   *piwan*   *pani*   *di-n-ə*
   that girl-ERG   that.OBL   man-DAT   drink.NON.   water.N   give-PFV-3SN
                                                    FIN

   'The girl gave the man water to drink.'

   (SDML data collected in Dhule district)

8 *amin khir khadi*

   we.ERG porridge.SF eat.PFV.3SF

   'We ate the porridge.'

   (SDML data collected in Dhule district)

Local Innovations in the Transitive-Perfective Clause

Ergative case marking only on the third person pronoun and variable verbal agreement with the case-marked subject/case-marked object / non-case-marked object noun phrase is observed in the speech variety of Sangameshwar in southern Ratnagiri district and also in Malwani, the speech variety identified with the southern district of Sindhudurg.

An example: Sangameshwar speech variety spoken in the Ratnagiri district in south-west Maharashtra. (Table 9.4A and B)[4]

The LSI evidence shows that, unlike Old Marathi (as well as Poona/Pune Marathi LSI: 1905, p. 34), case syncretism occurred in the first and second person singular and plural pronouns in Sangameshwar a hundred years ago. We compared the pronominal paradigms of the Sangameshwar speech variety as attested in the LSI and in the SDML and find no change in the nominal domain of the ergative construction.

Grierson (1905: 122) observes that Sangameshwari closely agrees with the Konkan Standard of Marathi; verbal agreement in the transitive-perfective clause in Sangameshwar variety/Standard Konkan is said to be predominantly with the object (1905: 67), even if it is inflected for case (as in Goan Konkani and in Gujarati). Our examination of the LSI-Sangameshwar data, however, suggests variability in verbal agreement: agreement with the subject is predominant (see sentences 9 to 12 below); agreement with object is also observed (see sentence 13, verb agrees with the non-inflected object NP *vāṭni*).

---

[4]Grierson makes a difference between the Konkan standard (which includes varieties such Agri, Bankoti and Sangameshwari in the coastal stretch from Thane to north Ratnagiri) and Konkani spoken in the region extending from Rajapur in Ratnagiri district up till Sindhudurg district.

Table 9.4 A: Pronominal paradigm of the Sangameshwar speech variety (based on LSI data; Grierson 1907, p.66). B: Pronominal paradigm of the Sangameshwar speech variety (based on SDML data)

Aspect	Person	Number	
		Singular	Plural
A: Pronominal paradigm of the Khandeshi/Ahirani dialect (based on LSI Vol. IX.3, p. 209)			
Non-perf	1	mi	əmi
Perf	1	mi,	ami
Non-perf	2	tũ	tumi
Perf	2	tu	tumi
Non-perf	3	to / ti	te
Perf	3	tyani/tini	tyanni
B: Pronominal paradigm of the Sangameshwar speech variety (based on SDML data)			
Non-perf	1	mi	ami
Perf	1	mi	ami
Non-perf	2	tu	tumi
Perf	2	tu	tumi
Non-perf	3	to / ti	te
Perf	3	tyani/tini	tyanni

9   *tya giresta-n hya-s ḍukrā tsaraya-s seta-var dhaḍ-l-an*

that person-ERG he-ACC pigs feed-DAT field.OBL-LOC send-PFV-3SM

'That person sent him to the field to feed pigs.'

(LSI 1905:125)

10   *bapᵊsa-n tya-s [....] miṭi marᵊ⁻l-an*

father-ERG he-ACC [...] embrace.SF hit-PFV-3SM

'Father embraced him.'

(LSI 1905:126)

11   *tya-nə   eka   gəd-ya-s   sad   ghət-l-an*

he.OBL-ERG   one.OBL   labourer-OBL-ACC   call.SF   throw-PFV-3SM

'He called a labourer.'

12   *leka-n   bapsa-s   pərət   bolnə̃   ke-l-an*

child-ERG   father-ACC   again   speech.SN   do-PFV-3SM

'The child once again spoke to the father.'

13 *məg*   *tya-nə*   *tyãs-ni*   *apʰlya*   *jinəgi-č-i*   *vãṭṇi*

   then   he-ERG   he-DAT   self.OBL   property.   division.3SGF
                                                                OBL-GEN-3SF
                                                                division.SF
                                                                division.3SGF

kərun   *di-l-i*

do-CP   give-PFV-3SF

'Then he divided his property and gave (his son) his share.'

(LSI 1905:125)

In data collected for the SDML project, we find variability in verbal agreement in the Sangameshwar villages. Further, the variability appears to correlate with the religion of the speaker. Non-Muslim collaborators in Sangameshwar use standard-Marathi-like agreement (with non-inflected object NP). Among Muslim collaborators in Sangameshwar (Karanjari, Amavali, Kondivare and Kasba villages), the verb agrees with the second person plural and third person (sg. or pl.) subject; elsewhere the verb agrees with the nominative object (Kazi, 2019). It is also worth noting that non-Muslims in Sangameshwar/Ratnagiri report Marathi as their home language while Muslims report Kokni[5] to be the home language (ibid.)

14 *tuj̃-ya*   *ḍæḍi-ni*   *tu-j̃ya*   *pəppa-ni*
AA   you-GEN-OBL daddy-ERG   you-GEN.OBL   father.OBL-ERG

paṛti   *ṭʰəw-len*   *həyt*
party.SF   keep-PFV.3PL   be.PRS.3PL
'*That's why your father has organized a party.*'

(Excerpt from the Prodigal Son Story collected for the SDML from Muslim collaborator in Kasba village by Kazi, 2019.)

In sentence 14 (collected in the Kasba village in Sangameshwar tehsil), the verb *ṭʰəw-len* agrees with the 3rd pl. ergative subject *ḍæḍi-ni* or *pəppa-ni* (3rd HON.). Similarly, in the sentences *tumi kagəd phaḍlew* 'You (pl) tore the papers,' *tumi porala nijəwlew* 'You (pl) put the child to sleep.' the verb agrees with the subject. Verbal agreement in the ergative clause thus appears to be both linguistically and socially conditioned. Our observation regarding social conditioning of the linguistic structure is strengthened by observations reported by Paradkar (2021: 144–145) for the Kokni-speaking Muslim diaspora in Cape Town, South Africa; the community is known to have migrated out of villages in Ratnagiri and Raigad districts around 1885.

---

[5] Kokni (Konkani) here refers to the speech variety of the coastal region of Maharashtra, i.e. the Konkan. This is not to be confused with Konkani, the official language in the state of Goa.

15   Cape Town Kokni Muslim Diaspora: Latwan (Ratnagiri) village variety

madʒja aisbapa-nis mɘna imana-ni balɘg-l-en

my mother father-ERG 1S.ACC honest-INS raise-PRF-3PL

My mother and father raised me honestly

The diaspora community in Cape Town has preserved variation which was present more than a hundred years ago in the input speech variety.

Variable Loss of Ergativity

Villages in the southern-most districts of Kolhapur, Sangli, Akkalkot tehsil in Solapur district, southern tehsils of Nanded district all show variable ergative marking on first and second person pronouns in addition to the third person pronouns; the verbal agreement is predominantly with the case-marked subject noun phrase. Note that all these regions adjoin the Kannada-speaking state of Karnataka (also the Telugu-speaking state of Telangana in the case of Nanded district). Ergativity is absent in Dravidian languages.

In the southern variety of Marathi spoken in the district of Kolhapur, overt ergative marking is present in all three persons (as in Old Marathi but unlike the contemporary standard variety). We will report on variation observed in the village speech varieties of Gadahinglaj and Chandgad tehsils of Kolhapur district. The actual pronominal forms differ: Chandgad variety has the forms *mya* (1st p.) and *tiya* (2nd p.) while the Gadahinglaj variety has *minɘ* (1st p.) and *tunɘ* (2nd p.). In both varieties, these pronominal forms variably occur with the forms *mi* (1st p.) and *tu* (2nd p.) attested in the standard speech variety. A further similarity between the transitive-perfective clauses of the two southern varieties is preferred verbal agreement with the subject NP which is unlike all other regional varieties of Marathi (but refer to Kokni spoken by Muslims in Sangameshwar under 4.1.3 above). The verb agrees with the person and gender of the subject NP (Table 9.5).

In sentence 16, the subject NPs (*hi* and *natu*) are not marked with the instrumental/ergative marker in perfective aspect and the verb 'to do' agrees with the subject.

Table 9.5 Pronominal paradigm of the Gadahinglaj (Kolhapur) speech variety (based on SDML data)

Aspect	Person	Number	
		Singular	Plural
Non-perf	1	mi	amʰi
Perf	1	mi/miya	amʰi
Non-perf	2	tu	tumʰi
Perf	2	tu/tiya	tumʰi
Non-perf	3	to/ti/te	tyani
Perf	3	to/tyanɘ	tyani
	3	ti/tinɘ	tyani

16   *hi BA kelin, natu pəndrawi kelyan*

     she BA do-PFV-3SF grandson 15th do-PFV-3SM

     'She (grand-daughter) has completed graduation and the grandson has studied until the 15th class.'

The subject in sentence 17 is marked with instrumental marker in perfective aspect, and the verb agrees with the subject.

17   *tyani baṭli anlelyani*

     they.ERG bottle.SF bring.PFV.3PL

     'They brought the bottle.'

This variant of the transitive-perfective construction is observed in most varieties of Marathi in the Marathi-Kannada border region (see also Kulkarni-Joshi, 2016 for data on Kupwar Marathi). The subject NP in both intransitive and transitive-perfective clauses (see examples 18 and 19 below) appears to be marked with the suffix -ne / -ni. The verb in both clause types agrees with such a subject. Could this be described as an extension of the ergative case marking to include subject NPs in non-perfective intransitive clauses? Alternatively, could the seemingly case-marked ergative subject NP have been reanalysed as a nominative subject NP thus permitting verbal agreement with the reanalysed nominative NP?

18   *tenə punyasnə alay*   (SDML data collected in Gadahinglaj)

     he Pune-from come.PFV.PRST.3SM

     'He has come from Pune'

19   *minə pepər wacayloy*   (SDML data collected in Gadahinglaj)

     I newspaper read.PROG.PRST.1SM

     'I am reading the newspaper.'

20   *moṭhya hɔspiṭᵉlat kam kəruca əsə ṭhərəvi-l-o mi* (SDML data collected in Chandgad)

     big.OBL. hospital.LOC work.SN do-PRED thus decide-PFV-1SM I

     'I decided to work in the big hospital.'

The second possibility, that the ergative case-marked pronominal form has been reanalysed as nominative, is strengthened by the occurrence of a pronominal form such as *teni*, used as an honorific (as in sentence 21), a pattern observed in the southern border dialects of Marathi which seems to be modelled on the Kannada construction in sentence 22. This usage was observed only in varieties of Marathi

Table 9.6 Summary of predominant regional patterns of ergative marking on the subject NP and verbal agreement in the transitive-perfective clause in representative varieties of Marathi. (The numbers 1, 2 and 3 indicate first, second and third person pronouns, respectively.) Note that standard-like ergative pronominal forms and agreement are variably present in all the regional varieties

	Old Marathi	Standard Marathi	Nagpur	Ahirani	Sangameshwar	South Kolhapur
Nominal domain (marking on subj. NP)	1, 2, 3 sg persons	3 sg, pl (no overt marking on 1, 2 persons)	1, 2, 3 sg persons	1pl 2pl 3 sg, pl	3 sg, pl	Nil (reanalysis of ergative subject NP as nominative)
Verbal domain (agreement)	Object	object	object	object	object and subject (community split)	subject

bordering the Kannada-speaking contact region. Arguably, the contact with a Dravidian language, Kannada has triggered this reanalysis in the southern varieties of Marathi. As was noted above, ergativity is absent in Kannada/Dravidian languages.

21 *pəppa teni alyat*   (SDML data collected in Gadahinglaj)

father he = HON. come.PFV.PRST.3PL

'Father has come.'

22 *tənde awəru bandidu*   (Kannada)

father he = HON. come.IMPF

'Father has come'

Summary: This section focused on describing broad patterns in the transitive-perfective clause in selected regional varieties of Marathi. The selected dialects included varieties spoken at the peripheries of the Marathi-speaking region today and the standard dialect. We noted variation across these dialects both in case marking the subject and in verbal agreement in the transitive-perfective clause. The variation is summarized in Table 9.6.

Intra-Dialectal Variation in the Transitive-Perfective Clause

The foregoing discussion suggests varying trajectories of change in both the nominal and verbal domains in various regional varieties of Marathi. In addition to the region-specific variants, we note that the standard-Marathi-like ergative construction has entered regional dialects and that it has a diglossic relation with the regional/local variants. (The likely pathways of this change will be discussed in Sect. "Sources and Pathways of Asymmetry in the Ergative Construction in Dialectal Marathi: Motivations for Change" below). Intra-dialectal variation (both inter-speaker and intra-speaker) is also noted in the SDML data. The rate and progression of standardization show regional variation too. The SDML data suggests that rate of standardization can be correlated with proximity of the village to an urban centre (town/city), speakers' age and education: the younger educated speakers in villages with easy access to nearby urban centres are leading the way to standardization. Secondly, not all linguistic features which identify a particular regional variety are equally affected by dialect change/standardization. The shift to the standard variant is accelerated for some linguistic features and more retarded for some others. To exemplify this process, we will cite the case of speech varieties of two villages in Vidarbh (Buldhana district): one of which is close to the town of Shegaon and the other which is situated away from urban contact (see Fig. 9.2). We will make use quantification of linguistic variation and its correlation with non-linguistic factors to draw inferences about language/dialect change.

This comparison involved two variable linguistic features–

(1) the Accusative-Dative (ACC-DAT) case-marker: local variants-*le* and *–l* vs. standard variant *–la*

(2) overt ergative case marking on the first and second person pronominal subject of the transitive-perfective clause (i.e. the ergative construction): local variants *minə/mya* 'I-ERG' and *tunə –twa* 'you-ERG.' This marking is absent in the standard dialect.

and two main sociological factors:

(i)   whether the speaker lives in a village close to the city or far from the city

(ii) whether the speaker is educated

(M32 and M27 are male speakers aged 32 and 27 years, respectively; F39 and F50+ are female speakers aged 39 and 50+, respectively).

The graphs in Fig. 9.2 indicate greater spread of the standard variants of both linguistic features in the village variety in close vicinity of Shegaon town. One might surmise that the forms *minə/mya* 'I-ERG' and *tunə –twa* '2-ERG' are on the path of becoming obsolete in the urban variety. Figure 9.2 also shows that the frequency of use of standard variants is greater in the speech of the graduate speaker. Education of the speaker does not appear to create much variation in the speech variety of the village situated away from the urban centre. Thus, it appears that dialect levelling through standardization will lead to some dialectal features becoming obsolete in urban varieties while particular features which index the regional speech variety are maintained (the use of the accusative-dative marker -le in the present case.)

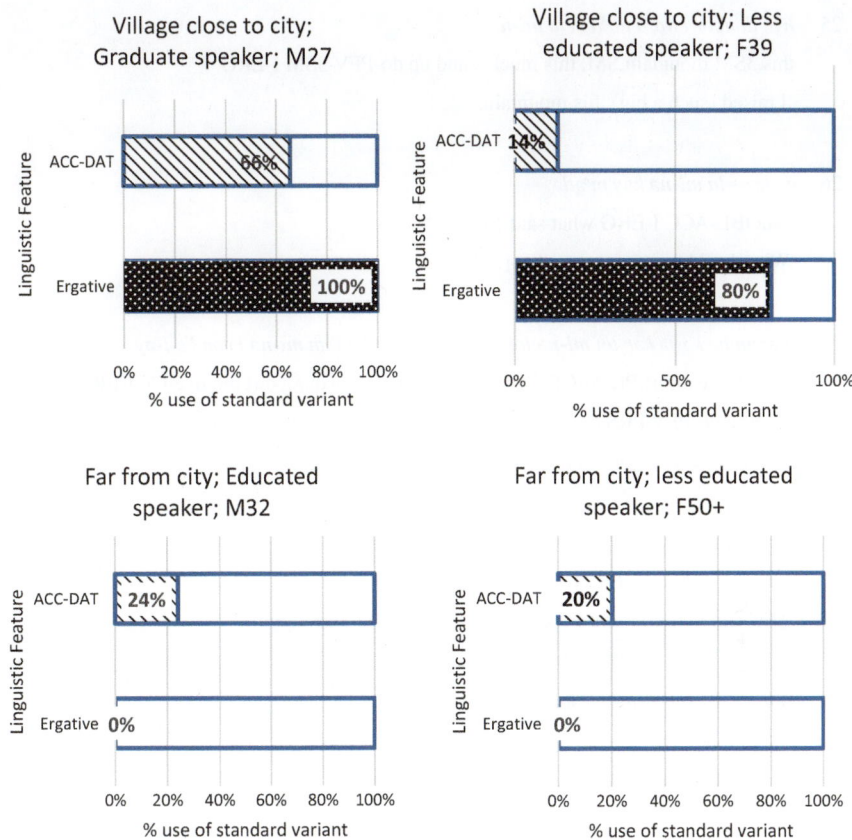

Fig. 9.2 Variant rates of standardization across speech varieties

Intra-Speaker Variability

Idiolectal (intra-speaker) variation too is attested in the SDML data. For instance, in the data collected in southern Maharashtra in Gadahinglaj taluka of Kolhapur district (village Hebbal Jaldyal), the following variability was observed in the interview speech of a female speaker aged 55 years:

23   ***mi-nə*** *ajpəryet he diwəs bəgitlə*

    I-ERG today-until these days see-PFV-3SN

    'I saw these days until today.'

24   *ti šenə kaḍʰun* ***mi-nə*** *pəiše bʰagiw-l-ə*

    those.F cow dung.PL remove-CP money I-ERG settle-PFV-3SN

    'I picked cowdung to earn money and settle (these expenses).'

25   *hyo ḍoṅgər ewḍʰa ubʰa kela **mi-nə***

this.3SM mountain.SM. this much stand up do-PFV-3SM I-ERG

'I raised (such a big) this mountain.'

26   *mulgya-la **mi-nə** kay mʰəṭlə*

son.OBL-ACC I-ERG what said-PFV-3SN

'What I said to my son was that […].'

27   *mʰənun he kəṣṭə kər-un **mi-nə** lokan-cə šan gʰaṇ kadʰun **mi-nə** jətən ke-l-əy*

hence these effort.PL do-CP I-ERG people-GEN cowdung dirt remove-CP I-ERG

preserve do-PFV-PRST

'I have done dirty jobs in order to save (money).'

28   ***mi** kaḍʰloy ki tu kaḍʰələs*

I remove-PFV-1S-PRST or you remove-PFV-3SGN-2SG

(He said to him), have I taken it out or have you taken it out

29   ***mi** tewḍʰə šeṇ kʰa-ll-ə səgl-ə*

I that much.3SN cowdung..SN eat-PFV-3SN all.3SN

'I took the blame.' (Lit. I ate all the cowdung.)

The occurrence of the first person singular pronominal forms *mi* and *minə* in the speech of this single speaker is presented in Table 9.7.

It was observed that the presence or absence of the ergative marking on the noun/pronoun is contingent upon the clause type (perfective or imperfective) and verb type (transitive or intransitive).

Samples collected from younger, educated speakers in this village show a complete absence of the structural alternative '*minə*.' Evidence for inter-speaker variation becomes evident especially on comparing the speech of older speakers with that of younger, educated speakers. We noted a strong preference for subject agreement among all speakers in this region. Yet, among the younger speakers we see a gradual shift towards standard-Marathi-like object agreement (28):

Table 9.7 Idiolectal variation in Hebbal Jaldyal (Dist. Kolhapur) Total number of tokens analysed = 51

	Perfective clause		Imperfective clause	
	Transitive verb	Intransitive verb	Transitive verb	Intransitive verb
minə	11	0	1	0
mi	14	6	9	10

Table 9.8 Pronominal paradigm of Gujarati (based on LSI data, Vol. IX.2).

Aspect.	Person.	Number.	
		Singular.	Plural.
Non-perf.	1.	hu.	ame, am.
Perf.	1.	mẽ.	ame.
Non-perf.	2.	tu.	təme, tam.
Perf.	2.	tẽ.	təme.
Non-perf.	3.	te.	Teo.
Perf.	3.	teṇe.	teoe.

28   *mi tu-la don kuraḍ-i dak-əw-l-ya*   (Female, educated speaker aged 25)

I.ERG you-DAT two axe.F-PL show-CAUS-PFV-3Pl.F

'I showed you two axes.'

Sources and Pathways of Asymmetry in the Ergative Construction in Dialectal Marathi: Motivations for Change

We noted above our observations regarding regional, inter-speaker and intra-speaker variability in a single morphosyntactic feature, viz. ergativity. The linguistic/sociolinguistic/socio-historical correlates of the observed change(s) in the dialects of Marathi may be examined to interpret the variability. In other words, the data may be interpreted in terms of constraints on dialect change in the Marathi region.

'Principles of language' as constraints on dialect change

Even as dialectal variability is becoming an integral part of mainstream formal theory in the guise of 'micro-variation,' attempts are being made to present formal accounts of the sources and pathways of asymmetry in the ergative construction. In this volume, for instance, Udaar looks 'inwards' for the source of linguistic variation. Through a careful analysis of ergativity patterns in some closely related languages of the Western Indo-Aryan belt, the author demonstrates that it is the inner structural constitution (transitivity, light verbs and the internal structure of verb phrases) of language that allows some domains of language to be susceptible to and some domains to be immune to variation. She thus proposes that linguistic variability is highly restricted by the 'inner working of the principles of language.'

Among other things, we observed that a split between local and non-local participants is manifested in the hierarchical agreement patterns in dialectal Marathi. Arguing against the traditional, purely historical account of the development of split-ergativity in language, Kiparsky (2008:15) demonstrates that such asymmetry in the ergative construction (i.e. split-ergativity) could be explained in terms of the language universal of 'animacy hierarchy' (or 'D-hierarchy,' see Fig. 9.3).

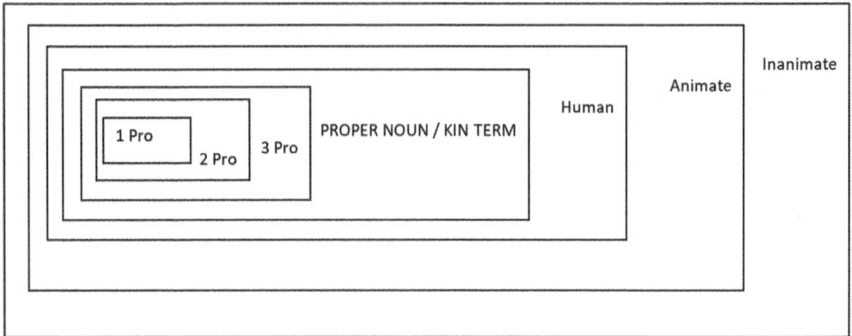

Fig. 9.3 Animacy hierarchy or D-hierarchy (*Source* Kiparsky, 2008: 9)

The ergative/nominative syncretism in the first and second person pronouns (high in the animacy scale) in the standard dialect of Marathi and in Ahirani and the overall tendency for agreement with the object NP (lower in the animacy scale) are some dialectological facts which can be accounted for by the scale. A comprehensive account of the Marathi dialectal data within this approach is not, however, the focus of this chapter.

Social Correlates of Dialect Change in Marathi

We discern an overall expansion in structural variation within the traditional dialects (regional varieties) of Marathi through the introduction of the standard variant and local innovations. Standard variants of the linguistic feature are in competition with the local variants (cf. Mufwene, 2001 in Sect. 1 above). As we noted above, the standard and local variants are in a diglossic relationship. Our discussion of inter-speaker variability (Sect. "The Ergative Construction in Marathi") suggests that traditional bilingualism/cross-border contact, speaker's education, place of residence (urban/rural), access to the standard variety, frequency of contact with urban speakers, etc., are possible social predictors of rate and direction of dialect change.

The distance among the regional dialects appears to be gradually decreasing both due the decreasing use of marked local linguistic variants and the introduction of standard variants (the process of *dialect levelling*), especially among educated and younger speakers. Greater access to formal/standard variety of Marathi through formal education and increased geographical as well as social mobility are the pathways by which standard variants have entered regional dialects. Thus, 'standardization' can be said to be an important mechanism of dialect levelling in the Marathi case. The likely contribution of other mechanisms, such as dialect mixture, supralocalization, etc., to dialect change also warrant examination. For instance, in the course of our fieldwork, we noted among speakers in rural Vidarbh a strong mental orientation towards Nagpur-Amravati in the Vidarbh region rather than towards the metropolitan cities in western Maharashtra (e.g. Mumbai, Pune). This strong regional emphasis correlates with a 'regiolect' whose linguistic characteristics include Nagpur-like ergative construction, the use of verb-conjunctive particle + RAH 'STAY' as the progressive construction, absence of gender marking on the third person imperfective verb form, etc. Rural communities in Kolhapur district have strong economic ties across the state border in Belgaum district (Karnataka) while they maintain strong socio-cultural networks within the home district. The consequences of this regional focus for the emergence of 'regiolects' in southern Maharashtra are also illustrative. The Hindus in rural Ratnagiri are clearly oriented towards employment in urban Mumbai, while the Muslims have relatively stronger local networks in the neighbouring villages. Such lifestyle differences too are reflected in language practices (cf. 4.1.3 above).

The role of language contact in determining the linguistic features of Marathi dialects must also be factored in: contact with neighbouring dialects of Hindi in the case of Vidarbh speech varieties, contact with neighbouring dialects of Gujarati in the case of the Khandesh speech varieties, contact with Goan Konkani and Kannada in the case of speech varieties in Sindhudurg and contact with speakers of Kannada and Telugu in the case of the southern varieties of Marathi. Synchronic facts and diachronic change in the dialect can be interpreted in the light of the social history of the region which resulted in the contact situation: e.g. membership of political denominations in the recent past. The inclusion of Vidarbh in the Central Province and the inclusion of tehsils in north Karnataka in the Bombay presidency of the British colonial rule facilitated bilingualism locally. Language contact plays a catalytic role in effecting dialect change. For example, change via analogical changes: the development of pronominal forms *mina* and *tuna* were presumably modelled on the third person pronominal form *tyana* in Nagpur region catalysed by overt ergative marking on all three persons in local varieties of Hindi. A second example is change via reanalysis: ergative subjects in the southern varieties of Marathi in contact with Dravidian were reanalysed as nominative, possibly under the influence of neighbouring Kannada.

An examination of the SDML dialect database leads to an important observation with regard to dialect change in the Marathi region. In the process of dialect levelling referred to above, traditional dialects are not directly replaced by the standard variety. Between the traditional variety and the standard is observed a linguistic space which is occupied by a 'dialect ladder' (cf. Hinskens, 2021)—a spectrum of structural alternatives in a diglossic relationship. For example, the post-dialect continuum in the Nagpur region includes the following structural variants for the ergative construction:

30	*mya khir khalli*	I-ERG porridge.3SF eat-PFV-SF	Local
	mina khir khalli	I-ERG porridge.3SF eat-PFV-SF	Regional
	mi khir khalli	I-(null) porridge.3SF eat-PFV-SF	Standard
	'I ate porridge.'		

Interim Conclusions and Some Suggestions for Future Research

An attempt was made in this chapter to provide an overview of the social dialectology approach to language (dialect) variation and change. Focusing on a single linguistic feature (the ergative construction), dialectal data from the SDML database for four regions at the peripheries of the Marathi-speaking region today were presented to describe varying trajectories of change (cf. 1.1, questions (i) and (ii) which social dialectologists seek to answer). The possible social correlates/motivations for the observed changes were discussed. The study also highlights the benefits of a dialect survey for uncovering challenging data and complex sociolinguistic patterns which must be explained.

What about the benefits of grammar studies for dialectological research? A key idea of this edited volume is to find meeting ground for the functionalists and formalists to examine variation in language. As the editor of the volume suggested, perhaps the regular patterns in dialectal data can be explained by grammar internal principles, while the deviations from the pattern are driven by grammar-external (social, historical, contextual) factors. This can be a systematic research programme for the near future, one which employs the strategy of 'same data—different analytical approaches.' Such a collaborative programme must begin by identifying relevant research questions and hypotheses (cf. Hinskens, 2021). A plurality of theoretical viewpoints is nevertheless a desideratum in the exploration of linguistic variability.

Notes
1. Data used in this paper were collected under the aegis of the 'Survey of Dialects of the Marathi Language', a joint project of the Deccan College, Pune and Rajya Marathi Vikas Sanstha, Mumbai. The author is the project head. She duly acknowledges the contribution of the project staff in collecting and analysing the dialect data: Dr. Manasi Kelkar, Dr. Prafulla Meshram, Mr. Sambhaji Jadhav, and Ms. Jayashree Bharambe..

References

Auer, P., Hinskens, F., & Kerswill, P. (Eds.). (2005). *Dialect change: Convergence and divergence in dialects of Europe.* CUP.

Bisang, W. (2004). Dialectology and typology—An integrative perspective. In B. Kortmann (Ed.), *Dialectology meets typology. Dialect grammar from a cross-linguistic perspective* (pp. 11–45). Berlin: Mouton de Gruyter.

Chambers, J., & Trudgill, P. (1998; first published 1980). Dialectology. Cambridge: CUP.

Chamoreau, C., & Léglise, I. (Eds.). (2012). *Dynamics of contact-induced language change (Language Contact and Bilingualism Series 2).* De Gruyter.

Hinskens, F. (2021). The future of dialects and the dialectology of the future: Some considerations, with special attention to the Dutch language area. *Taal en Tongval*. https://doi.org/10.5117/TET2020.1.HINS. Accessed on 14.4.2022.

Grierson, G. (1905). *Linguistic Survey of India, vol. 7. Indo-Aryan Family. Southern group.* Specimens of the Marathi Language. Calcutta. Reprinted 1968. Delhi: Motilal Banarsidass.

Grierson, G. (1907). *Linguistic Survey of India, vol. 4.3. Indo-Aryan Family. Central Group.* The Bhīl Languages, including Khāndēśī, Banjārī or Labhānī, Bahrūpiā, & c. Calcutta. Reprinted 1968. Delhi: Motilal Banarsidass.

Kazi, S. (2019). The Grammatical Sketch and Texts of Sangameshwari. Unpublished M.A. dissertation submitted to the Deccan College (Deemed University), Pune. Research funded under the project Survey of Dialects of the Marathi Language (SDML).

Kiparsky, P. (2008). Universals constrain change; change results in typological generalizations. In J. Good (Ed.), *Linguistic universals and language change*. Oxford: OUP.

Klaiman, M. (1987). Mechanisms of ergativity in South Asia. *Lingua, 71*(1–4), 61–102.

Kulkarni-Joshi, S. (2016). Forty years of language contact and change in Kupwar: A critical reassessment of the intertranslatability model. *International Journal of South Asian Languages and Linguistics*, De Gruyter, 147–174.

Kulkarni-Joshi, S., & Kelkar, M. (2020). Synchronic variation and diachronic change in dialects of Marathi. In T. Khan et al. (Ed.), *Alternative horizons in linguistics*. Munich: Lincom Europa.

Labov. W. (2003). Pursuing the cascade model. In D. Britain, & J. Cheshire (Eds.), *Social dialectology* (pp. 9). Amsterdam: John Benjamins.

Masica, C. (1991). *The Indo-Aryan languages*. Cambridge: CUP.

Mufwene, S. (2001). *The Ecology of Language Evolution*. Cambridge University Press.

Paradkar, R. (2021). *Language and transnational identity: A sociolinguistic account of the Kokni diaspora in Cape Town*. Doctoral dissertation submitted to Deccan College Postgraduate and Research Institute, Pune.

Peterson, J. (2022). A sociolinguistic-typological approach to the linguistic prehistory of South Asia: Two case studies. *Language Dynamics and Change, 1–50.*

Sankoff, G. (2006). Age: Apparent time and real time. *Elsevier Encyclopedia of Language and Linguistics*, Second Edition. Article Number: LALI: 01479. Accessed online on 29 April 2019.

Satam, S. (2020). Variation and change in the speech variety of Sawantwadi. *Bulletin of Deccan College Postgraduate and Research Institute, 80*, 135–145. Research funded under the project Survey of Dialects of the Marathi Language (SDML).

Siewierska, A., & Bakker, D. (2006). Bi-directional versus uni-directional asymmetries in the encoding of semantic distinctions in free and bound person forms. In T. Nevalainen, J. Klemola, & M. Laitinen (Eds.), *Types of variation: Diachronic, dialectal and typological interfaces* (pp. 21–50). Amsterdam: John Benjamins.

Trudgill, P., Britian, D., & Cheshire, J. (2003). *Social Dialectology*. Amsterdam: John Benjamins.

Tulpule, S. G. (1949). *Prachīn Marathi Gadya* [In Marathi]. Pune: Venus Book Stall.

Tulpule, S. G. (1963). *Prachīn Maraṭhi koriv Lekh [In Marathi]*. Pune University Press.

Tulpule, S. G. (Ed.). (1966). *Līḷācharitra (purvārdha,* Part 2) [In Marathi]. Nagpur-Pune: Suvichar Prakashan Mandal.

Tulpule, S. G. (1973). *Yādavkalīn Marathi Bhāshā,* 2nd edition. Pune: Venus Prakashan.

Walkden, G. (2017). The actuation problem. In A. Ledgeway & I. Roberts (Eds.), *Cambridge handbook of historical syntax* (pp. 403–424). Cambridge University Press.

Weinreich, U., Labov, W., & Herzog, M. (1968). Empirical foundations for a theory of language change. In W. P. Lehmann & Y. Malkiel (Eds.), *Directions for historical linguistics: A symposium* (pp. 95–195). University of Texas Press.

Sonal Kulkarni-Joshi is Sociolinguist and Professor in the Linguistics department at the Deccan College, Pune (India). She holds a Ph.D. from the University
of Reading (UK). Her research interests include language variation and change,
migration and language, language contact, dialectology and dialect mapping.
Sonal is currently heading a government-funded project for creating a digital
database of regional and social dialects of Marathi. The bilingual project website (under construction) can be accessed at www.sdml.ac.in. She has served as
Treasurer of the Linguistic Society of India (2005–2014). email: sonal.kulkarni@
dcpune.ac.in, Address: Dept. of Linguistics, Deccan College (Deemed University),
Yerawada, Pune [India] 411006.

Chapter 10
Parametrizing Ergativity: Insights from Western Indo-Aryan Languages

Usha Udaar

Abstract This chapter addresses the issue of language variation by showing that synchronic dialectal variations in closely related languages may have their source not only in the lexicon but also in the structure-building operation of narrow syntax. I study the phenomenon of ergativity in some Western Indo-Aryan languages (henceforth, WIALs) and analyse its varied manifestation in terms of overt case marking on transitive subjects and a change in the verbal agreement paradigm. All WIALs under consideration in this chapter are otherwise nominative-accusative, yet they show ergative-absolutive alignment in the perfective aspect. Through this chapter, I will point out that this 'break' from the nominative-accusative alignment is facilitated by transitivity and feature specification of the perfective verbs of WIALs. Thus, my objective in this paper is to consolidate the findings about ergativity in select WIALs and understand the underlying parameters that bring about the ergative pattern in the languages.

Introduction

The field of linguistic variation caters to one of the central questions of the modern linguistic theory addressing the fundamental opposition between what can be considered the essential language system, and what could be referred to as a by-product of actual usage of language by the speakers. In other words, a generative study of linguistic variation should be able to fundamentally reveal the variation allowed by the abstract mental construct of processes and elements which comprise the generative capacity of a speaker, and those brought about by the operations and products of that system as per the actual usage of language by speakers. In essence, this question points towards the primary dichotomy maintained in the

U. Udaar (✉)
Indian Institute of Technology Kanpur, Kanpur, Uttar Pradesh, India
e-mail: ushaudaar@gmail.com

© The Author(s), under exclusive license to Springer Nature Singapore Pte Ltd. 2023
P. Chandra (ed.), *Variation in South Asian Languages*,
https://doi.org/10.1007/978-981-99-1149-3_10

237

generative literature: the abstract, not directly observable construct and the concrete, observable sum of language production. This dichotomy is vital for any researcher who wishes to study linguistic variation. It should serve as the beginning point for an explanatorily adequate account of linguistic variation.

Linguistic variation has been at the centre of discussion regarding how languages function and subsequently change in the real world. The theory of Principles & Parameters and related works from the 1980s headed one of the distinguished movements in linguistics that accounted for the development of a detailed theory of Universal Grammar (UG) and explained the morphosyntactic variation at a cross-linguistic level. In the recent era of minimalism, linguistic variation is relegated to the periphery, limited to either the lexicon and/or the language-specific interface requirements (Baker, 2008; Borer, 1984). Thus, it is assumed that the core syntactic component remains uniform with a limited number of mechanisms that drive the syntactic operations. The variance between languages, however deeply observed, results from the language-specific lexicon and interface requirements. The phenomenon of linguistic variation assumes an even more intricate character as we approach the differences between dialects of a language. Barbiers (2009) notes that a study of dialectal variation provides an ideal laboratory-like condition where the overall structure of languages is similar (as in a control group) and a few variations can be used to deduce the finer interactions between elements involved in a linguistic operation.

This paper critically analyses the dialectal variation between some closely related languages of the Western Indo-Aryan belt. Through a detailed analysis of case and agreement operations in the domain of ergative alignment, I present evidence that variation may not be restricted to the peripheral elements of lexicon and/or PF/MF interface. Some variations may manifest in the computational system of human language itself, through diachronic processes of language change. Thus, I intend to answer the question about the locus of variation—whether linguistic variation in the present context is limited to the lexicon or happens at the syntactic level too.

This paper addresses the concerns about the presence of ergative case in some Western Indo-Aryan languages. Ergativity refers to a unique alignment where the subjects of intransitive verbs behave similarly to the objects of transitive verbs, rather than the subjects of a transitive verb in a language. As per Dixon (1994), if, in a language, the intransitive subjects and transitive objects are marked similarly for case, verbal agreement, and particles, it is an instance of morphological ergativity. On the other hand, some languages show 'deeper' ergativity by allowing only some arguments to participate in syntactic operations including control, relativization, and clausal coordination. Such languages that differentiate between intransitive subjects and objects in contrast with the transitive subjects in terms of syntactic operations of control, relativization, etc., are considered to manifest syntactic ergativity. As per Dixon (ibid.), ergative languages are said to be showing either morphological ergativity and/or syntactic ergativity. Most syntactically ergative languages would show both morphological and syntactic ergative patterns, while vice-versa is not true. Thus, morphologically ergative languages would show ergative patterns only in terms of morphological marking of case, particles, agreement etc.

Indo-Aryan languages show nominative-accusative alignment. That is, they treat their transitive subjects and intransitive subjects at par with each other in terms of case marking, verbal agreement, relativization, clausal coordination, etc. See examples given below.

1 jɔn   mɛri-ko   dekʰta   hɛ

John.3.m.sg.nom   Mary.3.f.sg.acc see.3.m.sg.hab be.3.m.sg.pres

'John sees Mary.'

2 jɔn   bʰag   jata   hɛ

John.3.m.sg.nom   run   go.3.m.sg.hab   be.3.m.sg.pres

'John runs away.'

In the empirical data given above, subjects of transitive (1) and intransitive (2) clauses carry an unmarked nominative case and trigger verbal agreement. In contrast, the object of the transitive clause (1) carries a marked accusative case and does not trigger agreement with the verb. Thus, we can say from the Hindi language examples given above that the language shows a nominative-accusative pattern. Yet, there are some Indo-Aryan languages where the nominative-accusative pattern is broken, and one can observe ergativity, albeit in a restrictive context. Such languages are said to be split-ergative. See the data given in (3) below.

3 hina-ne   mɛri-ko   dekʰa   hɛ

Hina.3.f.sg.erg   Mary.3.f.sg.acc see.def.perf be.def.pres

'Hina has seen Mary.'

In comparison with the empirical data discussed earlier, this construction breaks away from the nominative-accusative pattern. In comparison with (1) and (2), the subject here carries an overt case marker and fails to trigger agreement with the verb. As the ergative subject is overtly case-marked and does not agree with the verb, we can say that it behaves more like the object of the transitive clause. Therefore, we establish that in the perfective aspect Hindi (like other WIALs) is a split-ergative language.

In focus for this paper are many languages of the Western Indo-Aryan belt which display split-ergativity, where this break-away pattern is facilitated by the perfective aspect. One of the primary questions that I address through this paper is what facilitates this 'split' in a host of these otherwise 'nominative-accusative' languages. In this regard, I will be looking at the structural anomalies that bring about ergativity in WIALs. Hence, I will present my view on the Borer–Chomsky Conjecture (Baker, 2008) which states that the narrow syntactic component of Language, in general, is vastly uniform and immune to change. Therefore, any apparent linguistic variation should be attributed to external factors including the lexicon and the language-specific interface operations. I will demonstrate that slight changes in the feature inventory of an element participating in the structure-building operation of the computational system of human language may contribute to vast changes within the structure of the sentence itself.

In this chapter, I will present data from the following WIALs—Haryanavi, Mewati, Mewari, Marwari, Gujarati, Punjabi, and Marathi. These languages show perfective aspect-based split-ergativity, a feature found quite prominently in the WIALs. This brings us to the next question that I plan to address in the paper. While it is well-known that dialects arise out of a linguistic trend being restricted over a region, what is it that brings about micro-variations in dialects of closely related languages? As we will see in this paper, each of the aforementioned languages shows ergativity, in terms of differential marking of the subject of the transitive clause and a change in the verbal agreement pattern. Additionally, for each of these languages, this split-ergative pattern is found only in the perfective aspect. Yet, ergative case marking differs not only in terms of the kind of morpheme in use but also with respect to the kind of subject it appears on. When it comes to the verbal agreement, we will see that morphological variations are found there too. In some languages, the role of object DP will also differ as it may or may not be available be prominent in showing variation.

The chapter is organized as follows—Section "Introduction" begins with an introduction to the phenomenon of ergativity and provides examples detailing the difference between nominative-accusative and ergative-absolutive languages. Further, the author discusses varied instances of ergativity where in some languages the ergative-absolutive alignment is prevalent only in the morphological marking of relevant DPs, versus 'deep' ergative languages where only absolutive DPs are eligible for certain syntactic operations. Further, the question about the syntactic manifestation of ergativity—in terms of the position of ergative and non-ergative subjects—is discussed, and various views are provided to prove that morphological manifestation of case also results from deep syntactic operations. In the next subsection, I present novel data discussing the ergative paradigm in the Western Indo-Aryan languages under scrutiny in this chapter. This is followed by a brief discussion of various views on the rise and spread of ergativity in the concerned languages. Section "Parameters for Ergativity" explores the underlying syntactic reasons responsible for ergativity with respect to the two deciding factors namely transitivity and the structure of the perfective aspect. The author shows further how these two parameters are responsible for the presence or absence of ergativity in each of these languages. Section "Conclusion" provides concluding remarks.

About Ergativity

The phenomenon of ergativity, a rather prevalent occurrence across language groups, is taken to be a particular arrangement where the subjects of transitive and intransitive clauses manifest varying patterns of case marking and agreement morphology. A simple diagrammatic explanation of ergative case marking is shown below.

(4)   Nominative System   Ergative System

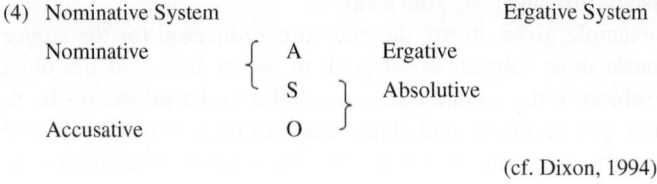

(cf. Dixon, 1994)

Note that in the figure given above in (4), A stands for transitive subject, S for intransitive subject and O stands for object. The diagrammatic representation given above shows that while nominative-accusative alignment treats transitive and intransitive subjects alike, ergative-absolutive alignment marks a difference between transitive and intransitive subjects. See data points (5)–(6) for an example of nominative-accusative alignment, and (7)–(8) for ergative-absolutive alignment in English and Dyirbal, respectively.

(5) John brings flowers.

(6) John sits on a chair.

Notice the unmarked subject 'John' in (5)–(6) that triggers verbal agreement marked by morpheme 's' on the verb. We can say that the subjects of transitive and intransitive clauses behave alike in English. Hence, English can be categorized as a nominative-accusative language. Let us now look at the following data points from Dyirbal:

(7)   yabu   banaga n^{y}u

      Mother-abs   return-$_{NONFUT}$

      'Mother returned.'

(8)   nguma   yabu-nggu   bura-n

      Father-abs   mother-erg   see-$_{NONFUT}$

      'Mother saw father.'   (Dixon, 1994)

Notice how the intransitive subject 'yabu' and the object 'nguma' do not carry a case marker in (7) and (8). On the contrary, the transitive subject 'yabu' is case-marked with the ergative case marker 'nggu' in (8). Hence, we can say that Dyirbal treats its intransitive subject at par with the object and marks its transitive subject differently than the intransitive subject. Thus, we consider Dyribal to be an ergative-absolutive language.

From a typological perspective, we are aware that there are widespread incidences of ergativity found cross-linguistically, but ergativity manifests through various means in different languages. Dixon (1994) reports that some languages differentiate between ergative and non-ergative subjects in terms of allowing special operations like movement, focus, scope, etc. For example, the nominative-accusative languages treat their intransitive and transitive subjects as syntactically similar and hence allow clause coordination as in (9).

(9) The boy$_i$ kissed a girl$_j$ and pro$_{i/*j}$ ran away.

In the English example given above, the clausal coordination for the subjects of transitive and intransitive subjects is allowed, to the exclusion of the object. Hence, the covert subject in the second clause may refer to the subject of the first clause. However, the 'pro' in the second clause may not refer to the object of the first clause. Thus, we have reasons to believe that the nominative-accusative language English treats its intransitive subject at par with the transitive subject.

On the other hand, ergative languages treat their intransitive subjects at par with their transitive objects and not the transitive subjects. In Dyirbal, for example, for operations like clause coordination, only the object NP (mother) may coordinate with the subject of the intransitive clause in both (10) and (11) given below

(10)   ŋguma   banaga-nyu   yabu-ŋgu   bura-n

        Father-abs   return-nonfont   mother-erg   see-$_{NONFUT}$

        'Father(S) returned and mother(A) saw him(O).'

        '*Father(S) returned and father(A) saw him(O).'

(11)	ŋguma	yabu-ŋgu	bura-n	banaga-nyu
	father-abs	mother-erg	see-nonfut	return-nonfut
	'Mother(A) saw father(O) and he(S) returned.'			
	'*Mother(A) saw father(O) and she(S) returned.'			

As discussed earlier in Sect. "Introduction", not all ergative languages are alike. Dixon (1994) discusses various types of ergative languages that manifest true and false ergativity, morphological and syntactic ergativity, and full and split ergativity. To state briefly, it is believed that only those languages that treat their intransitive subjects and objects alike similarly for the syntactic operations like clausal coordination (e.g. Dyirbal), relativization, control, etc., are truly ergative-absolutive. He states that there are many so-called false ergative languages that show ergative-absolutive alignment only in terms of morphological marking of case and verbal agreement. When it comes to syntactic operations mentioned above, they treat the subjects of transitive and intransitive clauses similarly. Hindi (a well-known WIAL) can be taken as an example of this kind of 'false' ergativity. See (12) given below.

(12)	jon$_i$-ne	bəkri$_i$	dekʰi	or	pro$_{i/*j}$	bʰag	gəya
	John.3.m.sg. erg	goat.3.f.sg. abs	see.f.sg.perf	and		run	go.m.sg.perf
	'John saw the goat and (John) ran away.'						
	'*John saw the goat and (goat) ran away.'						

It is evident from the example given above, that the object of the transitive clause and the subject of the intransitive clause behave alike in terms of carrying unmarked absolutive case and participating in the verbal agreement. However, when it comes to the syntactic operation of clausal coordination, it is the subject of the transitive clause which is interpreted for the missing NP argument of the intransitive clause, rather than the object of the transitive clause. Hence, Hindi, despite showing surface manifestation of ergative-absolutive alignment in terms of morphology, is nominative-accusative at the deeper, syntactic level.

Johns (1992), in fact, claims that there are no pure ergative languages. He discusses various instances of 'splits,' i.e. constructions where ergative-absolutive pattern fails to hold in ergative languages. Recall the case of WIALs (introduced briefly in Sect. "Introduction" of this paper), which are generally nominative-accusative languages, but show ergative-absolutive alignment in the perfective aspect. A pertinent question to ask at this juncture is about the reason behind the break in the nominative-accusative alignment. At the first sight, a nominative-accusative system for WIALs (which anyway show only morphological ergativity) looks fairly stable. Following the Inertia Theory of grammatical change proposed by Longobardi (2001), we understand that a language would not undergo change unless acted upon by external factors including phonological and semantic changes. In this regard, this volume addresses the issue of rise and spread of ergativity using the framework of social dialectology. Through her chapter titled 'Variation and Change in Dialects of Marathi: A social-dialectological approach,' Kulkarni-Joshi infers language change through a comparison between synchronic variation with historical sources. She demonstrates that the preservation and non-preservation of older patterns of language use (i.e. variation) can be traced and correlated with the social history of the regions. Thus, she effectively maps the linguistic variation caused due to contact with neighbouring languages/bilingualism, increased social and geographical mobility, and bi-dialectalism among educated dialect speakers. However, a language does not completely transform into another language when it comes into contact with another form. The process of language change is slow and deliberate. Following Longobardi (2001), we are also aware that the change starts from the outermost periphery (i.e. sounds) and slowly moves inwards (i.e. towards narrow syntax). However, it is also true that not all domains of languages are open to change. Since ergativity is related not only to the differential marking of the transitive subject—contra the intransitive subject and object; but also, to the verbal agreement, we have reasons to believe that the presence of split-ergativity is a mark of some internal syntactic changes. Additionally, the direct correlation between the perfective aspect and ergativity points towards changes affected by the grammar of the language. The forthcoming discussion about patterns of ergativity will also shed more light on the principal variations found in various languages of the Western IA belt. Thus, it is imperative to question the underlying grammatical reason for ergativity among WIALs. Hence, this chapter investigates the deeper reasons that justify the presence of ergativity in numerous languages that are otherwise nominative-accusative.

Returning to the basics, we looked at Dixon's (1999) proposal about ergativity, we had learned that transitive subjects are distinguished from intransitive subjects and transitive objects. As we explore the underlying reasons for presence of split-ergativity, we need to look at the syntax of ergative clauses. Do syntactically ergative languages provide different positions for subjects of transitive and intransitive clauses? Do these languages place their intransitive subjects and transitive objects in a similar position (to the exclusion of transitive subjects) such that only the non-ergative case-marked arguments can enter into A'-movement, participate in clausal coordination among other things? Why does only the subject of the transitive clause come up with an ergative case? Why do 'false' ergative languages come up with ergative morphology at all? What is the common basis of ergativity? Is ergativity a unified phenomenon, or an instance of disconnected occurrences that come to look like an ergative pattern at the surface level?

The generative literature on ergativity is filled with numerous proposals to understand this phenomenon. To begin with, let us first see what the generative literature reports about the syntactic position of the ergative subjects. Marantz (1984) reported that ergative case systems place their ergative agents in the thematic subject position. Hence, the ergative subjects appear inside the verbal phrase. This is the reason why they behave differently than the nominative intransitive subjects. In this regard, Ura (2001) claims that if an agreement relationship is established between finite T and DP, an unmarked structural case is assigned to the concerned DP. If the DP agrees with the T and moves to spec, TP position, it is said to carry the nominative case. Such a DP would also show the properties of a grammatical subject. However, if the agreement relationship between the finite T and the DP is established in situ (as in spec, vP), the object would carry an unmarked case (called absolutive), but the subject DP would not exhibit grammatical subject properties. This, as per Ura (2001), is the reason behind similarities between intransitive subjects and objects. The puzzle around ergative languages is that, besides syntactic ergativity, morphological ergativity is not uniform for ergative languages either. Hence, there are many languages (including WIALs) where the subject may show ergative case morpheme, but the verbal agreement pattern may differ. One such language is Warlpiri.) proposes that it is the nature of the ergative case which sets the transitive subjects apart from the absolutive/nominative case-marked arguments. Let us consider the following example from Warlpiri to clarify things further.

(13)   Maliki-rli   ngarrka   yarlku-rnu
       dog-ERG   man   bite-PAST
       'A dog bit a man'

As per Legate, ergative is an inherent case given alongside a θ-role to the external argument in the transitive clauses. When it comes to the structural case assignment, contra Ura (2001), Legate proposes that transitive vP licenses structural accusative case via agreement to the object DP. A diagrammatic representation of the sentence is given below for clarification.

(14).

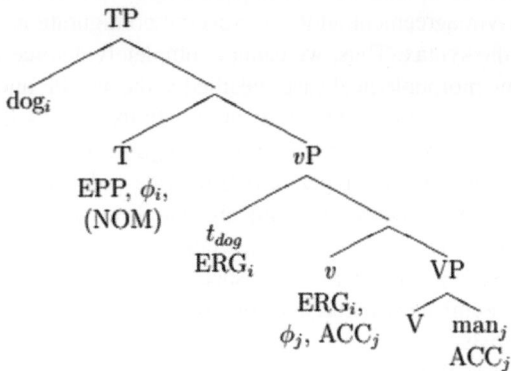

In the Warlpiri example given above, the transitive vP triggers φ-feature agreement with the object DP, resulting in object agreement and the licensing of accusative case. As Warlpiri lacks an accusative case suffix, it is morphologically realized as the default unmarked absolutive. The transitive v also assigns inherent ergative case to the subject 'dog.' Eventually, T triggers φ-feature agreement with the highest DP, i.e. the thematic subject 'dog.' The EPP feature of T attracts the subject DP to the spec, TP position, and the nominative case is not licensed on the subject as it already bears an inherent ergative case. Thus, the transitive subjects show different morphological marking of case than the intransitive subjects in Warlpiri.

As far as the morphological marking of ergative case morpheme is concerned, there is a set of proposals (Marantz, 1991; McFadden, 2010 among others) which states that case marking is an ornamental operation in language that does not bear any serious 'syntactic' consequence on languages. As per this view of the ergative case, languages follow a particular case markedness disjunctive hierarchy (see below)-

(15) Case Markedness Disjunctive Hierarchy

Lexical Case >> Dependent Case >> Structural (unmarked) Case >> Default Case

(Marantz, 1991: 247).

Thus, the narrow syntactic component only specifies certain situations where a case can be marked at the PF/MF interface in morphologically rich languages. Since the lexically governed case is specified in the lexicon, it appears with certain predicates and will be the first one to be marked if the situation warrants its use. The dependent case is the second to be assigned, where the dependent case requires a specific configuration when it c-commands a DP. The primary condition for dependent case marking is the presence of the concerned DP within the V+I domain. Ergative and accusative are assigned under this dependent case category for ergative-absolutive and nominative-accusative languages respectively. The structural case is considered to be a repercussion of agreement between a DP and a case assigning head like v and T, and so on. The major problem with this view of ergativity is that the morphological case is considered to be distinct from the abstract case which is operational in the narrow syntax. Even when we talk about case assignment via agreement and/or in specific configurations, these conditions are specified in the syntax. Thus, we cannot completely divorce the case assigned in syntax from the morphological case specified at the MF/PF interface.

A survey of the generative literature on ergativity reveals that the perfective aspect, indeed, conditions ergative-absolutive alignment in numerous languages. In this regard, Coon and Preminger (2012) provide a directionality table to map the cross-linguistic patterns for environments that allow ergativity. As per Coon & Preminger's findings, the ergative pattern occurs more frequently in certain conditions like the presence of the perfective aspect. Additionally, it is more likely that the third person nominals will carry the ergative case marker than the first or second person nominals.

See the fixed directionality scale below.

(16) Fixed Directionality of Aspectual and Person-based splits

(a). Fixed directionality of aspectual splits

←— ERGATIVE		NON-ERGATIVE —→	
perfective	≫ imperfective	≫ progressive	

(b). Fixed directionality of person splits

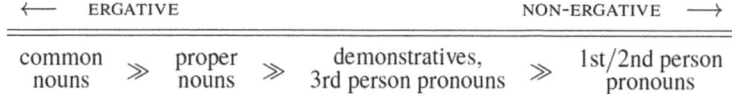

←— ERGATIVE			NON-ERGATIVE —→
common nouns	≫ proper nouns	≫ demonstratives, 3rd person pronouns	≫ 1st/2nd person pronouns

This observation makes us wonder why certain factors like perfectivity and third person are likely to facilitate ergativity. Indeed, the findings concur with the ergativity patterns found in WIALs. We will see (in the upcoming discussion) that ergativity among WIALs is facilitated primarily by the perfective aspect. For those WIALs which do not show ergative case marking for all transitive subjects in the perfective aspect, it is still more prevalent on the third person subject than on the first and second person subjects. Hence, one certainly wonders about the reason behind the directionalities. Is it for the underlying syntactic configuration of certain aspects and persons that numerous languages across the globe prefer ergativity in perfective aspect, and are more likely to mark their third person subjects with ergative case morphemes? Coon & Preminger claim that these observed tendencies result from a certain syntactic arrangement that exerts specific restrictions on the occurrence of ergative alignment in languages? The point is further supported by Laka (2017) who says that the term 'splits' is a misnomer for constraints levied by the syntactic component due to language-specific rules and phenomena.

As per Coon and Preminger's analysis, the phenomenon of split-ergativity is an outcome of the extended structure of the progressive aspect in Basque. To elaborate, the progressive aspect marked by the morpheme 'ari' leads to a split in the clause such that it embeds a locative-marked subordinate clause containing the lexical verb and its object. Following the dependent case analysis for ergativity, since the progressive aspect splits the clause, the subject does not have another DP for reference. Thus, the transitive subject in Basque is not marked ergative in the progressive aspect, and a split-ergative pattern is observed. Ergativity, however, is clearly seen in the perfective aspect as there is no clausal split. The language is a default ergative-absolutive language where the transitive subject is marked with ergative.

Ergative Patterns in Western Indo-Aryan Languages

Returning to the WIALs being discussed in this chapter, we must remember that, unlike Basque which is a default ergative-absolutive language that shows chance nominative-accusative pattern in the progressive aspect, we are dealing with a set of languages that are default nominative-accusative. These languages show ergative-absolutive pattern only in the perfective aspect. Thus, we wonder why the nominative-accusative pattern will be disrupted to give way to an ergative pattern. Before we explore the reasons behind the emergence of ergativity in the Western Indo-Aryan languages, I will first introduce the languages under discussion in this chapter namely Haryanavi, Mewati, Mewari, Marwari, Punjabi, Gujarati, and Marathi. Let us first locate these languages on the following map (Map 10.1).

The Haryanavi language is spoken primarily in the regions of the Haryana state, Delhi and Western Uttar Pradesh. For the present purpose, the author has focused on the variety spoken in and around West Delhi. Mewati, another language from the state of Haryana in Delhi, is a minority language spoken chiefly by the Muslim community of the Mewat district in Haryana. Mewari is spoken in Rajsamand, Bhilwara, Udaipur, Chittorgarh, and Pratapgarh districts of Rajasthan state, and Mandsaur, Neemuch districts of Madhya Pradesh state of India. The author has collected data from the Udaipur district and the empirical data presented here is from the fieldwork thus conducted. The next language Marwari is a well-known language originating in the state of Rajasthan. It is primarily spoken in the Jaisalmer, Barmer, Jodhpur and Bikaner districts of Rajasthan. The Marwari community is famous across India as a trading community, which explains the spread of Marwari language across India due to migration for trade by the concerned community. It was found by the author during her fieldwork that geographically distant dialects of Marwari may or may not show ergative patterns. Thus, the representative data used here was collected from native speakers of Marwari who belong to the Jodhpur district of Rajasthan. Punjabi language, along with Marwari, is spoken in regions of India and Pakistan. In comparison with Marwari, Punjabi is spoken by a greater population. The Punjabi empirical data provided in the chapter has been collected by Punjabi language speakers from the Delhi-NCR region. The next language to be considered in the chapter—Marathi is the official language of Maharashtra, and a co-official language in Goa state and the union territory

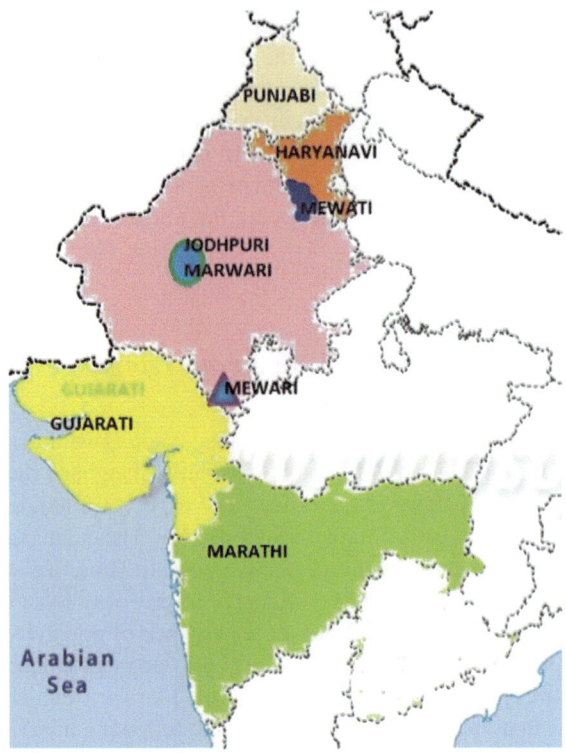

Map 10.1 Western Indo-Aryan languages

of Daman, Diu & Silvassa. Gujarati is the official language of Gujarat, a state in India. It is one of the 28 official languages of India and is spoken by 55.5 million speakers.

As a brief note, I would like to draw your attention to the fact that not all of these languages are given the status of a 'language.' While Gujarati, Punjabi and Marathi have received their fair share of recognition as independent languages and are well-studied in the linguistics literature, Haryanavi, Mewati and Mewari are treated as mere dialects and are rarely studied in linguistic literature. Marwari is the only language in this paper that is known to be a dialect, and yet, has received some attention in linguistics research. Nevertheless, each language brings something unique to the study by showing interesting variations in terms of how these languages manifest ergative patterns in the perfective aspect.

Let us begin with observing patterns of ergativity from some Western Indo-Aryan languages namely Haryanavi, Mewati, Mewari, Marwari, Marathi, Punjabi and Gujarati. Bhatt (2007) refers to the ergative paradigm as being marked by an overt case marker and object-verb agreement for Indo-Aryan languages. I present representative data from the concerned languages to show how ergativity manifests in each of these languages. Let us first begin with the ergativity pattern found in Haryanavi. See examples given below.

(17)   kalu   avɛga

        Kalu.3.m.sg.nom   come.3.m.sg.fut

        'Kalu will come.'   Haryanavi

(18)	kalu	lali-nɛ	bəjar-mɛ̃	dekʰɛga	
	Kalu.3.m.sg.nom	lali.3.f.sg.acc	market.loc	see.3.m.sg.fut	
	'Kalu will see Lali in the market.'				Haryanavi

(19)   kalu-nɛ   lali   bəjar-mɛ̃   dekʰi

        Kalu.3.m.sg.erg   lali.3.f.sg.acc market.loc   see.3.f.sg.perf

        'Kalu saw Lali   Haryanavi
        in the market.'

The first two constructions in the data set from Haryanavi display a nominative-accusative pattern. The intransitive (17) and transitive (18) subjects carry an unmarked nominative case and trigger verbal agreement. The object in (18) appears with an accusative case marker and does not show agreement with the verb. The pattern, however, changes in the perfective aspect as the transitive subject appears with an overt ergative case marker and fails to trigger verbal agreement. In the perfective aspect (see 19), the verbal agreement is triggered by the unmarked object. Thus, we can observe the split-ergativity in Haryanavi, where the language normally displays a nominative-accusative pattern; until we introduce perfectivity, where the ergative-absolute pattern is visible.

A similar pattern can be observed for Mewati as well. The intransitive (20) and transitive (21) subjects carry a covert nominative case and trigger verbal agreement. However, in the perfective aspect, the subject is marked with an ergative case and fails to trigger verbal agreement. In case of Mewati also, the subject-verb agreement is disrupted in (22).

(20)   kalu   avega

        Kalu.3.m.sg.nom   come.3.m.sg.fut

        'Kalu will come.'   Mewati

(21)   kalu   lali-ku   bəjar-mɛ̃   dekʰega

        Kalu.3.m.sg.nom   lali.3.f.sg.acc market.loc   see.3.m.sg.fut

        'Kalu saw Lali in the market.'   Mewati

(22)   kalu-nɛ   lali-ku   bəjar-mɛ̃   dekʰya
        Kalu.3.m.sg.erg   lali.3.f.sg.acc   market.loc   see.def.perf
        'Kalu saw Lali in the market.'   Mewati

The data given below shows ergative constructions in other WIALs.

(23)   kalu   bəjar-mɛ̃   načyo
        Kalu.3.m.sg.nom   market.loc   see.def.perf
        'Kalu saw Lali in the market.'   Mewari

(24)   kalu   lali-nɛ   bula   ryo   ε
        Kalu.3.m.sg.nom Lali.3.f.sg.acc   call   prog.m.sg   be.3.m.sg.pres
        'Kalu is calling   Mewari
        Lali.'

(25)   kalu-nɛ   lali-nɛ   bəjar-mɛ̃   dekʰyo
        Kalu.3.m.sg.erg   lali.3.f.sg.acc   market.loc   see.def.perf
        'Kalu saw Lali in the market.'   Mewari

(26)   ram   baṭi   kʰae   hɛ
        ram.m.sg.nom   bread.f.sg.acc   eat.prog   be.m.3sg.pres
        'Ram is eating food.'   Marwari

(27)   jon   məṭki   ucəyɪ
        john.m.sg.nom   pot.f.sg.acc   pick.f.sg.perf
        'John picked up the pot.'   Marwari

(28)   kalu   lali-nɛ   bəjar-mɛ̃   dekʰi ho
        Kalu.3.m.sg.nom lali.3.f.sg.acc   market.loc   see.3f.sg
                                                          be.3.m.sg.perf
        'Kalu saw Lali in the   Marwari
        market.'

Similar patterns of perfective aspect-based split-ergativity are found in other Western Indo-Aryan languages, as described variously in the works of Legate (2014), Mistry (1997), and Bhatt (2007). The aforementioned WIALs show ergativity across transitive constructions in terms of either object-verb agreement or the ergative case marker, or both, the forthcoming WIALs show differential marking of the subject with ergativity. As we will observe in the upcoming empirical data, Gujarati (29) corresponds to the previously mentioned WIALs in terms of showing ergative case markers on all subjects of transitive clauses in the perfective aspect. On the other hand, Marathi (30)–(32) and Punjabi (33)–(35) show object-verb agreement for all transitive constructions but mark ergative case only on the third person subjects in the perfective aspect.

(29)   men/ten/Siṭa-e   raj-ne   pajavyo

1/2/Sita.3.f.sg.erg   Raj.3.m.sg.acc   harass.3.m.sg.pst

'I/You/Sita harassed Raj.'   (Gujarati: Mistry,
                                                               1997)

(30)   mɪ   bɪčari-ne   səgla kam   kela

I.nom   poor-erg   all work   do-perf.1sg

'Poor little me did all   (Marathi:
the work.'   Legate, 2014)

(31)   tu   bɪchari-ne   səgla kam   kelas

you.nom   poor-erg   all work   do-perf.2sg

'Poor little you did   (Marathi: Legate,
all the work.'   2014)

(32)   liki-ne   aɲi   mi   keḷi   kʰalli

liki-erg   and 1.sg.nom   banana.npl.nom   eat-perf-npl

'Liki and I ate   (Marathi:
bananas.'   Legate,
                                                         2014)

(33)   mɛ-*ne   kuṛi-nu   vekʰeya

I-erg   girl.acc   see.def.perf

'I saw the girl.'   (Punjabi)

(34)   tu-*ne   kuṛi-nu   vekʰeya

You-erg   girl.acc   see.def.perf

'You saw the girl.'   (Punjabi)

(35)   o-ne   kuṛi-nu   vekʰeya

He-erg   girl.acc   see.def.perf

'He saw the girl.'   (Punjabi)

Summarizing the data given above, we can see that ergativity is a regularly occurring phenomenon in the Western Indo-Aryan languages under discussion in this chapter. All of these languages show a default nominative-accusative alignment. This pattern is broken in the perfective aspect, as the subject-verb agreement is disrupted and (with a few exceptions) the subject is marked with the ergative case marker. So far, I have shown that ergativity manifests in various forms in the languages of the Western Indo-Aryan belt. There are interesting variations in ergative-absolutive alignment not only in terms of the morphological form of the ergative case marker, but also in terms of their distribution across the person, verbal agreement, and form of object marking. While Haryanavi, Mewati, Gujarati and Mewari show aspect-based ergativity for all subjects, languages including Punjabi and Marathi further restrict ergative to the third person subjects. Stating that the ergative case marker is a prominent feature of ergativity does not suffice as we can see that Marwari fails to come up with any ergative marking on either subject. But it is considered to show split-ergativity as it shows object-verb agreement (alongside person-based subject-auxiliary agreement) in the perfective aspect.

While Haryanavi restricts the morphological case marker on the object DPs and shows object-verb agreement, Mewari repeats the syncretic case marker on the subject and object DPs, and shows a default verbal agreement pattern. In another comparison, Gujarati shows compulsory object-verb agreement irrespective of case marking on the subject and object, while Marwari does not mark its subjects with ergative case and shows multiple agreement pattern on the verbal complex. For Punjabi and Marathi, the subject DPs (marked or unmarked with ergative case) never trigger agreement. Instead, we find default agreement if the object DP is case-marked, and the presence of object-verb agreement, if the object DP remains case unmarked. A consolidated survey of ergative patterns from the concerned languages will help us understand the ergativity patterns and their unique manifestations in WIALs. Please see Table 10.1 given below for your reference.

As is evident from the data given above, the phenomenon of ergativity is highly diverse in these closely related languages. There is no unified operation, no clear pattern of case, and agreement to define ergativity. In fact, the safest possible definition for ergativity (at this stage) is to call it a break-away pattern from the default nominative-accusative pattern. A pertinent question to ask at this juncture concerns the reason behind this 'split' from the default nominative-ergative patterns. Let us look briefly at various perspectives about split-ergativity in WIALs.

Table 10.1 Ergative patterns in Western Indo-Aryan languages

Language	Subject marking	Object marking	Verbal agreement
Haryanavi	nɛ	–	Obj-verb
Mewati	nɛ	-/ku	Obj-verb/default
Mewari	nɛ	-/nɛ	Obj-verb/Default
Marwari	–	-/nɛ	Obj-verb + subj-aux
Gujarati	e (3P)	-/ne	Obj-verb
Punjabi	ne (3P)	-/nu	Obj-verb/Default
Marathi	e(3P)	-/la	Obj-verb/default

Why 'Split' Ergativity: Different Analysis

We have seen in the previous section that several Western Indo-Aryan languages display the phenomenon of split-ergativity in the perfective aspect. All of these languages are otherwise default nominative-accusative. However, something happens in the perfective aspect that all transitive clauses break away from the nominative-accusative pattern. We learned that ergativity in these languages is characterized by the presence of overt case marking on the subject of the transitive clause and the absence of subject-verb agreement. However, the puzzle deepens as we observe the differing patterns of ergative-absolutive alignment in these languages. So, it is imperative to question the source of ergativity. In this subsection, I will present a brief overview of the rise and spread of ergativity in WIALs.

If we view it from the diachronic perspective, Sanskrit (Old Indo-Aryan) was primarily a nominative-accusative language. The origins of most New Indo-Aryan languages under discussion in this paper can be traced back to Sanskrit. Thus, one needs to probe the underlying syntactic phenomena that led to this 'break away' from the default nominative-accusative alignment.' While it is true that a language undergoes many changes over a period of time, how susceptible is a language to change? Following the inertia theory of language change (Longobardi, 2001), we know that changes in the grammar of a language are far and few. Thus, even when a language changes over a period of time, one is more likely to encounter phonological and morphological changes than changes in the narrow syntactic component, which is more likely to remain undisturbed by diachronic language changes. Therefore, even if Sanskrit underwent profound changes from the Old Indo-Aryan to the New Indo-Aryan period, is it possible that it developed a new alignment altogether? This observation about language change resonates in a sense with the Borer–Chomsky Conjecture mentioned in Baker (2008) which states that 'all parameters of variation are attributable to differences in the features of particular items (e.g. the functional heads) in the lexicon.'

Udaar (2016) claims that ergativity in the concerned WIALs is not deep, syntactic ergativity. Rather, we are dealing with a case of superfluous, surface, morphological ergativity which does not keep intransitive subjects at par with the object DPs. The author claims that when it comes to syntactic operations like focus or relativization, the transitive and intransitive subjects are treated at par in the WIALs. Yet, the findings about the case and agreement phenomena in the generative literature point toward the fact that they are computed in the narrow syntactic component (Chomsky, 1982, Vergnaud, 1986, among others).

In the diachronic literature, the development of Indo-Aryan ergativity has been attributed to the passive constructions in Sanskrit (Dixon 1994; Bhatt, 2005, among others). These passive constructions contained a '-ta' participle used to mark past perfect participial forms and the subject carried an instrumental case marker '-ena.' Due to language decay and radical loss of Sanskrit case, this construction was reanalysed to represent an active voice construction. In the process,

Chandra and Udaar (2014) show that the syntax remained mostly unchanged as the instrumental subject still carried out the oblique function and the verbal agreement happened with the object. With the advent of New Indo-Aryan languages, Verbeke and Cuypere (2009) point towards '-nɛ,' a postposition used to mark accusative/dative in Old Rajasthani language, which was utilized in New Indo-Aryan languages like Hindi to mark the oblique subjects. In this chapter, we observe the use of the same postposition marker for case in Mewari, Marwari and Haryanavi (a descendant of Rajasthani spoken in Haryana and Delhi).

The historic account of the rise of ergativity in WIALs yet again takes into account factors including language decay, migration and language contact (as demonstrated by Kulkarni-Joshi in this volume). However, in this paper, my objective is to look at the deep syntactic reasons that make possible the presence of 'split-ergativity' in a number of closely related Western Indo-Aryan languages. In this regard, I further show that transitivity and activeness at the vP site are the two major factors that facilitate perfective aspect-based split-ergativity in these languages. The upcoming sections analyse two diagnostics for the WIALs.

Parameters for Ergativity

The discussion so far about ergative paradigms among WIALs shows that there are two important factors connected to ergativity—one is the link with transitivity. We have seen that the ergative alignment—the presence of overt case marker (except in Marwari) and absence of subject-verb agreement—is closely related to the transitivity of the clause. Secondly, we notice that, unlike the nominative-accusative alignment where the subject triggers verbal agreement, the vP site is the place of action in ergative clauses. The following subsections explain the primary requisites for ergativity among WIALs.

Transitivity

In this section, I will discuss transitivity as an important prerequisite for ergative alignment to manifest in the concerned languages. Let us begin with the primary definition of ergativity as given by Dixon (1994), which clearly shows that the ergative case appears only with the 'transitive' subjects (refer to 1). In another instance of support to the argument for transitive as a parameter for ergativity, Baker and Bobaljik (2017) conclude that ergative is an instance of the dependent case which requires the presence of a DP in the object position. The term 'dependent' case itself conveys the significance of another argument. In this sense, the presence of another (object) DP is crucial for the licensing of the 'dependent' ergative case.

To instantiate their claim, they give evidence from Shipibo where ergative appears on the derived (internal) subjects of constructions only after the introduction of another argument. See examples from Shipibo below.

(36)   Maria-ra mawa-ke
       Maria-PRT die-PRF
       'Maria died.'

(37)   Nokon   shino-n-ra e-a   mawa-xon-ke   (*shino-ra)
       my.GEN   monkey-ERG-PRT   me-ABS die-APPL-PRF   monkey.ABS-PRT
       'My monkey died on me.'

The Shipibo data given in (36) shows an unaccusative construction where the subject is unmarked. In this scenario, the subject is a lone argument in the clause. Hence, it is not eligible for a dependent ergative. However, with the addition of the applicative layer '-xon' on the unaccusative verb, there arises the possibility of adding an object DP. In construction (37), we can find that an object DP is present; thus, the ergative case marker becomes necessary on the subject.

Next, Baker and Bobaljik demonstrate a construction where the ergative is lost from the subjects in cases where the construction is detransitivized. The process of detransitivization effectively refers to removal (or making optional) of the referential object. See (38) and (39) for clarification.

(38)   ətləg-e   mətqəmət   (kawkaw-ək)   kili-nin
       Father-ERG   butter.ABS   bread-LOC   spread.on-3SG>3SG
       'The father spread the butter (on the bread).'

(39)   ətləg-ən   (kawkaw-ək)   mətqə-rkele-nen
       Father-ABS   bread-LOC   butter-spread.on-3SG>3SG
       'The father spread butter (on the bread).'

Note that the subject in (38) carries an ergative case marker, where the object is present. However, as the object becomes optional in (39), the ergative case marker disappears from the subject. Baker and Bobaljik attribute this loss of ergative from the subject in (39) to the incorporation object 'butter' into the verbal complex. Given the dependent analysis for ergativity, the configurational set-up fails to take off owing to the absence of object DP in the construction.

On similar lines, Deal (2009) assures of transitivity condition for ergativity, especially in a dependent context. However, her definition of transitivity relates to the importance of object agreement. As per her claim, in languages like Nez

Perce which show multiple agreement on the verbal complex, object agreement is the key to appearance of an ergative case on the subject. She instantiates her claim with the following constructions from Nez Perce.

(40) pit'ʼıin-im   pʼaa-yaˆx-na   picpʼıc-ne
      girl-ERG   3/3-find-PERF   cat-OBJ
      'The girl found the cat.'

(41) pit'ʼıin   hi-yʼaaˆx-na   pʼıcpic
      Girl   3SUBJ-find-PERF Cat
      'The girl found her cat.'

Note that the ergative is retained in (40) where the subject and object agreement is seen on the verbal complex. However, the ergative marker vanishes from the subject in example (41) as the verbal complex does not show object-verb agreement. Hence, as per Deal, transitivity is a parameter for ergative alignment, albeit understood in terms of necessary object agreement rather than only presence of an object DP.

As far as WIALs are concerned, it is clear that transitivity (in terms of object-verb agreement) is certainly a valid parameter and shows up prominently in the ergative paradigm. Let's begin with the Haryanavi data given below in (42)–(43), which shows that the appearance of ergativity is closely linked with the object-verb agreement.[1] Given the empirical data, the presence of an object is essential for ergative as it fails to appear on the intransitive subject in (42).

We find that the ergative appears only on the transitive subject in (42). However, the presence of object is not a sufficient condition for the presence of ergative case on the subject, as is evident from the data given in (44). In agreement with Deal (ibid.), object agreement is necessary for the ergative in case of Haryanavi.

(42) lalla   pəʈ   gya
      Lala-nom   fall   go.perf
      'Lala fell.'

---

[1] A reviewer points out that ergative case marking on the transitive subjects may be blocked by the presence of an intransitive light verb like 'čuka' in the perfective aspect. The presence of light verb will have syntactic repercussions and would require further insights into the structure of light verbs, the V_{trans}-$v_{intrans}$ combinations allowed by each language and their interaction with other elements in the syntax. Hence, it should be considered beyond the scope of this paper.

(43) lalla-nɛ   imli   kʰai

      lala-erg   imli.f.sg   eat.f.sg.perf

      'Lala ate imli.'

(44) lalla   imli   kʰavɛ   tʰa

      lala   imli.f.sg   eat.def.prog   be.m.sg.pst

      'Lala was eating Imli.'

The same observation holds for other WIALs, where object agreement is a necessity and features prominently in the patterns of ergative constructions. See Table 10.2.

Chandra et al. (2017) also provide clinching evidence to highlight the significance of transitivity parameter for ergativity in WIALs. They take an example from Punjabi, where unergative verbs may allow the subject to carry an ergative case in the perfective aspect (45), while the unaccusative verbs do not allow the ergative case marker on the subject (46).

(45) kuɽi-ne həsseya

      girl-erg laugh.perf.m.sg

      'The girl laughed.'

(46) kuɽi/*kuɽi-ne dıggi

      girl.nom/*girl-erg fall.perf.f.sg

      'The girl fell.'   Chandra et al. (2017)

As per Chandra et al., transitivity is an essential condition for ergativity to appear in Punjabi. In case of the aforementioned constructions, while both unergatives and unaccusatives appear to have only subjects, only the unergatives carry an underlying implicit object. See (47)–(48) to understand the difference.

Table 10.2 Verbal agreement in ergative constructions among WIALs

Language	Verbal agreement
Haryanavi	Obj-verb
Mewati	Obj-verb/default
Mewari	Obj-verb/Default
Marwari	Obj-verb + subj-aux
Gujarati	Obj-verb
Punjabi	Obj-verb/Default
Marathi	Obj-verb/default

(47) jɔn-ne ravən-di   hɔssi   hɔssi
      John-erg ravan-gen.f.sg   laugh.f.sg   laugh.perf.f.sg
      'John laughed Ravan's laughter.'

(48) *jɔn   digg   diggeya
      John.nom   fall.N   fall.perf.m.sg
      'John fell a fall.'

In case of unergatives, the object gets incorporated into the verb following Hale and Keyser, 1993. However, for Punjabi, it is shown that the implicit objects remain relevant even after incorporation into the verb. The implicitly significant role of objects is shown through the observation that the object can be modified using adjectives, and it governs verbal agreement (as in (47)). Thus, we find more convincing evidence from WIALs to prove that object agreement is crucial for ergative alignment. I will now discuss our next parameter that is vP-activeness in the next section.

vP-Activeness

Referring again to the fixed directionality of aspectual splits in (16) by Coon and Preminger (2012), we know that ergativity is more likely to surface in certain conditions like perfectivity than in the progressive aspect. As far as WIALs are concerned it has been widely established that these languages show an aspect-based split where ergativity appears only in the perfective aspect. This section provides clear insights into the role played by the composition and location of AspP in bringing about ergativity among WIALs. I attempt to understand the parametric settings that trigger ergativity in an otherwise nominative-accusative environment.

In the previous section, I have already shown that object agreement is crucial for ergativity. It should be noted at this point that the object agreement effectively happens inside the vP domain. There are many accounts linking ergative case marking to the vP domain itself. The most prominent proposals come from Laka (2017), Legate (2014), Udaar (2016), and Ura (2006) who unanimously conclude that ergative is assigned when the subjects are located in the specifier of vP. Given the requirement of object agreement and the position of ergative case licensing, it becomes clear that the vP plays a crucial role and is the main site of action. I will now investigate the ergativity paradigm to highlight the role of operations happening at the vP level.

Let us begin with a close comparison between the nominative-accusative and ergative-absolutive alignments in Hindi and Punjabi. See (49)–(52) given below.

(49) jɔn   roʈi   kʰa   rəha   hɛ
      john.3.m.sg.nom   bread.f.sg.acc eat   prog.m.sg   be.3.m.sg.pres
      'John is eating bread.'   Hindi

(50) jɔn-ne   roʈi   kʰa   li
      john.3.m.sg.erg   bread.f.sg.acc   eat   lv.f.sg.perf
      'John has eaten bread.'   Hindi

(51) munda   roʈi   kʰanḍa   e
      boy.nom   bread.f.sg.acc   eat.hab.m.sg   be.3.sg.pres
      'The boy eats bread.'   Punjabi

(52) munde-ne   roʈi   kʰaḍḍi
      boy-erg   bread.f.sg.acc   eat.f.sg.perf
      'The boy ate bread.'   Punjabi

If we carefully notice the verbal agreement pattern of the aforementioned WIALs, it can be seen that the person feature is represented for subject agreement in (49) and (51). On the other hand, the agreement pattern of (50) and (52) shows a clear absence of the person feature which is otherwise assumed to be located at the TP (Mahajan, 1990; Bhatt, 2005; Chandra & Kaur, 2017). This again points in the direction of vP as the main site of ergative case licensing.

Given the categorical participation of perfective vP in bringing about the split(-ergativity) in the nominative-accusative paradigm of WIALs, it is legitimate to investigate the events occurring at the vP level in the perfective aspect. In this regard, Udaar (2016) blames the defective nature of the participial perfective aspect for the manifestation of ergativity. Historically, the WIAL ergative construction is said to have arisen from a passive participial construction from the Old Indo-Aryan period (Stronski, 2009), where the subject carried a non-nominative, instrumental case marker and object-verb agreement was prominent. Chandra & Udaar (2014) further blame the loss of passive feature from the perfective vP for a possible reanalysis of the passive construction, and eventual upsurge of ergative structure. Returning to the WIAL ergative pattern in the present context, Udaar (ibid.) proposes that ergativity arises out of a structural phenomenon where the subject gets stranded inside the specifier of vP, unable to move up to the spec, TP position. Let us begin with following the structural representation given in (53).

(53).

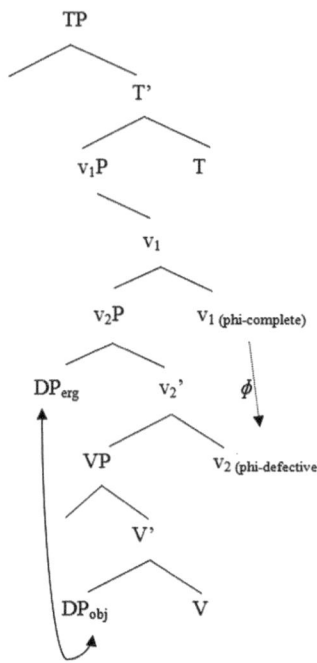

The analysis for ergativity among WIALs hinges primarily on the defective nature of perfective vP, which lacks a person feature. In the scenario given above, the object DP requires a structural accusative case from v2. However, that is not possible given the incomplete phi-feature set in v2. Hence, the v2 head borrows a complete phi-feature set from a higher aspectual v1P head. The v1P, in return also loses out on its specifier position due to the donated phi-set. Consequently, the object DP enters into an agreement with the (now phi-complete) v2 head and receives a structural accusative case. The subject, in turn, is left without a structural case because it cannot move up to spec, v1P, and consequently to spec, TP. Recall that the v1P had lost its specifier position due to phi-feature borrowing between vPs. Therefore, the subject eventually becomes stranded inside vP.

Given the prevalent conditions, a configurational set-up is triggered. The computational set-up contains of a structurally case-marked object DP and a subject DP stranded within the specifier of v2P. These conditions are ideal for a dependent set-up, and the subject becomes eligible for an ergative case. Therefore, the ergative constructions come into place where the object-verb agreement is prominent, the subject receives a dependent case instead of T-related nominative. At the PF/MF interface, the subject is located at the spec, vP position where it gets an overt case marker (Laka, 2017; Udaar, 2016). Hence, the ergative paradigm comes into effect. I shall now present another piece of evidence underlining the importance of vP-activeness for ergativity to appear in WIAL.

Marwari, one of the more well-known WIALs discussed in this paper comes up with a peculiar pattern for ergativity, where the ergative case marker is absent and a mixed agreement pattern prevails. Thus, we can see that Marwari presents a fascinating paradigm of ergative and has been noticed for its divergence from ergative pattern in other linguistics accounts. Khokhlova (2001) claims that Marwari is, in fact, undergoing a process of ergativity attrition. Patel (2007) also notices that Marwari closely resembles Kutchi Gujarati in terms of showing multiple agreement, such that while the verb triggers (person, number) agreement with object DP, the subject DP agrees in person with the tense auxiliary. See (54)–(55) for empirical evidence.

(54) mhāī sītā-ne   dekhī   hū

      I   Sita-acc saw.f am.1sg

      'I have seen Sita.'

(55) ve   sītā-ne   dekhī   hai

      they   Sita-acc   saw.f   are.3sg/pl

      'They have seen Sita.'   Magier (1983)

In this regard, Udaar (2015) also confirms the gradual loss of ergative paradigm from Marwari. She attributes this loss of ergative to reanalysis of perfective vP. Given that the structure and peculiar feature composition of perfective head is a historical construct, it is possible that the perfective head in Marwari became reanalysed as one containing a complete phi-feature head. See (56) for a diagrammatic representation.

(56).

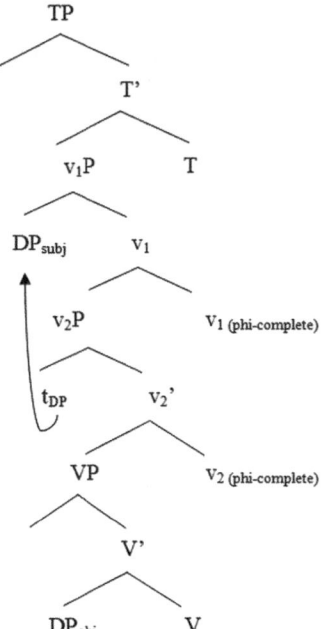

Given the complete phi-feature set of v2P in Marwari, there is no requirement of feature inheritance between the vPs. The v2P has sufficient phi-features to enter into an agreement relation with the object DP. The object DP, hence, receives a structural case from the v2P. Given that there is no feature inheritance and consequently no loss of specifier of v1P, the subject DP also moves to TP, and gets a nominative case. Marwari has effectively become a nominative-accusative system in the perfective aspect. In fact, the object-verb morphological agreement that is mistakenly assumed to mark ergativity is only a remnant of an old ergative construction. It is, therefore, opportune to assume that Marwari is a completely nominative-accusative system with no window for an ergative system.

Summarizing our understanding of operations leading up to ergativity in WIALs, we realize that the parameter of vP-activeness refers to the vP becoming main site of the operations for object agreement and subject case marking. Most WIALs under discussion in this paper get ergative due to the aforementioned operations. Contrastively, Marwari is a standalone test case study where the subject case marking does not happen inside the vP. Given the diachronic process of reanalysis of perfective vP into a non-defective verbal head leads to a completely nominative-accusative paradigm. The eventual loss of ergative from Marwari is actually brought about by the movement of some operations (read subject case marking via phi-feature agreement with T) into the TP domain. Hence, it is correct to assume at this point that restriction of verbal agreement and case licensing in the vP domain seems to be the key to ergativity. I will now present the last piece of evidence in support of the vP-activeness parameter.

Given the plethora of WIALs showing variation in ergativity, we observed another split within the aspectual ergative split, i.e. person split. WIALs like Punjabi and Marathi stand apart from other WIALs by restricting ergative case marker only on the third person subjects. The representative empirical data showing a person-based ergative split in Punjabi is given below.

(57) mɛ-(*ne)   roṭi   kʰaḍḍi
      1.m.sg-(*erg)   bread.f.sg.acc   eat.f.sg.perf
      'I ate bread.'

(58) tu-(*ne)   roṭi   kʰaḍḍi
      2.m.sg-(*erg)   bread.f.sg.acc   eat.f.sg.perf
      'You ate bread.'

(59) munde-ne/o-ne   roṭi   kʰaḍḍi
      boy-erg/3.sg-erg bread.f.sg.acc   eat.perf.f.sg
      'The boy/(S)he ate bread.'   (Chandra & Kaur, 2017)

As is evident from the Punjabi data given above, the ergative case marker fails to appear on the first and second person subjects. Only the third person subjects show a clear ergative case marker. However, it is interesting to note that the object-verb agreement pattern is carried across the constructions in (51)–(53), despite the absence of the subject case marker. A similar pattern is observed in Marathi; Table 10.3 summarizes the person-based split-ergative pattern of Punjabi and Marathi.

It is interesting to note here that despite the person split, the object-verb agreement is still crucial and present even with unmarked subjects in both Punjabi and Marathi. The languages stand out from other WIALs as the 1st and 2nd person subjects do not carry ergative case marker, and ergative appears on 3rd person subjects. The object-verb agreement pattern remains uniform across the board.

Here again, I concur with Laka (2017) who suggests that the apparent splits results from some language-specific syntactic mechanisms. To add to this, Chandra and Kaur (2014) propose that, in Punjabi, 1st/2nd person subjects carry an oblique case marker, and hence appear unmarked. On the other hand, the 3rd person subjects carry a proper ergative case and appear with a distinct case marker.

Punjabi reveals further operations inside the ergative paradigm which lead to certain person licensing condition. As is established by now, Punjabi treats its 1st and 2nd person subjects differently from the 3rd person subjects. Given the Punjabi differential subject marking (DSM), based on the DP's person feature, the 1st and 2nd person subjects move up to spec of a higher VoiceP and get oblique case marking. On the other hand, the third person subjects are treated differently and they remain in the spec, vP position. See (60) below.

(60).

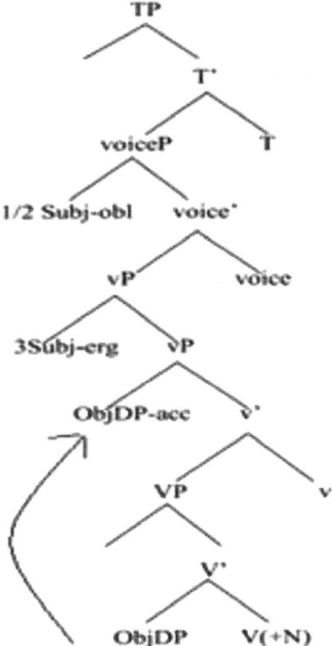

Table 10.3 Summarizes the person-based split ergative pattern of Punjabi and Marathi

Language	Subject marking			Object marking	Verbal agreement
Punjabi	-(1P)	-(2P)	ne (3P)	-/nu	Obj-verb/Default
Marathi	-(1P)	-(2P)	e(3P)	-/la	Obj-verb/default

The person-based split-ergativity in Punjabi can also be attributed to the vP-activeness parameter. In the previous paragraphs, we have already discussed the importance of vP as the site of all action including verbal agreement and case licensing, for the manifestation of ergativity. The latest evidence from Punjabi further adds to the investigation by showing that the ergative case marker appears on the subject only as long as it remains in situ. A clear departure from the default ergativity pattern is seen as soon as the 1st and 2nd person subjects move beyond the vP. However, the ergative pattern is still maintained owing to the defective vP in Punjabi, unlike Marwari.

In concluding this section, we can now justify that the manifestation of ergativity is highly dependent on the activeness of the vP site. We have so far seen that ergative constructions are typically marked by the prominence of object-verb agreement. Given the computational set-up of the WIALs, the absence of subject-verb agreement arises from the defective nature of the perfective verbal head. The ergativity paradigm is bound to manifest as long as the operations like verbal agreement and case licensing are restricted to the vP domain.

Conclusion

This paper observes the highly variant manifestations of ergative alignment in a multitude of Western Indo-Aryan languages namely Haryanavi, Mewati, Mewari, Marwari, Punjabi, Gujarati and Marathi. Given the wide variations within the ergative paradigm, it is hard to point out one phenomenon responsible for the landmark shift from default nominative-accusative alignment generally found in this language family.

I began with a review of prevalent literature concerning ergativity. An overall idea concerning the dependent ergative case considers transitivity as an important requisite for the alignment to occur. This means that the presence of an object DP is paramount to ergative case marking on the subject, and it is rightfully seen that ergative case appears only on the subjects of transitive clauses. A deeper investigation into the phenomenon of ergativity-transitivity interaction reveals the importance laid on object agreement. It is the object-verb agreement that defines the transitive condition in ergativity. I examine WIALs in this regard and realize the ergative, indeed, is clearly connected with the constructions where object agreement gains importance over the (non-existent) subject agreement.

Another parametric setting associated with WIAL ergativity concerns the aspect-based split. Here I identify vP-activeness as the prominent parametric setting leading to ergativity. Note that vP-activeness here refers to a plethora of syntactic operations, all happening within the realm of perfective vP. I concur with Laka (2017) who argues that the term 'split' is a misnomer, what we consider tendencies of languages leading up to specific case alignments result from language-specific syntactic mechanisms. For WIALs, I suggest that ergativity results from the syntactic operations triggered due to the feature composition of perfective vP and the necessity of object agreement. Therefore, ergative is only an outcome of the structure and analysis of vP in a specific language(s). The variations between vP result from either surface level preferences at PF or due to historical reanalysis of certain functional heads.

References

Baker, M., & Bobaljik, J. (2017). On inherent and dependent theories of the ergative case. The Oxford handbook of ergativity, 111–134.

Baker, M. C. (2008). The macroparameter in a microparametric world.

Barbiers, S. (2009). Locus and limits of syntactic microvariation. *Lingua, 119*(11), 1607–1623.

Bhatt, R. (2005). Long distance agreement in Hindi-Urdu. *Natural Language & Linguistic Theory, 23*(4), 757–807.

Bhatt, R. (2007). *Ergativity in Indo-Aryan Languages.* Retrieved from http://people.umass.edu/bhatt/papers/mit-nov2007-handout.pdf.

Borer, H. (1984). *Parametric Syntax.* Foris.

Chandra, P., & Udaar, U. (2012). Indo-Aryan ergativity: A case of Syntactic Intertia. In Paper presented at the 14th diachronic and generative syntax conference held at Lisbon, Portugal.

Chandra, P., & Kaur, G. (2017). Differential subject marking and person licensing condition. *Concentric: Studies in Linguistics, 43*(1), 25–46.

Chandra, P., Kaur, G., & Udaar, U. (2017). Optional ergativity with unergatives in Punjabi. *Taiwan Journal of Linguistics, 15*(2), 1–35.

Chomsky, N. (1982a). Some concepts and consequences of the theory of government and binding (Vol. 6). MIT press.

Conjecture (Baker, 2008)

Coon, J., & Preminger, O. (2012). Taking 'Ergativity' out of split ergativity: A structural account of aspect and person splits. *Lingbuzz* 001556.

Deal, A. R. (2009). The origin and content of expletives: Evidence from "Selection". Syntax 12:4, December 2009, 285–323, Blackwell Publishing Ltd.

Dixon, R. M. (1994). *Ergativity.* Cambridge University Press.

Johns, A. (1992). Deriving ergativity. *Linguistic Inquiry, 23*(1), 57–87.

Kaur, G. (2015). Person-based ergativity in Punjabi: Comparing transitive and unergative 1st/2nd person subjects. Indian Linguistics, 76–3.

Khokhlova, L. V. (2001). Ergativity Attrition in the History of Western New Indo-Aryan Languages (Punjabi, Gujarati, and Rajasthani). *The Yearbook of South Asian Languages and Linguistics*, 159–184.

Laka, I. (2017). Ergative need not split: An exploration into the TotalErg hypothesis. *The Oxford handbook of ergativity* (pp. 159–174). Oxford Handbooks.

Legate, J. A. (2014). Split ergativity based on nominal type. *Lingua, 148*, 183–212.

Legate, J. (2008b). Morphological and abstract case. *Linguistic Inquiry, 39*(1), 55–101.

Longobardi, G. (2001). Formal syntax, diachronic minimalism, and etymology: The history of French chez. *Linguistic Inquiry, 32*, 275–302.

Magier, D. S. (1983). Topics in the grammar of Marwari. Ann Arbor: UMI. (Doctoral dissertation, University of California at Berkeley; ix+356pp.).

Marantz, A. (1984). *On the nature of grammatical relations*. MIT Press.

Marantz, A. (1991). Case and licensing. In G. Westphal, B. Ao, & H. Chae (Eds.), *Eastern states conference on linguistics*, University of Maryland. Ohio State.

McFadden, T. (2010). Mapping out the syntax-morphology interface: how can we figure out when case assignment happens. Talk given at Generative Approaches to Contrastive Linguistics, 4.

Mistry, P. J. (1997). Gujarati phonology. *Phonologies of Asia and Africa, 2*, 653–673.

Stronski, K. (2009). Approaches to ergativity in Indo-Aryan. Lingua Posnaniensis, vol. LI/2009.

Udaar, U. (2015). Ergativity: A descriptive study of mewari & marwari ergative case. In Типология морфосинтаксических параметров (pp. 353–365).

Udaar, U. (2016). Ergativity in western Indo-Aryan languages. Ph.D. diss., IIT Delhi, New Delhi, India.

Verbeke, S., & Cuypere, D. L. (2009). The rise of ergativity in Hindi. Retrieved January, 23, 2011 from <http://biblio.ugent.be/input/download?func=downloadFile&fileOId=1132381>

Usha Udaar is Assistant Professor of Linguistics in the Department of Humanities and Social Sciences, Indian Institute of Technology Kanpur. She works on underexplored Western Indo-Aryan languages such as Haryanavi, Mewati, Marwari and Mewari. Her work, which tries to explain the mechanisms of micro and meso-level variation, has been presented and published in multiple fora.

Chapter 11
Cross-Linguistic Variations in the Processing of Ergative Case: Evidence from Punjabi

Mahima Gulati and Kamal K. Choudhary

Abstract Deducing processing parity in the face of linguistic variation has been a key ambition for neurolinguists as well as psycholinguists. However, the same has usually been tried only from the languages belonging to nominative-accusative alignment, and then there has been a general tendency to shoehorn ergative-absolutive languages into the mould. However, the handful of studies that have explored ergative case violations suggest that ergative languages seem to behave differently in comparison to the nominative-accusative type of languages. These studies have reported either an N400-P600 (Choudhary et al. 2009; Zawiszewski et al. 2011) or only positivity (Diaz et al. 2011) for ergative case violations. The present study in Punjabi is a replication of an experiment previously conducted in Hindi. The aim is to test if case-based violations are neurophysiologically equivalent in typologically similar language, or if typological variation have a bearing on the processing mechanism. In terms of the ERP component, in contrast to the previously reported N400-P600 pattern in Hindi, we observed only a positivity for both nominative as well as ergative case violations in Punjabi. We argue that this difference in the ERP components might have arisen owing to certain idiosyncratic properties of the language, namely the restricted use of the ergative case in Punjabi. Further, this neurophysiological difference is taken to be suggestive of the fact that ergative case might not be as strong a cue for Punjabi as it is in Hindi.

Keywords Language comprehension · Variation · EEG-ERP · Ergativity · Punjabi

M. Gulati (✉)
Department of Corporate Skills Development, New Delhi Institute of Management,
New Delhi 110062, India
e-mail: mahima.gulati@iitrpr.ac.in

K.K. Choudhary
Department of Humanities and Social Sciences, Indian Institute of Technology Ropar,
Nangal Road, Rupnagar, Punjab 140001, India
e-mail: kamal@iitrpr.ac.in

P. Chandra (ed.), *Variation in South Asian Languages*,
https://doi.org/10.1007/978-981-99-1149-3_11

Introduction

Linguistic diversity is known to pose a formidable challenge in establishing cross-linguistic generalizations both typologically as well as neurophysiologically. The role these variations play in understanding the underlying language processing architecture and in computing neurolinguistics theories, therefore, is non-trivial. In this regard, the two fields, namely neurophysiology and typology, seem to be inextricably entwined (For a detailed review, refer to Bornkessel-Schlesewsky and Schlesewsky (2016)). Given the interdependence between the two fields, a straightforward implication would be that insights from typologically diverse languages are acutely crucial in formulating an understanding about language and brain. While one is aware of the dangers of construing generalizations based on a small subset of languages, unfortunately up until recently, only a typologically narrow empirical base had been tapped onto. Interestingly, within this small subset that had been explored, typological variations did seem to result in neurophysiological variations (Carreiras et al. 2010; Polinsky et al. 2012; Bornkessel-Schlesewsky and Schlesewsky 2016). These studies therefore reveal the need to fill the gaps by diversifying the cross-linguistic coverage of neurotypological research.

It is only in the last decade or so that researchers have started taking into consideration language-specific grammatical properties such as morphological marking, word order variations and head finality inter alia. While all these are understood to be cues that aid incremental argument processing, languages reportedly vary in terms of which feature they may rely upon for computing 'who did what to whom' in a sentence (Bornkessel and Schlesewsky 2006; Bornkessel-Schlesewsky and Schlesewsky 2009; Alday et al. 2014; Alday et al. 2015). This variability in use of cues can be instantiated through the different languages. Consider, English, which is morphologically impoverished languages, and therefore speakers rely on the linear order of the constituents to formulate the interpretation. In contrast, speakers of morphologically rich languages like German and Hindi are known to rely more predominantly on case markings to deduce the 'who did what to whom.'

Within this domain of neurotypological research, case markers have received a reasonable deal of attention. From the processing perspective, case markers have been understood to be morphosyntactic information types that function as cues for argument interpretation during online comprehension, especially in verb final languages (Bornkessel-Schlesewsky and Schlesewsky 2009). Therefore, a lot of research in the past has been dedicated to first, identifying the neural correlates for processing arguments in the absence of the verb and second, to establish how informationally encapsulated and qualitatively significant different case markers are for incremental processing. However, since a significant amount of work is based on nominative-accusative languages, we have substantial processing insights for nominative, accusative, dative and genitive case (detailed account in the electrophysiology section below). The ergative-absolutive languages and thus the ergative case marker remains to be under-explored.

Neurophysiologically speaking, studies have revealed a general lack of parity (read variability) also in terms of the neural correlates engendered while processing case-based violations across languages, ranging from monophasic P600 (Diaz et al. 2011; Nevins et al. 2007) to monophasic negativity (Choudhary et al. 2009) to biphasic negativity-positivity patterns (Frisch and Schlesewsky 2001; Frisch and Schlesewsky 2005; Mueller et al. 2007; Choudhary et al. 2009; Zawiszewski et al. 2011). Additionally, different cases have been reported to modulate the amplitude of the effect, thus indicating qualitative differences in terms of the information they encode (Frisch and Schlesewsky 2001; Frisch and Schlesewsky 2005). Furthermore, the limited research from ergative languages seems to reveal processing disparities owing to the alignment type of the language (Carreiras et al. 2010; Polinsky et al. 2012; Bornkessel-Schlesewsky and Schlesewsky 2016).

Conclusively therefore, typological as well as neurophysiological variations need to be dealt with at length in order to ascertain the underlying processing architecture. Through this study, we probe into the same direction. We examine the processing routines adopted by the parser while processing nominative and ergative initial constructions in Punjabi, a split-ergative Indo-Aryan language. We intend to decipher if the two case markers modulate comprehension differently in real time. We then compare our findings with those reported by Choudhary et al. (2009) for Hindi, a typologically similar language.

Before we start the discussion on the processing of ergative case, we begin by revisiting the processing of case in nominative-accusative languages.

The Electrophysiology of Case

According to Chomsky's (1981, 1986, 1993) generative grammar, case filter is a prerequisite for all languages, thus every NP with phonetic content must be case-marked. The term 'case' here, refers to that which cannot be further reduced into any functional notion. More recent definitions of case, such as the one by Blake (2001), define it as 'a system of marking dependent nouns for the type of relationship they bear to their heads.' While case is understood and classified to be a morphological phenomenon, languages may employ it overtly in the form of markers or covertly, without any morphological case markings. Further, for languages that mark the case overtly, there is no parity in the way these case markings might be morphologically realized, with some languages like Latin marking it on the dependent (noun phrase), while those like Navajo too have the case realized on the head (verb) itself.

In keeping with the diversity exhibited by languages, researchers have vested interest in understanding how various cases are 'assigned'/licensed to arguments in this covert fashion. In this line, standard case theory categorizes case into two broad categories, structural case and non-structural case (Chomsky 1986). The two types vary in terms of the way they are licensed and the way they behave and theoretical literature is replete with evidence about the same. As far as the categorisation of case markers in these two classes is concerned, the nominative and the accusative case have unambiguously and constantly been considered structural in nature, but the categorization of the other cases is not as straightforward. Especially, for ergative case, researchers have a divide in opinion with some aligning it with the structural case (Wunderlich 1997; Ura 2000; Davison 2004) and others treating it as inherent case (Laughren 1989; Mahajan 1989; Harbert and Jacqueline 1991; Woolford 1993, 1997, 2001, 2006; Mohanan 1994; Butt 1995; Nash 1996; Massam 2002; Legate 2003) owing to its association with a particular theta position, the external argument, and the dative like behaviour in terms of preservation in A-Movement (raising constructions) in languages like Tongan (Hendrick 2004; Woolford 2006).

Interestingly, researches have reported processing differences in structural and inherent cases and have used these to make certain claims about the categorization per say. Hopf et al. (1998) conducted a study with ambiguous initial arguments, which were disambiguated only at the sentence final verb position in German. The authors reported that the parser works by a principle wherein it gives priority to assigning the structural cases (nominative and accusative) rather than a non-structural (dative) case, thus engendering an N400 for dative selecting verbs. Further, these results were replicated in Bader and Bayer (2006). Interestingly, Jacobson (2000) revealed that while in offline studies both structural (accusative) and inherent (dative) case violations in German are realized quite early and equally efficiently, in online tasks the violations of structural case were perceived more easily than violations of inherent case. Further, structural case reportedly engendered larger effect in comparison with the inherent case. One possible explanation for this preference for structural case can stem from the analysis proposed by Bayer et al. (2001), which stated that unlike structural cases, inherent (lexical) cases require an extra KP shell. Now, given that the human parser is known to economize, the preference possibly is for the minimal structure and thus for the structural (accusative) case in comparison to the inherent (dative) case.

However, this line of research was probably found untenable and thus remains to be under-explored. Instead, an orthogonal direction of research that deals with adjudging processing parities across case systems is what has garnered a lot of attention over the past few years.

Case systems define the way the core arguments subject (S), agent (A) and patient (O) arguments are treated across languages and are therefore used to classify the world languages. Different theorists have classified these case systems differently; however, the two most rampant alignment types are Accusative (S=A) and Ergative-Absolutive (S 6=A). The basis of this distinction is how the actor and the undergoer argument are treated across different types of constructions. One of the linguistic features that helps decipher which language type a language fall into is case marking.

Consider the following data set (1):

1. Exhibits alignment types
    a. He goes to school
    b. He likes Mary
    c. Mary likes him
    d. KuDi   darwaazaa   vekhdii   ai
        Girl-NOM.F   door-ACC.F   see.PRS.3SG.F   Aux
        'The girl sees the door'
    e. KuDii ne   darwaazaa   vekhiaa   e
        Girl-ERG.F   door-ACC.M   see.PFV.3SG.M   Aux
        'The girl saw the door'

English here exhibits an accusative alignment, such that it treats S and the A argument the same way (using the pronoun for 'he') but the P argument is treated differently (as in 'him' in 1 (c)), in contrast consider Punjabi, which has a split-ergative alignment, such that it exhibits morphological ergativity, by overtly case marking the A argument ('−ne' in 1(e)) but not the S or the P argument. This attribute of case not only helps ascertain the alignment of the languages of the world, but also to ascertain the grammatical/thematic role the arguments bear.

The exploration of case violations gained currency with Münte et al. (1997) study in German. The authors observed that the illicit use of genitive case-marked argument in the place of an accusative argument, as in (2) below, elicited a fron-to-central negativity 300–500 ms post stimulus onset, followed by a centroparietal positivity 600 ms post stimulus.

2. Example stimuli from Münte et al. (1997)
    Die Hexe benutzte ihren Besen/*Besens, um zum Wald zu fliegen
    'The witch used her broom/*broom's to fly to the forest'

This was furthered by another piece of evidence from a study by Coulson et al. (1998) with morphosyntactic mismatches using illicit case on arguments in English. As English is a morphologically impoverished language, the authors employed pronouns that bear remnants of the English case marking paradigm. The data set in (3) below presents the kind of sentences that were used.

3. Sample stimuli from Coulson et al. (1998)
    a. Genitive Case violation
        Ray fell down and skinned his/*he knee
    b. Accusative Case violation
        The plane took us/*we to paradise

The authors reported that the illicit use of nominative in the place of genitive as in 3(a) or accusative as in 3(b) rendered a biphasic LAN-P600 effect at the second argument position following the verb. This negativity seen around 300–500 ms post stimulus onset in the left anterior region, and was attributed to be a marker of a morphosyntactic mismatch. The positivity was observed 500–800 ms post stimulus onset in the centroparietal region and was understood to be an indicator of general ill-formedness.

Supplementary evidence from Frisch and Schlesewsky's (2001) study in German revealed that while case violations are intrinsically morphosyntactic in nature, they do have semantic underpinnings. The authors proposed that case markers, in the absence of the verb, help establish thematic relations between the arguments. The authors exhibit the same using verb final sentences (SOV) with either two nominative animate arguments or an animate nominative argument followed by an animate accusative argument. They observed that in comparison to the nominative-accusative construction, the double nominative construction engendered a biphasic centroparietal negativity-positivity (N400-P600) pattern at the second argument position. While the positivity was classically attributed to the brain perceiving a general ill-formedness owing to the case violation, the negativity was understood to be reflective of the inability to compute the thematic roles the arguments should bear. In a later study (Frisch and Schlesewsky 2005), the authors observed the same ERP signatures with varying amplitudes, in cases where two dative or two accusative arguments were used. Additionally, Mueller et al. (2007) replicated these results for native speakers of Japanese (a typologically distinct language).

While all the aforementioned studies involve exploring case violations, from languages with nominative-accusative alignment, the other end of the spectrum, i.e. languages with ergative-absolutive alignment, remains less explored. There are however a handful of studies that explore the processing of ergative case (for a detailed review on behavioural and ERP studies in ergative languages see Zawiszewski (2017)). From within this subset, we now discuss the studies that are relevant from the perspective of the present study. The first study that tried to explore ergative case violation was Choudhary et al. (2009), who tested case and aspect-based violations in Hindi, a verb final languages.

Choudhary et al. (2009) compared the processing both nominative and ergative case violation using simple transitive SOV constructions. The authors employed nominative and ergative initial constructions along with perfective and imperfective verbs, such that the grammaticality of the case employed at the first argument position could only be deciphered at the position of the verb. This is in keeping with the fact that Hindi being a split-ergative language permits both an initial nominative argument as well as an initial ergative argument, to be followed by an accusative argument. The grammaticality of the construction is then dependent on the form of the verb that appears at the penultimate position in the sentence. In the case of a nominative argument, by convention the verb should be in the imperfective aspect as exhibited in (4(a)). In contrast for construction with an ergative initial argument, the rule requires a verb in the perfective aspect as in (4(d)). In case the verb form is alternated, the result is a violation as observed in (4(b) and (c)).

4. Sample stimuli from Choudhary et al. (2009)

a.   shikshak   maalii-ko   dekh-taa   hai

teacher.NOM   gardener-ACC   see-IPFV.3SG.M   AUX.PRS

'The teacher sees the gardener.'

b.   *shikshak-ne   maalii-ko   dekh-taa   hai

teacher-ERG   gardener-ACC   see-IPFV.3SG.M   AUX.PRS

'The teacher sees the gardener.'

c.   *shikshak   maalii-ko   dekh-aa   hai

teacher.NOM   gardener-NOM   see-PFV.3SG.M   AUX.PRS

'The teacher has seen the gardener.'

d.   shikshak-ne   maalii-ko   dekh-aa   hai

teacher-ERG   gardener-ACC   see-PFV.3SG.M   AUX.PRS

'The teacher has seen the gardener.'

The authors measured the ERPs at the position of the verb and reported a classic centroparietal negativity for both the violation conditions. Additionally, for the ergative case violation, i.e. when the ergative argument was followed by a verb in the imperfective aspect (4(b)), the authors reported increased amplitude for the negativity and a late positivity. The authors attributed this negativity to be indicative of detection of a violation of an interpretively relevant rule and P600 to the general ill-formedness.

However, this becomes intriguing when we consider the study by Diaz et al. (2011), who explored double ergative case violation in Basque. This was based on the earlier reported set of experiments conducted in German by Frisch and Schlesewsky (2001, 2005). While the previous experiments explored double nominative, double accusative and double dative case violations, here the authors explored double ergative violation. The experiment included grammatical constructions with the subject in the ergative case and the object in the absolutive case or ungrammatical constructions wherein both the subject and the object were appended with ergative case markers, as enumerated in 5(a) and 5(b), respectively.

5. Sample stimuli from Diaz et al. (2011)

a.   Mikel-en   arreb-ek   egunkari-a   saski-a-n   ekarri

Mikel-Gen sister-the-ERG.PL newspaper-the-ABS.SG basket-the-in brought

d-u-te   kiosko-tik

it-root-they kiosk-from

'Mikel's sisters have brought the newspaper in a basket from the kiosk'

b. Mikel-en   arreb-ek   egunkari-*ek   saski-a-n   ekarri

Mikel-Gen sister-the-ERG.PL newspaper-the–*[Erg.PL] basket-the-in brought

d-u-te   kiosko-tik

it-root-they kiosk-from

The authors analysed the event related potential changes at the second argument position preverbally, to establish if using two ergative arguments did cause a thematic hierarchization problem. However, the ungrammaticality engendered only a late positivity and in a phenomenally large time window, i.e. 400–1250 ms. The authors attributed this late positivity to a general mechanism of detection of a case violation. Further, in their discussion, Diaz and colleagues visited the results of Choudhary et al. (2009) and attribute the absence of a negativity in comparison to Hindi to the difference in the alignments of the two languages. While Basque and Hindi are both ergative languages, Basque always exhibits an ergative alignment while Hindi exhibits a split-ergative alignment with the ergative surfacing only when the verb is in perfective aspect.

In another study in Basque, Zawiszewski et al. (2011) explored online comprehension of ergative case violations in native and non-native speakers of Basque. The speakers were either native speakers of Basque (native group) or native speakers of Spanish (non-native group). The participants had to adjudge the grammaticality of the constructions, which was basically dependant on the presence or absence of the ergative marker. The constructions therefore were same till the critical position, as exhibited in (6).

6. Sample stimuli from Zawiszewski et al. (2011)

Goiz-ean   ogia   erosi   dut ni-k/*ni   denda-n

morning-in bread bought have I-ERG/*I shop-in

'This morning I bought bread in the shop.'

ERPs time-locked to the second argument position post verbally revealed varied patterns for the native Basque and non-native Basque speakers. While the native speakers exhibited a biphasic N400-P600 pattern, the non-native Basque speakers engendered an N400 effect only. While this study was mainly pursued to tease apart the differences in the comprehension of native and non-native speakers, it brings out different connotations for us when we see the spectrum of ergative case violations. On the one hand, it suggests that maybe ergative case does provide some interpretively relevant information that other cases in nominative-accusative languages do not provide (thus engendering a centroparietal negativity). On the other hand, it puts the idea of processing parity into jeopardy with ergative case violations engendering different components within the same language in different studies.

To put it cohesively, the literature reveals a general dearth of cross-linguistic sample with a prevalent lop-sided coverage relying more rampantly on nominative-accusative languages. Second, there exists a multiplicity of ERP signatures that have been reported for case-based violations both within and across languages. Lastly, studies from ergative-absolutive languages do indicate that ergative case marker seems to be processed differently in comparison with the other subject case markers (Dillon et al. 2012; Choudhary 2011).

Through this study, we intend to add some more insight and to further the exploration of ergative case. We therefore examine the comprehension of simple transitive constructions in the perfective and imperfective aspect in Punjabi, a split-ergative Western Indo-Aryan language. The intention is to establish if the processing routines for the two subject case markers, namely nominative and ergative are indeed different. Next, we compare our findings with those reported by Choudhary et al. (2009), in order to ascertain processing similarities (if any) across typologically similar languages.

The Present Study

Given that the human brain is governed by economies of all sorts, it would be ideal for the brain to process a linguistic phenomenon similarly across languages. However, given the cross-linguistic disparity between the components engendered while processing the same linguistic phenomenon, this seems to be a far from the reality. So, in the present study, we test the next best hypothesis, i.e. if the brain functions similarly for the same linguistic phenomenon at least across typologically similar languages. In order to do so, we replicate the design employed in the study by Choudhary et al. (2009) in Hindi, a language typologically quite similar to Punjabi.

Both Punjabi and Hindi are Indo-Aryan languages, spoken predominantly in the northern parts of India, with Delhi, Madhya Pradesh and Uttar Pradesh being the epicentres of Hindi, and Punjab as the locus of Punjabi. Both languages are SOV, but while Hindi is rather flexible in its word order, Punjabi has a relatively strict word order, at least for the core constituents (Bhatia 1993). Also, both these languages exhibit a wide range of case markers, which are post-positional in nature. Some of these are morphologically overt while some are covert. Table 11.1 summarizes the case morphology in Punjabi.

Another facet that the two languages share is that both Hindi and Punjabi exhibit a split-ergative pattern. However, while Hindi exhibits an aspect-based split (Mahajan 1990), the split for Punjabi manifests across both person and aspect (Bhatia 1993; Butt and Deo 2001; Bhatt 2007; Kaur 2016). The case marking paradigm therefore varies not just on the basis of the aspect of the verb, i.e. imperfective or perfective, but is also governed by the person feature of the Actor argument, i.e. the case marking pattern aligns differently between a first/second person argument and a third person argument, be it a common noun, a pronoun or a proper name.

Table 11.1 Punjabi case spectrum

Case	Post-position	Realization
Direct	Nominative	Φ
Oblique	Accusative/Dative	-nüü
	Ergative	-ne
	Genitive	-da, -dii, -de, diāā
	Locative	-te
	Instrumental	-tõ
Vocative		óé/ve

For the purpose of this study, since we draw a parallel to Hindi, we explore the aspectual split that the two languages share. Aspectual split in principle implies that the languages exhibit different alignments in different aspects, i.e. both the case systems discussed in the previous section co-exist in the language but have a complementary distribution. So, while these languages have an accusative alignment in the imperfective aspect, they exhibit an ergative alignment in the perfective aspect.

Consider the data set in (7), which further exemplifies how the split manifests in Punjabi. In the imperfective aspect, the languages exhibit a nominative-accusative alignment, wherein the subject of a transitive and intransitive are treated alike, and different from the object of the transitive. Constructions in 7(a) (intransitive) and 7(b) (transitive) exemplify the same, with the two subjects taking the nominative case, while the object of the transitive takes accusative case (-nüü). In contrast, in the perfective aspect, the languages exhibit an ergative-absolutive alignment, with the two subject arguments behaving differently. As construction 7(c) (intransitive) and 7(d) (transitive) present, the subject of the transitive is obligatorily marked with an ergative case (-ne), while the subject of the intransitive verb still takes the nominative case.

7. Punjabi Data set

    a.   Maali ja   reya   ai

         Gardener(NOM) go PROG.M.SG AUX.PRS

         'Gardener is going.'

    b.   Maali   pathar-nüü   sutt-daa   ai

         Gardener(NOM) stone-ACC   throw-IPFV.M.SG AUX.PRS

         'Gardener throws the stone.'

    c.   Maali   gaya   ai

         Gardener(NOM) go.PFV.M.SG   AUX.PRS

         'Gardener is going.'

    d.   Maali-ne   pathar-nüü   sutt-iaa   ai

         Gardener-Erg   stone-ACC   throw-PFV.M.SG AUX.PRS

         'Gardener threw the stone.'

This obligatory subject case marking pattern akin to that seen in Hindi is the overt realisation of the split-ergative system. While this difference in case marking is at the first argument position, it is potentially guided only by the aspect on the verb. Further, while this case marking paradigm is rule governed for both these languages, it is also interpretively relevant in that it is the case marking that helps decipher both the grammatical as well as the thematic roles of the arguments in the construction.

In terms of the distribution of the case markers, theoretically speaking, a nominative argument in general has a wider expanse in comparison to the ergative argument. The latter is realized in relatively lesser sentential configurations (perfective aspect). Therefore, between the two cases (nominative and ergative), one would predict that during online comprehension, an ergative case-marked argument should lead to a more precise prediction of the sentential structure in comparison with a nominative argument (Dillon et al. 2012; Choudhary 2011). Probably thus engendering the neurophysiological differences that have been attested.

With this, we constructed the following experiment, using a 2*2 factorial design, wherein we crossed case at the first argument position (nominative and ergative) and aspect at the verb (perfective and imperfective) in order to generate four critical conditions as in Table 11.2. A condition was rendered grammatical if

Table 11.2 Behavioural results aggregated over conditions for all participants

Condition	Example	Acc	RT1	CQ	RT2
NI	**Lekhak chor-nüü phaD-daa si Writer(Nom) thief-Acc catch-IPFV.M.SG AUX 'The writer caught the thief.'**	91 (7)	433 (140)	92 (7)	1314 (264)
*EI	***Lekhak-ne chor-nüü phaD-daa si Writer-Erg thief-Acc catch-IPFV.M.SG AUX 'The writer caught the thief.'**	42 (33)	466 (167)	87 (8)	1414 (251)
*NP	***Lekhak chor-nüü phaD-iaa si Writer(Nom) thief-Acc catch-PFV.M.SG AUX 'The writer had caught the thief.'**	60 (32)	497 (163)	90 (7)	1375 (298)
EP	**Lekhak-ne chor-nüü phaD-iaa si Writer-Erg thief-Acc catch-PFV.M.SG AUX 'The writer had caught the thief.'**	93 (5)	416 (149)	91 (6)	1347 (286)

All values presented in the table have been rounded off.

As for the naming convention, Acc: mean acceptability; RT1: reaction time for acceptability task; CQ: mean accuracy; RT2: response time for comprehension question. For the condition names, N: Nominative; E: Ergative; I: Imperfective Aspect; P: Perfective Aspect. Further, for the electrophysiological analysis, the ERPs were time-locked to this position of the words in boldface.

the case and the aspect matched as per the rule (nominative-imperfective; ergative-perfective). Contrary to this, a condition was rendered ungrammatical, owing to either the misapplication of nominative case in the perfective aspect (nominative case violation) or to the misapplication of ergative case in the imperfective condition (ergative case violation). However, whether a sentence was grammatical or ungrammatical could only be deciphered at the position of the verb. It is for the reason that the verb was considered be the critical position for ERP analysis.

While the initial hypothesis was that if typologically similar languages are indeed processed the same way, then we should be able to reproduce the results reported for Hindi by Choudhary et al. (2009), i.e. an N400 for nominative case violation and N400-P600 for ergative case violations. Alternatively, if variation in structural configurations between the two languages, in terms of the distribution of the two case markers, is to play a role then one could expect to see deviation in the results. However, studies do exhibit the ergative case violations within the same language, namely Basque have exhibited different components (monophasic P600 (Diaz et al. 2011) and biphasic N400-P600 (Zawiszewski et al. 2011). Therefore, one cannot rule out the possibility of observing distinct neurophysiological components across languages, despite the fact that they may be typologically related.

Method and Material

Ethical Statement

The research protocol for the present study was approved by the Institute Ethical Committee (IEC), Indian Institute of Technology Ropar, where the experiment was conducted. Prior to the testing, informed and written consent were obtained from all the participants. All assessments were carried out in accordance with the approved guidelines and regulations.

Participants

Thirty-two native speakers of Punjabi (22 males) participated in the experiment after giving informed consent in writing. The participants were graduate or post-graduate students at the Indian Institute of Technology Ropar (mean age 24.68 years, SD = 4.6, Range = 18–35 years). Each participant was remunerated as per the allowance permitted by the ethical committee. All the participants were right handed (established via an adaptation of the Edinburgh Handedness Inventory (Oldfield 1971) and had normal or corrected-to-normal vision. They had all acquired Punjabi before the age of five but were fluent in at least one additional language (English) and had moderate fluency in Hindi.

Twenty-four participants (11 males, mean age 25.20 years) entered the final analysis as eight participants had to be excluded either due to low behavioural accuracy (error rate of >25% in any one condition) or excessive EEG artefact.

Material

The experimental material consisted of 60 sets of sentences in 4 conditions, as presented in Table 11.2. These 240 critical sentences were then divided into 2 lists (I and II) such that each list had 120 critical items wherein no lexical items were appeared more than twice. 120 filler sentences were additionally added to both these lists, to create two experimental sessions. The filler sentences added to the two lists were the same. The EEG data was recorded as each participant attempted one of these sessions with 240 sentences comprising of 120 critical (30 lexical items for each condition) and 120 filler sentences. Thus, taking into consideration all the sentences, each participant witnessed 120 grammatical and 120 ungrammatical sentences. Further, the sentences were counterbalanced and presented in a randomized fashion.

As for the experimental sentences, there were a total of four conditions, two of which were control conditions and the other two were critical conditions. The two control-critical pairs namely NI, NP and EI, EP, respectively, expressed the same proposition but exhibited either a case-aspect match (NI, EP) or a case-aspect mismatch (NP, EI). Structurally, every sentence began with a masculine animate common noun as the first argument, realized, either in the base nominative form (lekhak 'writer') or as an overtly ergative case-marked argument (lekhak-ne 'writer-ERG'). This was followed by an accusative marked masculine animate common noun (chor-nüü 'thief-Acc'), which was in turn followed by a verb (either perfective or imperfective) and an auxiliary.

A condition was rendered ungrammatical at the penultimate position, i.e. the position of the verb, owing to one of the two rule-based mismatches. The mismatch could either occur, when the nominative argument was followed by a verb in the perfective aspect, i.e. the nominative case violation as exemplified in NP or when an ergative marked argument was followed by an imperfective verb, i.e. ergative case violation as in EI. In contrast, NI and EP were the control conditions, wherein an imperfective verb correctly followed a nominative argument and the ergative verb was followed by a perfective verb thus exhibiting the perfectly grammatical constructions.

Procedure

The experiment was conducted in a dim light, sound attenuated room. The participants were made to sit a metre away from a computer monitor. The stimulus was presented in an RSV paradigm, in order to minimize the ocular artefact. Further, the stimuli were presented phrase by phrase (i.e. in the ergative conditions, arguments were presented along with the case markers) using E-Prime 2.0 software (https://pstnet.com).

Each trial began with a fixation cross that appeared in the middle of the screen for 1000 ms. This was followed by a 100 ms inter-stimulus interval and then an adverb was presented, which in turn was followed by the first case (un/) marked argument (NP1), second argument (NP2), the verb (V) and finally the auxiliary (AUX). Each of these frames appeared for 750 ms and had a 100 ms inter-stimulus interval. This longish time window for presentation was chosen because it was perceived to be comfortable for the participants (Bornkessel-Schlesewsky et al. 2020; Demiral et al. 2008).

The participant subsequently completed two behavioural tasks. In the first one, they evaluated the preceding sentence as grammatical or ungrammatical, while the second task was a comprehension question based on the previously read sentence. Herein, they had to testify if the proposition questioned through the comprehension question was exactly that expressed in the sentence they read previously or not. This was followed by an inter-trial interval of 1000 ms.

For both the tasks the participants had a response pad wherein the green button meant grammatical for the first task and perfectly matching for the second while the red button meant ungrammatical and not matching what they read earlier. While both of these tasks were a forced judgement task, the former was used to measure the acceptability of the participant, whereas the later was only used to measure the accuracy (thus attention) in order to identify the participants that would enter into the final analysis.

The experiment was conducted in 7 sets with a break following each set and took about 2 h to complete on an average.

Data Acquisition and Preprocessing

The electroencephalogram was recorded from 128 geodesically arranged electrode sites using the HydroCel Geodesic Sensor Net (Eugene, OR, USA) that arrays 129 (128 + VREF) Ag–AgCl coated electrodes over the surface of the scalp. The electrodes took care of the scalp surface distribution as well as covered the electro-oculogram sites, i.e. the outer canthi as well as under the eye so as to record eye movements as well as blinks. The data was digitized continuously at 500 Hz, with a vertex reference (Cz). The impedance was kept under 50kΩ as per the recommendation by the manufacturer. Further, in order to ascertain the elimination of all sort of noise the raw data was analogue filtered using 0.1 Hz high-pass filter. All EEG and EOG signals were amplified using the NET AMPS 400 EEG Amplifier.

For preprocessing, raw EEG data was exported into MATLAB (version 2017a; MathWorks, Inc., Natick, MA), and the data was processed using EEGLAB (Delorme and Makeig 2004) and the ERPLAB plugin (Lopez Calderon and Luck 2014) for EEGLAB toolbox.

The data was band-pass filtered at 0.3–30 Hz offline via Butterworth filter in order to get rid of the slow baseline drifts. This data was then re-referenced to the average of the two mastoids. Later, the electrodes on the lowest part of the face and the head were removed, resulting in 97 channels on the scalp for analysis. Data with obvious noise or non-physiological artefacts were identified by visual inspection and removed. This was followed by automatic rejection of the bad channels, using EEGLAG's pop_rejchan function. If a participant had more than 25% bad channels, they were rejected. Further, the data was filtered at a band-pass of 1–40 Hz and visually scanned to remove any data segments with any form of artefacts (muscular noise/drifts/slow drifts), before feeding it in for an Independent Component Analysis (ICA) (Iriarte et al. 2003) as per EEGLAB recommendations.

In the post-processing, the weights calculated during ICA were transposed onto the file with rejected channels and the systematic artefacts such as eye movements, eye blinks and muscular activities were identified and rejected using the SASICA plugin (Chaumon et al. 2015). The missing electrodes were interpolated from the remaining channels, using spherical splines. The continuous waveform was then epoched into single trials from −200 ms to 1200 ms relative to the onset of the verb. ERPs were then averaged per participant, per electrode, per condition and finally grand average was computed for all the participants.

Data Analysis

For the purpose of behavioural data analysis, we extracted each participants' acceptability judgement, the time taken to provide this judgement (RT 1), the computed evaluation for the answer to the comprehension question, and the time taken to answer the comprehension question (RT 2). This data was collated using E-Merge and the E-DataAid tool (Schneider et al. 2002) for E-Prime 2.0 software. It was later sorted using Excel. We calculated the aggregates per condition per participant, i.e. the mean acceptability for the acceptability judgement task and the mean accuracy for the comprehension tasks (in Table 11.2). The final data was only taken from participants who had a minimum of 75% accuracy in the comprehension question and if the data did not have too many EEG artefacts.

For the statistical analysis of the behavioural data, R Version 3.3.3 (R Core Team, 2017) was used to perform repeated measures ANOVA comprising of the two within-subject factors, namely the case at NP1 (nominative vs ergative) and the aspect at the verb (imperfective vs perfective) for the selected participants with subjects and items as random intercepts.

For the ERP analysis, the data from a total of 24 participants with at least 84% single trial epochs at the verb were included. ERPs were then calculated for each participant, electrode and condition time-locked to the onset of the verb. Followed by a grand-averaging of the ERPs across participants. Repeated measures ANOVA was performed for the single trial EEG data, quantified exclusively by mean amplitude measures per time window per condition. Since this is the first

ERP study conducted in Punjabi, therefore as has been the standard in the field, the intervals for statistical analysis selected during visual inspection (Choudhary et al. 2009; Bornkessel-Schlesewsky et al. 2011).

The analysis additionally included a topographical factor 'regions of interest' (ROI), which were generated with clusters of electrodes from 6 lateral and 3 midline regions. The lateral regions consisted of left anterior (20, 23, 24, 27, 28, 29, 34, 35), left central (30, 36, 37, 40, 41, 42, 46, 47), left posterior (51, 52, 53, 58, 59, 60, 65, 66), right anterior (3, 110, 111, 116, 117, 118, 123, 124), right central (87, 93, 98, 102, 103, 104, 105, 109) and right posterior (84, 85, 86, 90, 91, 92, 96, 97). The midline regions similarly included mid-anterior (4, 5, 10, 11, 12, 16, 18, 19), mid-central (6, 7, 13, 31, 54, 55, 79, 80, 106, 112) and mid-posterior (61, 62, 67, 71, 72, 76, 77, 78). These regions were chosen based on the likelihood of observing the effect based on previous research. Separate statistical analyses were performed for the lateral and the midline electrodes (Bornkessel-Schlesewsky et al. 2011).

Results

Behavioural Results

As is presented in Table 11.2, in general, the participants had a very high acceptability for both the grammatical conditions, with a condition-wise mean of 91% (S.D. 7) for the nominative control condition and 93.4% (S.D. 5) for ergative control condition. Contrary to this, the acceptability for the violation conditions were quite low, with a mean of 59.6% (S.D. 32) for the nominative case violation condition, i.e. when the nominative case was illicitly followed by a verb in the perfective aspect. Similarly, the acceptability for the ergative case violation condition was also low, about 41.9% (S.D. 33) when the ergative case-marked first argument was followed by a verb in the imperfective aspect.

A repeated measures ANOVA was then performed over the data with ASPECT and CASE as the within factors. For the acceptability task, it revealed a main effect of CASE ($F1(1,23) = 9.938$, $p < 0.01$; $F2(1,59) = 18.18$, $p < 0.001$), a main effect of ASPECT ($F1(1,23) = 21.34$, $p < 0.001$; $F2(1,59) = 53.99$, $p < 0.001$) as well as an interaction of ASPECT*CASE ($F1(1,23) = 52.76$, $p < 0.001$; $F2(1,59) = 387.1$, $p < 0.001$). Resolving the interaction by ASPECT revealed a significant effect of CASE for both the imperfective aspect ($F1(1,23) = 59.88$, $p < 0.001$; $F2(1,59) = 185.3$, $p < 0.001$) as well as for the perfective aspect ($F1(1,23) = 30.53$, $p < 0.001$; $F2(1,59) = 340.1$, $p < 0.001$).

For the reaction time for the acceptability task, repeated measures ANOVA revealed a significant interaction of CASE*ASPECT ($F1(1,23) = 12.88$, $p < 0.01$; $F2(1,59) = 18.87$, $p < 0.001$). Resolving the interaction revealed a significant effect for the perfective aspect ($F1(1,23) = 19.67$, $p < 0.001$; $F2(1,59) = 21.81$, $p < 0.001$).

Further, the interaction was marginally significant for the imperfective aspect but only for the analysis by item (F2(1,59)=4.438, p<0.05).

While the accuracy of the comprehension question was only used as a criterion for inclusion of participants into the analysis, we did run it for the statistical analysis. The results confirmed a tendency for CASE only by subject (F1(1,23)=3.583, p<0.1) and a marginal CASE*ASPECT interaction effect (F1(1,23)=7.002, p<0.05; F2(1,59)=4.725, p<0.05), which resolved for the CASE (F1(1,23)=7.846, p<0.05; F2(1,59)=3.632, p<0.1) only in the imperfective aspect.

Summary of Behavioural Results

The results from the acceptability task do confirm both descriptively as well as statistically that there is a substantial difference (drop) in the preference for the ungrammatical conditions. This reduced acceptability corresponds with an increase in the response time for these conditions, thus implicating that this is not a chance effect.

Further, while the acceptability of the ergative in the imperfective aspect is quite low, the acceptability of the nominative in the perfective aspect is a little higher in comparison. This is probably owing distribution of the structural configurations in which these two cases manifest (discussed in detail in the Discussion Section below). Furthermore, this acceptance for structure does manifest even in the accuracy rating for the comprehension question, with only the ergative case violation showing a marginal drop.

Electrophysiological Results

The grand-averaged waveforms derived from the ERPs time-locked to the onset of the verb were compared individually for the two aspects. Visual inspection revealed monophasic positivity for both the nominative as well as the ergative case violation conditions. Further, these positivities were observed in different time windows.

A repeated measures ANOVA was therefore conducted for the two time windows, i.e. 300–500 ms and 550–700 ms.

300–500 ms

A repeated measures ANOVA in the 300–500 ms time window revealed a significant interaction of CASE*ASPECT (F(1,23)=4.34, p<0.05), in the lateral region (Fig. 11.1).

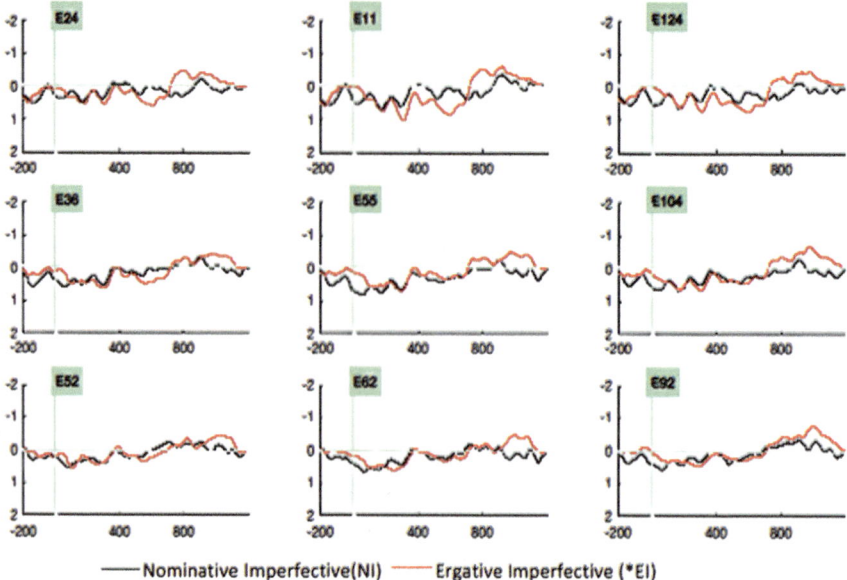

——Nominative Imperfective(NI) ——Ergative Imperfective (*EI)

Fig. 11.1 Verb in the imperfective aspect. Comparing imperfective control condition (NI (black line)) with the critical condition (EI (red line)) using Grand averaged ERPs (N = 24) time-locked to the onset of the verb. By convention, negativity is plotted upwards.

Resolving this interaction revealed a significant effect of CASE in the perfective aspect (F(1,23)=5.013, p<0.05).

For the midline electrodes, there was a tendency for the CASE*ASPECT (F(1,23)=3.35, p<0.08).

550–700 ms (Fig. 11.2).

A repeated measures ANOVA in the 550–700 ms time window revealed a significant interaction of CASE*ASPECT (F(1,23)=7.12, p<0.02).

These interaction when resolved, revealed a tendency of CASE in the imperfective aspect (F(1,23)=3.88, p<0.06).

For the the midline electrodes, we saw a significant interaction effect ASPECT*CASE (F(1,23)=4.86, p<0.04), however upon resolving there was no significant result (Fig. 11.3).

Summary of Electrophysiological Results

Overall, the electrophysiological data therefore implicated that the two violations rendered monophasic positivities. However, while this positivity was much earlier for the nominative case violation (i.e. in the perfective aspect), in the 300–500 ms

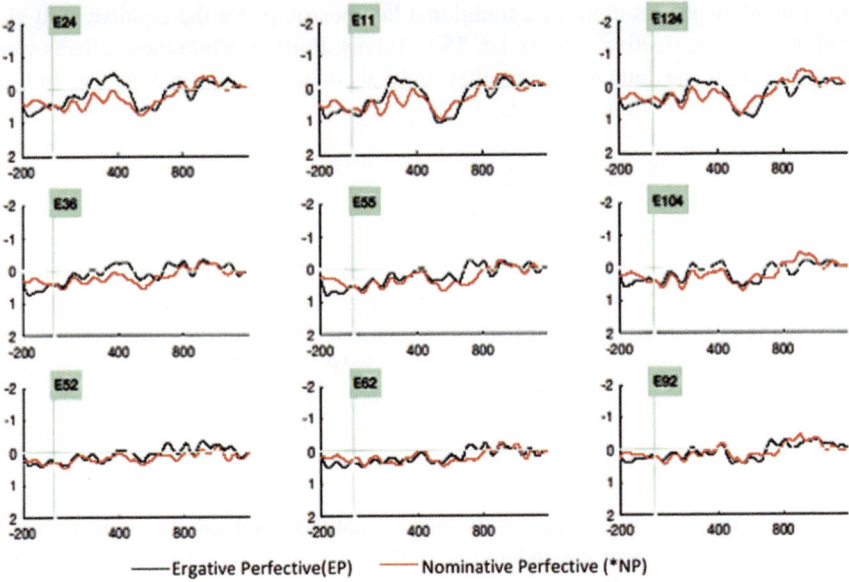

——Ergative Perfective(EP)   ——Nominative Perfective (*NP)

Fig. 11.2 Verb in the perfective aspect. Comparing perfective control Condition (EP (black line)) with the critical condition (NP (red line)) using Grand averaged ERPs (N = 24) time-locked to the onset of the verb. By convention, negativity is plotted upwards

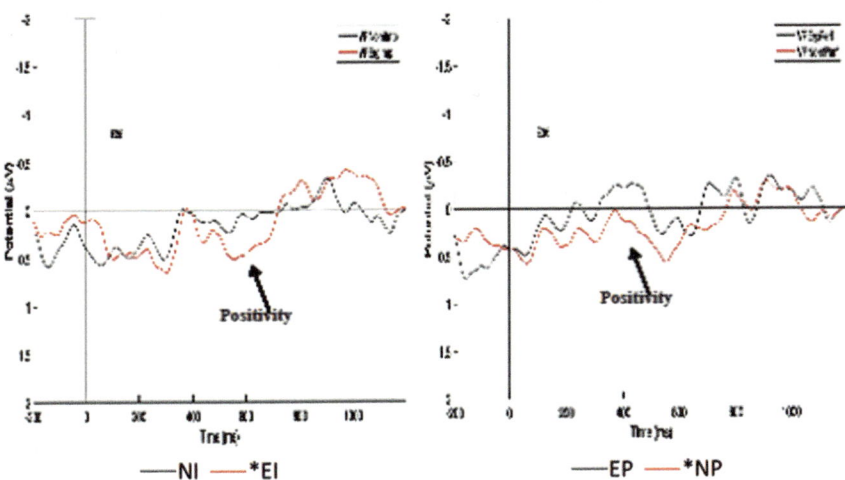

——NI ——*EI   ——EP ——*NP

Fig. 11.3 Aspect-based comparative analysis. A single electrode comparison of the Imperfective Aspect (left) and Perfective Aspect (right) using the grand averaged ERPs (N = 24) time-locked to the onset of the verb

time window, it was more of a traditional late positivity for the ergative case violation (i.e. imperfective aspect), i.e. 550–700 ms. Further, while these effects were
significant in the lateral regions they only seem to be marginal in the midline
region for both the time windows.

Discussion

The event related brain potentials from this study seem to suggest that typological
variations in languages do translate into neurophysiological variations. These variations are manifested in the form of distinct ERP components for the same violations across languages. To elaborate on the same, while ERPs time-locked to the
position of the verb in Hindi rendered an N400 (nominative case violation) and
an N400-P600 (ergative case violation) effect, the same manipulation in Punjabi
elicited only monophasic positivities, with variations in the onset latencies for the
two violation conditions. The results suggest that the illicit use of nominative case
in the perfective aspect engendered an early positivity in the time range of 300–
500 ms. On the other hand, the use of an ergative case-marked initial argument in
the imperfective aspect elicited a comparatively later positivity, in the 550–700 ms
time range.

Given the state of the art, these results are quite intriguing. First, not only is
the pattern that we observe different from the one recorded for Hindi, it is actually quite similar to the one reported by Diaz et al. (2011) for Basque in terms
of a monophasic positive effect at least for the ergative case violation. However,
in their analysis, Diaz et al. (2011) had attributed this difference in Hindi
(N400-P600) and Basque (P600) to the difference in the type of alignment, with
Basque being an ergative-absolutive language and Hindi being a split-ergative language. Now, given the results from Punjabi, this proposal seems to be questiona-
ble. Even though Punjabi is a split-ergative language like Hindi, its ERP patterns
for ergative case violation seem to align with those reported for Basque, a pure
ergative language. We can therefore assertively claim that the alignment type is not
a reason for the distinction in the ERP patterns.

Second, the difference in the biphasic N400-P600 pattern and the monophasic
P600 has often also been attributed to the difference in modality of presentation.
While in Basque, Zawiszewski et al. (2011) used a visual paradigm, and observed
a biphasic effect, Diaz et al. (2011) employed the auditory paradigm and reported a
monophasic effect. Contrary to this, results for Indo-Aryan languages suggest otherwise. While Choudhary et al. (2009) employed the auditory paradigm, and reported
a biphasic effect, we used the visual paradigm and report a monophasic effect.
Based on these counterfactual observations, one can therefore disregard the modality of presentation to be a precursor to the ERP component engendered in the study.

As for our electrophysiological data, despite the typological similarities
between the two languages, Hindi and Punjabi, we did not observe the N400 component for either of the violation conditions, as was the case in Hindi. Further, the

positivities that we observe are temporally quite distinct for the two violations and probably connote differences between the processing of the two constructions.

While these ERP results might seem contra-evidential, our claim is that there are certain processing similarities for the two constructions types in Hindi and Punjabi. First, the distribution pattern for P600 seems to be aligned in the two languages. Like Choudhary et al. (2009) who reported a P600 only for the ergative case violation, our results also attest the classic P600 effect only for the illicit use of the ergative case in the imperfective aspect and not for the nominative condition. Further, although the two violation conditions did not elicit an N400 effect in Punjabi, as they were reported to have in Hindi, the fact that we did not observe a different kind of negativity is important.

We therefore take this opportunity to claim that these case violations in Punjabi too are interpretively relevant (as proposed in Frisch and Schlesewsky (2001, 2005); Choudhary et al. 2009). However, we believe that the absence of an N400 is probably indicative of the fact that ergative case in Punjabi is not as strong an interpretive cue as it is for Hindi.

In a discussion of the strength and reliability of cues that aid online comprehension, it is important to point out that different languages might employee different cues in order to hasten incremental processing. Bornkessel and Schlesewsky (2006) enumerates several kinds of cues that help the native speakers to compute the prominence hierarchy and deduce 'who did what to whom' during online comprehension. These cues range from morphosyntactic cues such as case and word order to semantic cues such as animacy. Depending upon the type of the language, one cue might work better than the other (Bates et al. 1982; Macwhinney 2005). For instance, in a morphologically impoverished language such as English, speakers rely on the position of the arguments while trying to ascertain the actor and the undergoer of an action, in contrast, morphologically rich languages like Basque, replete with case markers, provide case as a cue to compute the same, while still other languages like Awtuw rely on animacy to compute the prominence hierarchy between the arguments. Further, certain cues might work more reliably than the others available within the language. For instance, Yokoyama et al. (2014) report that case markers are used as a preferential cue in Japanese when case and animacy information can both act as cues.

We can therefore argue that the difference between the electrophysiological components observed for Hindi and Punjabi are owing to the variations in the languages. First, in contrast to Hindi, Punjabi has a more rigid word order, at least for the core arguments (Bhatia 1993). Our results therefore in retrospect may indicate that the native speakers of Punjabi, probably take word order to be a more reliable cue than case. This bifurcation drawn for the presence (and absence) of the N400 component has in the literature also been traced back to the sequence independent and sequence dependence status of languages (Bornkessel-Schlesewsky et al. 2011). Sequence independent languages have been noted to be more prone to engendering N400, while sequence dependent languages are not. Therefore, while this is a plausible reason for the attested difference, it needs to be tested further before we can affirmatively conclude.

Another point of variation between the two languages is that while both the languages are split-ergative, Hindi exhibits only an aspect-based split while Punjabi has both aspectual as well as person-based split-ergativity. This therefore generates a greater variation in the subject case distribution of the two languages. While nominative case markers are quite widespread in Hindi, the ergative case marker occurs in a very specialized construction only, i.e. when the aspect is perfective, and therefore renders a specialized prediction (Choudhary 2011; Dillon et al. 2012). For Punjabi, this expanse is further restricted. Since Punjabi also has a person-based split-ergative pattern, the ergative marker effectively surfaces only in the third person in the perfective aspect (for a theoretical review, refer to Kaur 2016).

On the whole therefore, one could ascribe the absence of N400 to the difference in the word order flexibility and the scope of the structural configurations in which the case markers occur in the two languages.

These variations in the distribution of the subject cases also explains the observed pattern for the mean acceptability of the behavioural (grammaticality judgement) task. Since the use of a nominative argument in a perfective aspect in general an acceptable structural configuration (in the first and the second person constructions), native speakers find it reasonably acceptable even in the third person. However, since ergative with the imperfective is a never attested structural configuration it remains to be lesser liked by the native speakers.

Now going back to the positive component, as stated earlier, the configuration for the monophasic positivities rendered by the two violation conditions seems to be varied, with differences in their onset latencies. A few studies have in the past have addressed this issue of the onset variability of P600. These include Friederici et al. (2001), Phillips et al. (2005), Gouvea et al. (2010).

Friederici et al. (2001) explored garden path sentences and reported that onset latencies are subject to the completion of the 'diagnosis' stage before the reanalysis is initiated. Therefore, violations that are easier to reanalyse engender P600 with relatively early onsets while those which are harder to reanalyse have a delayed onset for the P600. Phillips and colleagues employed wh-dependencies and observed an early P600 for shorter wh-dependencies and a delayed one for longer wh-dependencies. The authors therefore attributed the latency shifts to the time taken for retrieval from memory, with the more distant retrievals taking longer, thus delaying the onset. Lastly, Gouvea et al. (2010) explored different kinds of violations and ascribed a more generic interpretation to onset latency variations, somewhat in line with Phillips et al. (2005). The authors claimed that onset latencies are indicative of the retrieval processes required in order for the structural building to begin.

In retrospect then, the three studies are somewhat unified in their account for onset latency shifts, with less prominent (more easy-to-handle) violations engendering relatively earlier positivities while those that are more prominent (thus harder-to-handle) eliciting the positivity with the more traditional onset and timing. This explains the onset distribution we attest in the present study.

As stated earlier, the use of a nominative argument in the perfective aspect is a structural configuration observed in the language. In contrast, an ergative argument in the imperfective aspect is outright bizarre and thus an overtly ill-formed construction. Therefore, while the nominative case violation is easier for the processor to parse, the ergative case violation is not. Hence, we observe the positivity with an earlier onset for the nominative case violation while it is later for the ergative case violation. Lastly, in terms of the functional interpretations of the component per say, we attribute the positivity in line with Bornkessel and Schlesewsky (2006), Bornkessel-Schlesewsky and Schlesewsky (2009) and Choudhary et al. (2009) to the detection of an ill-formedness.

Conclusion and Future Directions

The present study explored the processing of case in Punjabi. The experiment did not replicate the result previously reported for Hindi, a typologically similar language. Instead of a biphasic negativity-positivity or a negative pattern, we observed monophasic positivities for both nominative as well as the ergative case violations. Our findings are indicative of the fact that while similarities in typologically similar languages are treated similarly (in terms of the temporal distribution of the positive component), the idiosyncratic variations (word order flexibility) are also realized with the languages rendering effects in distinct cortical sites, which in turn engender distinct ERP components.

At a high level, since comparative studies are the best way to attest similarities and differences, there is a need therefore to divulge from exploring just macro differences (across alignment types) and to indulge in analysing meso-similarities and differences in order to formulate a language processing architecture.

At the moment, what we can say assertively based on the differences we observe between the processing of case markers in Hindi and Punjabi is that the neurophysiological differences observed in Punjabi are due to the fact that ergative case is not used as a stronger cue, as is the case in Hindi.

Further, another speculation, we make basis the observed neurophysiological differences, is interpreting these results along the lines of language change. While this is a post-hoc analysis, we believe that this could be the case for two reasons. First, languages have been reported to drift away from the ergative alignment and towards the accusative alignment (Bornkessel-Schlesewsky and Schlesewsky 2016). This disfavour for the ergative structure had typologically been reported by Nichols (1993), and also within the Indo-Aryan language family (Deo and Sharma 2006). Neurophysiologically also, the drift from ergative alignment towards nominative has been attested recently in Bickel et al. (2015), Bornkessel-Schlesewsky and Schlesewsky (2016). Second, as reported earlier, the acceptability patterns and the fact that Punjabi native speakers adjudge the extension of the first/second person pattern in the perfective aspect onto the third person as moderately acceptable, might thereof be taken to indicate the shift.

Having said this, we do acknowledge that further research is required to establish the sanctity both these claims, be it teasing apart the relative reliability of cues across languages, or the attrition of ergativity. Studies therefore need to take both typological as well as neurophysiological variations seriously and investigate how typological distinctions modulate the processing routine across constructions and across languages and language types.

Acknowledgements The work was supported by the Department of Science and Technology, Govt. of India through a project to KKC (SR/CSI/141/2012). We would also like to acknowledge Indian Institute of Technology Ropar for the research facility maintained through an ISIRD grant to KKC [IITRPR/Acad./2216]

Data Availability Statement The data sets generated for this study can be made available upon communication with the corresponding author.

Statement of Conflict The authors declare that this research was conducted in the absence of any commercial or financial relationships that could be construed as a potential conflict of interest.

References

Alday, P. M., Schlesewsky, M., & Bornkessel-Schlesewsky, I. (2014). Towards a computational model of actor-based language comprehension. *Neuroinformatics, 12*(1), 143–179. https://doi.org/10.1007/s12021-013-9198-x

Alday, P. M., Schlesewsky, M., & Bornkessel-Schlesewsky, I. (2015). Discovering prominence and its role in language processing: An individual (differences) approach. *Linguistics Vanguard, 1*(1), 201–213. https://doi.org/10.1515/lingvan-2014-1013

Bader, M., & Bayer, J. (2006). *Case and linking in language comprehension*. Evidence from German. Heidelberg: Springer.

Bates, E., McNew, S., MacWhinney, B., Devescovi, A., & Smith, S. (1982). Functional constraints on sentence processing: A cross-linguistic study. *Cognition, 11*(3), 245–299. https://doi.org/10.1016/0010-0277(82)90017-8

Bayer, J., Bader M. & Meng, M. (2001). Morphological underspecification meets oblique case: syntactic and processing effects in German. *Lingua, 111*, 465–514.

Bhatia, T. K. (1993). *Punjabi: A cognitive-descriptive grammar*. Routledge.

Bhatt, R. (2007). Ergativity in the Modern Indo-Aryan Languages, Handout of talk given at the MIT Ergativity Seminar. http://people.umass.edu/bhatt/papers/mit-nov2007-handout.pdf

Bickel, B., Witzlack-Makarevich, A., Choudhary, K. K., Schlesewsky, M., & Bornkessel-Schlesewsky, I. (2015). The Neurophysiology of language processing shapes the evolution of grammar: Evidence from case marking. *PLoS ONE, 10*(8), e0132819–e0132819. https://doi.org/10.1371/journal.pone.0132819

Blake, B. (2001). *Case*. In: Cambridge textbooks in linguistics (2nd ed.) Cambridge: Cambridge University Press. https://doi.org/10.1017/CBO9781139164894

Bornkessel, I., & Schlesewsky, M. (2006). The extended argument dependency model: A neurocognitive approach to sentence comprehension across languages. *Psychological Review, 113*(4), 787–821. https://doi.org/10.1037/0033-295X.113.4.787

Bornkessel-Schlesewsky, I., Kretzschmar, F., Tune, S., Wang, L., Genç, S., Philipp, M., … Schlesewsky, M. (2011). Think globally: Cross-linguistic variation in electrophysiological activity during sentence comprehension. *Brain and Language, 117*(3), 133–152. https://doi.org/10.1016/j.bandl.2010.09.010

Bornkessel-Schlesewsky, I., Roehm, D., Mailhammer, R., & Schlesewsky, M. (2020). Language processing as a precursor to language change: evidence from icelandic. *Frontiers in Psychology, 10*, 3013–3013. https://doi.org/10.3389/fpsyg.2019.03013

Bornkessel-Schlesewsky, I., & Schlesewsky, M. (2009). The role of prominence information in the real-time comprehension of transitive constructions: A cross-linguistic approach. *Language and Linguistics Compass, 3*, 19–58, 3. https://doi.org/10.1111/j.1749818X.2008.00099.x

Bornkessel-Schlesewsky, I., & Schlesewsky, M. (2016). The importance of linguistic typology for the neurobiology of language. *Linguistic Typology, 20*. https://doi.org/10.1515/lingty-2016-0032

Butt, M. (1995). *The structure of complex predicates in Urdu.* Stanford, Calif.: CSLI Publications.

Butt, M., & Deo, A. (2001). Ergativity in Indo-Aryan. In *Online KURDICA Newsletter for Kurdish Language and Studies, 5.*

Carreiras, M., Duñabeitia, J. A., Vergara-Martínez, M., de la Cruz-Pavía, I., & Laka, I. (2010). Subject relative clauses are not universally easier to process: Evidence from basque. *Cognition, 115*, 79–92. https://doi.org/10.1016/j.cognition.2009.11.012

Chaumon, M., Bishop, D., & Busch, N. (2015). A practical guide to the selection of independent components of the electroencephalogram for Artifact correction. *Journal of Neuroscience Methods, 250.* https://doi.org/10.1016/j.jneumeth.2015.02.025

Choudhary, K. K. (2011). Incremental argument interpretation in a split ergative language: Neurophysiological evidence from Hindi. (Unpublished doctoral dissertation). Max Planck Institute of Human Cognitive and Brain Sciences, Leipzig, Germany, Leipzig, Germany.

Choudhary, K. K., Schlesewsky, M., Roehm, D., & Bornkessel-Schlesewsky, I. (2009). The N400 as a correlate of interpretively relevant linguistic rules: Evidence from Hindi. *Neuropsychologia, 47*(13), 3012–3022. https://doi.org/10.1016/j.neuropsychologia.2009.05.009

Chomsky, N. (1981). *Lectures on government and binding.* Dordrecht: Foris.

Chomsky, N. (1986). *Barriers.* Cambridge, MA.: MIT Press.

Chomsky, N. (1993). A minimalist program for linguistic theory. In K. Hale & S. Keyser (Eds.), *The view from building 20: Essays in linguistics in honor of Sylvain Bromberger* (pp. 1–52). Cambridge, MA: The MIT Press.

Coulson, S., King, J., & Kutas, M. (1998). Expect the unexpected: Event-related brain response to Morphosyntactic violations. *Language and Cognitive Processes, 13*, 21–58. https://doi.org/10.1080/016909698386582

Davison, A. (2004). Structural Case, lexical case and the verbal projection. In V. Dayal, & A. Mahajan (Eds.), *Clause structure in South Asian languages* (pp. 199–225). Dordrecht: Kluwer.

Delorme, A., & Makeig, S. (2004). EEGLAB: An open source toolbox for analysis of single-trial EEG dynamics including independent component analysis. *Journal of Neuroscience Methods, 134*(1), 9–21. https://doi.org/10.1016/j.jneumeth.2003.10.009

Demiral, B., Schlesewsky, M., & Bornkessel-Schlesewsky, I. (2008). On the universality of language comprehension strategies: Evidence from Turkish. *Cognition, 106*, 484–500. https://doi.org/10.1016/j.cognition.2007.01.008

Deo, A., & Sharma, D. (2006). Typological variation in the ergative morphology of Indo-Aryan languages *10*(3), 369–418. Retrieved from https://doi.org/10.1515/LINGTY.2006.012

Diaz, B., Sebastian Galles, N., Erdocia, K., Mueller, J., & Laka, I. (2011). On the cross-linguistic validity of electrophysiological correlates of Morphosyntactic processing: A study of case and agreement violations in Basque. *Journal of Neurolinguistics, 24*, 357–373. https://doi.org/10.1016/j.jneuroling.2010.12.003

Dillon, B., Nevins, A., Austin, A., & Phillips, C. (2012). Syntactic and semantic predictors of tense in Hindi: An ERP investigation. *Language and Cognitive Processes, 27.* https://doi.org/10.1080/01690965.2010.544582

Friederici, A., Mecklinger, A., Spencer, K., Steinhauer, K., & Donchin, E. (2001). Syntactic parsing preferences and their on-line revisions: A spatio-temporal analysis of event-related brain potentials. *Cognitive Brain Research, 11*, 305–323. https://doi.org/10.1016/S0926-6410(00)00065-3

Frisch, S., & Schlesewsky, M. (2001). The N400 reflects problems of thematic hierarchizing. *NeuroReport, 12*, 3391–3394. https://doi.org/10.1097/00001756-200110290-00048

Frisch, S., & Schlesewsky, M. (2005). The resolution of case conflicts from a neurophysiological perspective. *Brain Research. Cognitive Brain Research, 25*, 484–498. https://doi.org/10.1016/j.cogbrainres.2005.07.010

Gouvea, A., Phillips, C., Kazanina, N., & Poeppel, D. (2010). The linguistic processes underlying the P600. *Language and Cognitive Processes, 25*, 149–188. https://doi.org/10.1080/01690960902965951

Harbert, W., & Jacqueline T. (1991). Nominative objects. In A. J. Toribio & W. E. Harbert (Eds.), *Cornell working papers in linguistics 9* (pp. 127–192). Ithaca, N.Y.: Cornell University, Department of Modern Languages and Linguistics.

Hendrick, R. (2004). *Syntactic labels and their derivations.* Ms., University of North Carolina, Chapel Hill.

Hopf, J. M., Bayer, J., Bader, M., & Meng, M. (1998). Event-related brain potentials and case information in syntactic ambiguities. *Journal of Cognitive Neuroscience, 10*(2), 264–280. https://doi.org/10.1162/089892998562690

Iriarte, J., Urrestarazu, E., Valencia, M., Alegre, M., Malanda, A., Viteri, C., & Artieda, J. (2003). Independent component analysis as a tool to eliminate Artifacts in EEG: A quantitative study. *Journal of Clinical Neurophysiology, 20*, 249–257. https://doi.org/10.1097/00004691-200307000-00004

Jacobsen, T. (2000). *Characteristics of processing morphological structural and inherent case in language comprehension.* PhD thesis, Max Planck Institute of Cognitive Neuroscience Leipzig.

Kaur, G. (2016). Person in Punjabi: Investigating Argument and Clitic Licensing. (Unpublished doctoral dissertation). Indian Institute of Technology Delhi.

Laughren, M. (1989). The configurationality parameter and Warlpiri. In E. Jelinek, L. Maracz, & P. Muysken (Eds.), *Configurationality: The typology of asymmetries* (pp. 319–366). Dordrecht: Foris.

Legate, J. (2003). Some interface properties of the phase. *Linguistic Inquiry, 34*, 506–516.

Lopez Calderon, J., & Luck, S. (2014). ERPLAB: An open-source toolbox for the analysis of event-related potentials. *Frontiers in Human Neuroscience, 8*, 213. https://doi.org/10.3389/fn-hum.2014.00213

Macwhinney, B. (2005). Extending the competition model. *International Journal of Bilingualism, 9*, 69–84. https://doi.org/10.1177/13670069050090010501

Mahajan, A. (1989). Agreement and agreement phrases. In L. Itziar & A. Mahajan (Eds.), *Functional heads and clause structure* (pp. 217–252). MIT Working Papers in Linguistics 10. Cambridge, Mass.: MIT, Department of Linguistics and Philosophy, MITWPL.

Mahajan, A. K. (1990). *The A/A-bar distinction and movement theory.* (Unpublished doctoral dissertation). MIT, Cambridge.

Massam, D. (2002). Fully internal cases: Surface ergativity can be profound. In A. Rackowski & N. Richards (Eds.), *Proceedings of AFLA VIII: The Eighth Meeting of the Austronesian Formal Linguistics Association* (pp. 185–196). MIT Working Papers in Linguistics 44. Cambridge, Mass.: MIT, Department of Linguistics and Philosophy, MITWPL.

Mohanan, T. (1994). *Argument structure in Hindi.* Center for the Study of Language (CSLI). Stanford, California.

Mueller, J., Hirotani, M., & Friederici, A. (2007). ERP evidence for different strategies in the processing of case markers in native speakers and non-native learners. *BMC Neuroscience, 8*, 18. https://doi.org/10.1186/1471-2202-8-18

Münte, T. F., Matzke, M., & Johannes, S. (1997). Brain Activity associated with syntactic Incongruencies in words and pseudo-words. *Journal of Cognitive Neuroscience, 9*(3), 318–329. https://doi.org/10.1162/jocn.1997.9.3.318

Nash, L. (1996). The internal ergative subject hypothesis. *North East Linguistics Society, 26*(5). Available at: https://scholarworks.umass.edu/nels/vol26/iss1/15

Nevins, A., Dillon, B., Malhotra, S., & Phillips, C. (2007). The role of feature-number and feature-type in processing Hindi verb agreement violations. *Brain Research, 1164*, 81–94. https://doi.org/10.1016/j.brainres.2007.05.058

Nichols, J. (1993). Ergativity and linguistic geography. *Australian Journal of Linguistics, 13*(1), 39–89. https://doi.org/10.1080/07268609308599489

Oldfield, R. C. (1971). The assessment and analysis of handedness: The edinburgh inventory. *Neuropsychologia, 9*(1), 97–113. https://doi.org/10.1016/0028-3932(71)90067-4

Phillips, C., Kazanina, N., & Abada, S. (2005). ERP effects of the processing of syntactic long-distance dependencies. *Brain Research. Cognitive Brain Research, 22*, 407–428. https://doi.org/10.1016/j.cogbrainres.2004.09.012

Polinsky, M., Gallo, C. G., Graff, P., & Kravtchenko, E. (2012). Subject preference and Ergativity. *Lingua, 122*(3), 267–277. https://doi.org/10.1016/j.lingua.2011.11.004

Schneider, W., Eschman, A., & Zuccolotto, A. (2002). *E-prime User's Guide.*

Ura, H. (2000). *Checking theory and grammatical functions in Universal Grammar.* Oxford: Oxford University Press.

Woolford, E. (1993). Symmetric and asymmetric passives. *Natural Language & Linguistic Theory, 11*, 679–728.

Woolford, E. (1997). Four-way case systems: Ergative, nominative, objective, and accusative. *Natural Language & Linguistic Theory, 15*, 181–227.

Wunderlich, D. (1997). Cause and the structure of verbs. *Linguistic Inquiry, 28*, 27–68.

Woolford, E. (2001). Case patterns. In G, Legendre, S, Vikner & J, Grimshaw (Eds.), *Optimality-theoretic syntax* (pp. 509–543). Cambridge, Mass.: MIT Press.

Woolford, E. (2006). Lexical case, inherent case and argument structure. *Linguistic Inquiry, 37*(1), 111–130.

Yokoyama, S., Takahashi, K., & Kawashima, R. (2014). Animacy or case marker order?: Priority Information for online sentence comprehension in a head-final language. *PloS One, 9.* https://doi.org/10.1371/journal.pone.0093109

Zawiszewski, A. (2017). Processing Ergativity: Behavioral and electrophysiological evidence. In J. Coon, D. Massam, & L. D. Travis (Eds.), (pp. 693–708). Oxford University Press.

Zawiszewski, A., Gutiérrez, E., Fernández, B., & Laka, I. (2011). Language distance and non-native syntactic processing: evidence from event-related potentials. *Bilingualism: Language and Cognition, 14*, 400–411. https://doi.org/10.1017/S1366728910000350

Mahima Gulati is currently Assistant Professor at the New Delhi Institute of Management, New Delhi. She has completed her doctoral degree from the Department of Humanities and Social Sciences, Indian Institute of Technology Ropar. Her dissertation titled 'The Role of Case in Incremental Argument Interpretation: Evidence from Punjabi' is an ERP study exploring the treatment of nominative and ergative case in Punjabi. She has formerly completed her Masters in Philosophy with a dissertation titled 'Sluicing in Hindi: A Psycholinguistic Study' from the Centre for Advanced Studies in Linguistics (CASL), University of Delhi in 2014. She did her Masters in Linguistics from the English and Foreign Languages University, Hyderabad in 2012, and her Bachelors in Literature from University of Delhi in 2009. Her areas of interest include exploring case and agreement from Linguistic, Neurolinguistic/Psycholinguistic and Cognitive Science perspective.

Kamal K. Choudhary is Associate Professor at the Department of Humanities and Social Sciences, Indian Institute of Technology Ropar. Kamal completed his Ph.D. from Max Planck Institute of Human Cognitive and Brain Sciences Leipzig, Germany/University of Leipzig, Germany. Before joining IIT Ropar, he worked as a visiting faculty at the Centre of Behavioural and Cognitive Sciences, University of Allahabad, India. He works primarily in the area of the neurophysiology of language comprehension. His broad areas of interest include Psycho/Neurolinguistics, Language and Cognition, Neurocognition/Neuroscience of Language comprehension. Currently, his research focuses on ergative languages.

Chapter 12
On Gender Micro-Variation

Pritha Chandra

Abstract This paper looks at dialect variation in Hindi 'dialects' Awadhi and Bhojpuri. Depending on the theory one adopts, small, micro-level differences between dialects are either taken to result from differential feature selections or from usage and input-based strategies. I instead propose that feature-level variation is tied to certain structural configurations, rather than to just discrete feature learning. Using gender variation data, I show that dialects that have a nominalizer, enable gender morphology; those which lack a nominalizer fail to display gender agreement. This correlation indicates specific structural signatures for gender morphology, while acknowledging the possibility that gender may be latent in every language, even those that do not morphologically realize gender. Language-learning children use these signatures to grasp structural schemas that are conducive to gender expression. This paper also shows how languages shift between nouns and adjectives and how gender expression via the nominalizing strategy lies at the intersection between these two categories.

Keywords Gender · Micro-variation · Features · Nominalizer

Introduction

While linguistic variation is apparent enough to warrant the ongoing extensive surveys and discussions of languages and dialects, its real import lies in the actual processes that underpin its very existence. What causes variation, is a question that linguists from different theoretical backgrounds, have tried to explain using their own methodological and philosophical assumptions. While some approaches (e.g. generative/minimalist) capture linguistic variability in terms of lexical or featural

P. Chandra (✉)
Indian Institute of Technology Delhi, New Delhi, India
e-mail: pritha@iitd.ac.in

© The Author(s), under exclusive license to Springer Nature Singapore Pte Ltd. 2023   295
P. Chandra (ed.), *Variation in South Asian Languages*,
https://doi.org/10.1007/978-981-99-1149-3_12

choices, others (usage and input-based theories—construction grammar, cognitive grammar) conceive it primarily as the outcome of the differential frequency rates of performance data. In the first tradition, the language-learning child selects a set of functional heads and features used to either trigger or offset the syntactic operations. The resultant structures are then given language-specific forms at the morpho-phonological component. For the latter, on the other hand, variability sets in when the language-learning child gets environmental input with different token frequencies that forces her to fix new schemas for her language. The former approach focuses more on preexisting features and featural compositions of heads, while the latter leans towards comparative token frequencies.

Irrespective of the adopted views, all accounts have a formidable challenge in the form of micro- or dialectal variation. Micro-variation or small-scale differences define mutually intelligible languages or dialects and happen generally at the level of features and feature values—such as person (first/second/third person values), number (singular/plural values) and gender (masculine/feminine/neuter values). Such differences are quite pervasive across the globe and are found even within varieties of a single language. A fundamental task for both groups is therefore to explain where this kind of variation comes from.

For the generativists, there is a direct answer since all variation, as per their theory, emanates from functional sub-choices (aka Borer–Chomsky Conjecture). Dialectal variation is the minimal change that can result from differential feature distribution. Depending partly on the data available to the language-learning children, two different varieties of the same language emerge in the minds of two different children—one with the given trait and the other without. The task is to show that children are indeed aware of feature-level units when they encounter external linguistic stimuli. If it is found that there are structural contexts that embed and determine featural values, then the generativist needs to rethink the exact mechanisms that are at play in micro-variation.

On the other hand, with the predominance of schemas and frequency in the learning process in the second camp, the learner is sensitive to holistic structures and not its constituent parts. The language learner's first task is to imbibe these schemas into her grammar and at a later point, to generate abstract structures and schemas by a schema/construction-comparative method. Variation results when the learner has access to data that either contest or attest an existing and dominant pattern in the grammar. The question that micro-variation places in front of these theorists is: what is the exact nature of the attained schema? How does the language learner get from the schema to the discrete feature that enables her to generate novel constructions using that feature?

In this paper, my primary claim is that dialectal variation, though seemingly minimal and restricted to feature-value differences, is directly linked to certain structural configurations; most specifically, to certain nodes. These structures signal that a certain feature can be expressed morphologically in the language, entirely contingent on the presence of certain structural signatures.

The presence of a structural signature for feature realization implies that a language-learning child is not on the lookout for discrete features in her linguistic input. It is the structure in which the noun and its feature are embedded, that she is primarily sensitive to. Thus, schema-based and usage-based learning models for micro-level variation cannot be entertained since they have no clear definition of a structural signature. Schemas are holistic and leave very little scope to identify structural signals within themselves—therefore, the idea that micro-variation dependent on such signals can happen through schemas must be discarded. For a generative account, on the other hand, the lesson to draw is that the mere presence of a discrete feature is not enough. In all possibility, the feature is always latent in the language—its morphological expression is tied to nodes and structures.

To understand this link between structure and feature realization, I examine gender variation data. Variation data help us understand how in the absence of the structural signature, the feature morphology also goes missing. Such differential expression can also happen within mutually intelligible languages and dialects. Using data from Awadhi, Bhojpuri (Indo-Aryan) and Kannada (Dravidian) dialects, I propose that the configuration essential to gender realization is a nominalizer or nP; gender representation happens only in those dialects where the said nominalizer is present.

The paper is structured in the following way. Section 12.2 introduces gender as a phi-feature. I then go on to discuss Awadhi dialectal gender variation in Sect. 12.3, highlighting the nominalized form necessary for the expression of this feature. Section 12.4 presents data from Old Indo-Aryan, Middle Indo-Aryan and old Kosali, the ancestor language of Awadhi which supports the idea that nominalizers are gender hosts. Additionally, the historical data also signals a clear noun-adjective-gender correlation, which is all tied to the n. This correlation is explained in Sect. 12.5. In the Sect. 12.6, comparison is drawn between Bhojpuri gender variation and Awadhi to further attest the nominalizer account for gender. Kannada gender data is discussed in Sect. 12.7, as a way to further substantiate our structure-based analysis for gender variation. The conclusion is in Sect. 12.8.

Introducing Gender

Gender is a member of the phi-feature set, along with person and number. Languages vary greatly on gender expression. While speakers of all languages have the concept of biological gender, not all have the morphosyntactic expression for it. Take for instance, the English sentence in (1), where both 'John' and 'Mary' trigger only number (singular) agreement on the verb. Different from this is Hindi (2), where 'John' and 'Mary' trigger not just number and person agreement, but also gender agreement. English does make a biological gender distinction for its third person, singular pronouns 'she' and 'he,' but they too fail to trigger gender agreement on the verb.

(1)   John/Mary likes mangoes

(2)   *John/Mary aam   pasand kartaa/kartii   he*

       John/Mary mango   like   do-masc./fem.   be.3p.sg.prst

       'John/Mary likes mangoes'

Differences between the two do not end here. English and Hindi also differ on grammatical gender. Hindi speakers extend masculine and feminine values to non-human and non-animate objects, as captured here through the following illustrations (3)–(4).[1]

(3)   *tumhaari*   *gaaRii aa gayii*

       your-fem. car   come go-fem

       'Your car has arrived'

(4)   *tumharaa*   *kapRaa*   *aa*   *gayaa*

       your-masc   dress-masc   come go-masc

       'Your dress has arrived'

In addition, there are nouns whose gender values are contextually decided, such as *dost* ('friend') in (5), which displays both masculine and feminine values on the accompanying predicate as well on the accompanying possessive pronominal.

(5)   *tumhari/tumharaa*   *dost*   *aa*   *gayii/gayaa*

     Your-fem./masc   friend-fem./masc   come go-fem./masc

     'Your (male/female) friend has arrived'

But the two-valued system of gender (or three-valued, including neuter) may not suffice when describing all world languages with gender systems. Gender values sometimes run into double digits; in such cases, scholars prefer to conflate them with noun classes (see Corbett 1991 for a thorough discussion). Unlike biological gender where gender values of nouns correspond directly to their conceived male/female features, extensions of gender to the inanimate world—either as grammatical gender or as noun classes—have no one-to-one association with any specific semantic character of the nouns. In other words, semantics is not a good heuristic for gender classification. While some languages have a two-tier gender system, driven primarily by semantics with males (animates) getting a+masculine value and females receiving a+feminine value, others denote one class of nouns with a+masculine value, with the rest of the nouns (irrespective of their+animate/-animate nature) receiving a+feminine value. There are other distributions as well, which are either partially decided by semantic factors, or are completely divorced from semantic considerations. In short, there are different ways to group noun classes based on gender values, and these are not necessarily based on semantic factors.

---

[1] English allows grammatical gender in restricted environments, such as the lexical items 'she-wolf' or when referring to inanimate objects with a feminine pronoun (e.g. 'The captain's ship sunk; he couldn't save her').

Given this rather random gender distribution of nouns, the diagnostic of gender is always indirect and happens via gender agreement on an accompanying item in the structure. This point is clearly stated by Corbett's seminal work on gender too, "All this means that the determining criterion of gender is agreement; this is the way in which genders are 'reflected in the behaviour of words'…Saying that a language has three genders implies that there are three classes of nouns which can be distinguished syntactically by the agreements they take (pp: 4)". Languages are therefore diagnosed as ±gender based on the morphological indicators present on their adjectives, verbs, adverbs, conjunctions, etc.

The implication for language acquisition is that the child cannot figure out the gender value of the noun solely based on the nominal form itself. The learner is instead, on the lookout for a more detailed form for the noun, or structures containing the noun such as the following:

(6)   a. $[_{TP} NP_{subj-masc} [V_{masc}]]$
      b. $[DP_{masc} AdjP_{masc} NP_{masc}]]]$

In the representation in (6a) which is part of the child's linguistic environment, the verb gets a masculine form upon agreement with the natural/grammatical + masculine subject. Since the noun has no direct way of signalling its gender value, the child's assessment of verbal morphology is crucial here to draw inferences about the noun's gender. The entire structure is therefore under scrutiny here. Similarly, in (6b), gender concord with the determiner and the adjective signals the gender value of the noun. The puzzle is: if a child was to start from these forms present in the linguistic input, how does she set about, from considering the entire structure to narrowing down on a single, discrete feature? Once the task of feature-selection is complete, how does the child use this information to create more structures of the same kind? This question is answered by looking at these critical nodes carefully—whether it is a D, a nominalizer, an adjective and understanding how they are intricately tied to the noun and features and more generally to other categories in the grammar. In later sections, I detail out such close connects and argue that category-feature overlaps allow the language-learning child to easily associate featural changes with structural signatures. The interrelations define our grammatical potential to express micro-level featural variation.[2]

---

[2]An anonymous reviewer shares the following Hindi example, to argue that the noun is an independent cue to grammatical gender. When asked if a pillow is 'good' (with the adjective either corresponding to the Hindi *acchaa*-masc or *acchii*-fem), the child responds with '*pillow koi boy hota he*!!' (Can a pillow ever be a boy?). To my understanding, there are two ways to interpret the child's response. Either the child is referring to the pillow as an inanimate object, and the inability to identify inanimate objects with the help of biological gender morphology, or the child is already aware of the grammatical feminine value ascribed to 'pillow' in Hindi and is ruling out the *acchaa* (good-masc) possibility. Either way, it is the gender inflection on the predicate that signals the noun's grammatical gender; the nominal form itself is neutral in this regard.

Awadhi Gender

Let me begin the discussion with gender inflection data from an Eastern Indo-Aryan language Awadhi. The language is primarily spoken in rural and semi-urban areas in the northern state of Uttar Pradesh in India and one of its varieties—Lakhimpur Kheri—has been previously documented by Saksena (1971). Picking up from that study, one understands that Awadhi is generally a gender-less language, having lost gender completely at an earlier stage. To state in more particular terms, there is no DP gender concord nor verbal gender agreement.

To test out whether this generalization holds true for all contemporary Awadhi varieties, we undertook a linguistic survey in some of the Awadhi-speaking regions over a period of two years. Our observations here on Awadhi gender are based entirely on the data obtained from that survey. See Map 12.1 for the Awadhi-speaking areas covered during the survey.

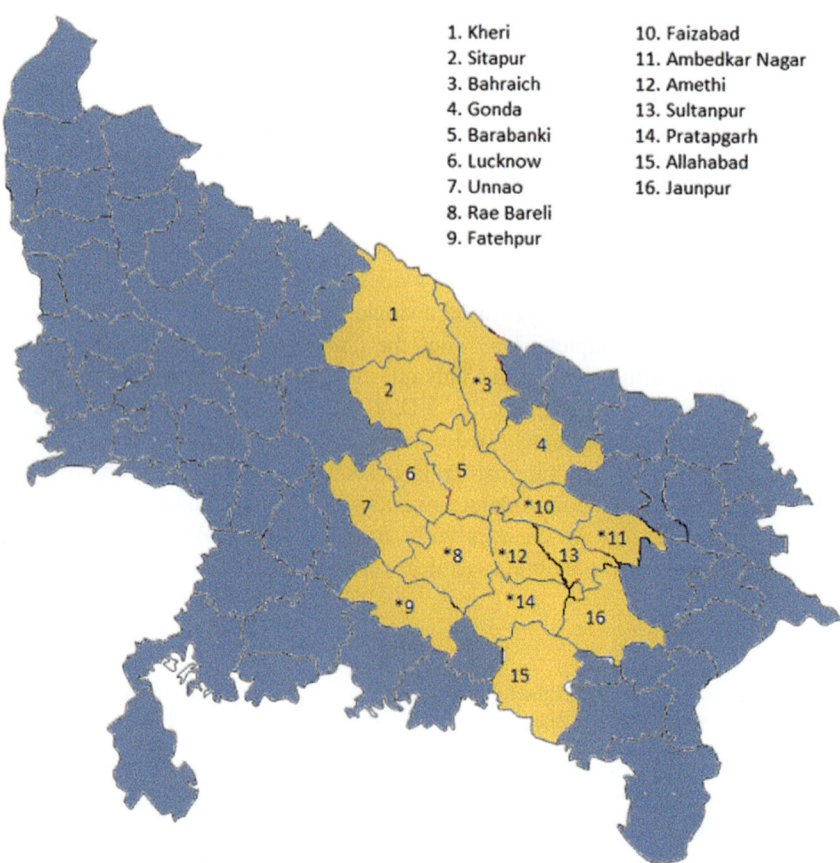

1. Kheri
2. Sitapur
3. Bahraich
4. Gonda
5. Barabanki
6. Lucknow
7. Unnao
8. Rae Bareli
9. Fatehpur

10. Faizabad
11. Ambedkar Nagar
12. Amethi
13. Sultanpur
14. Pratapgarh
15. Allahabad
16. Jaunpur

Map. 12.1 Awadhi-speaking areas

Awadhi is spoken in 15 districts (marked in yellow in Map 12.1), in the state of Uttar Pradesh. These districts are surrounded by Kannauji and Bhojpuri-speaking regions on the west and the east, respectively. Of the 15 districts, data was collected from 7 (identified with stars).

The survey shows that speakers of Awadhi dialects do not have long-distance verbal gender agreement. All speakers, barring some, produced structures such as (7), where the verb appears in its uninflected (for person, number, gender) form. However, a few bilinguals from Amethi district with knowledge of both Awadhi and Hindi used some such structures from the latter where the verb carried gender morphology. However, none of the other informants reported verbal inflection; we will put aside the issue of long-distance gender agreement for this paper and not pursue it further.

(7)   *u:*   *ekt^hi*   *bilari-ka*   *roj*   *marət*   *ba*
      he/she   one   cat.acc   daily   hit   be
      'He/She hits a cat daily'

However, we did observe considerable dialectal variation when it comes to gender concord. The dialects spoken in districts such as Amethi and Bahraich displayed gender morphology on the adjective (8a-b), which they possibly borrowed from mutually intelligible Hindi. The second strategy was found in dialects spoken in Ambedkar Nagar where a special *–ka/ki* morpheme is used to support gender morphology (9a-b). Yet in other dialects, such as those spoken in Fatehpur a special *-har* morpheme is used resist gender inflection (10a-b).

(8)   a   *u:*   *ləmbi*   *ləDki*
           that   tall-fem   girl
           'That tall girl'

      b   *u:*   *ləmba*   *ləDka*
           that   tall-masc   boy
           'That tall boy'

(9)   a   *u:*   *ləm-ki*   *ləDkiya*
           that   tall-nmz.fem   girl
           'That tall girl'

      b   *u:*   *ləm-ka*   *ləDkawa*
           that   tall-nmz.masc   boy
           'That tall boy'

(10) a *u:*   *ləməhər*   *ləDkiya*

          that   tall   girl

          'That tall girl'

      b *u:*   *ləməhər*   *ləDkawa*

          that   tall   boy

          'That tall boy'

Expressions such as those provided in (8) result from direct borrowings of adjectives from Standard Hindi. Given the superior status of the language and the dominant role it plays in mass media and education, speakers of lesser-known languages emulate several structures of Hindi in their own languages, and this extends to languages that are neither mutually intelligible nor belong to the same language family.

While assimilation of Hindi gender forms is a strong tendency, not all varieties directly borrow from the language. To make this point clearer, let us first consider the following adjectival/concord forms in Hindi:

(11)   *chhota/chhoti*   *ləDka/ ləDki*

       small-masc./small-fem   boy/girl

(12)   *bəRa/bəRi*   *ləDka/ ləDki*

       big-masc./big-fem   boy/girl

(13)   *sundər*   *ləDka/ ləDki*

       beautiful/handsome   boy/girl

(14)   *lal*   *bəs/ghar*

       red bus-fem./house-masc

As mentioned above, Hindi-like gender concord is available only in some districts where speakers directly incorporate them into their dialects. For many other Awadhi speakers, even while the Hindi data are available in their linguistic surroundings, direct borrowing is not allowed. Instead, they support gender concord by obligatorily appending a *–ka/ki* marker on adjectives. More such structures are provided in (15)-(16). Note here that the *ka/ki* adjectival forms can also be extended to inanimate nouns, suggesting a domain extension of gender in the languages. Biological gender forms are also used to express grammatical gender.

(15)   *sun(d)ər-ka/sun(d)ər-ki*

       handsome/beautiful (boy/girl)

(16)   *ləl-ka/ ləl-ki*

       red-masc./red-fem

       'the red one-masc./fem.(thing)'

It is worth mentioning at this point that this stratagem is not restricted to just Awadhi. It is also found in other Indo-Aryan languages such as Magadhi, Maithili, with which the former does not share a geographical border. These languages too do not have gender agreement, and speakers often use the *ka/ki* morpheme to display gender distinctions.

Let us look at the morpheme a little closely. Hindi also has a–*ka/ki* form with two primary functions: (i) as a genitive form (17a-b) and (ii) as a nominalizing suffix (18a-b). Consider:

(17)   a   *John-ki*   *kitaab*

            John-gen.fem. book.fem

            'John's book'

        b   *John-ka*   *ghar*

            John-gen.masc. house.masc

            'John's house'

(18)   a   *bəRki*

            big-fem

            'The elder one' (also 'elder daughter/sister,' etc.)

        b   *bəRka*

            big-masc

            'The elder one' (also 'elder son/brother,' etc.)

The first is mostly used in Standard Hindi, and the latter in provincial languages, or what are generally known as mutually intelligible dialects of Hindi (of which Awadhi is also considered to be one). We will consider the second form here, where the *ka/ki* form is essentially a nominalizer (18). The reason for terming it a nomimalizer is that when it is appended to an adjective such as 'big,' it transforms it with a special attribute-denoting noun. In (19), the adjective 'big' when attached to the nominalizer denotes 'the one that is big,' where 'big' means either 'big in size' or 'older in age/status.' Note that this structure is minimally different from the *ka/ki* carrying representation in Awadhi (15)/(16), where an overt noun is also included (20).

(19)   [$_{nP}$ [$_{AP}$ *bəR*] n *ki* [N *one*]]

(20)   [$_{nP}$ [$_{AP}$ *bəR*] n *ki* [N *ləRki*]]

Since Hindi already uses the *ka/ki* with multiple functions, a possible conclusion is that certain varieties of Awadhi have borrowed the form from Hindi. This borrowed form is then used for nominalizing the adjective. It is in this special context that gender concord shows up in these varieties. In all other cases, the language is strictly gender-less.

What we therefore see is a clear instance of a form adopted from a neighbouring language and used in the expression of inflectional markings in another language. For the particular phenomenon under consideration, it is gender inflection that makes a comeback with the nominalizing strategy. One could take this to also suggest that contra the commonplace assumption in generative grammar that differential feature subselection leads to language variation, it is the presence or absence of the right structure that is responsible for featural expression or its absence.

Another fall-out of the structural analysis of gender variation is that Awadhi had effectively never lost its gender feature. Rather, it is very likely that the gender feature was always part of the feature subset of every Awadhi speaker. However, it got manifested as gender concord only when the right configuration—headed by an *n*—was introduced into the grammar.

Indeed, the reason for why the *n*-head was lost at a certain point in the developmental trajectory of the language (and as we discuss in the following sections, even more generally, why adjectives, nouns and feminine gender got disconnected), needs to be studied carefully. Till far, the Awadhi data presented here indicate two things fairly clearly. The first is that micro-variation is due to some structural reasons, rather than just the absence or presence of a feature. The second is that both language contact and grammar-internal mechanisms can be at play for dialectal variation. We will have more to say on the structure-dependence of featural variation in the next two sections.

What is the *ka/ki* strategy then? Why are gender-less languages in the Indo-Aryan belt, in this case, Awadhi, adopting this mechanism to express gender? What I am going to suggest is that the *ka/ki* form is the correct signature for gender in these languages. This form anchors gender; its presence in the grammar is therefore vital for the expression of gender. As we delve into the *ka/ki* form in the next few sections, we will discover that the nominalizer allows category (noun to adjective) transition productively and was used in the prior stages of Awadhi (Old Kosali/Awadhi) and its ancestor languages Old Indo-Aryan and Middle Indo-Aryan. Its loss and reappearance play a significant role in the rise and fall of gender inflection in the language.

A Historical Support for the *N*

The exact structure of *ka/ki* morpheme and the reason behind the gender feature piggybacking on it become clear on looking at gender forms in ancestral varieties of the language and their development at different historical junctures. These stages are described below.

From a historical perspective, Awadhi descends from Old Indo-Aryan/OIA (1500 BC to 300 BC), which had both natural and grammatical gender agreement, though in much less frequency than number and person agreement. Gender agreement manifested on participial verbs, as shown in (21) below.

(21) ghṛtáṃ   vásanəh   pári   yasi   nirṇijəm
     ghee.masc.acc. wear.sg.masc.around travel.2sg bright garment.masc.acc
     'Wearing ghee, a bright garment, you circle around.'

                                        (RV 9.82.2d; Lowe 2015, pp: 1)

OIA also displayed gender concord, with adjectives appearing with the distinct feminine agreement morpheme –*i* (22). Masculine and neuter morphology were indistinguishable.

(22) ví   yáh   təstámbhə ródəsi: cit   urví
     asunder rel.sg.masc propped   world.fem   even   wide.fem
     'who has propped asunder even (the) two wide worlds.'

                            (RV 07.086.01; as cited in Kupfer 2002, pp: 208)

In short, OIA adjectives and (adjective-like) participial forms inflected for gender, suggesting a close connect between them and gender. Another interesting point to note is that certain OIA adjectives were in fact formed from neuter nouns (23).

(23) a   ápəs 'work'   ——>   əpás 'active'
     b   tárəs 'quickness' ——>   tərás 'quick'
                                        (Whitney 1896; pp: 156)

As shown above, OIA neuter nouns ('work' and 'quickness') transformed into adjectives by a stress shifting operation that displaced the stress from the first to the second syllable. What is noteworthy is that the same stress shifting operation is also used to shift between gender values (masculine to feminine). Some illustrations follow-

(24) a   ágru   ——>   əgrú
         'bachelor'   'virgin'
     b   krími   ——>   krimí:
         'insect (masc.)'   'insect (fem.)'

                                        (Whitney 1896: pp: 123)

These forms indicate that masculine to feminine variation in OIA was tied to structural changes. If one assumes 'masculine' as the default gender, the shift to 'feminine' value is via the same process that generates adjectives from nouns. An OIA speaker was most likely creating gender values (feminine, here) by deploying certain operations on existing forms. In other words, syntactic transformations played prominent roles in attributing gender values.

From the evidence presented, we infer about the link that exists between adjective formation and gender expression in OIA and its intricate connection with specific configurations. This specific configurational signature was required for both adjectives and gender expression. The question is: what common structure could underlie adjectives and gender? The OIA gender agreement data has some clear indicators. Gender agreement happened in OIA only on participial forms and never on tensed verbs. Similarly, gender concord also occurred on adjectives. Both adjectives and participial forms are nominalized structures—often coded in the literature as nPs.

Let us take up the following structural representation for the nominalizer in OIA. In (25), the noun (perhaps a concept embedded under N, in the sense of Borer 2001) is selected by a nominalizer n. The resultant structure is nP—a configuration that underlies both adjectives and gender expression.

(25) $[_{nP\,[+feminine]}\,[N\;n]$

The OIA nominalized structure in (25) supported gender expression. This was also the structure that allowed the generation of independent or derived adjectival forms (more on that in the next section).

This association continues through Middle Indo-Aryan/MIA (300 BC-1100 AD)[3] and Old Kosali/Awadhi (circa 1300 AD). In the words of Chatterji (1953: 45–46), '[a]s in MIA and OIA, the distinction between the noun and the adjective was but slight' in Old Kosali, and the [+feminine] value appeared only with adjectives, copulas and participial verbs.

The twelfth century Kosali text *Ukti Vyakti Prakaran* by Pandit Damodaran has ample illustrations that the language restricted its gender morphology to [+feminine] values. Only [+feminine] nouns triggered a distinct gender morpheme ($-i$) on the adjective. Chatterji (1953; pages 30–31) also provides illustrations of grammatical gender on adjectives.

In the following phases, Old Kosali gradually underwent a shift towards a gender-less system, and the [+feminine] marker took on a new function of a diminutive appearing on some inanimate nouns. This phase also saw the loss of gender concord in Awadhi, suggesting the concurrent loss of the n-head originally appended to Ns. The adjectives and nouns also got disassociated in the process, which is confirmed in the historical linguistics literature, with the last mention of the adjective-noun similarity noted till Old Kosali (Chatterji, ibid).

---

[3] See Cardona (1988, p. 178) for a discussion of MIA adjectives.

The lack of gender agreement in many varieties of current day Awadhi now finds an explanation. In OIA too, long-distance gender agreement was restricted to participial forms. When the current varieties of the language lost the nominalizer *n* form, there was simply no way to support gender morphology. In addition, the language also developed a phi-defective v/T head (as is currently attested in Awadhi and mutually intelligent languages such as Braj, Khari Boli that display uninflected verbal forms such as *marat* ('hit')). Such forms were unable to support person and number inflection as well. As for gender concord, since adjectives also lost the connection with the nominalizer, gender concord also went missing from the language.

The N-Adj-Gender Correlation

We now turn to address the common ground that we find between nouns, adjectives and gender values. The first question concerns why Western Indo-Aryan have this overlap between two categories. The second question is about the exact role of the *n* in phrases with both categories, and how that facilitates gender expression.

Existing literature on lexical categories has pointed out cross-linguistic overlaps between parts of speech, challenging the accepted divide between nouns, verbs, adjectives, etc. There are innumerable examples from the literature that report languages missing out on one of the primitive parts of speech/categories (nouns, verbs, adjectives); for reference, see Dixon (1982), Pustet (1989), Bhat (1994), Wetzer (1996), Stassen (1997) among others.

Baker (2005) is a more recent work that has dealt with this topic extensively, and so I take the liberty to cite directly from his work, of course limiting myself to only a few examples from the impressive list of cross-linguistic illustrations that he provides. More particularly, I will take up some examples from Mohawk, a North America Iroquoian language.

The traditional Iroquoian verdict is that Mohawk has no adjectives, with the putative adjectives appearing with the same agreement and tense/aspect prefixes as the intransitive verbs in the language.

(26)   a   *Ka-hutsi*   b   *t-a'-ka-ya't-a'-ne*

        NsS-black   CIS-FACT-NsS-body-fall-PUNC

        'It is black'   'It (e.g. a cat) fell'

Another overlapping property between adjectives and intransitive verbs of Mohawk is noun-incorporation—a process that has a noun and the verb combine to form a compound (cf. Mithun 1984; Baker 1996).

(27)   *Ka-wis-a-hutsi thika*
        NsS-glass-null-black that
        'That glass is black'

(28)   *T-a'-ka-wis-a'-ne'*   *thika*
        CIS-FACT-NsS-glass-fall-PUNC that
        'That glass fell'

These common properties are not unique to Mohawk. They are also attested in South Asian languages across the globe—such as Austroasiatic languages Kharia and Juang (cf. Peterson 2010) and the Dravidian language Malayalam (Menon 2016) that have also been reported for missing adjectives.

There are also reported similarities between nouns and verbs, with both taking up common affixes. In Mohawk, nouns and unaccusative verbs both have very similar inflectional patterns, with the referents and possessors of the noun marked the same as the themes and the affected goal/object of the verb. These overlaps led Baker (1996) to claim that nouns and unaccusative verbs have underlyingly the same structural representations.

That said, differences also abound between these overlapping categories, as Baker himself acknowledges. One of the prominent differences is that unaccusative verbs exclusively allow the incorporation of the theme argument. This property is not observed for nouns.

(29)   a   *ako-wis-e*   b   *t-a'-ako-hs-a'-s-e'*
             FsP-glass-NSF   CIS-FACT-FsO-Null-fall-BEN-PUNC
             'her glass'   'it fell on her; she dropped it'

Keeping in mind these and multiple other similarities and differences between lexical categories, Baker (2005) proposes the following features characterizing each—

(30)

a   Noun is $+N$ = 'has a referential index'

b   Verb is $+V$ = 'has a specifier'

c   Adjective is -N, -V

d   Preposition is part of a different system

From the above, it follows that verbs are structurally represented with a subject position. This is not a property that defines nouns, which are instead defined by their referential index. Finally, adjectives are neither nouns nor verbs, in that they do not feature subjects nor possess referential indices. With that information in the background, let us now proceed to analysing the noun-adjective-gender correlation found in Western Indo-Aryan languages.

Analysing the Category-Feature Overlap

Baker presents an elaborate exposition of the underlying structure of nouns, identifying the presence of a pair of referential indices as their defining characteristic. Referential indices are pairs of integers, where one of them, the first index, encodes the discourse referent signified by each nominal expression. The first index explains many properties that nouns are known for—such as their ability to form plurals, to serve as complements to determiners and quantifiers, provide antecedence to pronouns and appear in argument positions among others. These abilities are connected to the nouns bearing the referential index. However, carrying the indices also implies certain constraints imposed on nouns—such as the following (31)—

(31) The Noun Licensing Condition (NLC)

The second member of a referential index must be systematically identical to some dependent index in the structure that its bearer c-commands

A 'dependent index' is 'the index of an element that does not have intrinsic lexical content of its own: a theta-role, a pronominal, a trace, or a null operator' (pp: 153). This index functions to denote the concept of 'sameness' or 'difference' and locates the new discourse referent with something else in the structure. By this account, a noun's canonical function is not to refer, but to examine how similar or different referents are. Nouns therefore play a relational role, which is encoded via a second index on the noun. To illustrate, (32) is ungrammatical because there is a noun phrase which is set differently from the index provided on the verb 'sneezed.'

(32)   *The guests$_{[i,k]}$ sneezed$_{<Ag\ k>}$ a chicken$_{[n,\ m]}$

How are adjective different from nouns? Adjectives differ exactly on this count. According to Baker, they do not bear referential indices that could be used to denote 'sameness' or 'difference.' What then explains their overlap with nouns in some languages?

Recall, OIA had a way to connect the adjective with the neuter noun. Repeating for the reader's convenience, OIA neuter nouns (e.g. 'work') transformed into the OIA adjectives ('active') with a stress shifting operation.

(33)   ápəs   ——>   əpás
       'work'   'active'

The stress shifting operation was also deployed to shift from masculine to feminine (34).

(34)   ágru   ——>   əgrú
       'bachelor'   'virgin'

These schemes of things can be explained if we assume that the movement from neuter nouns to adjectives is possible with the introduction of a special n-head that carries a gender feature. Schematically (35a) to (35b).

(35)   a   [[$_{nP}$ [N n]   (neuter noun)
       b   [$_{AP}$ [$_{nP}$ n [fem [N]]]   (adjective)

In (35a), the neuter noun is not specified for any gender. When the n becomes marked for a gender value, as we see in (35b), it leads to a categorial shift, in that an adjective is formed. Note that the gender feature on the n is not interpretable, as one expects with features on noun which by definition are interpretable at the interfaces. Neuter nouns moreover are not specified for any gender. In (35b), therefore, it is simply the addition of an uninterpretable feature on an otherwise non-gendered noun. This addition is accompanied by the N losing its nominal features and instead giving rise to a category with a property (a gender feature).

What is the exact role of gender then? Gender as an uninterpretable feature on the n yields an adjective, when assigned as an interpretable feature, it modifies a noun. The connection between the noun, the adjective and gender is now evident. A n-head lies at the core of the similarities one finds these three constructs. The adjective and the noun are effectively the same, but for the interpretability/uninterpretability of their gender feature. The presence of the n, which is a functional head, allows the language to host an uninterpretable feature; when there is no n, the interpretable gender feature is either on the noun itself nor hosted on a separate gender head.

How does this connection play in the gender variation one finds from OIA to MIA to current day Awadhi? In OIA, the n played a prominent role and hosted a gender feature. That explained why adjectives and nouns exhibited significant overlap and also had gender expression. In MIA, the n was lost and so was the noun-adjective overlap and the morphological expression of gender. In current day Awadhi, a nominalized form *ki/ka* has been borrowed from Hindi and that has led to the resurgence of the noun-adjective overlap (*sundarkii/sundarkii laRkii* 'beautiful'/ 'beautiful one') and also the restricted appearance of gender morphology inside the DPs.

Bhojpuri Gender-Person Interaction

We now move to another language Bhojpuri that is classified as an Eastern Indo-Aryan language. The language lies adjacent to the Awadhi-speaking areas, as can be seen in Map 12.2. Bhojpuri provides an interesting contrast to Awadhi, but upon analysis, actually substantiates the structure-dependent analysis of gender variation.

Being an Eastern Indo-Aryan language, Bhojpuri should ideally lack gender agreement, as is true for many of its sister languages. But it defies this norm—it not only displays gender concord much like Awadhi, but most crucially, it also has long-distance verbal gender agreement. Since Bhojpuri gender concord -ka<u>l</u>ki structures are similar to those in Awadhi, I refrain from repeating them here. The nominalizer analysis that was provided for Awadhi can be easily extended to Bhojpuri. The patterns that need special attention are the long-distance ones.

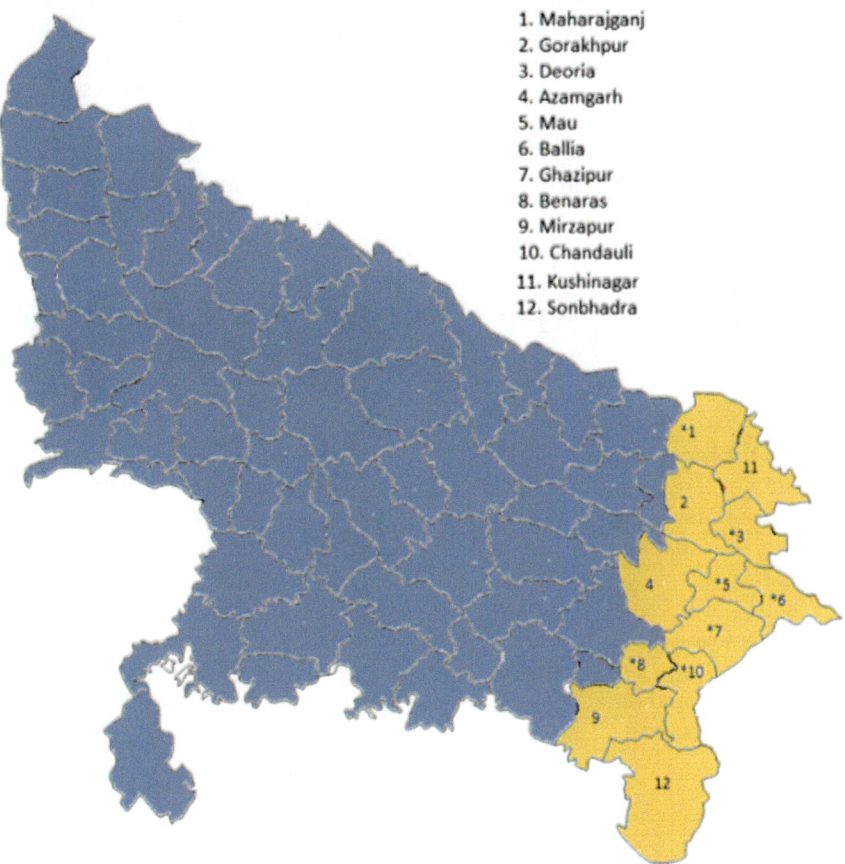

1. Maharajganj
2. Gorakhpur
3. Deoria
4. Azamgarh
5. Mau
6. Ballia
7. Ghazipur
8. Benaras
9. Mirzapur
10. Chandauli
11. Kushinagar
12. Sonbhadra

Map 12.2 Bhojpuri-speaking areas

One immediate question that arises is: why didn't Bhojpuri lose gender inflection with the other Eastern Indo-Aryan languages? If the predecessor languages underwent similar structural changes, which are evidenced in their often strikingly similar grammars, we expect gender erosion to have happened in Bhojpuri as well. In fact, Bhojpuri gender inflection is an excellent piece of evidence against the differential feature subselection. If the Old Eastern Indo-Aryan languages had lost the gender feature completely, we should incorrectly expect Bhojpuri too to lose its gender inflection. However, since that is not true, it is clear that gender was only suppressed in the older varieties due to a structural constraint. Once this structural constraint was removed, gender agreement made its way back into the Bhojpuri grammar.

I would however like to focus on one interesting aspect of gender inflection in Bhojpuri dialects which is seen in its interaction with the person feature. I tabulate the inflectional forms here for the Bhojpuri verb *maar* 'hit' (while also restricting myself to the singular paradigm) for the sake of brevity, instead of presenting the actual sentences. Take for instance, the forms of the verb in the Ghazipur dialect (Table 12.1).

Speakers of Ghazipur dialect display gender verbal agreement, with distinct morphology *–la* and *–li* for masculine and feminine values, respectively. Interestingly, person agreement is absent in all, but the first person feminine, which is marked distinctly with a *–ni* morpheme. On the other hand, dialects spoken in Chandauli, Maharajganj and Varanasi show slightly different patterns, which are displayed in Table 12.2. In these dialects, the variant form, where gender coexists with person is second person feminine—with a *–lu* morpheme. In all other cases, person agreement remains suppressed.

Yet, another dialect—the Deoria dialect—shows even more varied forms. These are given in Table 12.3.

Table 12.1 Ghazipur gender forms

First sg + Masc	First sg + Fem	Second sg + Masc	Second sg + Fem	Third sg + Masc	Third sg + Fem
marila	***Marini***	*marila*	*marili*	*marila*	*marili*

Table 12.2 Chandauli, Maharajganj, Varanasi gender forms

First sg + Masc	First sg + Fem	Second sg + Masc	Second sg + Fem	Third sg + Masc	Third sg + Fem
marila	*Marili*	*marila*	***Marilu***	*marila*	*marili*

Table 12.3 Deoria gender forms

First sg + Masc	First sg + Fem	Second sg + Masc	Second sg + Fem	Third sg + Masc	Third sg + Fem
marini	***marini***	***marilə***	***marilu***	*marila*	*marili*

Deoria forms are interesting because person agreement shows up only in the first and second person cases and coexists with gender. This is different from the previously stated cases, where person agreement showed up either in first person or in second person cases. The similarity however is that person and gender agreement do not coexist in any of these dialects for third person. The question we would like to ask is: are there structural reasons behind this variation? What explains the interaction of gender and person and their variation in Bhojpuri dialects?

As already mentioned in the previous section on Awadhi gender, OIA had gender inflection with participial verbs. Moreover, even at that stage, there was a clear link between gender value shift and adjective formation, which indicates that the nominalization strategy was critical to gender inflection. As time progressed, certain branches lost the nominalizer, which amounted in the loss of gender inflection. But interestingly, the feminine value (marker) remained in the later varieties (Old Kosali) of the Eastern Indo-Aryan branch. The same trend continues into current day Bhojpuri dialects as well, with the feminine holding the upper ground over the other gender values. This indicates that the subbranch ancestor of Bhojpuri never lost the participial form and consequently, the ability to host gender morphology on the verb.

But why is there this dependence of gender on first and second person pronominals? Do these person values provide a special structural context for gender expression in Bhojpuri? My contention is that these values play an indirect role in placing the noun in the right context so that its gender value is expressed. Person dependence is only a surface phenomenon; the actual structure instead has a nominalizing head in the main clausal spine.

It is a well-accepted assumption in the generative literature that first and second person values are licensed when the NP raises to TP/CP layer. The licensing is done as per Béjar and Rezac's (2003) *Person Licensing Condition*/PLC that states special licensing requirements for first and second person values of DPs against appropriate licensing heads. Third person pronominals are not entitled to the same and hence remain at vP-internal positions. Assuming that this condition applies universally to all languages, Bhojpuri first and second person pronominals too must raise to a higher projection in the clausal spine. This movement is captured in captured in (36), where the first/second person pronoun will move to the specifier of TP for person value licensing.

(36)

$$[CP[TP[nP_{[+feminine]}[vP\ NP\ V\ldots]]]]]$$

How does this movement affect gender expression in Bhojpuri? My contention is that there is a nominalizer head placed above vP in this language. This head is the authorizing structure for gender agreement here. When the NP raises to the higher heads for person licensing, it uses the specifier of nP as an escape hatch. A local spec-head relation between the two establishes gender agreement, which also gets reflected on the verb. Therefore, we have a case where the participial verb—where the v is selected by a nominalizer—hosts gender value when the noun hitchhikes a ride using a person feature. The actual structure for gender expression is an nP, much like Awadhi, but PLC helps out in moving the noun to the much-desired structural configuration. The contribution of the PLC in the actual expression of gender is substantiated by the fact that gender morphology goes missing on third person pronominals. Since these nouns remain inside vP, they are unable to locally agree with *n* and trigger gender agreement on the verb.

In summary, here is what the Eastern Indo-Aryan belt, as represented by Awadhi and Bhojpuri looks like. Awadhi has not lost the gender feature, but only the right structural conditions required to manifest gender. Dialectal variation ensues when some of its varieties borrow a nominalizer form from Hindi and adapt it to express gender in the nominal domain. This is also observed for Bhojpur for gender concord. Additionally, the language also has participial verbal forms that express gender agreement. Gender expression becomes possible when the noun uses the PLC to move to the domain of *n*. Bhojpuri long-distance gender agreement therefore happens in consort with person licensing.

The broad generalization we can create is that the re-emergence of gender inflection or its continuation from a previous variety, is driven by multiple structural factors. Over time, more research may reveal that some of these structural constraints are universal and not restricted to specific languages. An exercise in this direction is therefore a must. More and more languages, with and without gender agreement, need to be studied and analysed closely to figure out the actual reasons (universal or language-particular) for why gender is absent or present in a language.

As part of this exercise, let me now turn to a genealogically unrelated language—Kannada from the Dravidian language family. This makes an interesting case to study this multi-factor reasoning behind gender expression.

Macro-Level Variation: Kannada Gender

The Dravidian language Kannada is spoken primarily in the southern state of Karnataka, India. Nouns are (sometimes) marked with a masculine *–a* and feminine *–i* morpheme, as shown in Table 12.4. This suggests that Kannada nouns carry (interpretable) gender features. The data is from Mysore dialect.

One look at the pronominals forms in Kannada in Table 12.5 also shows that gender is only present with third person pronouns. There are no distinct gender forms for first and second person pronominals.

There is an additional twist here, especially when it comes to agreement with adjectives. The literature (Sridhar 1990) reports that the attributive adjectives do not inflect for gender (37a-c), but predicate adjectives do (38a-c).

Table 12.4 Kannada nouns

Boy	huduga
Girl	hudugi
Lion	simha
Lioness	simhini

Table 12.5 Kannada pronouns

	SG	SG	SG	PL	PL	PL
	M	F	N	M	F	N
1P	Aanu	nanu	–	navu	navu	–
2P	Ninu	ninu	–	nivu	nivu	–
3P	Avanu	Avalua	adu	avaru	avaru	Avvu

(37) a   *a:*   *tuNTa*   *huDug-a*

          that   naughty   boy-masc

          'That naughty boy'

      b   *a:*   *tuNTa*   *huDug-i*

          that   naughty   girl-fem

          'That naughty girl'

      c   *a:*   *tuNTa*   *huDug-a-ru*

          that naughty boy-masc-Pl

          'Those naughty boys'

(38) a   *avanu tuNTA(nu)*

          he   naughty.masc.sg

          'He is naughty'

      b   *avaLu tuNTa-Lu*

          she   naughty-fem.sg

          'She is naughty'

      c   *avaru tuNTa-ru*

          They naughty-Pl

          'They are naughty'

Extending the *n*-analysis to Kannada, the results are quite different from what we find in the Eastern Indo-Aryan languages. Here, unlike Awadhi, the *n*-head manifests only at the clausal level. There is no *n* attached to NPs. This differential distribution must be the reason behind the presence of gender values only on predicative adjectives.

What is interesting is that the literature already notes a clear correlation between predicative adjectives and gender. In fact, Sridhar (1990) conjectures that predicative adjectives in Kannada 'behave syntactically like nouns' and 'appear in their nominal form.' Attributive adjectives do not share this property. Translated into our adopted technology, this amounts to saying that there is an *n*-head when the adjective is placed on the clausal spine as a predicate.

Contradicting Sridhar, Baker (2003) claims that Kannada does not have gender inflection on predicative adjectives; rather the agreeing forms are pronominal in nature. His observation is that the canonical gender markers on the nouns—*a, i, a-ru* are never seen as agreement markers on the predicate adjectives, which are instead marked with *n(u), Lu* and *aru*—much like the endings that demonstrative pronouns take. This takes away any special status attributed to predicative adjectives. In other words, these agreeing items are attributive adjectives that modify pronominal elements. It is the pronominal part of this structure that agrees with the subject NP. Hence, Baker claims that gender agreement is nothing but person agreement.

One drawback of Baker's work is that it is unable to explain why despite the presence of a gender feature on nouns and third person pronouns as illustrated in Table 12.5, there is only 'person' agreement. If these nouns carry gender values (as shown in Table 12.4), what in his system suppresses gender agreement in favour of person agreement?

Second, his account does not give due consideration to the unique morphology with first and second person pronominals. As already mentioned, Kannada has 'gender' (or according to Baker, 'person') agreement with only third person pronouns. In the literature, the general assumption is that only first and second are 'true' person values; a third person value is equivalent to 'no person.' Therefore, if 'person' agreement is really as prevalent in Kannada as Baker claims, we expect it to show up with first and second person pronouns rather than with third person pronouns. Since there are no clear answers to these questions in Baker's analysis, I prefer to assume that Kannada does have gender agreement, albeit in restricted third person, predicative adjective constructions.

I therefore claim that Kannada has a gender feature with special licensing requirements, which are tied to (i) the presence of an *n*-carrying adjective and (ii) third person contexts. The Kannada *n*-carrying adjective is participial, in that it is not a full nominal and also has a V feature. This technically puts the adjective at the vP-domain and not at the DP-level. This explains why predicate adjectives and not attributive adjectives agree in gender with Kannada nouns.

The second issue about the restriction of gender agreement in third person contexts can be tackled thus. The predicate adjective cannot merge with a T, which is a 'true' person feature carrier. First and second person values are checked at the TP/CP level, and C and T heads do not host an uninterpretable gender feature. Only vP-level elements host gender feature, and therefore as expected, we have gender agreement only with third person pronouns that do not raise for PLC requirements to higher heads. Schematically:

(39) $[CP[TP[vP/ PartP\ nP_{[+feminine]}\ [vP[NP\ V \ldots]]]]]$
$\underset{+3P}{\uparrow}\underline{\hspace{2cm}}|\underset{Fem}{\underline{\hspace{2cm}}}|$

where does Kannada stand in terms of gender expression and variation? Kannada nouns are potential triggers for gender agreement. Just like Awadhi and Bhojpuri, there is a special head involved with gender agreement—the nominalizing head. However, Kannada's nominalizing head is also+V, making it a true participial head. In such cases, therefore, gender agreement cannot take place at the DP-level (i.e. no gender concord), but takes place at the vP-level (verbal agreement).

Conclusion

Languages typically vary at multiple levels—micro- (at the dialectal-level), meso- (between typologically related languages) and macro- (between typologically or genealogically unrelated languages). There is also nano-level variation, which considers specific lexeme/word-centred variation. While these levels are acknowledged by scholars from different theoretical backgrounds, there is still a lot unexplored on if and how these levels are related.

In the generative tradition, there is ongoing debate on how to connect them. While some scholars tend to assume that all kinds of variation essentially boil down to features, with the different variation levels emanating from the differential distribution and effects of features on functional heads (consider the *Parametric Hierarchy* of Biberauer & Roberts, 2012), some others (such as Baker, 2008) assume that macro-parameters are structural parameters (e.g. long-distance agree versus move) and micro- and meso-parameters are feature-triggered noisy differences between languages, with differential feature subselection playing a vital role in variation.

Both sides miss one crucial aspect of variation—that whether it is micro-level or macro-level variation, structural signatures are crucial determinants of variation. We have tried to illustrate this point with multiple dialects from Awadhi, Bhojpuri and Kannada. The micro-level gender concord variation between Awadhi dialects is with regards to a structural correlation with a nP nominalizer. Bhojpuri gender inflection is also tied to the realization of *n*-heads, albeit on the clausal spine and in cohort with person licensing. Kannada gender realization is contingent on *n*-heads, adjectives and person licensing. There is therefore a crucial dependence that feature expression has on structures. One important conclusion to draw from this study is that we should not disengage featural variation from structural variation. These two go hand in hand and must be studied together to understand linguistic variation better.

Acknowledgements   The author acknowledges the financial help from the Indian Council of Social Science Research, New Delhi, which facilitated wide-scale surveys among the native populace speaking Awadhi, Bhojpuri and many other related languages spoken in Uttar Pradesh and its neighboring states.

References

Baker, M. (1996). *The Polysynthesis Parameter*. New York: Oxford University Press.

Baker, M. (2003). *Lexical categories*. Cambridge University Press.

Baker, M. (2005). The Innate Endowment for Language: Overspecified or Underspecified. In Peter Carruthers, Steve Lawrence, and Steven Stich (eds). *The Innate Mind: Structure and Contents*. Oxford: Oxford University Press, pp. 156–174.

Baker, M. (2008). The Macroparameter in a Microparametric world. In T. Biberauer (Ed.), *The Limits of Syntactic Variation* (pp. 351–374). John Benjamins.

Béjar, S., & Rezac, M. (2003). Person Licensing and the Derivation of PCC Effects. In: A. Teresa Perez-Leroux, & Y. Roberge (eds.) *Romance Linguistics: Theory and Acquisition* Amsterdam: John Benjamins.

Bhat, D. N. S. (1994). *The Adjectival Category: Criteria for differentiation and identification*. Amsterdam: John Benjamins Publishing Company.

Biberauer, T., & Roberts, I. (2012). Towards a parameter hierarchy for auxiliaries: diachronic considerations. In: J. Chancharu, X. Hu & M. Mitrović (eds). *Cambridge Occasional Papers in Linguistics* 6, pp. 209–36.

Borer, H. (2001). Exo-skeletal vs. endo-skeletal explanations: Syntactic projection and the lexicon. Ms., University of Southern California, Los Angeles.

Cardona, G. (1988). *Pāṇini: His work and its traditions*. Part I: General introduction and background. Delhi: Motilal Banarsidass.

Chatterji, S. K. (1953). *Ukti-vyakti-prakarana: The oldest document in Kosali or Awadhi*, edited by Muni Sri Jinavijayaji. Bombay: Singh-Jain Series.

Corbett, G. G. (1991). *Gender*. Cambridge University Press.

Dixon, R. M. (1982). *Where have All the Adjectives Gone? And Other Essays in Semantics and Syntax*. Berlin, New York: De Gruyter Mouton.

Kupfer, K. (2002). *Die Demonstrativpronomina im Rigveda*. Frankfurt am Main: Peter Lang.

Lowe, J.J. (2015). *Participles in Rigvedic Sanskrit: The syntax and semantics of adjectival verb forms*. Oxford: Oxford University Press.

Menon, M. (2016). *Building adjectival meaning without adjectives*. Doctoral dissertation, University of Southern California.

Mithun, M. (1984). The Evolution of Noun Incorporation. *Language*, 60(4):847–894.

Peterson, J. (2010). *A grammar of Kharia: A South Munda language*. Leiden and Boston: Brill.

Pustet, R. (1989). *Die Morphosyntax des" Adjektivs" im Sprachvergleich*. Frankfurt am Maine: Peter Lang.

Saksena, B. (1971). *Evolution of Awadhi: A branch of Hindi*. New Delhi: Motilal Banarsidass.

Sridhar, S. N. (1990). *Kannada*. Routledge.

Stassen, L. (1997). *Intransitive predication*. Oxford: Oxford University Press.

Whitney, W. D. (1889/1896). *Sanskrit grammar*. Cambridge: Harvard University Press.

Wetzer, H. (1996). *The Typology of Adjectival Predication*. Berlin, Boston: De Gruyter Mouton.

Pritha Chandra is Professor of Linguistics in the Department of Humanities and Social Sciences at the Indian Institute of Technology Delhi. She works on inflectional morphology and structural phenomena from a generative linguistics perspective. Using data from a wide array of languages, her work primarily focuses on the mechanisms that underlie language variation—covering the entire gamut from micro-level to macro-level variation. Her research has been presented and published on different national and international platforms.

Printed by Printforce, the Netherlands